WITHDRAWN

DATE DUE

JAN 2 6 2001			

#47-0108 Peel Off Pressure Sensitive

BOOMER BASICS

BOOMER BASICS

~ ~ ~ ~ ~ ~ ~ Everything That You Need to Know about the Issues Facing You, Your Children, and Your Parents

ROBERT ABRAMS, WALTER T. BURKE,
TIMOTHY E. CASSERLY, AND BARBARA S. NODIFF

McGraw-Hill

New York San Francisco Washington, D.C. Auckland Bogotá
Caracas Lisbon London Madrid Mexico City Milan
Montreal New Delhi San Juan Singapore
Sydney Tokyo Toronto

McGraw-Hill

A Division of The **McGraw·Hill** Companies

The sponsoring editor for this book was Nancy Mikhail, the editing supervisor was John M. Morriss, and the production supervisor was Tina Cameron. It was set in Dante by Adobe.

Printed and bound by R. R. Donnelley & Sons Company.

McGraw-Hill books are available at special quantity discounts to use as premiums and sales promotions, or for use in corporate training programs. For more information, please write to the Director of Special Sales, McGraw-Hill, 11 West 19th Street, New York, NY 10011. Or contact your local bookstore.

This publication is designed to provide accurate and authoritative information in regard to the subject matter covered. It is sold with the understanding that neither the author nor the publisher is engaged in rendering legal, accounting, or other professional service. If legal advice or other expert assistance is required, the services of a competent professional person should be sought.
—*From a Declaration of Principles jointly adopted by a Committee of the American Bar Association and a Committee of Publishers.*

 This book is printed on recycled, acid-free paper containing a minimum of 50% recycled, de-inked fiber.

DEDICATIONS

Robert Abrams

To those in my life who make every day special: my wife, Linda; our parents, Sondra, Allan, Annette, and Joe; and our precious children, Dana and Tracey.

Walter T. Burke

For Mary; our wonderful children, Daniel and Laura; and to those loved ones who have gone before me, my parents, Walter and Kathleen, and my brother, Dan.

Timothy E. Casserly

To my parents, Jim and Fran; my children, Chris, Dan, and Ryan; and my wife and best friend, Shelly, for their continuous contributions of inspiration, love, support, and new material.

Barbara S. Nodiff

To my parents, Arnold and Lorraine, who supported a vision with inspiration to make it happen, and to my husband, Ed, who brings a new vision for our future.

CONTENTS

ACKNOWLEDGMENTS

This book is a collaboration of efforts well beyond those of the authors. Without the time, talent, and patience of many others, this reference guide could not have evolved over the past several years to its present form.

Sometime in the early 1990s, Bob Abrams suggested that given the varied circumstances and knowledge we had collectively experienced through our respective professional practices as well as in our own lives, it would be a good idea to find time to write a book. We told him that it is also a good idea to learn to play a musical instrument, eat less red meat, and reduce stress at work, but we have to make trade-offs. Nonetheless, he persisted; we made the time and, with the help of many others, proceeded with this guide, which we think will help many families with different issues and phases of their lives.

As we discussed our project with more friends, family members, and our colleagues and clients, we uncovered additional issues and planning concerns relevant to our audience. However, we also uncovered many areas about which we knew very little. Fortunately, we did know experts willing to help. David G. Wolinsky, M.D.; Philip Johnson, CFP; and the Honorable Ann M. Carrozza provided valuable input and recommendations for the "Health" and "Financial" portions of the book. Additional support from Robert Blancato, Rick Frishman, and Steve Klosk kept us moving in a positive direction.

Once we had a semifinished product, we thought it best to have a professional writer/editor review our work. We found the best of each in one person—Terri Porter. After several hundred hours of research and writing, Terri helped us mold what might have been a great book only in our minds into one that others could enjoy as well.

Another benefit of the collaborative process was the help we all had in recognizing the almost boundless amounts of information available on the topics that concern boomers. And although we accepted the fact that the book must be finite, we saw the opportunity to expand, revise, and update the content constantly through the Internet. Thanks to the creative and intensive Web browsing of Jeffrey Dorfman, Michelle Casserly, Ann Carrozza, and Daniel Burke, we were able to surf through oceans of useless information to find helpful, substantive sites and thus add this feature to our book.

Also, we needed assistance with fact finding, fact checking, and research on many ancillary issues for baby boomers. With the help of Rosemary Bailly, research assistants from the Albany Law School Government Law Center, Jerry Schwartz, Donna Glassman-Sommer, Kyra Morris, and many members of our respective firms, this got accomplished.

Overall, the collaborative process might have suffered or stalled in most cases as recently as a few years ago because we are separated by geography. But with the advent of e-mail, the Internet, overnight mail, faxes, scanners, and copiers, the geographical barriers have disappeared. However, a new and seemingly never-ending problem is how to utilize the latest technology efficiently while receiving drafts, comments, instructions, rewrites, and edits from several places and people at once. Thankfully, we have three people who could do that as well as keep track of where the most recent text being worked on was located. Thank you, Lorraine Takesky, Alicia DiGesare, and Cheri Terzian for knowing when to listen and when to ignore us at the right times.

Our vision for this book was shared and enhanced by our editor, Nancy Mikhail. Nancy's commitment to this book, as well as to us, will be forever appreciated.

Finally, we wish to thank our literary agent, Peter Miller, for believing in this project as much as we did and thus helping us get to this point where we can thank him in print.

The Authors

HOW TO USE THIS BOOK

Let's get the obvious out of the way: If you are truly a boomer, you will either intentionally bypass this section or read it and then ignore whatever we said. Old habits are hard to break.

Regardless of your individual preferences or biases, the following tidbits of information may prove to be helpful:

1. Have a good time reading the book—we enjoyed writing it. Although we suggest you read it from beginning to end, feel free to start where you like. We expect that as life happens, you will find most, if not all, of the topics covered will be of interest and assistance to you and your family for many years to come.

2. Throughout the book you will come upon "Insights" that will provide you with our personal experiences and suggestions. We hope they inform, amuse, and/or challenge you.

3. References to our Web site, <http://www.Boomerbasics.com>, abound throughout the book so that you can receive additional information about resources, products, and services that will also be of interest to you.

4. When you wish to supplement the information we have provided to you, you may wish to visit or contact one or more of the hundreds of Web sites or organizations listed throughout the book. The information available on them, combined with the information in *Boomer Basics* and <http://www.Boomerbasics.com>, will ensure that you have a comprehensive, if not exhaustive, foundation of the issues concerning you, your parents, and your children.

ENJOY!

REPRESENTATIONS AND DISCLAIMERS

We represent to you that we have designed this book to be a clearinghouse of information of concern and interest to baby boomers, their parents, and their children. We further represent that we have done our best, and we truly expect and believe that this book and our Web site will be a useful guide to you.

We cannot, however, guarantee the accuracy and timeliness of the information and resources referred to in this book given that laws, Web sites, organizations, and life in general are constantly changing. *Boomer Basics* is not intended to serve as a substitute for professional expertise. If you require legal, medical, or other expert advice for a particular situation, you should seek the services of a qualified professional.

INTRODUCTION

The greatest gift of all is the love we receive from and give to our children, parents, spouses, and significant others. May we always respect and advocate for their right to self-determination and autonomy to the greatest extent possible, and may we always be available to them if and when they need us to help implement their wishes and desires.

In the 1960s Mick Jagger sang, and we agreed, "Time is on our side, yes it is." Except for Dick Clark and Mick Jagger, most things have changed since then; now there seems to be too little time, and time is *not* always on our side.

It is not an age thing—yes, we are getting older—but we are not old. In fact, some of us are in the best physical, mental, and emotional shape of our lives. It's just that for most of us, we can now more readily relate to the Beatles' "When I'm Sixty-Four"; the father, rather than the son, in Cat Stevens's "Father and Son"; and the mother in Paul Simon's "Mother and Child Reunion." And whereas we and The Who used to be able to "see for miles and miles," we can now barely see unless we have our glasses on.

Even more illustrative of our age is that if our children read this, they'll want to know who (or what) "The Who" is. We have gone full circle. Didn't our parents ask us a few decades ago, when we were kids, who (or what) The Who was? But as we make the transition from concerns about being hip to fears about breaking one, this question doesn't really matter. What does matter is that such queries demonstrate our desire to communicate with our children and our parents and their desire to connect with us even if we don't always understand each other.

From one generation to the next, we appreciate and cherish the importance of family. We also accept that as we enter middle age, we have the unique and important responsibility to guide our children and assist our parents while we take care of ourselves and plan for our future.

As baby boomers (or just "boomers") growing up in the 1950s and 1960s, we had only ourselves to think about. Since then, our focus has widened, with thoughts of ourselves being sandwiched between concerns for our children and for our parents. Additionally, while these personal and intergenerational issues may sometimes feel infinite, the time we have to devote to them is all too finite. Because these pressures often force us to juggle many different, important duties at the same time and sometimes to decide which ones are most pressing and which can be set aside for later, boomers are sometimes (and in most cases, mistakenly) characterized as self-centered, shortsighted, or apathetic. In actuality, we consistently see boomers seeking new and innovative ways not only to address and prioritize these personal and familial challenges but also to do so in the most beneficial way for our families. However, finding the necessary resources often frustrates us or slows us down. It is the purpose of *Boomer Basics* to help put time on our side once again, "yes it is."

The term *baby boom generation* has been coined to describe those approximately seventy-eight million of us born between 1946 and 1964 in an environment of post–World War II optimism and economic growth. The number of Americans aged thirty-six to fifty-four is currently growing four times as fast as the number of any other age group in U.S. society. Because there are so many of us, we have been analyzed and dissected by everyone from demographers and marketing directors to physicians and financial planners. And just as they would like to categorize us neatly and succinctly so as to be more successful at selling us movies, cereal, shampoo, and life insurance, we would like to properly and efficiently address the issues concerning ourselves as parents, caregivers, and individuals. Given the wide range of entertainment, food, clothes, beauty products, and investment choices that confront us, we know that simplicity has disappeared from the superficial decisions we face, let alone the substantive ones. For example, forty years ago your choice of coffee included regular or freeze-dried instant, only one company handled long-distance calling, your range of sneaker options (now known as athletic footwear) spanned the spectrum from black to white (with nothing in between), and an interactive game meant "Twister." Now, each of these examples has witnessed entire industries built around them. With respect to the substantive issues, the complexity has expanded more radically, and the consequences of a wrong decision or inaction are much worse than ring around the collar, halitosis, or waxy buildup. As boomers, we recognize this, but we need some assistance to proceed.

In balancing our lives and obligations, we are constantly seeking more information to either do things on our own or, at least, participate in the decision-making process. As boomers, we have a heightened (and healthy) skepticism that has evolved gradually since the 1950s, from when we were very accepting and trusting of what Ike and Walter Cronkite told us, through the 1960s, when we began to look beneath the surface of what we saw and read and questioned words and acts of "authority" such as the Warren Commission, LBJ, and Nixon. In the following years, from Watergate and Nixon's proclamation that he was "not a crook" to the Clinton White House, where Bill neither inhaled nor had "sex with that woman," we have come to realize that almost nothing should be taken at face value. As such, we have become much more comfortable asking questions and reaching our own conclusions or at least having more informed impressions of an authority's statement or recommendation.

Being the first generation raised in front of the TV set, we see this same evolution reflected in our favorite shows. Initially, Father knew best and was not even second-guessed, and the FBI always proceeded with good intentions. We soon began wondering, however, why the Howells would have so many clothes on *Gilligan's Island* if they were only going for a three-hour cruise or how a father and his sons on *Bonanza* could all be about the same age or why on virtually any crime show (for example, *Dragnet, Mannix,* or *Adam-12*) the bad guys were typically minorities. During the 1970s we became less willing to ignore diversity and real life, so the shows addressing real-life issues became the popular ones (such as *All in the Family, M*A*S*H,* and *Hill Street Blues*). This trend has continued through today with the increasing popularity of *60 Minutes, Dateline NBC, 20/20,* and twenty-four-hour channels devoted to everything from news, sports, and weather to cooking, golf, and gardening.

But where the real-life programming falls short is in supplying the basics to our generation. And learning the basics can help us work toward solutions or, at least, relief. Granted, these complex intergenerational issues can only be simplified to a point, but you already know that. The ones who don't recognize the complexity or the need for involvement are not reading this book. They're either ignoring the issues or waiting for the problems to resolve themselves, much like the situations that Ralph Kramden, Columbo, Lucy, or Ben Casey often found themselves in where they reached an unrealistic solution by the end of the program. Unfortunately, in real life, these issues are more like TV shows today where some bad guys get away or the patient doesn't necessarily get better. However, our input can alter or affect the outcomes, and the more informed we are, the more effective and relevant that input can be. But like everything else, when we are looking to do the best that we can for our families, we need and want access to the basics to be able to develop a plan for ourselves and our family.

Boomer Basics was written to help you successfully address real-life opportunities and challenges. We will provide you with legal, financial, personal, and practical information that will help you deal with the unique issues and situations you have or may confront. We will also present you with hundreds of available resources from government, nonprofit, and proprietary on-line and off-line entities that offer you additional information, products, and services. References to <http://www.Boomerbasics.com> will take you to the ultimate Web site for those who care about relevant boomer issues and opportunities.

In the 1960s the Beatles sang, and we then naively agreed, that "All you need is love." But as we exchanged our albums and 8-track tapes for CDs, we began to understand why the Beatles also sang, "Help!" In advocating for and assisting our children, our parents, and ourselves, many times love is all we need. For those times, however, when love is not enough, *Boomer Basics* can provide the help we need to mitigate adversity, minimize anxiety, enhance our experiences, and celebrate our families' achievements.

OURSELVES

Over the past fifty years, our world has seen many changes. The pace of everyday life seems to be constantly quickening. As we try to leverage our time to cover more activities and responsibilities, we often get caught in the quicksand of modern-day life; those of us running in place feel lucky we haven't fallen behind.

But despite this accelerating change, the human basics have remained fairly consistent in that we want, first and foremost, what's best for ourselves and our families. Often, these goals can be achieved through our family relationships, which can supply an abundant source of strength, love, assistance, insight, support, experience, and fun. Granted, they also supply frustration, envy, heartache, guilt, sadness, and grief, but motivated by respect, love, or obligation, we seek to compromise or reconcile these feelings at varying times in our lives. Although these human basics have remained pretty constant from one generation to the next, it is only recently that they are being witnessed in such great abundance because many of us have children and our parents are living longer lives than were formerly the norm. Concurrently, mass communication and medicine have identified, dissected, interpreted, and reported our many traits, ailments, and relationships, not only raising our awareness but also labeling most of us with some new syndrome or dysfunctional trait as well.

The diversity of eighty million baby boomers (or "boomers" for short) makes it seem virtually impossible to find any commonality among us other than our birthdays being between 1946 and 1964. We take pride in celebrating our individuality and differences, but the common denominators exist both superficially and substantially. We don't like to acknowledge that gravity works as we see parts of our body moving downward, that leisure suits never looked good, that we now hear our favorite songs on the elevator, or that when someone asks, "What's your number?" we think in terms of cholesterol. We do not like complications especially where we see technology simplifying much of our everyday lives.

We would like to avoid anxiety in general and anxiety over our health in particular (it used to be when someone said "colon," we thought "punctuation," not "bran muffins"). We want to stay as we are indefinitely (which, depending on whether you are attractive or annoying, could be a good or a bad thing). We do not like unrealistic demands or deadlines (we know *stress* more as a noun than a verb). We do not like having so many things pulling at us and taking away time that we want to spend with our families.

What we do like, however, is to seek out choices and information. The volume of information and choices available—much like the issues, priorities, and distractions in our lives—can become overwhelming, but with some planning, education, and organization, we can better provide for the physical and financial well-being of our parents, our children, and ourselves.

This section explores options in light of ever-advancing developments in technology and profound changes in the home and workplace. It also examines issues relative to our financial affairs—the current state of our spending and saving patterns and whether (and to what extent) we need to make changes to ensure a comfortable retirement, as well as the effect of those decisions on our children, our parents, and our financial security; insurance for disability and long-term care; and planning adequately to ensure that our spouses and children are taken care of after we die.

Finally, we need to be mindful of our health, which is important to our family, our friends, and most particularly, ourselves. For those of us who care for our children or our parents, our effectiveness as caregivers will be adversely affected if we don't take care of ourselves. Although we often view ourselves as superbeings who can do it all, even the most stubborn boomers among us ultimately recognize that we're only human.

PERSONAL ~~~~~~~~

Get Organized!

We tend to live life on the fly—racing to get the kids to soccer or hockey practice, often helping with their homework, keeping track of dentist and doctor appointments, squeezing in the board meeting, and then taking

Mom shopping or playing golf with Dad—and, oh yes, when there's time, going out to dinner with our spouses on Saturday night just to remind each other of why we are doing all this. All this juggling requires sacrifice, prioritizing, and careful planning (not to mention an oversized calendar!). The same is necessary for the larger issues we face, and successful planning stems from a good sense of organization, which means putting an end to the piling (not filing) system, being able to access information quickly when you need it, and having alternate or backup procedures in case things don't go as planned. It's the same old story—you don't realize how ill prepared you are for a crisis until you find yourself unprepared in the middle of one.

Adequate planning can prevent a crisis from turning into a disaster. For a moment, imagine the unimaginable: You receive a phone call at work telling you that your spouse has been severely injured in a hit-and-run accident. Can you locate her health insurance card and policy to ensure that needed medical services are covered? If you need additional funds until her disability policy kicks in, do you know from which bank accounts you can withdraw or even how much money is in the checking account? Do you know where the power of attorney and health care proxy are (assuming you have them)?

The fortunate few among us can say, "Oh, yes, I know where all that stuff is," while the rest of us suffer from the "should've" syndrome: "I've been meaning to get to that," or worse, "I haven't got a clue." Even more difficult would be the call in the middle of the night from your mother: "Dad's in the hospital with a stroke. I'm so confused; I don't know where anything is." How would you begin to help her?

Despite your resolve to get a handle on all this information, even the best of intentions won't make it an easy job. To assist you in this unenviable but critical task, the Boomerbasics Crisis Information Checklist in the appendix will help you to organize information about yourself, your children, and your parents. (You can also click on <http://www.Boomerbasics .com> for this checklist).

Once you have completed the Boomerbasics Crisis Information Checklist, be sure to make a couple of photocopies of it. Keep a copy in your home and give a sealed copy (to preserve confidentiality) to your lawyer or a trusted friend or relative. Such duplication and notification protects against the loss of important documents in time of crisis. This same sheet will help your parents to be prepared as well. None of us likes to think about emergencies, but organizing now will take some of the sting out of the unexpected in the future.

RESOURCES

> **MyEvents.com**
> San Francisco, CA
> (415) 362-8700
> <http://www.myevents.com>

Summary: This site enables you to organize yourself, friends, family, or groups with whom you are involved. Simply stated, "MyEvents is a free service designed to help you manage your life by giving you a central place to keep track of the events and people important to you."

> **When.com**
> 501 E. Middlefield Road, MV-041
> Mountain View, CA 94043-4042
> (650) 937-4145
> <http://www.when.com>

Summary: From this site, which is also free, you can create a personal or group calendar and include event information. The When.com directory contains event information about finance, movies, books, cultural events, Web broadcasts, trade shows, and much more.

Physical Changes in Appearance and Performance

Did you ever think about how you look to other people? Assuming you are a forty-five-year-old boomer, do you think you look to them the way you imagine a forty-five-year-old looks, or do you think you look to them the *actual* way a forty-five-year-old looks? Don't you increasingly find yourself referring to a wider range of people, mostly younger, as being "our age"?

No matter how well preserved you keep yourself—both physically and mentally—your body goes through physical changes as you age. With the right frame of mind and the blessing of good health, you can deal with these changes in a positive manner. With the wrong frame of mind, you can look like a forty-five-year-old living in the body of a person the age of your parents or older.

Each of us will decide how we deal with these changes. Some of us may let nature take its course, while others will look to science, medicine, beauty aids, and our checkbooks to slow down or camouflage the aging process.

RESOURCES

National Institute on Aging Information Center
National Institute on Aging (NIA)
PO Box 8057
Gathersburg, MD 20898-8057
(301) 446-1752
<http://www.nih.gov/nia/>

Summary: The NIA conducts and supports biomedical, social, and behavioral research and training relating to the aging process as well as to diseases and other special problems and needs of the aged. The NIA also offers a series of brochures and fact sheets called Age Pages on specific diseases, disorders and conditions associated with aging. These publications can be obtained by contacting the NIA Information Center at (800) 222-2225 and also may be viewed on the NIA Web site.

American Academy of Facial Plastic and Reconstructive Surgery (AAFPRS)
310 S. Henry Street
Alexandria, VA 22314
(800) 332-FACE
<http://www.facial-plastic-surgery.org>

Summary: This site is maintained by AAFPRS, which is the world's largest association of facial plastic and reconstructive surgeons. Features on this site include a member directory, a guide to facial plastic surgery, and a patient information series.

RealAge Inc.
11468 Sorrento Valley Rd.
San Diego, CA 92121
(615) 812-3800
<http://www.realage.com>

Summary: RealAge is self-described as a "brand new, scientifically valued system that alters your rate of aging" and then teaches you how to slow down or reverse the process.

Personal Fitness and Health

It seems that every week, research data are reported that demonstrate the importance of diet and exercise to our physical health and overall sense of well-being. Although many consequences of aging are beyond our control, we can obviously exert a profound influence on our health and longevity by eating healthfully and engaging in regular exercise.

Studies have repeatedly shown that regular aerobic activity will not only lengthen our lives but also enrich the quality and enjoyment of our daily activities and relationships.

Exercise strengthens the pumping capacity of the heart and reduces levels of harmful low-density lipoprotein (LDL) cholesterol and fats in the blood. It reverses hardening of the arteries (atherosclerosis), which, if left unchecked, results in our nation's number one killer—heart disease. People who exercise regularly are also far less likely to develop cancer.

Anyone who has ever engaged in regular, vigorous, sustained activity has experienced benefits such as lower anxiety, less fatigue, and a sense of calm, all of which are the result of natural chemicals called endorphins that are released into the blood during every workout.

If the health and mood improvement benefits don't sell you, then how would you like to look and feel younger? By improving your posture, confidence, and outlook, exercise can result in an immediate boost to your looks. Over the long term, regular exercise can actually reverse some effects of aging such as bone loss (osteoporosis) and the loss of skin elasticity.

Activities such as lifting weights or walking with handheld weights will help replace the muscle we lose every year as mature (sedentary) adults. Who wants to build muscle? We all should, because each pound of muscle we have burns far more calories than does the fat that replaces it as we age. This is why adults tend to gain a few pounds every decade even if their dietary intake remains relatively constant. Think of added muscle as a fat-burning engine that continues to work off extra calories while we are at rest or even sleeping!

Hopefully, you are convinced of the importance of resuming or commencing a regular exercise program. But before heading to the gym, the best starting point is a complete physical checkup with your physician, which is especially important if you have been sedentary in the past or have certain medical conditions such as heart disease, high blood pressure, or diabetes.

Next, find something you like and can do. Walking is an ideal exercise for several reasons. A good pair of walking shoes is the only equipment needed, and even the least coordinated among us know how to do it. Because it isn't overly strenuous, this exercise will serve us well into old age. A twenty-minute walk every day could result in a ten-pound weight loss within one year.

In addition to walking, exercise options include jogging, aerobic dance, ballroom dance, hiking, cross-country skiing, jumping rope, running in place, cycling, and swimming, with the latter being an excellent choice for those with arthritis or other joint problems.

For optimum benefits, exercise sessions should last from thirty to sixty minutes, three to six times per week. It is a good idea to invest in a heart monitor to make sure your heart rate doesn't exceed 80 percent of your maximum heart rate. This can be determined by subtracting your age from 220. For example, a healthy fifty-year-old should not exceed 136 heartbeats per minute ($220 - 50 = 170 \times .80 = 136$).

Whichever activity you pursue, it is important to begin each session with a warm-up and to follow each session with stretching and a cooldown. This will prevent injuries and increase flexibility.

The toughest part about exercising is sticking with a program in spite of a busy schedule. It helps to clearly block out time for this purpose. Waiting until you have free time to exercise is analogous to saying you'll save all the money you have left over at the end of the month—in other words, it won't happen. In fact, you'll likely be out of shape and broke.

If you find yourself saying that you'd like to exercise but are too busy or too tired, it helps to change your mind-set. For example, if you have a really hectic day in front of you with time commitments to many different people, you should carve out some time in the morning to charge your batteries and thus better meet the challenges ahead. You will invariably get more accomplished during the day and will be able to give more to everyone around you by making this simple investment in your personal energy and health.

RESOURCES

Health World Online
Fitness Center
<http://www.healthy.net/fitness/index.asp>

Summary: Health World Online has created a family of sites whose goal is to be "your 24-hour health resource center" where you can access the information, services, and products to help design a wellness-based lifestyle. In their fitness center, you are provided information about fitness and your health, sports medicine, training, nutrition, and a variety of other topics.

American Council on Exercise (ACE)
5820 Oberlin Drive, Suite 102
San Diego, CA 92121-3787
(619) 535-8227
<http://www.acefitness.org>

Summary: The American Council on Exercise's mission is to promote active, healthy lifestyles and their positive effects on the mind, body, and spirit. ACE certifies fitness professionals and evaluates fitness products.

Lawrence Berkeley National Laboratory
University of California
<http://www.walkersurvey.com>

Summary: This Web site provides a free, on-the-spot analysis of your diet, physical activities, and lifestyle choices.

American College of Sports Medicine (ACSM)
PO Box 1440
Indianapolis, IN 46202-3233
(317) 637-9200
<http://www.acsm.org>

Summary: With the philosophy "healthier people make a healthier society," ACSM looks for better methods to allow everyone to live longer and more productively.

IDEA
(800) 999-4332
<http://www.ideafit.com>

Summary: IDEA's mission is to support the world's leading health and fitness professionals with credible information, education, development, and leadership to help them enhance the quality of life worldwide through participation in sure, effective fitness and healthy lifestyle programs.

National Strength and Conditioning Association
1955 N. Union Blvd.
Colorado Springs, CO 80909
(719) 632-6722
<http://www.nsca-lift.org>

Summary: This organization creates and disseminates knowledge about strength and conditioning to improve the lives of its members.

Diet

We are bombarded with often contradictory and supposedly expert diet and nutrition advice. It is very hard to keep track of whether margarine is good or bad, whether three glasses of wine would be even healthier than just the one with dinner many doctors recommend, or whether we are eating too many "carbs" (carbohydrates) or not enough.

The first step in evaluating the latest diet newsflash is to determine who released the study or reached the conclusion. A pharmaceutical company touting the benefits of the latest vitamin supplement—which it just happens to sell—may have as much (or as little) credibility as the movie star espousing the latest food combination miracle diet—which just happens to be the subject of her new book.

Once the source has been determined to be credible and objective, it is useful to know if the result was observed more than once.

The following dietary guidelines are based on numerous reputable studies and represent the best medical and scientific nutritional advice. The information provided here is merely an overview designed to connect the reader to the tools and resources that can help create a nutritious and satisfying diet to promote optimal health.

The single most significant dietary change we can make is to reduce our consumption of fat, which should comprise no more than 20 percent of our caloric intake. Foods that are high in fat often contain high levels of cholesterol and free radicals, which can actually speed up the aging process. Excessive dietary fat also causes atherosclerosis, which can lead to heart disease.

A high-fiber diet that includes fresh fruits and vegetables as well as foods high in whole-grain carbohydrates and soluble fiber such as oatmeal, oat bran, barley, and dried beans can be an effective guard against heart disease as well as many types of cancer.

Adequate protein intake ensures that our bodies have the necessary ingredients to make structural repairs, fight off diseases, and keep our hair, teeth, and bones strong. Small portions of protein throughout the day are also a great way to keep hunger at bay and prevent overeating.

RESOURCES

AMA Health Insight–Nutrition Information
American Medical Association (AMA)
515 North State Street
Chicago, IL 60610
(312) 464-5000
<http://www.ama-assn.org/insight/gen_hlth_nutrinfo/part3.htm>

Summary: The AMA provides excellent free information about eating right and staying healthy.

CyberDiet
<http://www.cyberdiet.com>

Summary: Cyberdiet features information on weight management, exercise, and keeping healthy.

American Heart Association
7272 Greenville Ave.
Dallas, TX 75231-4596
<http://www.americanheart.org>

Summary: The American Heart Association provides education and information on nutrition and exercise with a focus on heart attack and stroke prevention.

Health Answers
Healthway Online, Inc.
10435 Burnet Rd., Suite 122
Austin, TX 78758
(800) 794-2088
<http://www.healthanswers.com>

Summary: Comprehensive health education and resource site featuring expert advice.

Jobs and Careers

For many of us boomers, our work defines who we are. After all, we spend more time at our jobs than we do at anything else. And regardless of what we do, we care about doing a good job. We want to be proud of what we do and, to the extent possible, to enjoy going to work.

Many issues confront us in connection with our employment. The manner in which we address these issues will have both an immediate and a long-term impact on ourselves and our loved ones.

In addition to the traditional ways of finding a job through want ads in the newspaper, school placement services, personnel agencies, direct application to potential employers, and personal contacts, you can look to the Internet for employment opportunities, where several sites are available to identify job openings or offer career advice. The Web sites of many corporations and organizations now also include job listings.

RESOURCES

America's JobBank
U.S. Department of Labor
<http://www.ajb.dni.us/>

Summary: This Internet project, started by the U.S. Department of Labor to list available jobs nationwide, allows seekers to post résumés for employers to review. This site also has extensive information on labor and salary trends and job market conditions with resources to help you make the best career move possible.

> **College of William and Mary**
> Job Resources by U.S. Region
> Williamsburg, VA 23187-3329
> (757) 221-3240
> <http://www.wm.edu/csrv/career/>

Summary: Lists job finding resources by region.

> **Monster.com**
> (800) MONSTER
> <http://www.monster.com>

Summary: A huge job listings site with national exposure and plenty of related resources. National television advertising makes this site heavily trafficked. Monster.com is heavily used by technology-related firms and large corporations looking to expand their Internet presence.

> **Careerpath**
> 523 West Sixth Street, Suite 515
> Los Angeles, CA 90014
> (213) 996-0200
> <http://new.careerpath.com/>

Summary: Large database of available jobs and career advice. Allows for on-line searching of classified newspaper ads from across the nation.

> **Career Magazine**
> 4775 Walnut St., Suite 2A
> Boulder, CO 80301
> (303) 440-5110
> <http://www.careermag.com/>

Summary: On-line magazine covering career advancement and job hunting.

> **CareerLab**
> William S. Frank
> (303) 790-0505
> <http://www.careerlab.com/>

Summary: Career and job search advice, how-tos, and testimonials for corporations and individuals. CareerLab is produced by a consulting firm that provides career, outplacement, and human resources advice.

Ask the Headhunter
Nick Corcodilos
<http://www.asktheheadhunter.com>

Summary: Insider tips on job hunting, networking, and interviewing from an experienced headhunter.

Career Advice
PO Box 24938
Denver, CO 80224
(800) 559-6165
<http://www.careeradvice.com>

Summary: Job Search Counselor provides strategies on preparing for career transitions. The site contains numerous links to classified advertisements as well as headhunters.

HotJobs.com
24 West 40th Street, 14th Floor
New York, NY 10018
(212) 302-0060
(212) 944-8962 (Fax)
<http://www.hotjobs.com>

Summary: One of the largest job listings databases and résumé-posting services on the Web.

INSIGHT

Caveat emptor! Unscrupulous headhunters will often steal résumés that are posted on-line and send them out unsolicited in hopes of landing someone a job. Furthermore, some Web sites will copy résumés from others and add them to their database in an effort to bolster their holdings and attract more attention. Remember, once something is posted to the Web, it never dies, and a résumé posted today will still be floating around out there when you are preparing for your retirement party. Having your résumé pop in your human resources department in five years marked as "looking to change jobs" can cause embarrassment and hurt careers. At the very least, always date your résumés and ask Web sites to remove them after you have found a job.

In addition, because work is such a major part of our society, a variety of federal and state laws, as well as related court decisions, deal specifically with the workplace. Such laws address diverse issues such as family leave, discrimination, child labor, minimum wage, work conditions, and unemployment benefits.

Click on <http://www.Boomerbasics.com> for a comprehensive review of many of these issues as well as the text of key legislative initiatives.

Marriage, Divorce, Child Custody, and Child Support Issues

Marriage

Most boomers are or have been married, and contrary to popular belief, once married, the majority of boomers have stayed that way.

Marriages are subjected to many challenges including, but not limited to, financial pressures, drugs, sexual incompatibility, religious and social differences, in-law problems, child rearing and supervision, spousal power and control, and mental illness(es). (The last two challenges are not listed together for any particular reason.) The ability to deal with such pressures will often determine the ultimate success of the marriage.

Fortunately, if you have these or other issues in your marriage and you or your spouse desire to successfully address them, you can turn to professionals, clergy, and other individuals and organizations for help.

Divorce

As in any legal contractual arrangement, disagreements may develop between the parties in a marriage. In the case of divorce, the differences between the parties have damaged the relationship in a way (or ways) that may be irreparable. Leading causes of divorce include adultery, irreconcilable differences, and abuse. Regardless of the cause of divorce and the intense emotional baggage (sometimes rage) that is created within the environment leading up to it, the parties in a divorce must make decisions regarding division of property, spousal support (alimony), and child custody and support that may have lifelong repercussions.

Property

Property is defined as all marital assets, including the home, cash and other liquid assets, and personal property such as furniture and cars. Absent private agreement by the parties, the method used to distribute marital property will be determined by the laws of the respective states. Some states deem all property to be community property and thus divide it equally between the spouses after consideration of special and extraordinary factors; other states may conduct a more comprehensive review of the nature and origin of marital assets before determining how they will be distributed.

INSIGHT

Most states view assets that are commingled between spouses as marital property. For example, if you inherit $50,000 from your uncle and put it in a joint account with your spouse, it may be deemed marital property. If, on the other hand, you place it in an account in your own name, an argument can be made that it is your money alone and, therefore, property outside of the marriage. So if you're in a shaky marriage, or simply paranoid, you need to consider how to accept and record title to inheritances and gifts that are made to you personally and not to you as part of a couple.

An interesting phenomenon in modern-day boomer life is wrangling over whether a professional license(s) should be considered a marital asset. In many states, if a spouse earned a professional license during the marriage, anticipated future earnings stemming from that license may be included in the property settlement. For example, if a husband puts his wife through medical school while working at various jobs to pay tuition costs and then the wife divorces the husband, he may be able to claim an interest in her future earnings as a doctor.

Needless to say, the division and distribution of marital property can be analogous to a business dispute that involves a corporate dissolution. Where spouses are not able to resolve their differences in an amicable, reasonable, or efficient manner, lawyers, accountants, and other professionals ultimately receive a disproportionate share of marital assets.

Spousal Support (Alimony)

Determining whether one party should receive support from the other party is often a major battle in a divorce.

In the not-so-distant past, spousal support was a simple issue: A decision needed to be made as to whether the employed party (almost always the man) had to provide financial support to the nonworking, child-rearing party (almost always the woman). In most divorce situations today, the support issue is more complicated because both the man and the woman are working or are capable of working.

Once again, you need to be familiar with individual state laws to determine what rights and responsibilities you have in regard to receiving or paying alimony.

Child Custody

The primary battle in divorce cases is often over custody and how it will be structured, a decision (or series thereof) that is driven mainly by the realities of the familial relationship. Children often become pawns in the divorce battle when custody, support, and visitation issues are contested by parents; the court, however, must put the children's interests first and foremost when making a custody arrangement. Assessing where the children are in school; the nature of their activities, desires, and their relationship with their siblings; and the parents' work schedules, social life, and related issues are very important factors for the court to consider when deciding who gets custody.

INSIGHT

You should seek an attorney's advice to properly assert your rights in establishing and enforcing custody arrangements.

A variety of custody options exists. Legal joint custody is when both parents share not only the rights and responsibilities of raising their children but also physical custody. In joint custody, both custodians must confer when making major decisions regarding their children, such as rules that must be followed and what religion will be taught to them. This arrangement works best for parents who are willing and able to work at making decisions together for their children. Joint custody can be accomplished in two ways. In a pure joint custody arrangement, all decisions are shared equally. In the second form, all decisions regarding a certain issue are decided by one parent; for example, the mother may make all medical decisions, and the father may make all religious decisions. This may give the parents a way to reach acceptable compromises or delegations of authority as regards child-rearing issues. When unresolvable problems arise, the parents must go to court and present their respective cases so that the judge can make a decision. This can be a very expensive and time-consuming way of handling family problems, and the likelihood of court action should be considered thoroughly before agreeing to a joint custody arrangement.

In sole custody, one parent alone makes all the decisions. The noncustodial parent has no rights regarding the care and control of the child. This may be a practical arrangement if one parent plans on moving out of state or otherwise living a significant distance from the other.

Child Support

Children are expensive. The cost of raising a child from conception through college can range from tens of thousands to hundreds of thousands of dollars.

When parents divorce, the formal responsibility for child rearing is yet another issue often subjected to close scrutiny. Some states have created child support laws or guidelines that must be followed. Other states require that the parties reach a private agreement or that the matter be resolved by the courts.

Once support is established, the parties will have a legal obligation to make timely payments. Failure to do so can have serious ramifications, including civil and criminal sanctions.

RESOURCES
Marriage/Family Counseling

American Association for Marriage and Family Therapy (AAMFT)
1133 15th Street NW, Suite 300
Washington, D.C. 20005-2710
(202) 452-0109
<http://www.aamft.org>

Summary: The AAMFT is the professional association for the field of marriage and family therapy and facilitates research, theory development, and education.

Divorce

Divorcesource.com
<http://www.divorcesource.com>

Summary: Divorcesource.com is an informational Internet resource that includes state-by-state divorce information, attorneys, chat rooms, and related links.

Child Custody

Children's Rights Council
300 I Street NE, Suite 401
Washington, DC 20002
(202) 547-6227
<http://www.vix.com>

Summary: CRC is a national nonprofit organization that works to assure children meaningful and continuing contact with both their parents and extended family regardless of the parents' marital status.

Spirituality and Religion

After the "me" decade of the 1970s and the yuppie materialism of the 1980s and 1990s, many baby boomers find themselves in the new millennium looking for something more. Like the proverbial lost sheep, boomers are flocking to the religious/spiritual fold in record numbers.

Whatever road we choose, most of us are seemingly searching for something—a sense of belonging or connection to something much greater than ourselves, our life's purpose or spiritual path, a way to make sense of and cope with life's daily pressures, or a feeling of inner peace and contentment. Although some of us are returning to the religions we knew as children, others are embracing alternative religions or various aspects of the myriad New Age offerings, with their emphasis on integrating the body, mind, and spirit.

Balance is the watchword of many boomers who seek this elusive ideal through yoga, meditation, feng shui, and various remedies such as acupuncture, homeopathy, reiki, magnetism, and energy medicine. Books about angels, souls, contentment, living simply, living consciously, healing, and so on continually top the bestsellers lists. The Internet offers a wealth of information and resources on traditional, alternative, and New Age religious and spiritual interests.

RESOURCES

Note: These sites are illustrative of the type and scope of religious information available on the Internet. If you wish to seek information about a particular religion not listed, or if you desire more information about a religion that is included here, you can probably be on the Internet road to what you've been looking for by conducting a search of <http://www.[name of religion].org> or -.com>.

Christianity

OmniList of Christian Links Gold
Private site maintained by Keith Arthurs
<http://members.aol.com/clinksgold/index.html>

Summary: Links to resources on Christianity.

Not Just Bibles: A Guide to Christian Resources on the Internet
9700 SW Capitol Hwy., Suite 120
Portland, OR 97219
<http://www.iclnet.org/pub/resources/christian-resources.html>

Summary: More resources and information pertaining to Christianity.

Judaism

Torah.org
Project Genesis, Inc.
17 Warren Road, # 2B
Baltimore, MD 21208
(410) 602-1350
<http://www.torah.org>

Summary: A Web site dedicated to advancing the study of Torah.

DEI New Age Web Works
PO Box 4032
Felton, CA 95018
<http://www.newageinfo.com/res/welcome.htm>

Summary: A site dedicated to the rising popularity of New Age religions and spirituality.

Miscellaneous

Netguide
<http://www.netguide.com/Family/spirituality>

Summary: Features articles and information on every major world religion as well as online places of worship.

Profiles of World Religions
University of Virginia
539 Cabell Hall
Charlottesville, VA 22903
<http://cti.itc.virginia.edu/~jkh8x/soc257/profiles.html>

Summary: Provides historical and sociological information on religious movements to create a foundation for understanding and appreciation of all religions.

Yahoo!
<http://dir.yahoo.com/society_and_culture/religion/>

Summary: Connections to religious groups, articles, chat rooms, merchandise, and classified ads.

Doctors, Lawyers, etc.—Finding the Best Professionals for You

You can not always handle challenges and problems on your own. Sometimes you will need to resort to knowledgeable and dedicated professionals who can help you in a sensitive, competent, and efficient manner.

The increasingly complex nature of our society has led to a trend toward specialization among professionals. Lawyers, for example, tended to be general practitioners in our parents' days, but nowadays they are inclined to concentrate on a particular area of expertise. This seems to make sense; would you want a criminal attorney to handle an adoption? a divorce attorney to handle a complex corporate matter? or an elder law attorney to prepare an initial stock offering? Doctors serve as another example of this move toward a specific focus among professionals. Would you want a podiatrist to perform open-heart surgery? Would you want a dermatologist to perform brain surgery?

Suffice it to say that when you are working with a professional, you want to ensure that he or she has the skills, experience, commitment, and availability to perform the service(s) you desire at a price you can afford.

The following is a list of questions that you may ask a professional you may wish to retain:

- Where did you get your educational training?
- What type of experience do you have?
- Have you actually performed the types of services that I require at this time?
- May I speak with some of your other clients so that I may obtain their opinion of your work?
- Are you a member of any professional organizations? Do you participate in continuing education?
- How do you bill for your services? Will you provide me with a written retainer?
- Who is on your staff? If you are not available, who will help me?

The task of finding professionals that possess the requisite skills and ability has been made somewhat easier by the emergence of professional and consumer associations that provide such information and that, in some cases, certify that their members meet basic standards of performance and ethics.

RESOURCES
Medical

American Medical Association
515 North State Street
Chicago, IL 60610
(312) 464-4818
<http://www.ama-assn.org>

Summary: The AMA is a professional association of physicians and medical students dedicated to the health of the U.S. public. The AMA maintains the AMA Physician Accreditation Program, a voluntary, comprehensive program that measures and evaluates individual physicians against national standards, criteria, and peer performance. The AMA also maintains AMA Physician Select, which provides information on virtually every licensed physician in the United States and its possessions. And you'll find an "On-Line Doctor Finder" at the AMA Web site.

American Dental Association
211 E. Chicago Avenue
Chicago, IL 60611
(312) 440-2500
<http://www.ada.org>

Summary: The ADA is a professional association of dentists serving both the profession and the public. Its Web site has information on dental care, decay prevention, and finding a dentist.

Legal

American Bar Association
750 North Lake Shore Drive
Chicago, IL 60611
(312) 988-5000
<http://www.abanet.org>

Summary: ABA membership is open to lawyers admitted to practice and in good standing before the bar of any state or territory of the United States. ABA members represent approximately half of all lawyers in the United States. The ABA and Martindale-Hubbell have together established the ABA Network Lawyer Locator, which is available on the ABA Web site. The database contains over nine hundred thousand listings of lawyers and law firms (all information in the directory listings is gathered from the Martindale-Hubbell database).

Financial Planning

Institute of Certified Financial Planners
3801 East Florida Avenue, Suite 708
Denver, CO 80210-2544
(303) 759-4900
<http://www.icfp.org>

Summary: The Institute of Certified Financial Planners is a national professional membership association of certified financial planning licensees and candidates. Not every person who is described as a financial planner is a certified financial planning licensee. Most certified financial planning professionals have earned a four-year college degree in areas such as accounting, economics, business administration, marketing, or finances. Additionally, they have completed a course of study in financial planning at one of the colleges or universities that has registered its program with the CFP board.

National Association of Personal Financial Advisors (NAPFA)
355 West Dundee Road, Suite 200
Buffalo Grove, IL 60089
(888) FEE-ONLY
<http://www.napfa.org>

Summary: NAPFA is a professional association of comprehensive, fee-only financial planners that can help you find resources for yourself as a consumer as well as regulations for financial planners.

Accounting/Certified Public Accountants

The American Institute of Certified Public Accountants (AICPA)
1211 Avenue of the Americas
New York, NY 10036
<http://www.aicpa.org>

Summary: The AICPA is a national professional association of certified public accountants in the United States. To become a CPA, candidates must pass the uniform CPA examination; upon doing so, they qualify for a CPA certificate and license to practice public accounting. Each state has its own requirements that individuals must meet. CPAs in the United States are licensed by State Boards of Accountancy.

Securities Brokers/Dealers

National Association of Securities Dealers
1390 Piccard Drive
Rockville, MD 20850-3389
<http://www.nasd.com>

Summary: The National Association of Securities Dealers is the largest self-regulatory organization for the securities industry in the United States. You can lodge an official complaint on its Web site if you suspect that you have been wronged by a securities dealer.

North American Securities Administration Association (NASAA)
10 G Street NE, Suite 710
Washington, DC 20002
(202) 783-3571
<http://www.nasaa.org>

Summary: The North American Securities Administrators Association is the oldest organization devoted to investor protection in the world. You can find education links, updates, and policy positions from NASAA at its Web site.

Insurance

Alliance of American Insurers
3025 Highland Parkway, Suite 800
Downers Grove, IL 60515-1289
<http://www.allianceai.org>

Summary: The Alliance of American Insurers is a trade association of property and casualty insurance companies. Its Web site features updates on the insurance industry.

National Association of Life Underwriters (NALU)
1922 F Street NW
Washington, DC 20006
(202) 331-6000
<http://www.nalu.org>

Summary: According to its Web site, NALU represents more than one hundred thousand sales professionals in life and health insurance and other related financial services. Its purpose is to sustain and improve the business environment in the life and health insurance profession.

FINANCIAL ~~~~~~~~

Developing a Financial Plan

Although some may argue that our desire for conspicuous consumption now is leaving little money for our future, poor saving habits are not the only financial problem that some in our generation may face. Our sheer numbers will work against us when we become retirees. For example, Social Security and other social welfare programs such as Medicaid and Medicare may go bankrupt or become seriously curtailed in the not-so-distant future.

Some of you may not be too concerned because we boomers will be the legatees of a record $10 trillion in inheritance from our parents—an amount that equals roughly $130,000 per baby boomer. If this sounds too good to be true, it's because for most of us, it is—approximately two-thirds of this inheritance will go to only 10 percent of us. For the rest of us, in the absence of proper planning, any sums that do come our way likely will be consumed by our living longer and surviving more illnesses—in other words, by covering higher nursing home, home care, and medical expenses.

Now for the good news: We boomers have proven ourselves to be the most educated and resourceful group in the history of the world. With the right resources, we can and will assert our individual and collective wisdom to ensure financial security for ourselves and our loved ones.

To help us in this endeavor, in addition to the information available at <http://www.Boomerbasics.com>, you can receive free or low-cost assistance from a multitude of private and governmental organizations. Be it for altruistic or proprietary reasons, each of these entities can provide us with tools we need to address our current and future financial needs. Before we list these available resources, you should note the functions that many of these organizations will enable you to perform.

Education

To many of us, financial terminology and concepts are analogous to, or even a part of, a foreign language we don't understand. For example, don't the "-tion" words such as *amortization, depreciation, capitalization, deviation, valuation, contraction,* and *appreciation* sometimes confuse you? Do you understand basic and complex investment strategies that can help you achieve your objectives? Have you given thought to planning and paying for your child's education? The answer to all of these questions is "probably." But have you done anything about it besides putting it off?

At the risk of stating the obvious, we did not learn or care about many of these issues when we were in school and, in many cases, through our young adult life. We now need to self-educate, a task that is made a lot easier with the accessibility of several world-class Web sites as resources.

Planning

Think of all the things for which you need to plan: everyday living, retirement, education for children, vacations and other special events, your estate, and much more. Many of these sites guide you with a potpourri of checklists and advice for both short- and long-term goals. Many of you will find planning for these important issues to be a cleansing experience in which you evaluate, quantify, and address the needs and desires of yourself and your loved ones.

Personalized Calculations and Considerations

Because we are all different in our spending and saving habits, our aversion to risks, and the priority of our goals and objectives, a plan that works for one person may not be appropriate for another. Therefore, we need to review our individual situations; calculate our own best personal financial plan; and ensure that our objectives are reasonable and attainable and, if not, decide where to compromise and modify our plan. To help us in this endeavor, many sites provide the tools to perform the necessary calculations, including, but not limited to, the following: retirement planning, paying for college, personal budget, loans and mortgages, investments, insurance matters, and tax planning.

Implementation

Once you've developed your plan, you can implement it through many of the goods and services offered via the Internet. For many, the search may simply be for a qualified advisor(s). For those so inclined, it might be for actual products. A great example is insurance, for which you can get comparable quotes that will help you secure appropriate coverage at a competitive price. Another example is investments; you can learn about investment opportunities as well as purchase investment products on-line. Regardless of whether you seek professional guidance, handle the planning yourself, or do some of each, you can probably find it on the Internet.

INSIGHT

It's worth the time, cost, and effort to plan for your financial future and security. The pessimists who report daily on the anticipated financial demise of the boomer generation clearly underestimate our resolve and commitment.

RESOURCES

Note: The following sites can provide you with a representative sample of the type(s) of comprehensive financial Web sites, sometimes referred to as *portals,* that offer information, services, or products regarding issues of financial importance to boomers and their loved ones.

> **Cyberinvest.com**
> 3620 Third Ave., Suite 201
> San Diego, CA 92103
> (619) 295-5408
> <http://www.cyberinvest.com>

Summary: Among the information, services, and products you can get from this site, you will find especially useful the feature titled "Linksoup," which connects you to Web sites covering a wide range of areas including banking, bonds, investment, taxes, and financial news. Cyberinvest also has a variety of other special features, including "Guide to Investing Super Sites" and "Cool Tools."

Financenter.com
1860 East River Road, Suite 200
Tucson, AZ 85718
(520) 299-9009
<http://financenter.com>

Summary: This site is well recognized for its 110 calculators that address personal financial issues involving automobiles, credit lines, retirement, stock, home, budgeting, insurance, mutual funds, credit cards, savings, Roth IRAs, and bonds.

Money Central Investor
Microsoft
One Microsoft Way
Redmond, WA 98052-6399
(425) 882-8080
<http://www.moneycentral.com>

Summary: The comprehensive content available in this site includes the following categories: "Investor," "News Desk," "Banking and Bills," "Saving and Spending," and "Family and College." There are several special features as well including technical support, an article index, and a tool index. As with many of other similar sites, you can also enjoy access to stock quotes and the stock exchange ticker and create your own portfolio to track your investments.

Quicken.com
<http://www.quicken.com>

Summary: In addition to the routine information, services, and products found on most similar sites, this site offers special features, such as the (financial) "book of the month," the "problem solver," and "today's highlights." The departments maintained in this Web site include investments, home and mortgage, insurance, taxes, banking and credit, small business, retirement, life events, and saving and spending. When you click on the Quicken.com index, you'll truly appreciate the range of financial topics listed.

T. Rowe Price
Shareholder Correspondence
PO Box 89000
Baltimore, MD 21289-0250
(800) 225-5132
<http://www.troweprice.com>

Summary: This site offers a variety of financial information, services, or products regarding retirement, IRAs, college funding, tax strategies, and business matters. The site provides daily news updates as well.

Charles Schwab
101 Montgomery St.
San Francisco, CA 94104
<http://www.myschwab.com>

Summary: If you seek it, you can probably find it on this comprehensive site. The following is a brief list of what you will find here: investment tips and research; assistance with life events, such as tax, retirement, college, and estate planning, which includes educational programs with expert speakers and related planning tools; market snapshot; and the MySchwab homepage, where you can create your own personalized financial home-page.

INSIGHT

In addition to the information that you can get by clicking on <http://www .Boomerbasics.com> and the previously mentioned sites, almost all financial-related businesses have established or are in the process of establishing an Internet presence. You can probably easily locate the Web site of your bank, mutual fund, retirement plan, and any other entity with which you do business, and you will likely be treated to a wealth of information if you do. As you probably have figured out, it becomes a matter of business survival to not only have an Internet presence but also to provide Web site visitors with interesting and useful information at little or no cost.

Consumer Debt—Avoid It If You Can

Before addressing what you should be doing, we'll start with what you should not be doing: Do not put yourself voluntarily into debt! Consumer common sense is based on the theory that you shouldn't borrow money to buy things you cannot afford, especially things you don't really need. When it is not likely that you will ever be able to pay back the loan or when the total interest you will end up paying back on the loan is so substantial that it will equal or even exceed the amount you paid for the item you purchased, you need to exercise consumer common sense. Unfortunately, the high amount of personal bankruptcies in our country demonstrates that many people, including boomers, who as a class are the most educated people in the history of the world, do not practice consumer common sense.

Ponder this amazing statistic from the U.S. Federal Reserve: In 1998, U.S. citizens amassed $1.3 trillion in outstanding installment debt. The intentional accumulation of debt has become a way of life for many people in the United States. Ironically, this phenomenon is often encouraged by business and financial institutions that target both wealthy and poor people with a propensity to borrow. These companies make tremendous profits from the interest payments they receive from the loans they make. This is why banks, credit card companies, stores, and the like aggressively offer credit cards to as many people as possible because they know the interest that consumers pay on credit cards far exceeds what they would pay on any other type of loan.

Don't be a willing participant in the terminal debt trap. If you are paying off substantial debt service on your credit cards, you need to rethink your spending habits because such debt takes a long time to disappear. If you are planning for your retirement, you don't want to be paying for things you bought years ago.

INSIGHT

Do _not_ borrow money for the sake of borrowing money or for convenience. Consider the cost for you to borrow the money; calculate the total cost of the product and anticipated interest. There is no worse feeling than paying something off long after you purchased or enjoyed it (for example, a vacation) and—

it gets even worse—when you figure out that the total repayment far exceeded the item's original value. For example, if Ralph Kramden charges $2,000 for a vacation on his credit card and takes three years to pay it back at 16 percent interest, he will eventually pay in excess of $2,500, with the final payment being sent off long after the vacation ended. Ralph now asks himself if the vacation was worth the expense of paying for it and then some after the fact.

Although some people knowingly invite or accept a life of debt because they want or believe they deserve certain things, other people are forced into debt for compelling reasons such as health problems requiring immediate treatment, family emergencies, unemployment, and so on. For people truly in need, alternatives to going into debt may be available, such as medical assistance from the government, especially for children and the elderly.

Click on <http://www.Boomerbasics.com> for additional information regarding consumer debt and page 87 of this book regarding bankruptcy issues.

If you are concerned about your credit status or would like to review credit standing, you can, for a small fee, request this information from several companies. If you have recently been denied credit, you may be entitled to receive this information for no cost. Remember that you have the right to dispute items on your credit report that you believe to be inaccurate.

RESOURCES
Credit Report Information

> **Equifax, Inc.**
> PO Box 740241
> Atlanta, GA 30374-0241
> (800) 997-2493
> <http://www.equifax.com>

Summary: You can order your Equifax credit report on-line, request it in writing, or order it by phone.

Trans Union
PO Box 403
Springfield, PA 19064
(800) 888-4213
<http://www.transunion.com>

Summary: In addition to providing you with your credit report, Trans Union provides you with a summary of consumer rights.

Debt Management and Counseling

The Center for Debt Management
119 Camp Sargent Road
Merrimack, NH 03054
<http://www.center4debtmanagement.com>

Summary: The Center for Debt Management maintains this 500-page Web site that provides information to families and individuals who are employed but in debt. From the index of features, click on either "Debt Counseling Services" or "Debt Management Services."

Debt Relief Counseling Service
234 Aquarius Drive, Suite 109
Birmingham, AL 35209
(888) 211-6144
<http://www.drcs.org/>

Summary: Debt Relief Counseling Service is an IRS-recognized, nonprofit organization dedicated to helping people regain control over debt.

Debt Counselors of America
<http://www.dca.org/>

Summary: The Debt Counselors of America is a nonprofit organization that provides a broad array of information on regaining financial independence.

National Foundation for Consumer Credit
8611 Second Avenue, Suite 100
Silver Spring, MD 20910
(800) 388-2227
<http://www.nfcc.org>

Summary: A network of nonprofit agencies that provide money management education, budget counseling, and debt repayment plans.

Saving for Future Expenses / Planning for Retirement

As we enter into the new millennium, any true boomer will remember calculating in grade school how old he or she would be at the turn of the century. We all know how quickly time has flown to get us to this point, and it will move even more quickly as we head toward our retirement years. Hence, the planning for retirement begins now!

In the following sections we will provide you with the basics to help you examine when and how well you can retire. In part, reaching your goals will be a by-product of how well you can save and, equally importantly, of how well you utilize the planning tools available through your employer, the IRS, and your financial advisors to leverage your savings through and beyond your retirement years. By reviewing your retirement objectives, identifying potential sources of retirement income, and knowing how best to have your retirement savings paid out to you someday, you will be much further along in reaching, or hopefully exceeding, your goals.

Nearly everyone expects that they can live on less once they reach retirement, and it's true. By that time, expenses related to such things as mortgages, child care and education, and working and commuting will usually have disappeared. In all, the generally accepted benchmark for a comfortable retirement income used by most financial planners is approximately 70 percent of what you currently earn. Calculating your expenses during retirement, your fixed sources of retirement income, the shortfall between the two, and the amount of money needed to fund the shortfall is all part of the process of planning for the future.

First, estimate retirement expenses for one year—remember, that's approximately 70 percent of current expenses. That is just the beginning!

Now multiply that figure by the number of years you hope to live after retirement (be optimistic). As a guide, you should consider that the U.S. Department of Health and Human Services reports that in 1998 the average life expectancy was 73.1 years for men and 79.1 years for women. The result of these calculations shows how much you will need to take care of yourself.

Second, figure out the fixed sources of income you will have at the time of your retirement. To compute this, you'll need to find out the value of any retirement accounts you now have. As part of this analysis, you should also figure out how much Social Security benefits you will be receiving; click on <http://www.Boomerbasics.com> for information on how to do that.

Any additional assets, such as cash-value life insurance, real estate, valuable personal properties (for example, antiques), or business/shareholder interests, may be liquefied to provide capital and added to what you've already accumulated toward retirement. Liabilities (debts) on these assets should be subtracted when determining the assets' actual value.

Options for decreasing the cost of retirement include delaying the time at which you retire, working part time after retiring, relocating to a less expensive locale, or creating a less expensive retirement lifestyle. With all this to consider, remain undaunted—it is possible to estimate where you stand in planning for retirement.

So far, you have computed your total retirement years' expenses and total retirement years' assets. Another consideration is inflation. Yes, we're bound to carry on some day about what a dollar used to buy. To illustrate its effects over different time horizons at various rates, click on <http://www .Boomerbasics.com>. The extent to which the former exceeds the latter is the amount of additional income you will need. Before figuring out what you need to do to generate that amount of money, consider how much of the gap may be adjusted by adopting cost-reduction strategies such as those mentioned previously.

Now you need to determine how much money you need to save presently to generate the amount of income you'll need when you retire. This process is undoubtedly a little complicated, but with some patience and perseverance, you can come up with the magic number. Doing so now will help you to avoid a lot of personal grief and panic upon realizing, the day after your retirement begins, that you've run out of money before you've run out of steam.

INSIGHT

Almost all of the comprehensive financial Web sites listed on pages 30–32, as well as numerous other off-line and on-line services, will provide you with the necessary tools to quantify your retirement needs and objectives.

Potential Sources for Retirement Income

As our parents who are retired can attest from their personal experience and as we discussed just previously, you want to ensure, if possible, that you have enough income to cover your expenses in retirement and avoid substantial depletion of your assets. In fact, you want your assets to generate income when they can.

There are many potential sources of retirement income. In this section, we will discuss the following sources: Social Security, qualified employee benefit plans, profit-sharing plans, individual retirement accounts (IRAs), Roth IRAs, Keogh plans, simplified employee pensions (SEPs), and 401(k) and 403(b) plans.

Social Security

You are painfully aware of the amounts deducted from your pay for Social Security. However, the money you are paying into the federal Social Security system pays for those who are now retired. Down the road when you retire, those who are working at that time will pay for your benefits. Sounds good— all those young people working for your benefit. Unfortunately, the critical mass of boomers creates special problems in this regard. In 2010, there won't be enough workers to pay the retirees. No one knows the solution to this dilemma, but it looms very large over the future of the federal plan.

Whether you can count on that monthly check is certainly still an open question, but for planning purposes, you can fill out a form at the local Social Security Administration office or visit its Web site to find out what you would receive if you stopped working (and contributing) now and retired at age 65. If and when you do qualify for a Social Security check, many current rules will probably still be in effect. Normal retirement is generally believed to start when you reach the age of sixty-five, and early retirement age is sixty-two, but the rules for baby boomers are changing. For many of us, Social Security checks won't start until we are sixty-six or sixty-seven.

If you retire later than the minimum age, you'll get more (current increases are 0.33 percent for each month a person delays beyond normal retirement age). Your spouse and dependents may also get payments because a number of variations and circumstances affect eligibility. For example, spouses receive a reduced amount (unless their own earnings are greater); divorced spouses also need to have been married to the retiree for more than ten years and be over the age of sixty-two before they can collect. A divorced spouse can receive benefits from an ex-spouse's Social Security benefits if he or she is caring for the ex-spouse's minor child. Overall, the best advice is to check with the Social Security Administration using your particular facts and circumstances. You may learn of some benefits to which you did not know you were entitled.

RESOURCES

Social Security Benefits
SSA Office of Public Inquiries
6401 Security Boulevard
Room 4-5 Annex
Baltimore, MD 21235-6401
<http://www.ssa.gov/>

Summary: The Social Security Administration will provide a personal earnings and benefit statement (PEBES). Simply answer the on-line questionnaire, and your benefit statement will be mailed to you. From the main screen, click on "benefit statement."

For further information, click on <http://www.Boomerbasics.com> and refer to "Resources" on pages 316–317 in the "Financial" section of Part Three, "Our Parents."

Qualified Employee Benefit Plans

Qualified employee benefit plans, usually provided by an employer, pay out distributions on a certain date, either upon retirement or at the end of employment. There are two basic types of these plans: defined contribution and defined benefit. As its name might suggest, in a *defined contribution plan,* contribution to the plan is decided by formula, not by actuarial data. This method distributes earnings and losses of the plan assets to the employees and lessens the company's costs. In contrast, a *defined benefit plan* has a definite payout amount; any plan that is not a defined contribution plan or an individual account falls under this description. If there is not enough money in the account to pay the promised benefit, the employer must pay additional money to cover the shortfall.

Both a defined contribution plan and a defined benefit plan could pay out in the form of an annuity or a lump sum. Annuities and lump sum payments are covered in the following section, "Payout at Retirement."

RESOURCES

U.S. Department of Labor
Pension and Welfare Benefits (PWBA)
200 Constitution Avenue NW, Room N-5656
Washington, DC 20210
<http://www.dol.gov/>

Summary: The U.S. Department of Labor site provides many regulations and publications on employee benefit and pension issues among the many areas it oversees.

Profit-Sharing Plans

Profit-sharing plans, another type of defined contribution plan, are also tax deferred. Basically, such plans allow you to share in your employer's profits, which are paid into a retirement fund under your name where you are typically offered investment options in stock or bond mutual funds. Loans and withdrawals for emergency expenses generally are not permitted. The plan usually has a vesting period, which means that to be guaranteed money, you must continue working for the same employer for at least a minimum number of years. Once the money vests, it becomes yours, so it can move with you if you leave the employer.

Individual Retirement Accounts

An IRA is an account that you may have already established for your retirement savings. If not, you may wish to consider doing so because of the tax-deferred advantages. Basically, you may make tax-deductible contributions of up to $2,000 of earned income into an IRA each year until the year you reach seventy and one-half years of age. You may also put away an additional $2,000 per year of your earned income for your non-income-earning spouse. If you or your spouse are not covered by an employer's retirement plan, then your IRA contributions are generally tax deductible. Even if you or your spouse is covered by an employer's retirement plan, subject to certain income limitations, you may still deduct some or all of your IRA contributions.

Click on <http://www.Boomerbasics.com> to determine whether you fall within these income tax limits for deductible IRA contributions.

In addition to the contribution rules, you should be aware of several withdrawal rules. In the event you withdraw money from your IRA, it is taxed as ordinary income at that time. If you withdraw funds from your IRA before you reach the age of fifty-nine and one-half years, the withdrawn funds will be subject to a 10 percent federal tax penalty. You may avoid the penalty if you fall within certain exceptions, such as for reasons of disability, payment of higher education expenses, purchase of a new home (up to $10,000 lifetime limit), or to cover certain medical expenses.

Although you are penalized for taking money prior to reaching the minimum age, you may also be penalized if you do not start taking money by the time you're seventy and one-half. Upon reaching that age, there are several rules to follow, but basically you must begin taking annual withdrawals for the term of your life expectancy no later than the April after attaining the age of seventy and one-half years. Click on <http://www.Boomerbasics .com> for further details as to what amounts may be withdrawn, how to extend the deferral period, and the alternatives available for calculating the amounts to withdraw.

RESOURCES

Bank America Corp.
<http://www.bankamerica.com>

Summary: This site provides a list of frequently asked questions about IRAs. From the main screen, click on "personal finance."

> **The Vanguard Group**
> PO Box 2600
> Valley Forge, PA 19482-2600
> (800) 871-3879
> <http://www.vanguard.com>

Summary: This site answers questions on IRA contributions, deductions, transfers, and rollovers.

Roth IRAs

Congress recently enacted legislation establishing the Roth IRA, which is a variation of the contributory IRA. Named after its chief sponsor, Senate Finance Chairman William B. Roth Jr. of Delaware, the Roth IRA allows an individual to contribute up to $2,000 per year of after-tax savings. Whereas the traditional IRA takes in pretax dollars and grows tax free until withdrawal, at which time it is taxed, the Roth IRA receives after-tax contributions and grows tax free but is never taxed again, even upon withdrawal. As such, there are no minimum distribution requirements upon attaining the age of seventy and one-half years as there are with the typical contributory IRA discussed previously. However, some withdrawal rules do apply. As with the traditional IRA, you may not make withdrawals before you reach the age of fifty-nine and one-half, although withdrawals of up to $10,000 (lifetime limit) may be made for first-time purchase of a home. In all cases, a Roth IRA must be in existence for five years before any withdrawals are made to get the tax-deferred benefits.

Another planning consideration is the possibility of converting your traditional IRA to a Roth IRA. In the event you wish to do this, the cost of conversion will require that income taxes must be paid on the untaxed amounts withdrawn. As unappealing as it may sound to pay income taxes sooner than you have to, it may make economic sense to gain the long-term benefits of the Roth IRA, as the tax deferral will continue in your account and ultimately be withdrawn on a tax-free basis during retirement or by your heirs. In any event, you must take into account the number of years until retirement, your present and projected tax brackets, and your overall financial plan when deciding whether or not it makes sense to convert to a Roth IRA at this time.

Finally, a Roth IRA may not be available to everyone, as certain income limitations apply. Briefly, if your adjusted gross income exceeds $110,000 as a single filer or $160,000 as a joint filer, you cannot make a Roth IRA contribution. Also, if you make more than $100,000 in a year, you will not be able to convert your old IRA into a Roth IRA.

Because this legislation is relatively new, it is important that you click on <http://www.Boomerbasics.com> to get the most up-to-date information available as Congress continues to write guidelines with regard to the administration of Roth IRAs.

RESOURCES

Roth IRA Website Homepage
<http://www.rothira.com>

Summary: The Roth IRA Web site is sponsored by Brentmark Software, Inc., and was established to provide technical and planning information on Roth IRAs to practitioners and consumers.

Strong On-line
<http://www.strong-funds.com/strong/retirement98/roth/rothind>

Summary: This Web site is maintained by Strong Investment Services and features a Roth conversion analyzer. From the main screen, click on "Roth IRA Conversion Calculator."

Smith Barney Investment Update
<http://www.salomonsmithbarney.com/inv_up/arts/two.html>

Summary: Explains factors to be taken into consideration when determining whether a conversion to a Roth IRA is appropriate.

Keogh Plans and Simplified Employee Pensions

Keogh plans are tax-deferred investment plans available if you are self-employed full time or if you are self-employed part time and get retirement coverage through an employer. You can set up a fund that contains up to 15 percent of your self-employment income, with a maximum of $30,000 per year.

Similar to Keogh plans but easier to set up and administer, SEPs are attractive if you are self-employed with no other employees in your business.

INSIGHT

Your local bank or mutual fund should be able to set up either a Keogh or a SEP for you at little or no charge.

RESOURCES

Small Business Advisor
Information International
Great Falls, VA 22066
(703) 450-7049
<http://www.isquare.com/retire.htm>

Summary: A quick overview of Keogh basics from the Small Business Advisor.

401(k) or 403(b) Plans

The hallmark of 401(k) and 403(b) plans is that they allow you to make pre-tax contributions from your salary that may be matched by your employer. These employer-sponsored plans are defined contribution (formula) plans. A 403(b) plan is used by not-for-profit employers with or instead of a 401(k) plan. These plans' numerical names refer to the sections in the Internal Revenue Code that allow for and describe their operation.

A typical 401(k) allows you to contribute up to 6 percent of your pretax pay. The employer may contribute a fixed percentage, for example, 50 cents for every dollar you contribute. If this is the case, take full advantage because you will rarely find a 50 percent return on your money in other investments. Employee contributions are capped each year but can still be quite enough to provide a considerable retirement nest egg if contributions continue for an extended period.

Both plans are portable, meaning that if you leave your employer, your contributions can go with you.

RESOURCES

The Investment FAQ
<http://www.invest-faq.com/articles>

Summary: This site offers information about investments and personal finance, including the use of 401(k)s and related investments.

401(K) Forum

625 Third St.

San Francisco, CA 94107

(415) 547-1120

<http://www.401kforum.com>

<http://www.kafe.com>

Summary: As you explore these sites, you will receive valuable information. Special attention is paid to the various levels of knowledge of site visitors.

Benefits Link

1014 E. Robinson St.

Orlando, FL 32801

(407) 841-3717

<http://www.benefitslink.com>

Summary: This site describes itself as a free on-line publication about all kinds of employer-sponsored benefit plans in the United States. You will find information and articles about 401(k) and 403(b) plans on this site.

Quicken

<http://www.quicken.com>

Summary: Discusses various aspects of 403(b) plans, including eligibility, contributions, withdrawals, and changing jobs, in the form of a reference guide.

Payout at Retirement

Once you decide to start using your retirement savings, there are a variety of options to consider. As you would expect, the IRS is a factor in all of the options, but otherwise the decisions on how and when to have your IRAs, pensions, savings, and the like paid to you should be based on you and your family's unique circumstances, needs, and objectives. This section will illustrate that you can do more than simply follow the lead of the person who retired just before you.

Use of Principal

For reasons that probably relate back to the Great Depression, most people are reluctant to use up principal after they retire. In fact, they should not be reluctant to use their hard-earned savings provided they have made a thorough and realistic analysis of their retirement needs and resources, as they are unlikely to ever outspend their life expectancy, real or on paper.

Lump Sum versus Annuity

Most private retirement plans defer the decision concerning payout until you retire. In general, the choice between a lump sum or an annuity should not be made lightly, as it is usually irrevocable and has potentially serious consequences. Surprisingly, many people don't think about the choice of payout until the retirement party is set and the human resources office is wrapping up its paperwork; until that moment, their minds have been on the final celebration and foisting all responsibility onto that junior person who has been preening for his or her job. Think about it now while time is still your ally.

An *annuity* is the payout of a fixed amount in periodic payments over the lifetime of the annuitant. An annuity can be single (for just one person's life) or joint (for more than one person's life). A *single-life annuity* pays out at a higher rate but leaves nothing to a spouse or family members. A *joint and survivor annuity* is one that pays through the joint lifetimes of both people, typically spouses.

Annuities are good for people who do not have a high tolerance for risk and like the idea of a fixed check each month. Although investing in any annuity plan is quite hassle free, the down side is that you lose the flexibility of what you can do with your money and the amount you receive. You are locked into a predetermined amount, and you do not have access to the capital to address unforeseen changes in circumstances. Another drawback is that such lifetime annuities cannot be passed to heirs. Once you or the other beneficiaries die, the annuity ends. The payments end even if you die soon after retiring with plenty of unused retirement funds. However, you can never outlive your payments.

Receiving your payment in a lump sum—the payout of the entire amount at one time—may be better than receiving it on an annuity basis most of the time because the long-term return on the annuity is often lower than if you prudently reinvest the lump sum. Reinvesting in a diversified portfolio may allow you to maintain your purchasing power in the marketplace by keeping up with inflation, as opposed to annuities, which remain fixed throughout your lifetime.

The disadvantage of a lump sum is the responsibility of managing it. Investments by their nature involve some risk, and no guarantee exists that you will get a greater return on your investment than you would receive through your fixed annuity. Many retirees do not want to deal with such decisions. Professional money management can eliminate the pain of decision making, although it cannot guarantee investment returns.

If you choose a lump sum, the immediate decision will be whether to receive it all at once or defer some tax consequences by rolling over all or part of it into an IRA. The answer to this question depends on your vision of retirement. Consider the reality of the financial situation, your age at retirement, your expected lifestyle, and whether you intend to create a legacy.

If you don't need the funds immediately, then reinvestment is the best strategy. As just mentioned, reinvestment can be tax deferred by rolling over into an IRA, or you can pay the income tax up front and reinvest the proceeds. When you roll over the lump sum, all the usual rules about withdrawal of IRAs will then apply. The money remains tax deferred until withdrawal. However, withdrawals could push you into a higher income tax bracket, so foresight is needed.

By not rolling over to an IRA, the lump sum is taxable as income in the year you receive it, which, again, could push your extra income into a higher tax bracket.

INSIGHT

The tax code changes constantly; it is best not to rely on advice contained in any printed material that isn't dated for the current tax year.

INSIGHT

Usually, we think of income taxes in connection with the federal government, but state taxation can take a bite, too. State income taxes vary considerably. If you are thinking of moving after retiring, check out the income tax rates of your planned retirement state; you might want to roll out the money when you move into the low tax state.

The Federation of Tax Administration provides information regarding state individual income tax rates on their Web site: <http://www.taxadmin.org /fta/rate/tax_stru.html>.

Age and Health Factors

If you retire early, you'll need to consider the additional time you'll be relying on retirement funds to support yourself and, thus, how much more money you'll need. Early retirement means you may have to wait before receiving retirement plan payouts, either because you won't yet be eligible or because of the substantial penalties (for example, 10 percent) for early withdrawal. Social Security also pays less if you apply for benefits early, which makes sense since the longer payout period means essentially a bigger payout.

INSIGHT

Retiring boomers can expect to live into their eighties. This is great news if you have a substantial nest egg, but most boomers don't have the savings they need; it's therefore likely that many of us may be working into our seventies. If you want to avoid that fate or if you want to retire early, focus on the following:

1. **Early retirement incentives offered by an employer**
2. **Health insurance and the availability of retiree health benefits or COBRA continuation until you become Medicare eligible**
3. **Social Security benefits and payouts of retirement plans**
4. **The tax status of your payouts**
5. **The effect on your taxes and Social Security benefits of working after retirement age**

Any retirement strategy must consider the possibility of the retiree encountering chronic or fatal illnesses, debilitation, and incapacity. Taking care of your health and knowing the likelihood of certain illnesses in your family are reasonable moves toward safeguarding your retirement plans, but one way or another, boomers must cope with disability, sickness, and death. Although health, health care proxies, living wills, powers of attorney, various health and life insurance policies, and estate planning are covered in other parts of this book, they are also part and parcel of any thorough retirement plan. Likewise, they should be part of your parents' plan.

Investment Planning

Having given some thought to where you want to be financially when you retire, you are undoubtedly contemplating how you can get there. Various investment options are discussed on the following pages.

How to Make Your Money Work for You

Whether you are your own advisor, rely on a professional one, or have chosen a mutual fund, two investment concepts are fundamental: diversification and risk management. Diversifying your money by choosing a mutual fund with an appropriate portfolio or a number of diverse mutual funds—or by just spreading out your investments—can lessen the inherent risks of investing. By determining the level of risk you can afford to take, you can invest in stocks or mutual funds whose objectives support that goal.

Think of risk taking as a matter of fair give and take. If you risk nothing, you get nothing in return. If you risk everything, you can double your money or lose it all. Somewhere in between is the right level of risk for each of us. When we're young, we can more readily afford risks because there's still time to recoup our losses. When we're past retirement, we cannot afford to lose because there's little chance to replace lost savings.

There are three major investment risks: inflation, market, and management. Inflation—the increase in market costs—is really beyond your control. Market and management risks are partially the result of your own decisions. The market is what is out there; you could have a safe market and a prudent manager, or you could be embroiled in a volatile high-yield market and a dice-rolling mutual fund. Luckily, both market and management can be researched. Look to what stocks have been consistent winners, where the trends are, and what funds (and fund managers) have done for the past five years. Don't invest in a fund until it has a proven track record. There are lots of good mutual funds out there; a little research will go a long way.

INSIGHT

Investment specialists boil down good investing tactics to five rules:

1. **Never stop investing and invest in growth stocks (stocks that have good earning potential).**

2. **Diversify.**
3. **Don't touch your principal.**
4. **Add to your principal (at least 3 or 4 percent a year) to keep abreast of inflation.**
5. **Get a mix of taxable and tax-exempt or tax-deferred investments and use the taxable income first when you retire.**

Certificate of Deposit

A *certificate of deposit (CD)* is essentially a bank account in which you promise not to use the money for a designated period of time, such as six, twelve, or twenty-four months. In return, the bank provides a slightly higher interest rate than it would for a savings account. Like all bank accounts, CDs yield taxable income and are insured by the Federal Deposit Insurance Corporation (FDIC) for up to $100,000. Banks often will offer CDs for IRAs, which means there's no taxable income—you just have to keep renewing your agreement to keep your CD in the IRA account.

Money Market Account

A *money market account* is a bank account that invests your money in various short-term instruments such as certificates of deposit, Treasury bills, and government securities. The yield changes daily, but a money market account is an almost risk-free investment. In exchange for promising to maintain a minimum amount in the account, you get interest rates slightly higher than those for savings accounts, check-writing privileges, and the usual FDIC protection up to $100,000. The low interest rate will not offer the higher yield of monies placed in more long-term investments, so money markets are used primarily for short-term (less than six months) needs.

Annuities

Fixed annuities, like those in retirement plans, are contracts with an insurance company that are purchased with after-tax savings but provide tax-deferred accumulation of interest and fixed payments for life. The accumulated earnings are taxed as income when paid out. They are commonly considered complementary to a retirement plan, but because they do not grow with inflation, they may be undesirable as the mainstay of a retiree's lifestyle.

Stocks

Stock represents ownership in a corporation and participation in corporate profits through dividends. They can increase dramatically in value or plummet and become worthless. It all depends on the company itself and the investment community's perception of a corporation's future.

Bonds

Bonds represent debt owed by the issuer to the owner of the bond. Bonds usually pay out interest in six-month periods, with the principal paid out to the bondholder upon the bonds' maturity.

U.S. Series EE Bonds

Series EE bonds are likely the ones your aunt gave you for grammar school graduation. EE bonds offer interest rates similar to those provided by banks, along with safety of principal, federal income tax deferral, and no state and local income taxes. To get an earlier return, you can roll the EE bond into a Series HH bond, which will provide periodic payouts to the bondholder. Government-backed bonds usually have the advantage of being state tax–free. Because this advantage makes a real difference in the actual yield on your investment, it's a good idea to understand the real value of government bonds in comparison to private investment strategies.

Treasury Bills and Municipal Bonds

U.S. Treasury bills can be purchased directly from the U.S. Treasury or through a bank in a variety of denominations. These bonds are very secure, so the interest rate is minimal. Interest is taxable by the federal government but not by state or local authorities.

Municipal bonds issued by state and local governments or public authorities are free from federal and state (if you live in the issuing state) income tax and are thus a truly tax-free investment. Even here, however, the government has been edging toward including some of the yield in taxable income through various phaseouts of exemptions, deductions, and the alternative minimum tax.

Corporate Bonds

Like government bonds, corporate bonds protect your principal (but don't guarantee it) and provide a steady stream of income. They can be safer than stocks in the same corporation and generally have a better return than CDs or money market accounts. In times of less profit, corporations can cut back on dividends, but they must pay the interest owed on bonds before paying out a dividend.

INSIGHT

Bond ratings change in response to the fiscal health of the bond issuer. The ratings range from AAA to unrated. You can get the ratings of bonds from Moody's or Standard and Poor's. Bonds are only as valuable as the surety of their ultimate payback of principal. You should check the previous five years' bond rating on the company or government agency that is issuing the bond before deciding to invest.

RESOURCES

U. S. Department of the Treasury
Office of Public Correspondence
1500 Pennsylvania Avenue, NW
Washington, D.C. 20220
(202) 622-2000
<http://www.publicdebt.treas.gov/bpd/bpdmap.htm>

Summary: The Bureau of Public Debt has plenty of information on T-Bills, notes, and savings bonds that is updated daily by the Department of the Treasury, including information on buying directly from the U.S. Treasury and calculating the value of any U.S. savings bonds you may have had since your child's birth, baptism, bar mitzvah, or graduation.

Mutual Funds

Mutual funds are a large pool of diversified stocks or bonds managed by an investment company. Investors buy into a fund and let the fund's money managers do the hard work of picking the actual stocks or bonds. The manager's duty is to make the fund's total return (dividends and appreciation) as high as possible within a level of risk consistent with the fund's stated investment policy and objectives. As always, the higher the return, the higher the risk to your principal. Therefore, as with bonds, it really is necessary to look at the track record of a fund and its management.

It's also important to know the types of stocks in which a particular fund invests and the fund's stated objective (for example, growth, income, or both). You should consider these objectives in determining what level of volatility and risk you find comfortable. If the objective of the fund is growth, the immediate return may be lower while you carry the risk of watching and waiting for the growth of the portfolio to occur over time. If the goal is income, the fluctuations in your account value may be diminished, the immediate return will be evident, but the total rate of return on your investment may not be as high.

Considering that thousands of mutual funds are available with differing styles, objectives, and costs, you may want to discuss the options with an advisor or even have an advisor oversee your investments. If you are doing the picking, find funds that fit your comfort level for risk and have consistent management and above-average returns (after expenses) over at least the past three- to five-year term. If you pick a fund with a proven track record and follow the prudent rules of investment, mutual funds can be one of the best means to balance risks and return.

Impact of Taxes

The benefit of pretax and tax-free yields can be seen when you look at taxable equivalents. For example, for a person in the 28 percent income tax bracket, an investment with a tax-free yield of 5.5 percent has an equivalent taxable interest rate of 7.64 percent. Conversely, if the same person can invest in a taxable bond yielding 7.75 percent, they are better off paying the taxes. Although it may feel good in the short term to pay less to the IRS, what matters most is how much you are left with after taxes.

RESOURCES

Alliance for Investor Education
<http://www.investoreducation.org/>

Summary: The Alliance for Investor Education is a not-for-profit organization that provides a broad array of objective investment information.

The American Association of Individual Investors (AAII)
625 N. Michigan Ave.
Chicago, IL 60611
(800) 428-2244
<http://www.aaii.com/>

Summary: AAII is a not-for-profit investor education and research organization.

The American Stock Exchange
Investor Services/Nasdaq Web Site
1735 K Street, NW
Washington, D.C. 20006
<http://www.amex.com>

Summary: The NASDAQ stock market Web site provides market information (with an approximately twenty-minute delay). From the homepage, click on "investor services" for a great deal of basic investment information.

Deloitte & Touche LLP
Center of Excellence
700 Walnut Street
Cincinnati, OH 45202
<http://www.dtonline.com/>

Summary: This is a comprehensive guide to personal finance produced by Deloitte & Touche LLP.

Fortune
<http://www.fortuneinvestor.com/>

Summary: This Web site is maintained by *Fortune* magazine. Many investment services are provided here, such as a financial news wire service and professional analysis of hundreds of mutual funds as well as a market tracker. This is a subscription-based Web site, but the first thirty days are free, after which time much free information is still offered.

Financial Web
<http://www.financialweb.com/>

Summary: This Web site provides free stock quotes, mutual fund information, sophisticated technical analysis, and market research.

Multex Investor
<http://multexinvestor.com>

Summary: In addition to being a leader in providing on-line investment information and research, Multex Investor offers a variety of special and unique services, including the "Analyst Corner," where recognized financial professionals provide valuable insights; "Let's Talk," where Multex Investor users can exchange their thoughts and information; and "Investment Ideas."

Bonds OnLine
7251 W. Mercer Way
Mercer Island, WA 98040
<http://bondsonline.com>

Summary: Although not all of the information is provided free of charge, those interested in fixed-income bond markets will find this site helpful.

INSIGHT

In addition to the Web sites just mentioned as well as the comprehensive financial Web sites listed on pages 30–32, you can surf the Web for thousands of sites that provide investment-related information. You must always question the veracity and usefulness of the information that is being provided on these sites. You need to determine if the provider of the Web site is making information available in a manner that furthers its commercial or other self-serving objective. In regard to all Web sites that provide free information, the old adage applies: "Nobody does anything for free."

Estate Planning

The word *estate* can be misleading, as many people associate it with wealth. However, everyone who owns anything—whether real estate or personal property such as cash, clothes, or collectibles—will have something in their estate when they die.

What to do with this property is called *estate planning*. Even if your only cherished possession is a slightly used lava lamp and your record album collection, you may well want to pass those on to someone. On top of this basic notion of legacy, estate planning deals with how to preserve what you own, either for your own use or for bequests to charity or to your family. Estate planning also refers to how you control your property and, lastly, to how you can ensure that the people at the IRS don't become your largest beneficiaries.

In 1997, the federal government phased in an increasing estate and gift unified credit from $600,000 to $1 million through the year 2006. Many would say this figure ends their need to plan. Some think they are nowhere near that mark, but remember—that figure includes any lifetime gifts made to an individual in a given year that amounted to more than $10,000; it includes everything in your possession or control, which can add up faster than you can say "car, house, cash, bank accounts, stocks, bonds, insurance, furniture, collectibles, and trusts."

Even if the IRS won't get its hands on your estate, you still need to decide who will. However, most of us boomers still don't take advantage of this right to decide on what should be done. Often, it is left to others, such as your state government, to dictate what will happen. In our crusade to stay forever young, we boomers, like our parents before us, often try to overlook the inevitable. As you consider how you should plan, it may also be time to review what your mother and father might need to do. (Be sure to check Part Three, "Our Parents," in this regard.) It's not pessimistic to say that someday you and your parents won't exist—it's just true. But to soften the inevitable, you and they could make death, and not taxes, the only sure thing.

Goals of Estate Planning

Assuming that you are ready to proceed with your own (rather than the government's) estate plan, you can do some preliminary thinking.

A good estate plan has four basic goals:

1. To ensure that you maintain your standard of living and that you will be properly provided for throughout your lifetime
2. To make sure that your wealth reaches the individuals or organizations you select, in the manner in which you choose, with minimum shrinkage from federal and state transfer taxes and administration expenses

3. To allow you to select who will handle various administrative and management functions on your behalf, both during life and after your death
4. To control your family's future

Basic Strategies

By following a number of strategic planning steps, you may be able to minimize or even eliminate estate taxes and settlement costs and ensure that your assets are distributed according to your wishes. Those steps are as follows:

Goal Evaluation

Determine who you want to inherit your assets and how you want your property distributed. Once your objectives are clear, you can incorporate strategies designed to help meet your individual goals.

Estate Inventory

List all of your holdings and place a fair market value on the assets. Subtract the sum of your debts from the value of your assets to determine your gross estate. This is the amount you could leave to your heirs.

Will and Trust Preparation

Your will or revocable trust is the cornerstone of your estate plan; it will determine who will receive your assets and how those assets will be distributed.

Family Gifts

Lifetime gifts to your family can reduce your taxable estate and provide personal satisfaction. Currently an individual can transfer up to $10,000 per person each year without reporting the gift or paying taxes, as will be discussed later.

Charitable Giving

Contributions to a qualified charity may result in a current income tax deduction, can be made gift tax free, and may also reduce estate taxes.

Estate-planning strategies often involve more than just executing a will. You can make arrangements for the accumulation and handling of assets while you are alive and upon your death; draft inter vivos ("between living persons") trusts to manage your assets during and after your lifetime to support your children until they are of age and to shelter your estate from taxes; make gifts to people or charities to reduce taxes; incorporate life and disability insurance into your plan to provide liquidity; and more.

Voluntary and Involuntary Plans

The basic transfer vehicles from which you can choose when planning your estate are as follows:

1. *Intestate succession,* which amounts to having *no* estate plan
2. *A last will and testament* or possibly a *living trust*

Some people might add the use of *will substitutes* as an additional transfer technique; these include such assets as life insurance, qualified retirement plans, and jointly held property, all of which pass to designated beneficiaries by operation of law and outside of your will or intestate succession. These will be discussed in more detail later.

Dying without a Will

If you die without a will (that is, intestate), the courts will take control of your estate and distribute your assets according to the intestacy laws of the state in which you resided at the time of your death. In other words, a state legislature becomes your estate planner when you die intestate. The statutes are designed to accomplish the desires of a majority of a state's citizens and may not match your goals. For example, in New York, if you do not have a will and you are married but without children, your spouse will receive your entire estate. Likewise, if you do not have a will and you are married with children, your spouse will receive $50,000 and one half of the remainder of your estate, and your children will receive the other half of the remainder.

Another disadvantage, particularly so where your spouse has predeceased you, is that the court will appoint a guardian for your children with respect to their share of your estate. The court may not name an individual or individuals that you would want to take responsibility for your children, and having a court-appointed guardian can provide complications in estate management. For example, any money used to pay for your children's education, clothing, and living costs would require prior approval of the court, *even if your spouse is the guardian.* The law further requires annual accountings of income and expenses to the court, and investment of the funds by the guardian will be limited to choices approved by the court. If the guardianship should last for any significant length of time, the investment limitations imposed by the court may not allow your children's funds to grow at an acceptable rate of return.

Also, without a will, the court will appoint a personal representative, or administrator, of your estate. This may be a relative if one is willing or able to serve, or the court may appoint an administrator of its choice. Because your personal representative will cost your estate a percentage of the estate assets in commissions, most people find comfort in selecting someone they know and trust to oversee the administration of their estate.

Finally, if you die intestate, your estate will not have the benefit of any tax planning to minimize the oftentimes confiscatory effects of federal and state death taxes. Remember that estate taxes, unlike income taxes, are elective. You can plan to avoid estate taxes or elect to pay by doing nothing.

Probate and Nonprobate Assets

Most estates include probate assets and nonprobate assets (previously referred to as will substitutes), and you should be aware of the impact of both. *Probate assets* are those owned in your own name that require a determination by the court as to where the assets should go (for example, a bank account or residence titled in your name alone).

Nonprobate assets are those that transfer automatically to another person or designated beneficiary upon your death. Examples of nonprobate assets include

- Assets held in a revocable living trust
- Assets held jointly with your surviving spouse or with another as joint tenants with a right of survivorship
- Proceeds of an insurance policy in which beneficiaries other than your estate are named.
- Balances of retirement plans, IRAs, or Keogh accounts and tax-deferred annuities, which may be payable to designated persons rather than your estate

For those assets that go through probate (or administration), probate involves two procedures:

First, the Surrogate's Court (sometimes referred to as the Probate Court) in the county where you resided at the time of your death determines whether a particular instrument is your will and whether it will be held to be valid to transfer your assets. If you die intestate, the court determines your legal heirs by reference to the applicable state law on intestate succession.

Second, the court oversees the process of settling your estate, including

- Supervision of the actions of your personal representative, either your executor or administrator
- Ruling on the legitimacy of any creditors' claims against your estate
- Supervision of the transfer of your remaining property to the beneficiaries named in your will or to your heirs if you died without a will
- Overseeing a guardian's use of any property that is left to minor children until they reach the legal age of majority (eighteen years of age in many states)

Court supervision of the probate process helps ensure that the directions left in your will are carried out properly. The probate process can take as little as a few weeks or as long as several years (for example, if your will is contested or if you own additional real property in other states). A properly drafted estate plan that is kept up to date will minimize probate delays and expenses. It can provide for the prompt appointment of executors, guardians, and trustees; payment of expenses and taxes; settlement of claims; continuation of business interests; and the avoidance of will contests and unsubstantiated claims.

Planning Alternatives

Why You Need a Will

One of the most effective ways to direct the distribution of your property according to your own wishes is to make a will. However, many individuals assume that wills are only for very wealthy people or for people who want to set up trusts or save estate taxes. The fact is that whether you are young or old, married or single, and are a parent or not, if you have financial assets, you generally should have a will! Many of us can readily accumulate a substantial estate consisting of life insurance, equity in home, savings and investments, and retirement plan assets.

Unfortunately, three out of four U.S. citizens die without leaving a will, probably because no one enjoys contemplating his or her own death. However, if you have worked hard throughout your life to build a solid financial foundation and to provide for the security of your family, shouldn't you be the one to decide how and by whom your assets will be distributed after your death?

The primary reason for making a will is to provide instructions on how your assets are to be distributed among your beneficiaries. A will is a written document that performs the following functions:

- Outlines how you wish to distribute your assets, including specific gifts of your tangible personal property
- Designates an executor or personal representative who is responsible for taking inventory of your property; preserving your estate; paying creditors, administrative expenses, and death taxes; and disposing of the remainder of your property among your beneficiaries
- Appoints guardians for minor children in the event of the death of both parents
- Establishes trusts to protect assets in special circumstances

You can use your will to establish a *testamentary trust* (also called a *trust under will*) that will ensure that your assets are held, managed, and distributed in the manner specified by you. You can direct that the trustee manage certain assets for the benefit of your family or other beneficiaries and distribute trust income and principal at specific times and in the manner you have set forth in your will. For example, if you are concerned that your spouse may remarry after your death and change his or her will to include the new spouse, you can create a trust that provides income and principal for your spouse during his or her life but preserves the remaining principal for your children upon his or her death. Likewise, if you are leaving assets to children, you may want to use a trust to ensure that they do not receive the funds until they reach a certain age or level of maturity and then only for certain purposes you specify such as support, maintenance, and education.

Avoiding Probate

There are certain reasons why you may wish to avoid probate:

- If you desire privacy, trust documents are generally not filed with the court (but be aware of exceptions, such as when a pour-over will, one that leaves everything to your trust, is used)
- If you own property in more than one state that will require an expensive ancillary administration in the other jurisdiction
- To provide for uninterrupted management of your assets
- To avoid certain probate expenses and undue administrative delays
- To provide a certain sense of relief, knowing that everything has been taken care of prior to your death

An effective way to avoid probate is by employing an inter vivos or revocable living trust, which can provide for the management of your assets during your lifetime and for the proper disposition to your beneficiaries upon your death. Each state may have its own variations for living trusts, but generally you may change or revoke the terms of the trust at any time and may designate anyone you like—a professional manager, your spouse, or a child—as trustee. You can be your own trustee during your life and while you are competent. This type of trust is also useful if you become incapacitated or incompetent because the successor trustee will be able to manage your assets and provide for your needs without court intervention.

Estate Costs and Taxes

Two obligations must be paid from your estate before your assets can be fully distributed to your heirs—administrative costs and estate taxes.

Administrative Costs

Administrative costs vary widely from state to state but usually are estimated at 3 to 8 percent of an estate's gross value. The biggest administrative costs are executor's fees and legal fees, but there are also filing fees, appraisal fees, publication fees, bond fees, and legal costs for unexpected legal services such as will contests and real estate transactions. Before proceeding further, it is important for you to understand the basic federal transfer tax systems in general, and in particular, two key tax provisions—the unified credit and unlimited marital deduction, which form the basis of many estate-planning strategies.

Transfer Taxes—The Unified Gift and Estate Tax System

Basics

The estate tax is an *excise* tax on the transfer of property from a decedent. Under federal law, a unified transfer tax is applied cumulatively to all gifts that are made during an individual's lifetime and then to all assets that are owned at death. This is a single, progressive tax ranging from a marginal rate of 37 percent to maximum rate of 55 percent (see Table 2.1).

The federal estate tax is a tax based on the fair market value of all property interests that each individual owns or has rights to at death. These property interests include not only property passing under your will or by state laws of intestate succession but also property known as will substitutes, which pass by operation of law. As previously mentioned, these include real property held in joint names, joint bank accounts, retirement plans, and insurance policies. In particular, death proceeds from a life insurance policy owned by the decedent on his or her life or policies in which the decedent-insured had certain so-called incidents of ownership are also included in the gross estate.

Whether or not your estate goes through probate, it will be taxed depending on the size of the estate and whether or not your spouse survives you. It is a common misconception that assets that avoid probate, such as life insurance, pension benefits, and jointly owned property with a right of survivorship, are not taxed in your estate. Probate and estate taxes are separate and distinct considerations. In summary, your estate for federal estate tax purposes includes

Table 2.1   **Unified Rate Schedule of Federal Gift and Estate Tax**

Tentative Tax Base	Tentative Tax	Excess (%)
675,000	220,550	37
Over 1,000,000	345,800	41
Over 1,250,000	448,300	43
Over 1,500,000	555,800	45
Over 2,000,000	780,800	49
Over 2,500,000	1,025,800	53
Over 3,000,000	1,290,800	55
Over 10,000,000	5,140,800	60
Over 17,184,000	9,451,200	55

- Property held in your own name
- Half of the value of property you hold jointly with your spouse
- The full value of property you hold jointly with someone other than your spouse, unless you can overcome the presumption that the asset does not entirely or in part belong to you
- The face value of life insurance you own on your life or over which you hold incidents of ownership (regardless of the beneficiaries)
- Property over which you have a general power of appointment
- Pensions, IRAs, annuities, and other plans owned by you with a death benefit to others

These items together comprise your *gross estate,* which equals the value of all property subject to estate taxation.

Deductions

Your personal representative may deduct from your gross estate the administrative costs of the estate, funeral expenses, the value of debts you owe at the time of death, and charitable donations (the charitable deduction is unlimited). In addition, the *marital deduction* (discussed later) allows you to leave an unlimited amount of property to your spouse tax free, but as we will see, it then becomes important to plan for payment of taxes at your spouse's death, for when your spouse dies and the property passes to your children or other heirs, it will be taxed at even higher rates.

Lifetime Gifts

The federal unified transfer tax, or unified gift and estate tax system, potentially taxes each item of property you transfer to someone else, either while you are alive or upon your death. However, for lifetime gifts, an annual gift tax exclusion, which is currently indexed for inflation, facilitates lifetime transfers of property. Each individual has the ability to transfer up to $10,000 to any donee, and to an unlimited number of donees, free of gift taxes; this tax exclusion is now indexed annually by increases to the cost of living based on 1997 figures but rounded to the next lowest multiple of $1,000. Thus, no adjustment will occur during 1999.

A married individual can make a $20,000 gift and split the gift tax exclusion with a spouse even if the entire gift comes from only one spouse's assets. As mentioned, the number of donees permitted is unlimited, but if the gift is other than outright, certain conditions must be met to qualify for the annual $10,000 exclusion. The gift must be a gift of a *present interest,* meaning the recipient must be able to use the gift once it is made. Most gifts to trusts are gifts of a future interest and therefore do not receive this tax-exclusive treatment. You can also consider educational bills, nursing home bills, and medical bills as additional annual exclusion gifts over and above the $10,000 per donee if you pay such bills directly to the university, nursing home, or physicians on behalf of the donee. (For further information on gifting, see both Part Two, "Our Children," and Part Three, "Our Parents.")

The Applicable Credit Amount

Under current law, each individual is entitled to a federal gift or estate tax credit of $220,550, which is equivalent to the estate tax liability on an estate valued at $675,000. This amount rises slowly until it reaches $1,000,000, as follows:

Year	Applicable Credit Amount ($)
1999	650,000
2000–2001	675,000
2002–2003	700,000
2004	850,000
2005	950,000
2006 and later	1,000,000

Applying the credit at death allows you to effectively pass the first $675,000 of assets (in 2000) to your heirs and beneficiaries without federal estate tax. As previously mentioned, if estate assets, including any prior taxable gifts, exceed $675,000, minus administration fees, funeral expenses, outstanding debts, legal fees, and executor's fees in 2000, the federal estate tax begins at 37 percent, reaching a maximum of 55 percent.

The Unlimited Marital Deduction

A married couple can defer any or all federal estate taxes on the death of the first spouse by passing an unlimited amount of property to the survivor, provided the recipient spouse is a U.S. citizen. At the death of the surviving spouse, however, taxes will become due and payable on the full value of the combined estates. Because the surviving spouse is entitled only to an individual unified credit, the estate will receive only a single federal exemption on property valued up to $675,000. Thus, use of the unlimited marital deduction to defer federal estate taxes at the death of the first spouse will result in additional estate taxes due nine months after the death of the surviving spouse. However, planning opportunities to minimize these estate taxes and provide liquidity to pay them will be described later. An example on page 75 illustrates the technique known as a *credit shelter trust,* which allows spouses to maximize the use of both of their estate tax credits rather than only protecting $675,000 (in 2000) from estate tax.

The Generation-Skipping Transfer Tax

Depending on the size of your estate and the beneficiaries you choose, there may be another tax to plan around. The *generation-skipping transfer tax (GSTT)* is an additional transfer tax designed to take away the benefit of using a trust—or similar device—to pass property through successive generations within a family without paying an estate tax at each generation. It is a flat tax pegged at the top bracket for the federal estate tax—now 55 percent. Because the tax is levied *in addition* to the applicable gift or estate taxes, it is possible for the combined taxes to exceed the value of the transferred property!

There are some escape hatches to avoid the GSTT. Many gifts that qualify for the $10,000 annual exclusion will also be immune from the GSTT; a cumulative lifetime and testamentary $1,010,000 GSTT exemption also exists. This exemption may be used on behalf of one grandchild, for example, or spread among several grandchildren. Thus, grandparents could leave $2,020,000 to their grandchildren free of GSTT penalties (but subject to normal gift or estate taxes).

Three types of generation-skipping transfers would be taxable events in addition to regular transfer taxes. If property is gifted or left directly to a grandchild, this is called a *direct skip.* One can, instead, create a trust with income and principal payable to a child and grandchildren during the child's life and then provide for distribution of the principal to the grandchildren. Any payments to the grandchildren during the child's life are known as *taxable distributions;* when the last of the children dies or his or her interest in the trust ends, a *taxable termination* occurs, which would be a taxable event for GSTT purposes. As previously stated, up to $1,010,000 of these payments are protected from the GSTT owing to the $1,010,000 GSTT exemption under federal transfer tax laws.

Taxable Gifts versus Testamentary Transfers

It may make sense for some individuals with very large estates to make a taxable gift and pay the transfer tax currently rather than have their estate pay the applicable transfer taxes. Taxable gifts are taxed *exclusively*, whereas testamentary transfers are taxed *inclusively* (that is, the tax is levied on the money used to pay the tax). Also, an individual must live three years after paying the gift tax, or the amount of the payment will be added back to the taxable estate. Of course, this will push the estate into a higher estate tax bracket.

EXAMPLE

Paying Federal Transfer Tax during Lifetime versus at Death

Archie, single, fifty-five years of age, and widowed, wishes to use $2,000,000 of his assets to benefit his daughter, Gloria. The remainder of his large estate will be left to charity at his death. He has already made a $675,000 "exemption equivalent" gift to Gloria. Archie would like to know whether it is better to use $2,000,000 of his assets during his lifetime or at death. To keep things simple, he would like to assume a 50 percent marginal tax bracket for the initial analysis. He is in good health.

	Lifetime Gift ($)	Transfer at Death ($)
Assets Used	2,000,000	2,000,000
Gloria Receives	1,333,333	1,000,000

INSIGHT

Archie's total cost of making a gift will include the $666,667 gift tax. He should be certain that he will not need these funds for his own support.

Gloria will also benefit from the future appreciation on the $1,333,333 gift, which will be out of Archie's estate. The longer he lives and the greater the appreciation on the funds, the larger this benefit will be.

The Use of Trusts in Transfer Tax Planning

What Is a Trust?

A *trust* is basically a fictional legal entity that is created by an agreement under which an individual you select, known as the *trustee,* holds and manages property for your *beneficiaries.* You, as *grantor, settlor,* or *creator* of the trust, dictate the terms of the trust, and the trustee is then responsible for carrying out your written instructions as set forth in the agreement.

Thus, a trust is a legal arrangement through which you give property to your trustee to manage and use for the benefit of whomever you name. There are two main types of trusts:

1. *Testamentary,* which go into effect when you die.
2. *Living (inter vivos),* which take effect during your lifetime. Living trusts may also be revocable or irrevocable.

Trusts are vehicles to provide for certain actions to take place with the best possible consequences—both tax and nontax. Inter vivos trusts should generally be prepared in conjunction with a pour-over will to ensure that upon your death any remaining assets in your name inadvertently left outside the trust will be transferred (i.e., poured over) into the trust for distribution to your designated beneficiaries in accordance with your wishes as expressed in the trust instrument.

The living trust is funded by transferring the title to all or a portion of your assets into the trust name. If the trust is *revocable,* you retain complete control of the assets and can change the terms of the trust at any time. If it is *irrevocable,* you give up all rights to the property and cannot amend the trust terms.

A well-conceived family wealth plan using trusts can also provide asset protection and divorce protection benefits for descendants. With proper planning, a trust structure can be created for the benefit of your descendants that will insulate the family wealth from creditors and ex-spouses, erode the impact of transfer taxes on vast wealth, and then can be enjoyed and controlled by the family in perpetuity. A strong argument can be made that all gifts or inheritances should be made in trust unless the size of the transfer does not justify the expense of setting up a trust. For mature, competent family members who would receive the property outright were it not for the benefits that can be derived through the receipt of property in trust, a trust can be designed to give the primary beneficiary the functional equivalent of outright ownership, including undisturbed control over the property. In the hands of a proficient attorney, trusts are extremely flexible arrangements that can help your family cope with various problems, both anticipated and unanticipated, that have occurred or may occur in the future. Customized design of a trust can in almost every instance achieve your goals, even when it is desired that virtually all major decisions be lodged in the hands of the trust beneficiaries.

Although it has always been a worthwhile consideration, asset protection and liability planning is becoming a more integral part of the business- and estate-planning process. Indeed, because of the generally litigious nature of our society, coupled with the increasing success plaintiffs are enjoying and the proliferation of divorces, creditor protection is often the motivating factor; from some boomers' perspectives, it is an essential element in the planning process. In addition to the traditional estate-planning techniques used to pass wealth to the desired persons with a minimum of taxes and costs, the estate plan should be structured so that the family wealth passes in a manner that will render it undesirable, unattractive, and unreachable by creditors, including spouses in the context of divorce. An irrevocable trust set up by someone other than the beneficiary provides the ultimate in creditor protection because if you don't own it, nobody can take it away from you. Historically, it has been the general rule in almost every state that the creator of a trust can dictate who may receive the beneficial enjoyment of the property and the extent and circumstances under which this enjoyment may be obtained. As a result, unless trust property is distributed to a beneficiary, it will likely be protected from the beneficiary's creditors.

Advantages and Disadvantages of Living Trusts

A revocable trust arrangement generally offers several advantages over a will. It can help you

- Manage and protect assets during your lifetime
- Provide continuity in the management of your affairs after your death
- Control how and when assets are to be distributed
- Avoid the costs and delays of probate
- Ensure privacy in the handling of your affairs
- Reduce taxes or expenses when properly designed

Although there are many benefits to trusts, there are also some disadvantages. Most trusts, particularly irrevocable trusts, involve some degree of loss of flexibility or control over your assets, and trusts are initially more expensive to prepare and implement than wills.

Types of Trusts

The following are more detailed descriptions of some of the more common types of trusts.

Revocable Living Trust

In addition to the benefits set forth previously, a revocable living trust can ensure your own personal and financial welfare in the event that you become incapacitated during your lifetime. You will be able to select someone to make decisions and act on your behalf should you become incapable of making your own management decisions. In addition, you may appoint a professional manager, maintain complete control over the trust property, receive income from the trust, transfer property to your heirs, provide privacy for your family, and reduce estate settlement expenses.

Irrevocable Living Trust

This is a method to transfer ownership of an asset without giving the recipient unbridled access to the money or property. If you relinquish all rights to income and principal from the trust as well as the power to change the trust agreement in any manner, then the asset will *not* be considered part of your taxable estate. You name the recipient of the assets, including income and principal beneficiaries. Because the transfer is considered a gift to the trust, a gift tax may be imposed unless the transfer qualifies for the previously discussed gift tax annual exclusion, or you use some or all of your unified credit.

Irrevocable Life Insurance Trust

One popular use of an irrevocable living trust is to have a trust own the life insurance policies on your life, thereby removing the proceeds of such policies from your taxable estate because you neither own nor control the asset at the time of your death. If the death benefit proceeds will not be included in your taxable estate, they will be available to provide liquidity to accomplish estate objectives. The cash may be used to buy nonliquid assets from the estate or loan money to the estate, thereby eliminating any need for distress sales of estate property or excessive borrowing that might be needed to pay estate taxes.

An irrevocable life insurance trust should be used when it is desirable to remove life insurance proceeds from the taxable estate and effect the management of the death benefit proceeds. If your estate is over $650,000 (in 1999; $675,000 in 2000) or, in the case of a married couple, if your combined estate is over $1,350,000 (the combined exemption equivalent amounts), you should begin to think about using such trusts. Those with larger estates and those with closely held business, real estate, or other illiquid assets should seriously consider using them in almost all cases.

You need to understand that if transfers of existing employer-sponsored and personal policies are made to an irrevocable trust, the insured must survive the transfer by three years for the policy proceeds to avoid estate taxation. Gift taxes on payments of premiums may also have to be paid if the trust is not properly drafted. A frequent objective of such trusts is to minimize any gift tax consequences. Two techniques that will accomplish this are using annual exclusion gifts with Crummey powers (a withdrawal power given to the trust beneficiary that gets its name from the federal court case allowing such an arrangement, *Crummey* v. *Commissioner*) or using portions of your federal estate exemption equivalent. Simple assignment and change of beneficiary forms are all that is required to effect the transfers. For new policies, the trustee should be the applicant, owner, and beneficiary of the new policy. In either situation, cash gifts are generally made to the trust by the policy donor. The trustee then pays the insurance premiums due each year.

If it is an estate-planning objective to transfer existing policies out of the taxable estate of the insured, the insured must give up all incidents of ownership in the policies. This means that the person who gives up the policy must not retain control over the use of the policy in any way (for example, the right to name a beneficiary or to borrow against the policy).

Transferring the insurance to your spouse will not accomplish transfer tax savings because the death benefit would become part of his or her estate. You must transfer such policies to your children or other beneficiaries or to irrevocable trusts for their benefit or the benefit of your spouse.

You should use a special type of insurance known as *survivorship whole life* to provide liquidity sufficient to pay death taxes at the death of the second of two spouses. In most estate-planning situations where the unlimited marital deduction is used to defer taxes until the death of the second spouse, this would be the most opportune time to provide such liquidity from life insurance. Survivorship whole life can permit dramatic leveraging of the annual exclusion, the $675,000 exemption equivalent, and the $1,010,000 GSTT exemption.

Survivorship whole life is most commonly written as a level premium permanent insurance product covering two lives. The premiums are generally substantially lower than comparable single-life products for two reasons. First, because two people must die before benefits are paid, benefits are usually paid later than for a single-life policy. Thus, the mortality cost of insuring two lives is much lower than that of insuring one life. Second, the insurance industry has responded to market needs by formulating a product that creates maximum death benefit leverage by requiring smaller premiums than more traditional whole-life products.

To summarize, the irrevocable life insurance trust can provide income for your heirs, avoid probate, reduce estate settlement expenses, prevent life insurance proceeds from being valued in your gross estate, and provide funds to pay estate taxes and other estate settlement costs at deeply discounted rates.

EXAMPLE

Using Annual Exclusions and Exemption Equivalents with an Irrevocable Life Insurance Trust

Ward and June established an irrevocable life insurance trust to benefit their son, Theodore. The trust is the applicant and owner of a survivorship whole-life policy. Ward is fifty-five years old, and June is fifty-two. The $1,000,000 policy is illustrated to require premium payments of $30,000 each year for ten years and then vanish.

Ward and June will transfer $30,000 per year to the trust for ten years. After a short period of time (for example, thirty days) the trustee of the trust, Mr. Haskell, will pay the insurance premium with the $30,000.

Because the trust was drafted with Crummey powers, the first $20,000 transferred each year will qualify for the gift tax annual exclusion. The remaining $10,000 per year will utilize $5,000 of each of Ward's and June's exemption equivalent amounts.

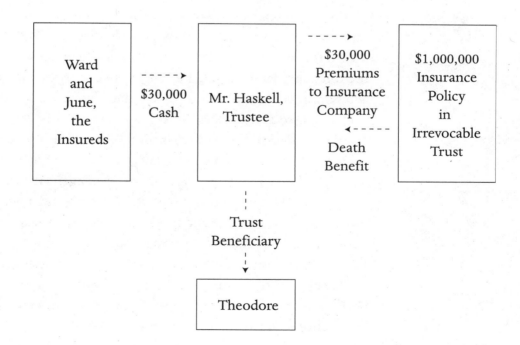

Use of the irrevocable trust allows Ward and June greater control over disposition of policy proceeds than if Theodore had owned the policy outright.

INSIGHT
Gift tax returns must be filed each year.

Bypass (Family) or Unified Credit Shelter Trust
If you are married and have a net worth of over $675,000, then you can adopt what is often referred to as an *A-B trust plan, credit shelter trust plan,* or *bypass trust plan.* The purpose of this plan is to utilize both your and your spouse's unified credits. As we have stated, both you and your spouse may each transfer up to $675,000 free of federal transfer taxes. If the estate is left to the surviving spouse using the unlimited marital deduction, then only $675,000 can later be transferred to your beneficiaries tax free.

By designing an estate plan that divides the estate upon the death of the first spouse, both unified credits will be used. Again, the unified credit allows the exemption equivalent amount of $675,000 of property that one may pass to others, either through lifetime transfers or death, free of transfer taxes. The opportunity to benefit from the unified credit is on a "use it (during life or upon death) or lose it" basis. If, for example, all property in an estate passes to a surviving spouse, the ability to pass the $675,000 of property to the heirs free of transfer taxes is lost. This $675,000 will be taxed at the top marginal tax bracket in the estate of the second spouse to die. In addition, there is a phaseout of this benefit for estates that range from $10,000,000 to $21,040,000. The bypass trust can produce federal estate tax savings of approximately $200,000 to $400,000 for a married couple and allow for the transfer of up to $1,350,000 to children or other heirs without any federal estate tax. This type of trust arrangement, which is funded at the death of the first spouse, can permit the surviving spouse to manage the investment of trust assets and receive income and principal from the trust if desired. It will provide for the trust property to be transferred to your designated beneficiaries at the death of your surviving spouse, eliminate estate tax liability on the future appreciation in value of trust assets after your death, avoid probate of such assets in the estate of your surviving spouse, and reduce estate settlement expenses.

The $675,000 Exemption Equivalent and Tax Savings with a Bypass Trust

Ricky and Lucy have a net worth of $2,500,000. Ricky has a $2,000,000 investment account in his name, while their $500,000 house is in Lucy's name. They do not own any life insurance. Their wills leave everything to each other and then to their son Ricky Jr. They live comfortably on the income from their assets and would like to leave as much of their estate as possible to Ricky Jr.

Without Planning—assume Ricky dies first.

	FIRST DEATH Ricky	SECOND DEATH Lucy
Gross Estate	$2,000,000	$2,500,000
Marital Deduction	2,000,000	0
Taxable Estate	0	2,500,000
Estate Tax	0	1,025,800
Unified Credit	(220,550)	(220,550)
Net Tax	0	805,250

With Planning—Ricky leaves $675,000 to a bypass trust for Lucy in his will and everything else to her directly. This leaves $1,325,000 to Lucy via the unlimited marital deduction. Ricky's taxable estate is then $675,000.

	Ricky	Lucy
Gross Estate	$2,000,000	$1,325,000
Marital Deduction	1,325,000	0
Taxable Estate	675,000	1,325,000
Estate Tax	220,550	480,550
Unified Credit	(220,550)	(220,550)
Net Tax	0	260,000
Difference—Federal Tax Planning Advantage		545,250

Marital Trust

You can provide for your spouse without leaving your property directly to him or her through a *marital trust*. You may appoint another individual to act as trustee for your spouse, with your spouse as the beneficiary, and if certain technical requirements are met, the trust assets will qualify for the marital deduction and thus pass free of estate tax to your spouse.

Other trusts that may be useful under certain circumstances include the following.

Qualified Terminable Interest Property Trust

With a *qualified terminable interest property trust (QTIP)*, you dictate how your property will be distributed upon the death of your surviving spouse. This trust is generally used in the context of second marriages when the testator wishes to provide for the surviving spouse for life and give the remainder to the children of the first marriage. Your spouse must receive the income from the trust for life and may receive some rights to principal, but the trust agreement must be carefully drafted to satisfy a myriad of highly technical legal requirements. However, if properly drafted, the property transferred to the trust will be eligible for the unlimited marital deduction.

Qualified Personal Residence Trust

The *qualified personal residence trust (QPRT)* allows you to transfer your residence or a vacation property to a trust on a highly leveraged transfer tax basis and still collect income from or use the property for the term of the trust. This type of trust is often used to freeze the value of estate assets for estate tax purposes.

Minor's Trust

If you and your spouse both die, a testamentary *minor's trust* can hold your assets for your children until they reach a certain age, provide management of the assets, and pay income and principal as you direct for such purposes as their support, maintenance, and education. (See Part Two, "Our Children," for more detail on this type of trust.)

Charitable Trusts

Charitable remainder trusts can help an individual obtain income tax deductions, increase diversification of an investment portfolio without incurring an immediate capital gains tax, increase cash yield generated by assets, and decrease the size of the estate. They work best for older individuals who find themselves holding low-yielding, highly appreciated assets and who have charitable-giving objectives. Assets are transferred by an individual to a trust and then sold to be reinvested in higher-yielding assets. Generally, an individual and perhaps a spouse may receive income for life, with the remainder going to a charity after the death of the last income recipient. The value of the property given to the trust is often replaced for the heirs with a life insurance policy in an irrevocable life insurance trust. A charitable lead trust provides a charity with the income from your principal, paid over a certain amount of time, after which the remainder passes to your heirs at greatly reduced transfer tax costs.

Dynasty Trusts

A *dynasty trust* is designed to permit the passage of significant wealth through multiple generations without the imposition of transfer taxes at each generational level even though the trust beneficiaries have a beneficial enjoyment in the trust property virtually equivalent to outright ownership. A taxpayer places property into a trust, electing to allocate a sufficient amount of his or her GSTT exemption against the transfer so that the trust is wholly exempt from the generation-skipping transfer tax. Additionally, the dynasty trust provides asset protection and divorce protection benefits. Asset protection and liability planning have become a more integral part of the business- and estate-planning processes. Indeed, because of the litigious nature of our society, coupled with the increasing success that plaintiffs are enjoying and the proliferation of divorces, creditor protection is often the motivating factor for many clients; from some clients' perspectives, it is an essential element in the planning process.

You might consider asking yourself, "What have I done to protect my children's and other descendants' inheritances from divorce, creditors, or bankruptcy?" With more marriages in the United States ending in divorce than by death and with the increased attention being given to asset protection strategies, this query is often a material motivating factor in having people immediately move forward with the estate-planning process. An irrevocable trust, set up by someone other than the beneficiary provides the ultimate in creditor protection. As stated previously, if you don't own it, nobody can take it away from you. Historically, the general rule has been that the creator of a trust can dictate who may receive the beneficial enjoyment of the property and the extent and circumstances under which this enjoyment may be obtained. As a result, unless trust property is distributed to a beneficiary, it will be protected from the beneficiary's creditors. The same is not true when the creator of the trust makes himself or herself a discretionary beneficiary.

This trust is designed to last the maximum term permitted by law and to be managed with the avoidance of wealth transfer taxes as a primary consideration insofar as consistent with the objective of providing comfortably for the trust beneficiaries. Distributions will be permissible but might not be made even though retention might be undesirable from an income tax–planning standpoint. The trustee should take into account the transfer tax considerations prior to such distributions and should be encouraged to provide the use of trust assets rather than to make distributions in the absence of a compelling reason to deviate from this policy. The trust beneficiaries will be expected to pay for their own consumables. Thus, the trust will form an asset pool providing multigenerational benefits for the descendants of its creator. The spouse of the creator may be included among the beneficiaries, but careful attention must be given to the income tax consequences, because the grantor will be taxed on the income unless distributions may be made to the spouse only with the consent of an adverse party.

The primary transfer tax savings with respect to the assets in a dynasty trust are (1) the trust assets, if retained in the trust, are not subject to transfer taxes for the duration of the trust, and (2) the accumulation of income inside the trust will increase the transfer tax savings because the income retained will also escape transfer taxes.

Also, the acquisition of a large life insurance policy inside a dynasty trust can leverage the benefits of the life insurance product.

Charitable Giving

Assets transferred to a charity are not included in your taxable estate. The charity must be approved by the federal government. A qualified charity is either a federal, state, or local agency that has a public purpose; a religious, charitable, scientific, literary, or educational organization; a war veterans' association; a fraternal lodge; or a cemetery. The provision of services cannot be deducted as a charitable contribution, so the IRS doesn't want to hear about your volunteer work or any donated professional services. If you get anything in return for your donation, such as tickets to a benefit concert, the fair market value of the tickets must be taken off what you claim to have contributed.

Basically, in order to facilitate a gift to a charity, you can give money outright or set up some form of trust. The two most frequently used charitable trusts combine a transfer to a noncharity (such as children) with a charity. A *charitable lead trust* is a trust in which income from principal is paid to a charity for a period of time, and then the trust pays the principal to someone else. A *charitable remainder trust* is a trust in which income is paid to someone other than the charity for a period of time, and the remainder is then given to a charity. Another variation on the trust concept is the *charitable remainder annuity trust*.

RESOURCES

Charitable Giving
Tips on Charitable Giving
<http://www.bbb.org/about/tipsgive.html>

Summary: The Philanthropic Advisory Service of the Better Business Bureau provides sound advice on charitable giving.

Leave a Legacy
PO Box 12097
Berkeley, CA 94712-3097
(888) 747-0454
<http://www.leavealegacy.org>

Summary: The mission of this organization is to promote interest and plan charitable giving through wills and estate planning. The organization works with professional advisors and nonprofit groups to encourage plan giving. The site offers answers to frequently asked questions with regard to planned giving.

> **Independent Charities of America**
> (800) 477-0733
> <http://www.independentcharities.org>

Summary: This Web site is designed to connect charitable individuals with needy organizations. It contains a charity search engine that can be used to locate potential recipients.

> **Charitable Choices**
> 1804 S Street, NW
> Washington, DC 20009
> (888) 410-1999
> <http://www.charitablechoices.org>

Summary: Charitable Choices provides information on qualified charities that are approved by the United Way.

> **The National Philanthropic Trust**
> 165 Township Line Rd., Suite 3000
> Jenkintown, PA 19046-3593
> (888) 878-7900
> <http://www.nptrust.org>

Summary: The National Philanthropic Trust is a public charity formed to encourage charitable giving through gifts. This site provides thorough information on tax and nontax benefits of philanthropy.

Life Insurance

Overview

Life insurance is insurance on your own life that provides funds for the life of another, such as a spouse or children, in the event of your death. Life insurance money may also be used to cover burial costs and to avoid or pay estate taxes. The basics on insurance are covered in Part Two, "Our Children."

There's no limit to the amount of life insurance you can take out on yourself, except that insurance companies usually place a ceiling on the amount they're willing to offer in insurance. How much insurance you should have is a function of how much you can afford and what situation you want the proceeds to cover. Types of expenses you may want to consider are funds for last expenses, readjustment of family members, dependency period income, mortgage payments, education, and lifetime income for a spouse.

INSIGHT

When you decide how much insurance you want to provide, it's important to gaze into the misty future while keeping in mind that situations almost always turn out differently than foreseen. Policies that permit changes can give you the opportunity to respond to the unexpected. For instance, you could be paying premiums to ensure that your child gets through college, but he or she may marry and decide not to go to school. In the meantime, your spouse develops a serious mental incapacity. If your insurance plan lets you change with the times, you are able to plan for the short run and still keep options open.

After figuring out the type of policy and the reasons for getting life insurance, you need to do some comparative shopping.

Click on <http://www.Boomerbasics.com> for a listing of insurance-rating services that can give you comparisons. Be sure to review the ratings for a ten-year span. An A+ rating in six of the last ten years suggests the long-term stability you should want to have in an insurance provider.

INSIGHT

Make sure you compare similar policies. Some states have companies that offer price comparisons by calling an 800 number. Click on <http://www .Boomerbasics.com> for a listing of these companies.

You also need to compare premium payments for similar policies. You'll need to adjust payments to factor in any dividend payback the company makes to the policyholder. Payment of a dividend means that it is a *participating policy*. *Nonparticipating policies* may have lower premiums but can actually cost more in the long run.

RESOURCES

Insurance Online
<http://www.insweb.com/>

Summary: This Web site is maintained by Ins Web Services, a licensed insurance agent. It serves as an insurance marketplace, providing quotes from participating companies, but also provides a lot of free insurance information. From the main screen, click on "Insurance 101" for a thorough explanation of often bewildering insurance terms.

Tips on Purchasing Life Insurance
<http://www.newyorklife.com/viewer/wsh-nyl/pfstchtp.html>

Summary: This Web site is maintained by the insurance carrier New York Life but provides a great deal of free information on what to do prior to purchasing insurance as well as how to select a reputable agent.

Consumer Insurance Guide
<http://www.insure.com/>

Summary: Insure.com, which does not sell life insurance, maintains this independent education site. From the main screen, click on "Life" to access a complete array of life insurance information, including valuable consumer information tips.

Life Insurance Trusts for Child Beneficiaries
<http://www.insure.com/life/trusts.html>

Summary: This section within the Insure.com Web site explains why a parent may wish to consider setting up a trust with life insurance.

Budget Life
<http://www.budgetlife.com>

Summary: Contains an easy to use on-line insurance calculator and can match users with independent insurance agents.

Tax Consequences

Dividends from the life insurance contract are taxable income. The proceeds of the insurance payout at your death are received by the beneficiary free of income tax but will become part of your taxable estate unless you divest yourself of the incidents of ownership. This is the same idea as retained control over the property, which also results in property being included in your taxable estate.

Releasing control is often done by setting up an insurance trust that pays the premiums and can change the beneficiaries. Payment of the premiums won't be considered control by the IRS, but being able to cash in the policy, borrow on it, or change the type of coverage or the beneficiaries will be considered incidents of ownership and result in the entire sum failing to pass outside of your taxable estate. Releasing control and keeping control are closely examined by the IRS. Professional advice can be well worth the fees for the estate tax savings that can result.

Selecting the proper kind of insurance and the proper amount of coverage for you can be a difficult process. However, it can also give you peace of mind that your loved ones will be protected should something happen to you. See Part Two, "Our Children," and Part Three, "Our Parents," for more information on insurance.

RESOURCES

Life Insurance
Insurance Company Ratings
<http://www.insure.com/ratings/index.html>

Summary: Insure.com maintains this site as an educational service. From the main screen, click on "S&P insurance company rating" for a detailed Standard and Poor's rating based on the long-term financial health of a company.

A.M. Best's Ratings
<http:// www.ambest.com/ratings/access.html>

Summary: An independent rating service, A.M. Best rates the financial strength of insurance companies and the related security of holding company debt and preferred stock.

Disability Insurance

As will be discussed in Part Two, "Our Children," disability is as hard to contemplate as death, but given that disability is more likely than death through your working years, not doing so really leaves a gaping hole in your estate plan. Check the section on disability insurance in Part Two.

RESOURCES

Disability Insurance Basics
<http://www.insuremarket.com/basics/disability/disbasics.htm>

Summary: This Web site is maintained by Quicken Insure Market, which is comprised of participant insurance carriers. A lot of good information is contained here, including coverage term explanations and advice on selecting appropriate levels of coverage.

Disability Insurance: How It Works
<http://www.insure.com/health/disability.html>

Summary: Insure.com, which does not sell insurance, maintains this Web site, providing information on disability insurance options.

Long-Term Care Insurance

Catastrophic illness that requires long-term rehabilitative care is likewise not a pleasant thought, but as we age, the possibility of such illness is no longer merely an idle thought. Just as our parents need to think about preparing for that possibility, it behooves us to look into long-term care insurance for ourselves. See the section on long-term care insurance in Part Three, "Our Parents," for details on policies.

Other Considerations in Estate Planning

It would be impossible for this section to do more than introduce you to estate planning. Many legal and tax requirements apply to the general principles discussed, and legal guidance should always be sought before taking any action.

With that in mind, following are several important points to consider in planning your estate:

- If you leave assets directly to minor children, the guardian (including the child's surviving parent) must keep records of even routine use of the inheritances and apply to the court for any unusual expenditures on the child's behalf. Instead, you may be wise to bequeath your property to a trust established in the children's names, and in most cases, name their designated guardian as trustee.

- If you give your personal representative broad powers to settle disputes or sell property as he or she sees fit, the personal representative will not have to seek permission from the court for each activity.

- If you plan to be married, you may wish to consider a prenuptial agreement to control the disposition of your assets in the event of divorce or death (most often a special consideration in a second marriage). This may be particularly important in certain circumstances, such as if you own a closely held business or wish to bequeath all or a portion of your estate to children from a previous marriage.

- It is wise to avoid provisions likely to be ruled invalid or to cause a challenge from neglected heirs. In most states, for example, you may not totally disinherit a spouse, but if you seek to totally disinherit a child, we recommend that it be unequivocally indicated in your will that this is your intent. Also, bequests that appear as favoritism or slights may cause challenges to the will or, just as damaging, lasting ill feelings in your family.

- There is little that can be done after death to relieve your estate from taxes if you have not properly planned the disposition of your estate.

- Anytime your life or circumstances change dramatically, your estate plan should be reviewed and, if necessary, updated. Changes in the following areas may alter your desires significantly:
  — Marital status
  — Ownership or value of property
  — Birth of a child
  — Tax law changes
  — Income or employment status
  — Business ownership
  — Relocation

At a minimum you should have your estate plan reviewed every three to five years. In doing so, you should consider the following:

- Keep your affairs in order and maintain an inventory of all of your property. Take some time to educate your personal representative about the property and where you keep your inventory or leave a copy on file in your lawyer's/advisor's office.

- Your will is effective until you change or revoke it. You may alter your will by executing a new one or by adding a *codicil,* an amendment to your will that is executed with the same formalities as a will. If you make changes to your will by writing on the document itself, you may invalidate the entire will.

- Designating a beneficiary of your life insurance policy does not take the place of a will. Life insurance is but one asset which needs to be considered in your overall estate plan. Under certain circumstances, it is advisable to transfer ownership of your life insurance either to a trust or to the beneficiary. If you create a trust for your children during life or in your will, be sure to designate the minor's trust as your beneficiary.

- If you own your house and checking account jointly with your spouse, those items will not be probated, and the survivor will have immediate access to the account. This is not necessarily true for all assets, however, as those assets held individually will be subject to probate.

- Married couples should work closely together in estate planning so that family objectives can be met regardless of who dies first.

- Do not have a beneficiary serve as a witness to your will. If the beneficiary is needed as a witness in order to validate your will, he or she may not be able to collect an inheritance.

- If you think your estate might shrink or grow, use percentages instead of dollars to divide your assets.

- You generally may not exclude your spouse completely from your will without your spouse's consent. In New York, for example, in such case a surviving spouse is entitled to an "elective share" of the estate, which amounts to the greater of $50,000 or one-third of the net estate, including testamentary substitutes.

- The best assets to give as gifts are those that are gaining in value because future appreciation will be excluded from your estate for tax purposes.

Bankruptcy

Although it is not a replacement for responsible fiscal behavior (in other words, don't use it as a credit card bailout), bankruptcy can help you to salvage what's left and get you back on your feet if that's where you need to get before thinking about the future.

There are two types of consumer bankruptcy: chapter 7 and chapter 13. The difference between the two is the result to the debtor. In chapter 7, the debtor's property, other than certain exempt assets, is sold to pay off the dischargeable debt. This wipes the slate clean, and the chapter 7 debtor no longer owes those debts. In chapter 13, the debt is not wiped away; the debtor enters into a payment plan and, using future income, pays off the debt over a three- to five-year period. Chapter 13 is meant for persons with a regular income and a limited amount of debt—no more than $250,000 in unsecured debt and less than $750,000 in secured debt.

To file for either chapter 7 or chapter 13 bankruptcy, you must first complete a detailed petition with as much data and information about your financial situation as possible. Don't leave anything out! This could cause your case to be dismissed and possibly result in criminal charges against you. Once the form is accurately and truthfully completed, you must file the petition at the bankruptcy court for the jurisdiction where you live. There is a filing fee, usually between $130 and $160. Courts allow petitioners to pay this fee in installments. Once you've filed, creditors cannot try to collect or foreclose without court approval.

In a chapter 7, if there are debts you wish to pay, such as a car loan, you can reaffirm that debt and file a statement with the court. After the petition is filed, the court will hold what is known as a *section 341* (of the U.S. Bankruptcy Code) *meeting*. Creditors attend the meeting and can ask you questions about your debt and your assets and attempt to get you to reaffirm your debt to them. You must attend, or your petition will be dismissed. After the hearing, the court appoints a trustee, who technically owns your property. The trustee actually is there to hold on to your property while deciding which assets are exempt and which should be sold to pay off your debts. Whatever money is made by sale is paid to your creditors in the order determined by the court. Once this is done, the trustee files a report, and the case is closed. Your debts are gone except for the ones that you reaffirmed or that were not dischargeable. These nondischargeable debts usually include such debts as student loans and taxes.

The process with a chapter 13 is almost the same. When you file the original petition, you must also file a plan showing how your creditors will be paid. You have to start paying the creditors in accordance with that plan within thirty days of filing. The court also has to approve the plan, and your creditors can raise objections. Courts are not unreasonable about this; if you meet certain criteria, your plan will be approved. As a final failsafe, if a chapter 13 proves unworkable, the court can permit its conversion into a chapter 7.

INSIGHT

To file for bankruptcy, you must have at the very least more liabilities than assets. Also, it's important to recognize that purchases made immediately prior to (or after) filing will not be discharged. No spending sprees are allowed. So if there is a necessary expenditure, it may pay to put off filing until you can be sure that the debt will be discharged.

INSIGHT

Although some people suggest that you can file for bankruptcy without legal assistance, we suggest you hire a lawyer! A mistake can get your petition thrown out of court. For a moderate fee, a lawyer can make sure you get those debts discharged and, in some cases, even have your creditors return property they've taken from you. With the stakes this high, there's no reason not to do it right. There may seem to be a contradiction between filing for bankruptcy on one hand and on the other hiring a professional who charges a fee for doing the legal work for you, but bankruptcy lawyers understand that contradiction, and they are prepared to make suitable arrangements to accommodate their bankruptcy clients.

RESOURCES

**Bankruptcy Laws: Free Information on Chapter 7 or 13
Personal Bankruptcy Laws**
<http://www.bankruptcyresource.com/>

Summary: A good overview of bankruptcy laws with answers to many common questions. This site provides a thorough comparison of chapters 7 and 13 of the Bankruptcy Code. The site is maintained by the Bankruptcy Laws Resource Center.

HEALTH ~~~~~~~~

aking care of your health is a simple goal but a complex reality. Our medical options range from the mainstream to the far-out. We have miracle drugs, new and promising daily research pronouncements, a veritable garage full of replacement body parts, alternative medicine, homeopathy, osteopathy, naturopathy, and more. Choosing a treatment can represent a daring leap of faith, a stubborn adherence to tradition, blissful ignorance, a prudent and wise decision, or an illogical wish—depending on who's giving you an opinion. Nevertheless, there is a mainstream, and its waters are deepest in the middle, so for the most part, illness has a course to safe harbor.

In this section, we will provide you with a multitude of resources that offer comprehensive and useful health-related information, services, or products. We also identify and describe medical conditions and health issues of special concern to boomers.

Access to and Availability of Health-Related Information, Services, and Products

Our parents grew up in a paternalistic society in which doctors (sometimes with input or direction from the government) generally had sole possession of medical information and resources and had significant (if not total) input regarding a patient's medical decisions. Our parents generally had (and may still have) blind faith in the medical community.

We boomers, on the other hand, are not so trusting. We grew up in an era in which we questioned authority, including medical professionals. We are comfortable in demanding information and explanations from our physicians, and we often pursue second opinions.

In this light, we can marvel in "boomer delight" given our almost unlimited access to medical information and resources. The ongoing development of the Internet has further enabled traditional and e-commerce companies, as well as the government, to educate, guide, and assist us in learning about and meeting our health care needs.

The following is just a short summary of the types of health information, services, and products that are readily available to you, essentially 24/7 (twenty-four hours a day, seven days a week) over the Internet.

Comprehensive Health Information

Any and all medical conditions are explained, defined, illustrated and discussed in a detailed manner.

Diagnosis

Some sites will offer you a diagnosis after you have listed your symptoms via e-mail. Alternatively, you may be able to chat directly with a physician or health care professional regarding your medical concerns.

Procedures and Treatment

Once you have familiarized yourself with a particular medical condition, you can learn all about diagnostic procedures and routine, experimental, and alternative treatments.

Health Profile and Medical History

If you so desire, you can complete a health profile or medical history that you can keep as an icon on your homepage and update as your medical status changes. Some sites will review your medical history and e-mail you a list of risk factors you should consider as well as other health-related suggestions. E-commerce health-related sites may market applicable products directly to you.

Referral or Physician/Provider Locator

You can find comprehensive lists of physicians and other health care providers who practice in your community on many sites. You can also find information about your physician or health care provider, including issues such as professional standing, affiliations, and results of government surveys and evaluations.

Anatomy and Physiology

If you would like to learn more about the human body—pictures and all—you can click on several Internet sites.

Educational Programs and Seminars

From your computer, you can attend lectures by famous (and not-so-famous) physicians and other health care professionals. Most lectures include an opportunity for the audience to chat with the guest speaker.

Videos, Vignettes, or Illustrations

If you would like to view a particular medical procedure, surgery, or even the birth of a child, many sites will provide you with such visuals—you need only supply your own popcorn and refreshments.

Health Communities

Internet communities where you can communicate with other people who have similar medical conditions or concerns are very popular and often very helpful. Members of the community can share valuable information including personal experiences, recommendations regarding physicians and other health care providers, effects of mainstream and experimental drugs and procedures, and moral support. Although such communities can be helpful, their members should not rely solely on such information, as its reliability will vary from one member to the next.

Health Care Stores (Malls)

You can buy almost any health-related product you can imagine over the Internet. From medication to prosthetics to birth control to diapers, what you need or desire is but one click away. Remember, many of the excellent health care sites entice you by providing free helpful information, thus giving them the opportunity to sell products to you.

INSIGHT

Don't be lazy when it comes to the health of you or a loved one. You can and must be an informed, involved, and knowledgeable consumer. Your well-being and that of your loved ones may depend on it.

RESOURCES

Private and Nonprofit Organizations

> **AccentHealth.com**
> 2203 N. Lois Ave., Suite 1100
> Tampa, FL 33607
> (813) 349-7100
> <http://www.accenthealth.com>

Summary: AccentHealth is a media company that provides health care information to consumers and health professionals. On its Web site, information is provided about the latest health news from the *New York Times,* healthy lifestyles, fitness, health conditions, and tests and procedures. Additional services provided on this site include "Find a Doctor" and a customized health profile.

> **Adam.com**
> 90 Tehama St.
> San Francisco, CA 94105
> (415) 541-9164
> <http://www.adam.com>

Summary: Adam.com is an on-line provider of health, medical, and wellness information that has established licensing arrangements with many other Internet sites. Special features provided on this site include health-related chat rooms; tools, including diet, nutrition and fitness calculators, and a health quiz; a health encyclopedia with corresponding illustrations; a custom-designed health newsletter; and a personalized health report.

> **AmericasDoctor.com**
> 11403 Cronridge Drive, Suite 200
> Owings Mills, MD 21117
> (888) 88AMDOC
> <http://www.americasdoctor.com>

Summary: Initially launched on America Online in September 1998, AmericasDoctor.com provides numerous services, including "Ask-A-Doc," where consumers can ask questions of health care professionals on-line. Other services include a health events calendar, daily features, and a medical mall.

AMA Health Insight
American Medical Association
515 North State Street
Chicago, IL 60610
(312) 464-5000
<http://www.ama-assn.org>

Summary: The creators of the AMA Web site describe it as "the patient's advocate and the physician's voice. It sets standards for the profession of medicine." The goals of the AMA involve providing information on medical practice and being an advocate to physicians and their patients as well as setting standards for medical ethics, practice, and education. The Consumer Health Information section of this site includes an area from which you can access and obtain information ranging from facts about diseases to finding a particular medical specialist or hospital in your area.

American Psychiatric Association (APA)
14000 K. St. NW
Washington, DC 20005
(202) 682-6000
<http://www.psych.org/>

Summary: The APA Web site includes sections on public information on mental illness, choosing a psychiatrist, medications, resources, and more. Information relating to public policy advocacy is available as are links to many related organizations.

drkoop.com
7000 North Morac, Suite 400
Austin, TX 78731
(888) 795-0998
<http://www.drkoop.com>

Summary: drkoop.com provides its users with a variety of information, services, and products, including the opportunity to participate in interactive communities, such as over one hundred thirty chat support groups. Among the comprehensive services available on this site you will find "cool tools" such as a drug checker, personal insurance center, local health resources, and a physician locator.

Drugstore.com
13920 SE Eastgate Way, Suite 300
Bellevue, WA 98005
(800) 378-4786
<http://www.drugstore.com>

Summary: You can purchase products that address your health, wellness, personal care, pharmacy, and (almost) all other needs on this site. It also provides information, newsletters, and "expert" advice. Drugstore.com shoppers can "personalize the shopping experience with personal shopping lists, e-mail reminders for replenishing regularly used products and private e-mail access to pharmacists and beauty experts for questions."

Healthatoz.com
66 Witherspoon St., Suite 345
Princeton, NJ 08542
(609) 409-8200
<http://www.healthatoz.com>

Summary: Healthatoz.com's goal is to help consumers better manage their health by assisting them in customizing their health from A to Z to suit their personal health needs and interests. To achieve this objective, visitors to this site can create a portable family health calendar and health organizer to keep track of important health information, medical opportunities, diet, medication, and other relevant information. This site's many other features include opportunities to ask questions of health experts, and on-line librarians, as well as information about healthy lifestyles.

Intelihealth.com
(888) 244-4636
<http://www.intelihealth.com>

Summary: Home to Johns Hopkins Health Information, this site offers a comprehensive selection of information, products, and services, including a physician locator, disease and condition guide, drug resource center, medical directory, medcite, and links to other health-related Web sites.

Medicinenet.com
19651 Alter
Foothill Ranch, CA 92610
(949) 380-9800
<http://www.medicinenet.com>

Summary: Medicinenet.com was created by physicians and high-tech executives to provide information and products to consumers. Special features listed on this site's directory include information on diseases and treatments, procedures and tests, first aid, medications, and poison control centers, as well as archives on health facts and news.

Mental Health Net
570 Metro Place North
Dublin, OH 43017
(614) 764-0143
(614) 764-0362 (Fax)
<http://www.mentalhelp.net/>

Summary: Mental Health Net, launched in 1995, is an on-line community that provides mental health news and resources. Features include information on most types of psychiatric disorders, psychotropic medications, and available treatment resources. It also has an on-line question-and-answer page where specific questions can be posed to professionals.

OnHealth
808 Howell St., Suite 400
Seattle, WA 98101
(206) 583-8665
<http://www.onhealth.com>

Summary: OnHealth describes itself as an independent consumer health information company. This popular site provides a variety of services, including news and reports, opportunities to pose questions to experts, references, interactive tools, live shows, on-line community, local health directory, shopping, and "my wellness manager."

PlanetRX
349 Oyster Point Blvd., Suite 201
South San Francisco, CA 94080
<http://www.planetrx.com>

Summary: PlanetRX exists to allow its users to fill prescriptions, shop for products, and get answers and advice. PlanetRX offers a variety of services, including but not limited to easy-to-read information on medical conditions and prescriptions and over-the-counter medications and drugs and other products and a secure record of your family's prescription and health care services.

The Health Network
1440 South Sepulveda Blvd.
Los Angeles, CA 90025
(310) 444-8123
<http://www.ahn.com>

Summary: This site is known for having hosted a telecast of the world's first live birth on the Internet. In addition to featuring live medical events, The Health Network provides medical information, health news, health tests, a health mall, health communities, and a variety of other services.

Thriveonline.com
Thrive Partners
221 Main St., Suite 480
San Francisco, CA 94105
<http://www.thriveonline.com/>

Summary: Thriveonline.com describes itself as "devoted to health, fit, and sexy living." Its five main areas are "Health," "Shape," "Eats," "Outdoors," and "Passion." The site's features include programs, chats, experts, vital resources, and a community of people with whom to interact. The site boasts a health library as well as a weight loss center.

WebMD
(888) 728-3702
<http://www.webmd.com/>

Summary: The creators of WebMD describe themselves as "an Internet-based health care network that connects physicians, hospitals, third-party payors, and consumers to a virtual world of medical information, tools and services." Special features for consumers include a health and medical library, on-line chat events, a self-care advisor, message boards, and health-related news.

Women's Health Interactive (WHI)
PO Box 271276
Ft. Collins, CO 80527-1276
<http://www.Womens-health.com>

Summary: The mission of WHI, as stated in its Web site, is "to be a unique, interactive learning environment where women gain knowledge and mastery of their health through the multi disciplinary resources that are offered for consumers and women's health professionals." The site provides information on women's health issues, providers, and specialized health services available to women.

Government Organizations

Centers for Disease Control and Prevention (CDC)
1600 Clifton Rd. NE
Atlanta, GA 30333
(404) 639-3311 (CDC operator)
(800) 311-3435 (CDC public inquiries)
<http://www.cdc.gov/>

Summary: The mission of the CDC is to promote health and quality of life by preventing and controlling disease, injury, and disability. A major focus of the CDC is the cause(s) and impact of infectious disease. The CDC Web site offers a diverse collection of information and resources. Of special interest to consumers is "Health Topics A to Z," where you can receive information ranging from health-related gender issues, occupational health, food-borne illness, senior health, and much more in both English and Spanish. From this site, you can also link to state and local health departments.

National Institutes of Health (NIH)
Bethesda, MD 20892
<http://www.nih.gov/>

Summary: The NIH's mission is to uncover new knowledge that will lead to better health for everyone. On its site, you will learn about the many research projects it has initiated or supported as well as have an opportunity to review the results of the research. You will also find health hotlines, publications, special programs, and a variety of other useful and interesting information. Consumers will find the feature "Medlineplus" very useful as it provides a variety of resources, including dictionaries for definitions of medical terms, information regarding health organizations, directories for finding doctors, and databases for articles.

Healthfinder.org
Office of Disease Prevention and Health Promotion
Office of Public Health and Science
Office of the Secretary
U.S. Department of Health and Human Services
Washington, D.C.
<http://www.healthfinder.org>

Summary: Healthfinder, a site developed by the U.S. Department of Health and Human Services, describes itself as a free gateway to reliable consumer health and human services information and can lead users to selected on-line publications, clearing houses, databases, Web sites, and support and self-help groups.

INSIGHT

The health Web sites just listed represent a few of the many sites dedicated to health-related issues. We urge you to familiarize yourself with these sites and use them with the caveat that you should always make important medical decisions with the input and guidance of your personal physician. In all likelihood, you can find most of what you're looking for through traditional and on-line organizations. When you need more information or help finding what you need, click on <http://www.Boomerbasics.com>.

Health Issues of Special Concern to Boomers

When we were younger, people we knew who were diagnosed with a serious illness or who died were almost always people our parents' age or older. Now, as we boomers have aged, that someone who has been afflicted with or succumbed to a serious medical condition or illness may be a member of our own generation.

We've all heard about or known boomers who have suffered from heart disease—such as the forty-year-old father of three young children who dropped dead on the basketball court. How many of us know women who have been diagnosed and treated for breast cancer, with those seriously affected left no option but to have one or both breasts removed? And how many of them did not survive in spite of their best efforts?

In most cases, these boomers believed themselves to be in good medical condition, as did their loved ones. Sadly, in some cases, serious illness or death may have been avoidable had they received annual physical exams or were more sensitive to their medical needs and family history.

Although we can dismiss those boomers who have died or become seriously disabled as being but a small percentage of the total boomer population, it's hard to dispute that as we get older, our susceptibility to such illnesses and diseases substantially increases. None of us can or should think that we are immune to heart disease, cancer, or other potentially deadly diseases.

We owe it to ourselves and our loved ones to be as knowledgeable as we can about such diseases and to ensure that we lead a healthy lifestyle. To help us all in this endeavor, we have consulted with our trusted friend, colleague, and fellow boomer, David Wolinsky, M.D.

Dr. Wolinsky, or David to his friends and fellow boomers, offers us information and guidance in regard to caring for the heart as well as a discussion of cancer-related conditions. With David's assistance, we conclude this chapter with an overview of relevant boomer medical issues, including a look at menopause, impotence, insomnia, and alternative medicine. You will also find the discussion of health issues covered in the "Health" section of Part Three, "Our Parents," of interest to people of boomer age as well.

Caring for the Heart

Atherosclerotic disease, or hardening of the arteries, is the leading cause of death in the United States. As we boomers enter our forties and fifties, many of us are seeing our parents suffering the complications of heart attacks or strokes. Often these illnesses are sudden and catastrophic, and we may be ill prepared to help our parents understand these diseases and help them make decisions.

The complications of atherosclerosis are less likely to affect boomers themselves; however, the diseases that lead to atherosclerosis, such as diabetes mellitus, hypertension, and hypercholesterolemia (high blood cholesterol), can and must be aggressively treated because they pose threats to health in and of themselves. This will not only prevent complications of the diseases themselves, but also reduce the likelihood of developing atherosclerotic cardiovascular disease. In addition, lifestyle modifications, such as smoking cessation, dietary modifications, and institution of weight loss and exercise programs, must be initiated to reduce cardiovascular risk.

How Atherosclerosis Develops

To take steps to reduce cardiovascular disease, one must understand how the disease develops and progresses. Three coronary arteries supply the heart; two carotid arteries and two vertebral arteries supply the brain; the aorta, with its branches, supplies the rest of the body; and all of these arteries are subject to atherosclerosis. As previously mentioned, many key risk factors can predispose one to developing cardiovascular disease:

- Diabetes
- Hypertension
- Hypercholesterolemia
- Smoking
- A family history of premature coronary heart disease
- Being a middle-aged male or postmenopausal female

Coronary artery disease may begin to develop during your teens and twenties. Those predisposed may develop a fatty streak within an artery. With time (usually twenty or more years) this streak develops into a plaque that can begin to narrow the artery. These plaques are composed of fats called *lipids* and fibrous tissues similar to those that form scars. There are various lipid components, but the most dangerous form is LDL cholesterol, which gets converted to an oxidized or activated form and then wreaks even more havoc within the artery. As the lipid plaque grows, several things can happen. The plaque may develop a fibrous cap, which will keep it stable. Blood flow may be reduced to some degree, but the artery remains open. This is called a *stable plaque.* If excessively rich in LDL, however, the plaque may crack or rupture. This rupture exposes the cholesterol in part of the blood vessel wall to substances that bring in platelets and activate a clotting cascade. Such a cascade can cause rapid and dramatic occlusion of an artery, leading to sudden death or *myocardial infarction* (heart attack), which can be almost instantly fatal. In the brain, components of these plaques may break off and travel downstream, cutting off blood supply to a portion of the brain and thus causing a *cerebral vascular accident* (stroke).

Coronary artery disease is widely present. One and a half million heart attacks occur annually, and 500,000 deaths per year result from coronary heart disease. There are 250,000 cases of sudden death each year from this cause, at least two-thirds of which occur in people with no known prior heart disease. It is for these reasons that preventive measures need to be instituted to reduce cardiovascular risk. Over fourteen million people in this country suffer from angina or have had a heart attack. As we head into the millennium, much needs to be done to reduce the incidence of coronary heart disease in this country. Fortunately, many options have become available for preventing the development of and treating the manifestations of atherosclerosis.

Diabetes Mellitus

Up to 7 percent of the population may have diabetes, which has two forms. Type 1 usually appears in teenage years and often requires insulin therapy. Type 2 diabetes appears in middle age and beyond. Whereas type 1 diabetics are insulin deficient and require insulin administration, type 2 diabetics may merely be insensitive to insulin, which causes their bodies to make more insulin in compensation. The higher levels of insulin contribute to the development of cardiovascular disease, which is two to four times more frequent in diabetics than in nondiabetics. In addition, the other standard risk factors for heart disease, such as hypertension and high blood cholesterol, have a more malignant effect in diabetics and therefore need to be controlled more aggressively.

What Is Diabetes?

Diabetes is defined by high serum blood sugar. Anyone with fasting blood glucose greater than 126 is considered diabetic. People with sugars between 110 and 125 are considered to have abnormal glucose tolerance, or prediabetes. People with two-hour postprandial sugars (as determined in blood tests drawn two hours after a standard oral sugar load) of 140 to 200 are also considered to have abnormal glucose tolerance. People with impaired glucose tolerance have a variety of metabolic abnormalities similar to those of diabetics and need to be treated quite aggressively with respect to risk-factor modification to reduce their likelihood of developing cardiovascular disease.

People suffering from a clinical syndrome called *insulin resistance (IRS)* are obese, hypertensive, and have borderline high blood glucose levels and disordered cholesterol metabolism as defined by low levels of HDLs and high levels of triglycerides. Their obesity is characterized by increased abdominal girth as opposed to excess fat distribution in the chest and hips. An increased waist-to-hip ratio is a trademark for the disease. These people are at high risk of developing heart attack, stroke, or heart failure, and they need to be both identified and educated by their physician to promote risk-factor modification. Treatment does not necessarily require blood glucose–lowering medicines but does require control of other metabolic abnormalities.

INSIGHT

People with insulin-resistance syndrome should have their blood pressure lowered to 130/85. People over 120 percent of their ideal body weight need to lose at least 10 to 15 percent of their total body weight; should be considered for aggressive cholesterol-lowering treatment, including medications; and must begin an exercise program.

Who Should Be Tested for Diabetes?

All men and women over the age of forty-five should be screened by testing blood sugars every three years.

The following people, however, are considered at higher risk and should be either tested at an earlier age or more frequently:

- Obese people weighing more than 120 percent of their desirable body weight
- People with first-degree relatives with diabetes
- High-risk ethnic groups (African Americans, Hispanics, Native Americans, Asians)
- Women who delivered a baby that weighed greater than nine pounds or had gestational diabetes
- Hypertensive people with blood pressure greater than 140/90
- People with cholesterol abnormalities having HDL levels less than 35 or triglyceride levels greater than 250
- Any patient who has shown impaired fasting glucose or impaired glucose tolerance on a prior blood test

Just as high-risk people need to be screened more carefully for overt diabetes, diabetics need to be screened more carefully for coronary artery disease. Stress testing is the most common form of such screening and should be carried out in the following subgroup of diabetics:

- Any diabetic with any type of suspicious chest pain
- Diabetics who have other forms of vascular disease, such as carotid artery blockages or evidence of peripheral circulation disease
- Sedentary diabetics over the age of thirty-five who wish to begin an exercise program
- Diabetics with two or more of the following risk factors for coronary artery disease:
  - Cholesterol greater than 240
  - Blood pressure greater than 140/90
  - LDL greater than 160
  - HDL less than 35
  - Smoking
  - A family history of premature coronary disease

INSIGHT

Although the motto "know your number" most recently refers to cholesterol values, it is equally important to know your blood sugar. If your doctor doesn't tell you, then ask. If it hasn't been drawn, then ask to have it drawn. As in all phases of cardiovascular risk-factor reduction, the patient must play an active role, which means knowing what information must be obtained.

High Cholesterol

The second major risk factor for developing cardiovascular disease is *hypercholesterolemia,* or high cholesterol. Cholesterol is found in almost all cells. It is required to give integrity to cells and must be present for the synthesis of many hormones, such as cortisone, estrogen, and testosterone. The body synthesizes cholesterol from other substances, and a small amount of cholesterol is obtained from dietary intake. However, fat consumption in most diets is such that the body makes much more cholesterol than it needs. This excess cholesterol is incorporated into the blood vessels and may lead to the development of atherosclerosis as described previously.

People metabolize fat and cholesterol differently; genetic predisposition is the most common reason why people have high blood cholesterol levels. Although it is possible to have high blood cholesterol levels without manifesting any vascular disease, in general the higher your serum cholesterol levels, the more likely you are to develop coronary artery disease.

The Framingham study is the most famous epidemiologic study on the development of coronary artery disease and the effect of coronary risk factors. The entire population of Framingham, Massachusetts, has been followed for the development of heart disease, and multiple data has been derived from this study. Both the Framingham study and the Multiple Risk Factor Intervention (MRFIT) study have shown a linear relationship between cholesterol and coronary risk.

LDL Cholesterol

Cholesterol is transported throughout the body in packets called *lipoproteins.* Dietary fat is converted into *chylomicrons,* which in turn becomes VLDLs (very low density lipoproteins). The most dangerous form of lipid is the LDL (low-density lipoprotein), which is better remembered as the **L**ousy cholesterol. LDL appears to trigger the development of unstable atherosclerotic plaque by bringing cholesterol into the blood vessels and incorporating it into the plaque. Lowering LDL lowers cardiac risk.

New information is now available regarding subtypes of LDL. Pattern A LDL is large and light, like a Nerf ball, and is far less atherogenic than type B LDL, which is small and dense, like a golf ball. Type B LDL is often associated with the insulin-resistance syndrome described previously and is also seen in people who are overweight, which may be the reason why these people are so susceptible to the development of coronary artery disease. Routinely, total cholesterol, LDL, triglycerides, and HDL levels can be measured in a lab. To ascertain the subtype(s) of LDL, a test called *LDL electrophoresis* must be carried out. This is not a routine blood test but must be specially ordered by a physician when necessary. This usually is not covered by health insurance but in some settings is quite valuable in further defining risk.

HDL Cholesterol

HDLs, or high-density lipoproteins, are responsible for removing cholesterol from the circulation and into the liver where it can be eliminated. High levels of HDL, which you can easily remember as **H**appy cholesterol, are associated with a lower risk of vascular disease; low levels of HDL, with higher risk. Again, low HDL is one of the hallmarks of insulin-resistance syndrome. Lowering LDL with drugs is relatively easy and effective at lowering cardiac risk. Raising HDL, though effective, is much more difficult.

Triglycerides

Triglycerides are the third major lipid subgroup. They may be related to the risk of cardiovascular disease in diabetics and in women but are less of a risk for men. Dietary indiscretion, obesity, and poorly controlled diabetes contribute to high levels of triglycerides, but such levels can be lowered with appropriate dietary management.

Multiple formulas and ratios have been proposed to assess for the risk of coronary disease. The HDL–to–total cholesterol ratio and the absolute LDL levels appear to be the most predictive.

Testing and Treatment

The NCEP (National Cholesterol Education Program) is a division of the NIH and has defined criteria for cholesterol testing and treatment. Random cholesterol and HDL levels can be drawn at any time. These tests do not require a fast. A fasting lipid profile requires an eight- to twelve-hour fast and at least a twenty-four-hour abstinence from alcohol.

INSIGHT

Ask your doctor what your cholesterol levels are and ask what needs to be done to lower those levels if they are too high. Is changing your diet enough, or will medications need to be added? Be sure to ask when your cholesterol profile will be drawn again.

INSIGHT

As we get older, cholesterol levels tend to rise. Recheck even the lowest cholesterol levels every five years and recheck mildly elevated cholesterol levels every one to two years if you're not taking medication to control those levels.

Several multisite national and international studies have been done to prove the beneficial effects of lowering cholesterol with *statins,* a class of drugs that cause a dramatic reduction of LDL and total cholesterol levels in the bloodstream.

The 4S (Scandinavian Simvastatin Survival Study Group) studied patients who had already suffered a coronary event. There was a 34 percent reduction in future coronary events noted if LDL was reduced to target levels of 100 or less with Simvastatin.[1]

In the CARE (Cholesterol and Recurrent Events) study, the use of Pravastatin (Pravachol) in patients with defined coronary disease but relatively normal cholesterol levels (mean cholesterol 209, mean LDL 139) dramatically reduced recurrent events by 31 percent.[2]

---

1. Scandinavian Simvastatin Survival Study Group, "Randomized Trial of Cholesterol Lowering in 4,444 Patients with Coronary Heart Disease: The Scandinavian Simvastatin Survival Study (4S), *Lancet* 344 (1994): 1383–89.

2. F. Sacks et al., "The Effect of Pravastatin on Coronary Events after Myocardial Infarction in Patients with Average Cholesterol Levels," *New England Journal of Medicine* 335 (1996): 1001–9.

The WOSCOPS (West of Scotland Coronary Prevention Study) showed that the use of Pravastatin (Pravachol) in patients with high cholesterol but no history of myocardial infarction produced a 31 percent relative risk reduction of coronary death and nonfatal heart attack.[3]

The AVERT (Atorvastatin versus Revascularization Treatment) study showed that the use of high-dose Atorvastatin (80 mg daily) was more effective than balloon angioplasty at reducing recurrent events in patients with known angina.[4] Atorvastatin (Lipitor) is the most powerful statin on the market today, lowering LDL levels 30 to 50 percent.

Side effects of statins are very rare; the most common are mild forms of gastrointestinal distress. Liver function test abnormalities may occur, but these can be monitored by serial blood tests. Whenever cholesterol levels are drawn, liver functions tests are drawn simultaneously. Another side effect is *myosotis,* a muscle inflammation that presents with muscle aches and usually responds to withdrawal of the medicine.

Niacin is another drug useful in treatment of high cholesterol. It is the most effective drug available for raising HDL cholesterol levels. In addition, it can lower total cholesterol and lower LDL to a degree, but the later effects are much less powerful than those obtained with the use of statins. Side effects include flushing and bloating, but these can be reduced by taking the drug with an aspirin and a small low-fat snack late in the day. Other side effects include hepatitis. Niaspan, a once-daily form of niacin, appears to have the best combination of efficacy, safety, and a low-risk profile. Cholesterol metabolism is most active in the evening, so it is recommended that statin or Niaspan be taken at that time.

For those people who cannot take statin or niacin, other drugs are available. Lopid and Tricor are two examples of *fibrates,* drugs that may lower triglycerides and raise HDL. They have a lesser effect on LDL, and their efficacy in reducing coronary morbidity and mortality is less well defined.

Though many people require medications to lower cholesterol, this does not eliminate the need for dietary restriction of fat. All people with

---

3. J. Shepherd et al., "Prevention of Coronary Heart Disease with Pravastatin in Men with Hypercholesterolemia," *New England Journal of Medicine* 333 (1995): 1301–7.

4. B. Pitt et al., "Aggressive Lipid-Lowering Therapy Compared with Angioplasty in Stable Coronary Artery Disease," *New England Journal of Medicine* 341 (1999): 70–76.

cardiovascular risk or disease should follow the American Heart Association diet, which can be found in the association's cookbook. Both step 1 and step 2 diets have been defined in Table 3.1.

Table 3.1   *American Heart Association Diet*

	Saturated Fat (g)	Fat (g)	Cholesterol (mg)
Step 1	8–10	30	300
Step 2	Less than 7	30	200

National Institutes of Health, "National Cholesterol Education Program Second Report of the Expert Panel on Detection, Evaluation, and Treatment of High Blood Cholesterol in Adults (Adult Treatment Panel II)," NIH Publication 93-3095 (Bethesda, MD, 1993).

A step 1 diet can be expected to reduce cholesterol by 3 to 14 percent, and a step 2 diet can be expected to reduce cholesterol an additional 3 to 7 percent.

INSIGHT

Do not be misled by advertising. The key to low-fat dieting is reduction of saturated fat and total fat in the diet. Hearing that a food may have no cholesterol might not mean much, as such foods may still be high in fat and saturated fat. Intake of a variety of unhealthy products high in saturated fat must be limited in a cholesterol-reducing diet.

Cholesterol lowering requires partnership between patients and health care providers. A variety of other resources are available to help deal with this chronic problem. Contact the local American Heart Association for dietary information or seek out the National Heart, Lung and Blood Institute (NHLBI) or American Heart Association Web sites for more information (see the "Health" section of Part Three, "Our Parents," pages 350–381, for these Web sites). Do not hesitate to see a dietician for more specific information.

Hypertension

The third major risk factor for coronary artery disease is hypertension, which affects fifty million people in the United States. Hypertension can lead to many grave health problems such as congestive heart failure, kidney failure, stroke, and increased risk of coronary atherosclerosis. Blood pressure control is easily obtainable with proper medical therapy. This requires compliance with medications and acknowledgment by both the physician and the patient that serious side effects can and do occur with medication. Minor side effects occur often and might necessitate frequent dosage adjustments.

INSIGHT

Forty percent of people with high cholesterol have hypertension, and 45 percent of hypertensive people have high cholesterol. The combination of the two risk factors increases coronary risk and therefore requires more aggressive treatment of both.

In 1997 the U.S. government released *JNC-VI*, a monograph that defined the various stages of hypertension and gave treatment guidelines. Hypertension severity was defined as shown in Table 3.2.

Table 3.2 **Stages of Hypertension**

Rating	Blood Pressure
Optimal	120/80
Normal	130/85
High Normal	139/89
Definite Hypertension	
Stage 1	140–160/90–99
Stage 2	160–179/100–109
Stage 3	Greater than 180/110

National Institutes of Health, Joint National Committee on Prevention, Detection, Evaluation and Treatment of High Blood Pressure, "The Sixth Report of the Joint National Committee on Prevention, Detection, Evaluation, and Treatment of High Blood Pressure (JNCVI)," NIH Publication 98-4080 (Bethesda, MD, 1997), 16, 17, 29, 49.

Effective blood pressure control results in a 27 percent reduction of the risk of heart attacks, a 36 percent reduction of the risk of strokes, and a 49 percent decrease in the risk of congestive heart failure.

INSIGHT

Blood pressure control must be achieved slowly. Often, people attribute side effects to a new medication when in fact the symptoms are attributable to the fact that their bodies are not yet acclimated to a lower blood pressure. Also, do not expect major changes in blood pressure within one to two days of starting new medication. A new drug or new dose often requires one to two weeks for peak effect. Be patient and stick it out. Talk to your doctor or a nurse regularly.

Many types of antihypertensive medications are available. Because it is difficult to take medications more than once a day, your doctor should try to put you on a regimen of once-daily drugs. In addition, many people cannot be controlled with a single drug. Initially it would be appropriate to try to increase the dosage of the given drug, but a second medication must often be added to the regimen.

Obesity

One-third of U.S. citizens are overweight. Obesity contributes to increased cardiac risk by raising blood pressure and cholesterol levels and by making diabetes less easily controlled. Obesity is the most dangerous cardiac risk factor for women over the age of sixty. Being more than 30 percent over your ideal body weight triples the risk of death. A key assessment of cardiac risk is the waist-to-hip ratio. Apple-shaped bodies, with weight concentrated around the waist, appear to predispose one to cardiac risk more than pear-shaped bodies, with weight centered around the hips. Management of obesity requires diet and exercise.

Exercise is fun! Set realistic goals for exercise. It does not need to be high intensity to be effective. Studies have shown that walking for 10 minutes four times per day is almost as effective as doing a single 40-minute session. To burn 2,000 calories per week, walk 400 minutes per week.

INSIGHT

When initiating an exercise program, have a reasonable three-month goal and make small, steady increments along the way. Set yourself up for success, not failure.

Twenty to 40 percent of people discontinue exercise within six months. In part, this is because they have set unrealistic goals and become discouraged. Vary your program, exercise with other people, and cheer each other on.

Smoking

Smoking five cigarettes a day doubles your risk of dying from a heart attack. **There is no cutting down, only quitting, when it comes to reducing cardiac risk.** A variety of smoking cessation programs are available. The use of a prescription drug called Zyban or Nicorette gum may be helpful in increasing your success at quitting smoking. Make sure to consult with your physician before using any treatment.

Women and Heart Disease

In general, coronary artery disease is felt to be a man's disease. In fact, it is not. One-third of women have hypertension, one-quarter of women have high cholesterol, and one-quarter of women are overweight. Whereas only one in twenty-six women die from breast cancer, one-third to one-half of women die from heart disease. One-third of women over the age of sixty-five have coronary artery disease, which increases to 55 percent at age seventy-five. And when a woman does suffer a heart attack, it tends to be much more deadly, in part because women are usually older and have other medical problems at the time of their event.

Before menopause, estrogen protects women against coronary artery disease by keeping HDL levels up and cholesterol levels down. Natural estrogen is an anti-oxidant and anticoagulant and helps to dilate small blood vessels. Unfortunately, estrogen levels plummet after menopause, at which time risk-factor modification should be carried out as aggressively in women as it is in men. One year after a woman stops smoking, her cardiac risk is reduced by one-fourth. In three to five years, she has risk equivalent to that of a nonsmoker even if she has already suffered a heart attack. Estrogen replacement therapy remains a controversial and unresolved issue. Many studies have suggested that estrogen replacement therapy reduces cardiac events. For example, a study that examined women who had had a prior cardiac event found that estrogen replacement therapy caused a dramatic reduction in event rates among the study's subjects. In people who had not had a prior heart attack, the event risk was reduced 42 percent by initiating estrogen replacement therapy.

Because taking estrogen can pose some health risks, including the possibility of an increase in breast cancer, consult with your physician on the best treatment for you. Currently, the Women's Health Initiative is the most comprehensive study on the beneficial effects of estrogen to date. Unfortunately, we will not have the final results of this study for another five years. In the meantime, women must weigh the risks and benefits of estrogen replacement therapy; certainly if multiple coronary risk factors are present, including a positive family history, this would favor its use. Adding progesterone may lower the risk of uterine cancer but blunt the beneficial effect on cholesterol. Comprehensive discussion must be carried out involving internists, gynecologists, and where indicated, cardiologists.

Diagnostic Testing

Now that you have done all the right things, how do you find out if you have a problem? First and foremost, if you are concerned about symptoms, don't wait. Go to the doctor and get an electrocardiogram (EKG) or, if indicated, an exercise stress test. EKGs, in fact, are not useful for the diagnosis of coronary disease unless you are having acute symptoms. They will show whether or not you have had a heart attack, but in the absence of symptoms, more sophisticated testing is needed.

A stress test that employs a treadmill is a simple way to screen for coronary disease. Using graded exercise (from slower and gentler to faster and more intense) heart rate, blood pressure, and EKG are monitored. The principal warning sign to observe is the *ST segment depression* (a specific electric wave for an EKG), which may show that the heart is not receiving enough blood flow under stress. The more severe the changes and the earlier they occur, the more unfavorable the prognosis. Stress testing is not a black-and-white test. There are various degrees of positivity and negativity, including absolute false positives and false negatives. In order for stress testing to be most accurately used, it may need to be ordered appropriately. A study from Duke University classified people as high, medium, or low risk based on stress testing, with a four-year survival rate of 79 percent, 95 percent, and 99 percent, respectively.

Stroke

Whereas coronary artery disease is the number one killer in the United States, stroke (or *cerebral vascular accident,* as it is more formally known) is one of the major causes of disability. Six hundred thousand strokes occur yearly, with a 25 percent annual mortality rate. Strokes are especially devastating within the African-American population. With each ten-year period after one reaches the age of fifty-five, the risk of stroke doubles.

Stroke is caused when the blood supply to a particular portion of the brain is cut off. Symptoms are related to whatever portion of the brain is involved. The vascular blockage may come from clot formation within a main vessel, such as the carotid artery or its branches. In addition, cholesterol plaques may break off from the aorta and go to the brain, causing blockage of small vessels. Another cause of stroke is an embolus, in which case a small blood clot may break off from the heart and go to the brain, again, impairing blood supply.

The most common cause of embolic stroke is *atrial fibrillation,* an irregular rhythm of the heart that is associated with lack of organized contraction of the *atria,* or upper chambers of the heart. As the atria do not contract efficiently, blood swirls around inside them, causing the formation of small blood clots that may later break off and go to the brain, causing stroke. Atrial fibrillation is a disease of increasing prevalence. It may be chronic or occur intermittently. Risk factors for the development of atrial fibrillation (and hence, stroke) include the presence of underlying heart muscle dysfunction, valvular heart disease, enlarged cardiac chambers, congestive heart failure, and underlying coronary artery disease.

In patients with atrial fibrillation, anticoagulant drugs may be administered to prevent clot formation or propagation. Acutely, heparin may be given intravenously in the hospital. Chronically, coumadin, an oral anticoagulant, is used. When taking coumadin, a blood test called the Protime/Internationalized Normalized Ratio (PT/INR) must be done with relative frequency to allow for dosage adjustment. Too high an INR increases the risk of bleeding, but too low an INR reduces the drug's efficacy.

INSIGHT

Drastic changes in your diet, particularly regarding the consumption of green leafy vegetables, and a change in medications, particularly antibiotics, dramatically effect the PT/INR. If your diet changes significantly or if drugs such as antibiotics are added to your regimen, the cardiologist should be notified and a PT/INR should be obtained.

Reducing the Risk

Modifying or reducing risk factors for stroke can help you avoid this health problem. In major clinical trials, stroke was reduced by 27 percent in association with the use of statins. Reduction of diastolic blood pressure yielded a 40 percent reduction of stroke risk; reduction of systolic blood pressure yielded a similar decrease. In the elderly, blood pressure reduction may bring about a 50 percent reduction of stroke risk.

The last twenty years have brought about changes in the way cardiovascular disease is treated. Primary prevention involves lowering the risk of cardiovascular events in patients who have risk factors but have never had defined disease such as heart attack, stroke, angina, or congestive heart failure. Secondary prevention consists of treatment and reducing the likelihood of developing repeat clinical events. We have become effective not only in prevention but also and more importantly have become more adept at treating the acute manifestations of diseases such as heart attack and stroke. This has reduced short-term mortality and allowed long-term survival to improve as risk-factor control becomes more effective. These treatments require significant effort on the part of both the patient and the health care provider and, as previously noted, require intense cooperation to be most effective. Still, information is a powerful tool in allowing us boomers to manage health issues for ourselves and our parents.

RESOURCES

In the "Health" section of Part Three, "Our Parents," you will find resources that address heart disease (page 361), diabetes (page 351), and strokes (page 363).

National Cholesterol Education Program
NHLBI Information Center
PO Box 30105
Bethesda, MD 20824-0105
<http://www.nhlbi.nih.gov>

Summary: The National Cholesterol Education Program provides current research findings as well as suggestions for lowering cholesterol through diet and exercise.

Mayo Clinic
4500 San Pablo Road
Jacksonville, FL 32224
(904) 953-2000
<http://www.mayohealth.org/mayo/9709/htm/hyperten.htm>

Summary: Discusses lifestyle and drug treatment options for high blood pressure (hypertension).

Keeping Cholesterol under Control
Food and Drug Administration
5600 Fishers Lane
Rockville, MD 20857
(800) INFO-FDA
<http://www.Fda.gov>

Summary: The U.S. Food and Drug Administration publishes this comprehensive educational site that describes causes and effects of high cholesterol levels as well as treatment options.

Cancer

"You've got cancer" . . . probably three of the most paralyzing words in our vocabulary. Despite the many fears that still surround the "C word"—principal among them, that a cancer diagnosis is equivalent to a death sentence—cancer treatments and prognoses have come a long way. In fact, rather than being viewed as incurable, cancer is treated in most cases as a chronic illness that, with the appropriate treatment, can be managed for many years.

Even though it's the second leading cause of death (behind heart disease) in the United States, over five million Americans who were diagnosed with cancer five or more years ago are alive today, and most of them are considered cured (with no sign of the disease and with the same life expectancy as someone who never had cancer).

INSIGHT

If you or a loved one has been diagnosed with cancer, one of your best allies is information: It allows you to ask the right questions and to make informed choices. Along with the wealth of information you'll find through <http://www.Boomerbasics.com>, numerous printed resources and several toll-free numbers are available. An excellent sourcebook for cancer information is *Choices* by Marion Morra and Eve Potts (Avon Books, 1994). Another topnotch resource is the Cancer Information Service ([800] 4-CANCER), where trained professionals are on call to answer your questions about cancer and to help you decide what steps to take—either for yourself or on your parents' behalf.

RESOURCES

American Cancer Society (ACS)
(800) ACS-2345
<http://www.cancer.org>

Summary: The American Cancer Society sponsors programs in research, patient services, prevention, detection and treatment. Call for information or to find the local ACS chapter.

University of Pennsylvania OncoLink
OncoLink Editorial Office
University of Pennsylvania Medical Center
3400 Spruce Street—2 Donner
Philadelphia, PA 19104-4283
<http://cancer.med.upenn.edu>

Summary: OncoLink is an Internet information resource that was developed in affiliation with the University of Pennsylvania Cancer Center. It is a very good source of cancer information.

National Cancer Institute (NCI)
National Institute of Health
Bethesda, MD 20892
<http://www.nci.nih.gov>

Summary: The NCI coordinates the U.S. government's cancer research program and operates a Web site for cancer patients and the public with news and information on its programs and resources.

A discussion of the more than one hundred forms of cancer is simply beyond the scope of this handbook. The most common ones are described in the following sections.

Breast Cancer

The statistics are scary enough: Breast cancer is the most common cancer among U.S. women, and one woman in eight will develop breast cancer in her lifetime (assuming a life span of eighty-five years). But nothing compares to the fright of finding a lump in your breast or being told your mammogram looks "suspicious."

As with all cancers, early detection significantly increases the odds that the cancer can be treated effectively. In addition to the yearly mammograms recommended for women over fifty, all women should self-examine their breasts once a month.

Click on <http://www.Boomerbasics.com> for guidelines on how to do a breast self-exam along with a discussion of the risk factors and symptoms of breast cancer.

Colon and Rectal Cancers

Colon cancer and the importance of preventive screening took center stage in 1998 when New York Yankee outfielder Darryl Strawberry was diagnosed with the disease. If the cancer is caught early enough, when it is still localized, survival rates are high: 91 percent of these patients will still be alive after five years. The problem is that too few cases (37 percent) are diagnosed at a localized stage because colorectal screening is underused.

Doctors recommend that anyone over the age of fifty should be screened regularly for colorectal cancer. Screening includes an annual fecal occult blood test (FOBT) based on a stool sample, a flexible sigmoidoscopy every five years, and a total colon examination by colonoscopy every ten years or by a double-contrast barium enema (DCBE) every five to ten years.

The sound of words such as *sigmoidoscopy, colonoscopy,* and *enema* is unsettling enough, never mind the images they evoke. But cancer paints an even uglier picture. If you or your parents are among the 59 percent of people over the age of fifty who have never had a sigmoidoscopy or similar procedure, urge them to see their doctor *soon.*

Click on <http://www.Boomerbasics.com> for information on the risk factors and symptoms associated with colon cancer, what's actually involved in each of these screening procedures, related diagnoses, and treatment options.

Lung Cancer

Lung cancer is the most common cause of cancer death among U.S. men and women. Unlike certain other cancers, lung cancer is difficult to detect at an early stage because an effective screening test has not yet been developed. Even the symptoms are hard to pin down because they may vary depending on the cancer's location and growth pattern.

Most lung cancer (80 percent) is caused by cigarette smoking, although exposure to other environmental factors such as secondhand smoke and asbestos also increases the risk of developing it. If you are a smoker, you can still cut your risk for lung cancer as soon as you stop smoking (after 15 years without a cigarette, you'll have the same level of risk as a nonsmoker).

That lung cancer is the most preventable type of cancer will offer you little comfort if you or a loved one has already been diagnosed as having the disease. Surgery, radiation therapy, and chemotherapy are the usual treatment options, but the search is ongoing for effective screening tests and treatments to make lung cancer more manageable.

Click on <http://www.Boomerbasics.com> for information about the different treatments currently available for lung cancer and for the latest research on potential alternatives, including opportunities to participate in clinical trials of promising new treatments.

Prostate Cancer

By the age of sixty, most men have experienced problems associated with an enlarged prostate gland. However, a prostate *problem* doesn't necessarily signify prostate *cancer.*

The risk of prostate cancer increases with age (men over sixty-five comprise about 80 percent of the new prostate cancer diagnoses each year). It's found in about 30 percent of men over sixty and is the second most common cause of cancer-related deaths among U.S. men.

Because there are essentially no early warning signs of prostate cancer, most such cancers usually are discovered through a digital rectal examination, which is recommended annually for all men over the age of forty. Though not the most dignified of examinations, the few minutes it takes literally could save your life—especially when you consider that the five-year survival rate for men with early-stage (localized) prostate cancer is 100 percent! When contrasted with the 31 percent survival rate after five years once the cancer spreads beyond the prostate gland, that should be all the evidence you need to get an exam if you haven't had one in the last year.

If you have been diagnosed with prostate cancer, any decisions about treatment (usually surgery, radiation, or hormone therapy) should be based not only on your medical history, age, and the stage of the disease but also on the benefits, risks, and possible side effects of each treatment.

Click on <http://www.Boomerbasics.com> for information about treatment options for prostate cancer, including a discussion of the advantages and disadvantages of each.

Alternative Treatment

For a variety of reasons including religious beliefs, medical complications, and a lack of effective traditional medical intervention, some patients and their families seek alternate types of treatment. Although alternative treatments may not meet the medical needs or desires of traditionalists, they may in some cases have a positive medical or psychological benefit to patients and their families.

RESOURCES

National Center for Complementary and Alternative Medicine (NCCAM)
National Institutes of Health
<http://nccam.nih.gov>

Summary: The stated mission of NCCAM is to conduct and support basic and applied research and training and to disseminate information on complementary and alternative medicine to practitioners and the public.

Insomnia

Insomnia is simply defined as the inability to sleep. A 1996 report by the National Sleep Foundation states that one in every three U.S. adults loses a significant amount of sleep each month. Insomnia has multiple causes, many of which are related to stress or illness. Research in this area has increased over the years to the point that sleep centers have been established to try to identify the nature of sleep disturbances. Specific treatment intervention may include counseling, medication, or a change in diet.

RESOURCES

Sleep Well
<http://www.stanford.edu/~dement/>

Summary: Produced by a researcher at Stanford University, Sleep Well is a source for both general and academic sleep disorder–related information.

Sleep Net
<http://www.sleepnet.com/>

Summary: Sleep Net provides discussion forums and links to other related sites.

American Sleep Disorders Association (ASDA)
<http://www.asda.org/>

Summary: The ASDA is a professional medical association representing practitioners of sleep-related medicine and research.

Restless Legs Syndrome
4410 19th Street NW, Suite 201
Rochester, MN 55901-6624
<http://www.rls.org/>

Summary: Provides information on a common symptom of poor sleep.

National Institutes of Health: Sleep and the Elderly
National Institutes of Health (NIH)
Bethesda, MD 20892
<http://text.nlm.nih.gov/nih/cdc/www/78txt.html>

Summary: This site provides an analysis of sleeping patterns in the elderly and how to combat problems.

Menopause

Menopause is arguably the single most significant life change experienced by half of all adults. The following description of this stage of life should be of interest not only to women but also to men whose lives will also be affected to varying degrees by it. With increased awareness by all family members as well as ever-advancing scientific developments, this process need not be as worrisome or difficult as it is sometimes portrayed and perceived.

Menopause is commonly described as the cessation of a woman's menstrual cycle. Although technically accurate, this description fails to convey the complexities of this multifaceted life change, which is characterized by profound physiological, emotional, and cosmetic metamorphoses.

At the close of a woman's reproductive years, ovarian egg production stops, and estrogen levels fall to imperceptible levels. The average age for this is fifty-two. There are many consequences to the changed hormone levels, but none is more characteristically associated with menopause than the so-called hot flashes, which are experienced to some degree by 85 percent of all menopausal women. Characterized by a dramatic sensation of heat in the upper body, these flashes may be accompanied by an increased pulse and sweating. When they occur at night, insomnia frequently results. The precise cause of hot flashes is unknown, but researchers are actively studying the phenomenon. In the interim, some helpful strategies include avoiding very warm conditions and dressing in layers so that needed temperature adjustments can easily be made.

Another common physiological and cosmetic change associated with this life change is an increased tendency to gain weight. The loss of estrogen is thought to influence the body's metabolic rate. Many women report that during and following menopause, they gain weight even though their activity level and caloric intake remain constant. One useful strategy in combating this insidious (and unfair!) weight gain is to eat five to six small meals throughout the day rather than three regular-sized meals. As the body matures (and this is true for men, too), we have a decreased capacity to metabolize large quantities of food ingested at one sitting. The result is stored fat. It is preferable to wake up our metabolisms at more frequent intervals, thereby increasing our metabolic rate and burning more calories.

Menopausal women are also at an increased risk for heart disease, the leading cause of death for this age group. This risk is also directly related to the loss of estrogen, which protects a woman's cardiovascular system during her reproductive years. Experts recommend that menopausal women continue or begin an exercise program (after consulting a physician). Regular exercise decreases the occurrence of hardening of the arteries (atherosclerosis), which is the most important factor in heart disease.

Another serious health problem experienced during menopause is bone loss, or osteoporosis. Although there is no cure for this disease, it is highly preventable. Including calcium-rich foods such as yogurt, green leafy vegetables, sardines, milk, cheese, and broccoli in the diet will help keep bones strong. In addition, drugs such as fosamax and calcitonin and estrogen replacement therapy may slow the progression of osteoporosis. Many women also take calcium supplements. As well, exercises such as jogging, walking with weights, or lifting weights can actually stimulate new bone cell production.

In addition to the many physiological changes that accompany menopause, most women experience mood disturbances such as irritability and depression. The degree of emotional changes experienced is to some extent related to a woman's perception of this stage of life. Increasingly, we as a society are moving toward an image of women in their fifties and beyond as vital and vibrant. This is an excellent time for women to evaluate their life and appreciate the positive consequences of maturity such as increased wisdom and self-worth as well as increased emotional strength. Women at this stage of their lives invariably have much more self-confidence than they had twenty years previously, and nothing can make a woman sexier or more attractive than a positive outlook.

In addition to regular exercise and a balanced, healthful diet, many women are turning toward the promising hormone replacement therapies that are now available. Doctor-prescribed estrogen replacement as well as the newer combination estrogen/progesterone replacement therapies can prevent, lessen, or reverse the physiological and emotional consequences of menopause. Most striking is current evidence that hormone replacement therapy can reduce a woman's risk of heart attack by 50 percent!

When accessing the many tools available to help enrich this time of life, it is important to keep in mind that menopause is not a disorder but rather a natural process of womanhood marked by many potentially positive changes.

RESOURCES

North American Menopause Society (NAMS)
PO Box 94527
Cleveland, OH 44101
(216) 844-8748
<http://www.menopause.org/faq.htm>

Summary: NAMS is a nonprofit organization that provides for research into menopause.

Menopause
Women's Health Center
(203) 735-1806
<http://www.menopause-online.com/>

Summary: Resources for dealing with and understanding menopause.

Always
<http://www.always.com/>

Summary: A community-oriented Web site for women by the makers of Always.

Menopause: A Women's Rite of Passage
<http://www.yoni.com/cronef/menopause1.shtml>

Summary: Information about changing cultural attitudes toward menopause.

Impotence

Impotence, also known as erectile dysfunction, is the consistent inability of a man to obtain or sustain a penile erection during sexual intercourse. Its causes include diabetes, atherosclerotic cardiovascular disease, and a variety of neurologic diseases. In addition, impotence may be psychologically based or may result as a side effect of many medications. Whatever the cause, impotence is very difficult for most men to talk about, may lead to decreased self-esteem, and often places a strain on relationships. It is important to seek medical attention to determine the cause of the impotence. Treatment may include medication, counseling, or use of prosthetic devices. Viagra (sildenafil) is very effective but must be used with caution in patients with cardiovascular disease or hypertension. It is contraindicated for any patient who uses nitroglycerin.

RESOURCES

Impotence
HealthGate Data Corp
25 Corporate Drive, Suite 310
Burlington, MA 01803
<http://www.bewell.com/hic/impotence/>

Summary: Definitions, diagnosis, and treatment information on impotence.

Impotence Resource Center
American Foundation for Urologic Disease (AFUD)
(800) 433-4215
<http://www.impotence.org/>

Summary: AFUD is dedicated to providing timely information on a variety of male urologic problems.

> **Impotence World Association (IWA)**
> Impotence Institute of America
> (800) 669-1603
> <http://www.impotenceworld.org>

Summary: The IWA provides a reference of available treatments for coping with impotence. Its Web site states that it "has served as the nation's only non-profit, nonvested health association exclusively dedicated to impotence education."

INSIGHT

The medical issues and conditions discussed in this section are a representative sample of the health challenges faced by us boomers and our loved ones. With your access to <http://www.Boomerbasics.com>, the multitude of organizational and Web site references listed in this section, and good old-fashioned boomer resourcefulness, you can and should be an informed health consumer, patient, and advocate.

OUR CHILDREN

As baby boomers, we have experienced a tremendous change in technology and, in turn, an increased pace in our everyday lives. Some advances offer us greater efficiency at work and at home, while others simply provide us with a wider variety of diversions and entertainment. Along with these increased efficiencies and opportunities, our obligations and duties to our parents and children seem to have expanded as well.

Whether it is information, transportation, communication, or recreation, we have witnessed an accelerating development of products and services available to us over the past forty years. We have gone from Etch-a-Sketch and Rock'em Sock'em Robots to virtual reality golf and skiing. Schools that hand-cranked copies of tests on ditto machines (who could forget that smell!) can now copy, collate, and staple hundreds of pages on one machine in a very few minutes. Whereas before most households had one black-and-white television with three channels that could be changed only by getting out of your chair, we now have multiple televisions that offer over one thousand channels by remote control. In the 1950s, one rotary telephone was sufficient. Now we have phones everywhere—not only in our homes but also in our cars and pockets so that calls can be made and received anytime and anywhere!

Research once meant looking up a topic in the *World Book Encyclopedia,* and current events included the election of John F. Kennedy or the Beatles' invasion of the United States. Now, world news and comprehensive, up-to-date information is immediately available on the Internet and television. We could easily fill this book with lists of once-revolutionary technological developments that we now take for granted, but the most important thing about all these advances is that they make our lives at work and at home easier and more efficient in many ways, with one exception—raising our children. In spite of the many great advances bringing ease, speed, and dependability to our lives, nothing has really advanced or changed the process of raising our children to be kind, caring, successful adults. This process takes time—and we want to spend time with our children because few things give us greater pleasure.

Although we have the benefit of disposable diapers, videos, juice boxes, and portable cribs in raising our own children, we must still expend as much time and energy as our parents did—and should there come a time when you are confident in your parenting skills and that all is going well, it can vanish quickly when your child becomes a teenager. But we have a responsibility to our children, and we have the benefit of hindsight in that we know the cost of ignoring the advice of our parents. As much as we otherwise seek immediate gratification and simplicity, we want to spare them any long-term harm, hurt feelings, or adversity. As a result, we tell our kids what they must do rather than settling for what they want to do. We try to walk the line between prompting and encouraging them as opposed to nagging them (although they would say there's only one side to that line).

It's easy to become accustomed to saying no more than yes. Because our children are works in progress, we have to proceed with the hope that the long-term benefits will be worth the short-term whining. But along the way, the rewards to us, whether it be cheering as they play in a soccer game; congratulating them on a good report card; watching them learn how to draw a picture, snap their fingers, play the piano, or make us laugh; or just having them fall asleep on our shoulder, can be so gratifying that we embrace our responsibility to raise healthy, happy, well-adjusted and financially secure children.

While we juggle our many responsibilities, we somehow still manage to find time to love our children, yell at them, indulge them, embarrass them, and spoil them, even repeating, probably with some degree of horror, our parents' words that we swore we would never use: "You'll thank me some day!" or "This hurts me more than it does you" or "Stop putting those raisins in your nose!" We constantly strive to do what is best for them in the long run. This section won't reveal how to do that job, but hopefully it will help you formulate the issues and goals of caring and providing for your children.

The focus of this section is on the personal, financial, and health-related challenges and issues facing us as parents. Occasionally, certain matters may be unique or isolated to some parents, but more often the issues addressed herein are universal to all of us.

PERSONAL ~~~~~~~~

Having Babies

For most, parenthood has pretty low barriers to entry. It doesn't require any specialized knowledge or training, heavy equipment, large capital investment, or outside connections. (Seeing how easy it can be, it seems like some better warnings of what lies ahead should have been posted.) As a result, the act of conceiving a child can easily be taken for granted. (The politics, discussions, bargaining, and, possibly, begging that might precede the act itself are beyond the scope of this book.) But for many couples it can be heartbreaking not being able to conceive a child because of health issues, age, or some other circumstance. Fortunately, alternatives exist for bringing children into the family. Whether by way of conception or adoption, there are several alternatives for parents to consider, and the following sections will discuss each of them.

Infertility Issues

Infertility affects over six million people in the United States, and it can strike men as well as women. For men, the most likely cause is a low sperm count. For women, causes vary, but some common ones are blocked fallopian tubes, endometriosis, or other diseases. Treatment programs range from more traditional ones such as surgeries and hormone therapy to more high-tech procedures such as in vitro fertilization. Many hospitals and, more recently, clinics dedicated to fertility treatments offer a variety of treatment programs. In some cases, alternatives may also include artificial insemination and surrogate mothering.

Before embarking down this difficult and emotionally charged road, explore all your options thoroughly. First, have a physical to determine if, in fact, the problem is infertility. Second, whether you decide to pursue conventional or high-tech therapies, investigate carefully what your insurance carrier or health management organization (HMO) will cover. Not all coverage is the same, and not all states require insurance carriers to cover reproductive treatments; click on <http://www.Boomerbasics.com> for a list of states that mandate insurance coverage for some or all reproductive treatments. Third, consider to what extent you wish to pursue treatments. In addition to the expense, these treatments are invasive procedures, and the chances of successfully conceiving and carrying a child to full term decrease over time. Fourth, check the credentials and success rate of the hospital or clinic that you use. Finally, find a support group or organization, or even a counselor, who can help you and your spouse, if you have one, through this very difficult time.

Fertility Drugs

The primary treatment for women who are infertile owing to ovulation disorders is the use of fertility drugs. A number of fertility drugs are available to either help women who do not ovulate on their own or who have irregular ovulation cycles. As with any drug, there are often side effects. And one unique side effect can be the risk of multiple births. In any event, many resources offer information about the various drugs, how they work, possible side effects and the symptoms to which they would apply.

In Vitro Fertilization

In the event that treatment is unsuccessful, there are alternatives for couples to have a biologically related child. The most popular among the alternatives is in vitro fertilization (IVF), although it accounts for only 5 percent of all infertility treatment in the United States.

In IVF, the embryos are fertilized outside of the woman's body. More particularly, the eggs are surgically removed from the ovary and mixed with sperm in a petri dish. Once the eggs are fertilized and dividing into cells, they are placed in the woman's uterus. By doing so, the fallopian tubes are avoided. This procedure has been successful to the point where the average delivery rate for IVF is now about the same as it is for a reproductively healthy couple having a baby (that is, about a 20 percent chance of conception in any given month).

The cost of IVF, on average nationally, is about $7,800. However, many times the procedure is covered by insurance plans. In fact, twelve states currently require insurers to cover some or all of the cost of IVF. Therefore, it is recommended that you check both your state laws and your health insurance policy to determine the scope of any coverage if you wish to try this medical procedure.

RESOURCES

RESOLVE, The National Infertility Association
1310 Broadway
Somerville, MA 02144-1779
(617) 623-0744
<http://www.resolve.org>

Summary: Resolve is a nonprofit organization whose mission is to provide timely, compassionate support and information on infertility issues through advocacy and public education.

American Society for Reproductive Medicine (ASRM)
1209 Montgomery Highway
Birmingham, AL 35216-2809
(205) 978-5000
<http://www.asrm.com>

Summary: ASRM, formerly The American Fertility Society, is a nonprofit organization providing information relating to fertility, sterility, conception control, reproductive biology, and relevant endocrinology.

The American Surrogacy Center, Inc.
638 Church Street
Marietta, GA 30067
(770) 426-1107
<http://www.surrogacy.com>

Summary: This site offers information regarding surrogacy and egg donation along with other infertility-related issues. It also offers several on-line support services.

Adoption

For women over the age of forty, the chances of giving birth plummet to 8 percent. Men, too, have increasing fertility issues as they get older. Nonetheless, with little regard to age, boomers want to start families. The bottom line is that more boomers are adopting children.

Several avenues exist for adoption; they can be arranged privately or through a private or public agency, either domestically or internationally.

RESOURCES

National Council for Adoption (NCFA)
1930 17th Street NW
Washington, DC 20009-6207
(202) 328-8072
<http://www.ncfa-usa.org>

Summary: The NCFA is a charitable organization that provides information and education on adoption and also conducts research and advocacy on adoption issues.

National Adoption Information Clearinghouse (NAIC)
330 C Street SW
Washington, DC 20447
(888) 251-0075
<http://www.calib.com/naic>

Summary: The NAIC was established by Congress in 1987 and is a service of the Children's Bureau, Administration on Children, Youth and Families in the U.S. Department of Health and Human Services. The NAIC provides professionals and the general public information on all aspects of adoption and maintains an adoption literature database of adoption experts; listings of adoption agencies, crisis pregnancy centers, adoptive parent support groups, and search support groups; excerpts and full texts of state and federal laws on adoption; and other adoption-related services and publications.

Avenues for Adoption

Private Adoptions

In a private adoption, the adopting parents seek out a child on their own by contacting physicians, networking through friends and colleagues, or by advertising in newspapers, alumni magazines, and other print media. Some states don't allow private adoptions, and others paint a fine line between private and black-market adoptions. Although the birthmother generally cannot profit from the adoption, she can accept money for medical expenses.

Private adoptions have obvious potential problems. A birthmother can change her mind, or she may want contact with the child. Although private adoptions eliminate agency fees and scrutiny by strangers, they may also eliminate the assistance of professionals in addressing concerns that might arise.

Private agency adoptions are handled by private organizations, churches, or not-for-profit groups. Both adoptive parents and birthparents approach the agency separately, and the agency matches children to families.

If you wish to pursue a private adoption, your legal rights to do so will vary from state to state. Click on <http://www.Boomerbasics.com> for state-specific rules regarding private adoptions.

Involvement of Public and Private Agencies

Public agency adoptions are processed by governmental social services or welfare agencies. Some of the children available for adoption through a public agency have been placed there voluntarily by their parents. Although the number of children, particularly older kids, in foster care has risen dramatically, adoptions of these children unfortunately have not kept pace. States are trying to facilitate adoptions by speeding up the application process. Cooperative agreements between the adoptive parents and birthparents and shortened periods in foster care are part of statewide efforts to increase adoptions of children in foster care.

Public agency adoptions can be preceded by a period of foster parenting, or you can act as a foster parent for a limited time without committing to an adoption. Agencies will interview you and inspect your home before certifying you as a foster parent. Foster parents are paid a monthly stipend for providing care. If you are interested in helping older children, you may want to consider foster care before leaping into adoption.

In both public and private agency adoptions, prospective parents generally can expect to undergo an initial application process and home study, complete parent preparation classes, and submit various records and documents. The criteria for qualifying to receive a child are generally very stringent and thorough.

When that process is complete, the prospective adoptive parents are placed on a waiting list. When a child becomes available for adoption, the agency facilitates the completion of the legal adoption process. Some states provide for interim foster care, either by the adopting parents or others, until the paperwork is finalized.

Special Circumstances

Single and Same-Sex Partners

Some states, such as New York and Hawaii, permit same-sex couples to adopt; others allow only couples of the opposite sex to adopt. Where same-sex adoptions are not allowed, adoption by one partner of a same-sex couple may be possible. The nonadopting parent is put at a disadvantage, however, insofar as he or she may have no rights regarding the child if the couple breaks up.

A single person attempting to adopt may face similar problems. In addition, many agencies attempt to limit single parents to the adoption of special-needs children. Laws differ from state to state and even among different agencies in a given state.

Click on <http://www.Boomerbasics.com> for information on each state's adoption laws.

International Adoption

When the family seeking to adopt goes to a foreign country in search of a baby, additional concerns arise. The international adoption process involves a foreign government's laws regarding the release and emigration of its children as well as federal immigration laws and state adoption laws. The foreign country's residency requirements for the adopting parents in the child's country of birth are of particular concern. The U.S. Immigration and Naturalization Service (INS) participates in the process to ensure that the child has a home in the States and will not become a state ward. The INS issues the visa that permits the child to enter this country.

INSIGHT

In 1993, many nations signed the Hague Convention, which provided participating countries with voluntary guidelines designed to make the rules of adoption among countries more uniform and stable. It's a good idea to find out whether the country you are considering has signed this agreement.

Click on <http://www.Boomerbasics.com> for a list of parent support groups for issues regarding infertility and adoption and a list of public and private agencies in your state that provide adoption services locally or with a foreign country.

The Legal Process

The last step in the adoption process is the court proceeding to make you the legal parent of your adopted child. Each state has different rules regarding this process.

Click on <http://www.Boomerbasics.com> for state-specific rules regarding the legal adoption process. Given the serious nature of the proceeding and its permanent consequences, you would be wise to consult an attorney to guide you through the process.

Locating a Birthparent after the Adoption

At some point, most children who are adopted become interested in learning the identity of their birthparents. States can have their adoption records entered into the Adoption and Foster Care Analysis and Reporting System (AFCARS). This system holds information from four reporting sources in the United States: public agencies, private agencies, tribal agencies, and independent individuals. AFCARS permits children born in the United States to conduct searches about their lineage. The search becomes more complicated in international adoptions.

A growing trend is cooperative adoptions, in which the biological parent stays in contact. As this trend continues, it may be possible to tailor the information and contact between an adoptive child and the birthparents into a beneficial structure that works for all concerned.

Click on <http://www.Boomerbasics.com> for state-specific laws governing disclosure of information regarding birthparents.

INSIGHT

Whether your child is born to you or adopted, you need to consider what to name him or her. Whether that name will influence your child's success in life is not known. However, many people believe that the name you bestow will help pave a road to success for your child. Some psychological evidence seems to indicate that children with more popular names have an easier time in school and with peers. There are, in fact, several very famous boomers with popular names, such as William (Gates) and Michael (Jordan). However, there are also famous boomers with names such as Oprah, Madonna, Spike (Lee), and the baby formerly known as Prince. Whether or not the name makes the kid remains to be seen with your own child.

The following are some resources to supply you with ideas:

<http://www.Babynamer.com>
<http://www.4Babynames.com>

Caring for an Infant

Tips and Resources on Infant Care

Bringing a child into the world today is quite different than it was even ten years ago. Most parents now work and must find day care for their children. Even two-parent homes are usually faced with the reality of two full-time, out-of-the-home jobs. This applies to boomers especially because of the added responsibilities of taking care of their parents and children and the financial stress this prospect brings. Nonetheless, some basics do not change.

Considerations including which birth method is appropriate for you, bringing your child home from the hospital, choosing a safe and secure day care provider, and making your home safe for your children all remain very important. The following are some suggestions and resources to help make these decisions easier for you.

RESOURCES

Zero to Three: National Center for Infants, Toddlers and Families
734 15th Street, Suite 1000
Washington, DC 20005-1013
(202) 638-1144
<http://www.zerotothree.org>

Summary: Zero to Three is a national, nonprofit organization dedicated to advancing the healthy development of babies and young children.

American Academy of Pediatrics
141 Northwest Point Boulevard
Elk Grove Village, IL 60007-1098
(847) 228-5005
(847) 228-5097 (Fax)
<http://www.aap.org>

Summary: The American Academy of Pediatrics is a professional association dedicated to the health, safety, and well-being of infants, children, and young adults. Its Web site features a wide variety of information for parents on its "You and Your Family" page.

Babyproofing the House

Making sure that your home is a safe environment not only for your newborn but also for your children as they get older is extremely important. Many boomers may remember the days of playing with mercury in the science classroom, which has now been found to be carcinogenic. Substances once thought to be safe or harmless years ago, such as lead-based paint, are producing effects on our bodies that might not show up for years, including issues with fertility. Additionally, the atmosphere we live in contains more known dangerous substances than it once did. When we grew up who knew about an ozone layer? Making sure children are aware of these dangers at home and in the environment is extremely important to protect their well-being in both the short and the long term.

One easy tip (depending on your knees) for babyproofing your home is to take a child's-eye look at things—crawl around and see just what looks good from their point of view. While doing this, ask yourself whether you notice anything that could fall on, butt, burn, poke, strangle, choke, poison, suffocate, or tip over on your child (or that your child could similarly damage). From our viewpoint many everyday items look harmless, but they may be attractive as playthings or destinations from a child's perspective. This should be done every couple of months as your child grows to make sure everything is in check.

Safety Checks

Many aspects of the home environment can seem innocuous but in fact can be very dangerous to toddlers who love to put things into their mouths. In much the same way you would evaluate a day care environment for your child, analyze your home. For example, does your home have any poisonous plants or shrubbery that is within reach of children? Are the outlets covered with blank plates or inserts to prevent a child from sticking things inside them? Are your animals friendly with children or appropriately tied up? All of these items should be checked for safety depending on the age of the children in your home and the access they have to these things. It is also important to make sure you have a first aid kit stocked and available at a moment's notice. Also, keeping emergency phone numbers on hand for you or your sitter can save time during an emergency.

For older children, make sure that they know what to do in case a piece of their clothing catches on fire (stop, drop, and roll) and that they know the evacuation route when a fire alarm goes off. Ensuring that the fire alarms in your home are properly working by periodically testing them (when you change the clock, for instance) and changing the batteries is also an excellent preventative measure in the home.

RESOURCES

Most of the general health sites listed in the health sections of "Our Children" and "Ourselves" (pages 217 and 90, respectively) offer information on babyproofing and safety issues.

Healthcenter.com
<http://healthcenter.com>

Summary: Click on "Family Center" and then "Baby Proof Home" for valuable information on babyproofing your home.

Child Care

Bringing a child into a family is quite different today than it was when Lucille Ball or Wilma Flintstone did it. Most single parents and, in two-parent homes, often both partners, typically work full-time outside the home. Consequently, parents must arrange for child care.

Over the past few decades, the percentage of children receiving care and education from people other than parents has grown to the point that most children receive some type of nonparental care prior to first grade. According to the U.S. Department of Education and Statistics, as of the spring of 1995, approximately six out of ten children under the age of six who had not yet attended kindergarten were receiving some type of care and education from persons other than their parents. This translates to almost thirteen million kids in various in-home and center-based arrangements with relatives and nonrelatives. Although getting into the right day care or preschool probably won't make or break the career path of your child, it can affect how prepared your child is for school. Given the wide range of options and costs, from a relative to someone who takes care of a small group of children in his or her home to a child care center to a caregiver who comes into your home, the following questions can give you some guidance.

Finding Care

- Are the caregiver and the environment suitable to your child's needs?
- Does the caregiver enjoy children and have the energy to keep up with preschoolers?

- Are they patient and do they respond maturely to crisis, conflicts, or even simple whining?
- What are their credentials (including how long they have worked with preschoolers)?
- Is the caregiver responsive to the individual needs of different children?
- Will your child get enough attention? Check the ratio of children to caregiver and ask whether a primary caregiver will be assigned to your child.
- Does their child-rearing philosophy (as regards, for example, discipline, feeding, toileting) agree with yours?
- Do they mind having you stop in at any time, or must visits be scheduled?
- Is the facility clean, safe, and filled with appropriate toys and activities for your child's age?
- Do the other children like it there?

There is very little uniformity in terms of how credentials are awarded to child care providers. The rules and regulations vary considerably, not only from state to state but even from county to county in some areas. Because many people feel they are capable of running a child care center based on the fact that they have been around a lot of kids or raised their own, it is not unusual to find day care centers offering mediocre or poor care.

RESOURCES

Administration for Children, Youth and Families (ACYF)
U.S. Department of Health and Human Services
<http://www.acf.dhhs.gov/programs/acyf/>

Summary: The Administration on Children, Youth and Families oversees several federal programs that promote the well-being of our children. When you enter this site, you can receive information about the Head Start program and other programs administered by the ACYF.

Careguide.com
1160 Battery, 4th Floor
San Francisco, CA 94111
(415) 474-1278
<http://www.careguide.com>

Summary: By clicking on this site, you can receive information about thousands of child care centers, preschools, and family care centers located throughout the country.

National Child Care Information Center (NCCIC)
<http://www.nccic.org>

Summary: The NCCIC is run by the U.S. Department of Health and Human Services and not only provides information on how your state licenses child care providers but also allows you to check on any complaints or infractions filed against a particular provider.

National Association for Education of Young Children (NAEYC)
(800) 424-2460
<http://www.naeyc.org>

Summary: The NAEYC is a private industry-sponsored group that gives a seal of approval to child care centers.

In-Home Care

Having someone come into your home and care for your child or children may be the best choice if you have a very young child or several children with different schedules. However, there are several considerations and many ways that in-home care can be done. An in-home caregiver can live in your home, come and go according to set hours or, depending on your arrangements, be available for sporadic hours. With in-home care, it is completely up to you to set the framework of the caregiver's responsibilities, which can include light housework or errands in addition to watching your children.

In-home caregivers are flexible not only in the variety of tasks they may perform but also in regard to their level of training or focus. A nanny, for instance, may be found through an employment agency and may have formal training for childcare. The American Council of Nanny Schools has a listing of programs that meet its criteria. Nannies' duties and abilities vary depending on your needs (for example, whether you need live-in help or just during the day).

Another type of in-home caregiver is the au pair. Government-approved programs allow younger women from Europe to come to the United States and study while living with a family and taking care of their children. Using a governmental program is the best route to take, and with the recent tightening of immigration laws, it's practically the only way to acquire an au pair. There are specified guidelines regarding the amount of work they are required to do and the compensation they are to receive.

If you choose to look for someone on your own to come into your home and care for your children, the following tips are important and helpful in allowing you to choose a competent and responsible person:

1. Screen applicants by telephone before meeting with anyone
2. Ask for references and follow up on them
3. Interview the caregiver personally
4. Ask very specific questions about any prior positions, including the age of the children, the children's attachment to them, their specific duties, and why they are no longer caring for those children
5. Focus questions during the interview on your children's needs, depending on whether your child is in middle school or an infant requiring day-long care
6. Don't offer a position on the spot; instead, think it over and discuss it with your spouse or friends before making a decision

Another important consideration when deciding to employ an in-home caregiver is that you will become the employer of that individual and are responsible for his or her Social Security and other income tax withholdings. Unfortunately, this means filing forms with the IRS. The current form is Schedule H in the 1040 form, entitled Household Employment Taxes. However, you yourself may be entitled to some income tax credits. To determine this benefit, Form 2441, Child and Dependent Care Expenses, needs to be filed with the complete amount you spend on childcare reflected. These forms can be ordered directly from the IRS by calling (800) 829-FORM. Although ignoring these rules is preferred by many parents, individuals who choose not to pay their caregiver using the proper channels can be liable for back taxes and penalties for any amount of the time the caregiver worked. It is important to contact your accountant, the IRS, or other local agencies when choosing in-home care to ensure you are in compliance with applicable requirements.

INSIGHT

In addition to tax considerations, you should ensure that your homeowners insurance will provide you with coverage in connection with incidents or accidents involving your in-home "employee" caregiver as well as your obligation to provide workers compensation and other benefits.

Day Care

If you choose a day care environment, it is important to make sure that it is safe and appropriate for your child. Naturally, you will have an initial reaction of some type when visiting a day care center, but more objectively, the following is a checklist of twenty questions that can be used when taking your child to a day care center or someone else's home to determine if the setting is appropriate for your child.

1. Is the diaper-changing station far away from food-handling areas, and is there a diaper-changing policy?
2. Are children required to wash their hands before eating and after?
3. Are there fire escape doors in all rooms of the facility and regularly performed fire drills?
4. Are fire extinguishers and working smoke alarms on the premises properly located?
5. Are there no attractive hazards, such as matches or cigarette lighters, in sight?
6. Are there gates or some type of barrier in doorways and stairwells?
7. Do you see childproof locks on all cabinets or doors containing toxic or dangerous materials?
8. Are there proper floor coverings for crawling and falling infants (throw rugs are easy for toddlers to fall on)?

9. Are there safety devices on unused electrical outlets?

10. Are heating appliances such as baseboards, space heaters, radiators, and fans (including electrical cords) properly cared for?

11. Do you see any flaking paint?

12. Is medication properly stored (for example, in a locked box kept in the refrigerator), and are first-aid kits accessible?

13. Does the caregiver know CPR, and has he or she taken a first-aid course?

14. Are there any poisonous plants?

15. Is there a fenced-in outdoor play area free of any dangerous materials?

16. Are there locks to any doors leading to a swimming pool?

17. Are heavy objects, for example, bookcases, plant stands, and television stands, properly fastened;

18. What pets, if any, are on the premises, and what are their dispositions?

19. What is the policy for when a child is sick? Is there an isolation area for sick children?

20. Are emergency numbers prominently posted?

Make sure that you provide the caregiver with the names, addresses, and telephone numbers of persons who can take care of the child if you are unavailable. Some states even have laws that permit parents to authorize a third person to make decisions on the child's behalf when the parent is unavailable.

Click on <http://www.Boomerbasics.com> for state-specific laws that allow you to designate an agent to make decisions for your children on your behalf as well as state-specific rules about day care programs and for a list of resources that will help you learn how to identify a safe and reliable day care program.

Beginning School

A child's first day in kindergarten represents a rite of passage not only for the child but for his or her parents as well. It is a special day, a day in which the child's anticipation is exceeded only by the parents' disbelief that they have a child old enough to begin school.

If you think the beginning of school is a shock, wait until your child enters college. At that time, you will be amazed at how young the college students look (compared with you). You will also be shocked at how much college costs (page 198).

With the onset of technology and the availability of day care, nursery schools, and other social and educational programs offered to preschool-aged children, many kindergartners start school with basic math and reading skills; others do not. Regardless of where they start on the first day of kindergarten, most children soon develop the basic skills they require to become successful students.

Each child is unique and develops in his or her own way. Do not panic if your child is not able to do all the things the other children can do, and do not allow yourself to fall into unfettered exuberance if your child appears to be superior to other children in many areas. In time, you will learn a lot about your child, as will his or her teachers and other concerned persons. If you believe that your child is gifted, turn to page 146, or if you are concerned that your child has learning problems or disabilities, see page 147.

In a variety of publications, the U.S. Department of Education sets forth a combination of skills that your child will require for success in school: good health and physical well-being, social and emotional maturity, language skills, the ability to solve problems and think creatively, and general knowledge about the world. You can contact the U.S. Department of Education by regular mail or e-mail or visit its Web site for detailed information on ways you may best assist your child.

As educators will attest, the commitment of parents to work with and support their children in school activities is extremely important. Statistics and research clearly show that all children want to learn and they respond positively and successfully when their parents are involved in the learning process.

In addition to helping your child with school work, you need to further support your child in other related areas, such as ensuring that your child eats nutritionally balanced meals and gets the requisite amount of sleep.

When your child succeeds in school, you feel wonderful. Your commitment to your child's educational development will serve as motivation for your child to reach his or her maximum potential.

RESOURCES

U.S. Department of Education
400 Maryland Avenue SW
Washington, DC 20202
(800) USA-LEARN
<http://www.ed.gov>

Summary: The U.S. Department of Education publishes information for teachers, parents, students, researchers, and policy makers having a stake in education. Many publications are available in full on its Web site.

You should also review the resources listed in "Children and the Internet" (see page 165). These resources provide you with information on how you can help your child not only succeed in school but also enjoy doing so.

Gifted Children

If your child demonstrates superior abilities in academic areas and, to a lesser extent, in artistic or athletic endeavors, the child may be described as *gifted*. We've all been bored by those parents who think anything their child does is exceptional, but just as we must be careful about diagnosing children with attention deficit disorder (ADD) on the spot because they are hyperactive or have a short attention span, so, too, we should distinguish between children who have superior abilities and those who seem extraordinary for other reasons—perhaps, for example, because of particular personality characteristics.

Whether designated as ADD or gifted, both types of children will benefit when their uniqueness is recognized and accommodated. With gifted children, the emphasis lies in enhancement rather than competition. If you believe your child has exceptional talent in one or more areas, he or she may in fact be gifted. Contact your child's school to set up an evaluation or special program to help develop your child's talents. Acceleration, enrichment programs, resource rooms, pull-out programs, mentors, independent study, advanced placement, and internships are some of the ways in which schools can help gifted children.

Click on <http://www.Boomerbasics.com> for a list of publications on helping gifted children achieve their potential.

RESOURCES

The Council for Exceptional Children (CEC)
1920 Association Drive
Reston, VA 20191-3660
<http://www.cec.sped.org>

Summary: The CEC is the largest international professional organization dedicated to improving educational outcomes for individuals with exceptionalities, students with disabilities, or the gifted.

National Parent Information Network (NPIN)
ERIC Clearinghouse on Disabilities and Gifted Children
<http://www.npin.org>

Summary: The NPIN is a project cosponsored by the ERIC Clearinghouse on Disabilities and Gifted Children. The purpose of NPIN is to provide information to parents and those who work with parents to foster the exchange of parenting materials. The special section titled "Internet Resources for Parents and Those Who Work with Parents" will link you with many excellent organizations and Web sites.

A Public and Appropriate Education for Children with Disabilities

All children are special. All children have a right to a public and appropriate education.

In the "olden days," when we boomers were in school, children with developmental or learning disabilities as well as those with physical and emotional challenges often were either kept out of school or received their "education" in the school's basement outside the view of the other children and teachers.

Fortunately, as we became more aware of the needs and capabilities of children with special needs, laws were passed to protect their rights and to provide them with an appropriate public education. Examples of these laws include the *Individuals with Disabilities' Education Act (IDEA), Section 504 of the Rehabilitation Act of 1973,* and the *Americans with Disabilities Act (ADA).*

If you are the parent of a child who needs special educational services, you must be familiar with these and other laws. You must be an advocate for your child and ensure that he or she receives the assistance and accommodations required to meet his or her maximum potential.

RESOURCES

Americans with Disabilities Act Document Center
<http://janweb.icdi.wvu.edu/kinder>

Summary: This Web site contains copies of the Americans with Disabilities Act of 1990, regulations, and technical assistance documents. It also contains hot links to other Internet sources dealing with the ADA and related issues.

Disabilities Studies and Service Center (DSSC)
<http://dssc.org>

Summary: A department of the Academy of Education Development, the DSSC administers the following programs: the National Information Center for Children and Youth with Disabilities (NICHCY), the Federal Resource Center for Special Education (FRC), the National Transition Alliance (NTA), and the Technical Assistance Center for Professional Development Partnerships. You can link to these and many other helpful programs and organizations from the DSSC site.

Technical Assistance Alliance for Parent Centers
Alliance Coordinating Office
4826 Chicago Avenue South
Minneapolis, MN 55417-1098
(888) 248-0822
<http://www.taalliance.org/>

Summary: The task of the alliance is to provide technical assistance and coordinate parent training and information projects under IDEA. Its Web site offers numerous links to other excellent sites that are divided into several categories, including Accessibility and the Internet, Legislative Resources and Government Sites, Multicultural and Translated Resources, National Disability Agencies and Organizations, and Technology Resources.

> **U.S. Department of Education**
> Office of Special Education and Rehabilitation Services
> 400 Maryland Avenue SW
> Washington, DC 20202
> (202) 205-4873
> <http://www.ed.gov> (Site for U.S. Department of Education)
> <http://www.ed.gov/offices/OSERS/> (Office of Special Education and Rehabilitation Services)
> <http://www.ed.gov/offices/OSERS/IDEA> (IDEA '97)

Summary: The U.S. Department of Education, through its own and related Web sites, provides a variety of information regarding educational programs and services available for children with disabilities and their parents.

Learning Problems

Attention Deficit/Hyperactivity Disorder

Although at one time or another any child will display some or all of the symptoms of ADD/HD, a child diagnosed as having ADD/HD must display at least eight of the following behaviors for at least six months, and the behavior must begin before the age of seven:

1. Restlessness
2. Having difficulty remaining seated when required to do so
3. Being easily distracted by extraneous stimuli
4. Having difficulty awaiting turn in games or group situations
5. Often blurting out answers to questions before they have been completed
6. Having difficulty following instructions from others

7. Having difficulty sustaining attention in tasks or play activities
8. Frequently shifting from one uncompleted activity to another
9. Having difficulty playing quietly
10. Often talking excessively
11. Often interrupting or intruding on other's games
12. Often not seeming to listen to what is being said
13. Often losing things
14. Often engaging in physically dangerous activities without considering consequences

Before you voice your concern that this list of behaviors applies to just about every child who has been told to sit still at the dinner table or declare "Our baby has ADD/HD," please note that the actual number of children who display enough of these symptoms frequently enough to be diagnosed with ADD/HD is only between 2 and 5 percent of all school-aged children in the United States.

A determination as to whether your child has ADD/HD will take into account medical, psychological, or behavioral causes for the behavior. Sometimes the cause is simply allergies, diet, a nervous personality, or an unknown social situation. If ADD/HD is diagnosed, one course of treatment is administering medication such as Ritalin. Whether to use medication is a decision you should make only after a professional has diagnosed your child as having ADD/HD and assessed the severity of the disorder. If treatment is recommended, you may want a second opinion, because many ADD/HD children are treated effectively without medication.

A school counselor or social worker should be able to provide you with helpful information or direct you to a local organization that can provide you with support.

Click on <http://www.Boomerbasics.com> for a list of publications on ADD/HD and a list of national organizations that can provide you with more information and support.

RESOURCES

The National Information Center for Children and Youth with Disabilities (NICHCY)
PO Box 1492
Washington, DC 20013-1492
(800) 695-0285
<http://www.nichcy.org>

Summary: The NICHCY is a national information and referral center that provides information on disabilities and disability-related issues for families, educators, and professionals, including free publications and fact sheets on ADD/HD. Its focus is children and youths.

Children and Adults with Attention Deficit/Hyperactivity Disorder (CHADD)
8181 Professional Place, Suite 201
Landover, MD 20785
(301) 306-7070
<http://www.chadd.org>

Summary: CHADD is a national nonprofit organization for children and adults with ADD/HD and provides support and information for those affected by this condition. CHADD offers fact sheets on ADD/HD and related issues, including treatments, legal rights, and parenting challenges.

Dyslexia

Dyslexia is not a disease. It is a learning disability that results from differences in the structure and function of the brain whereby problems in processing information arise. Contrary to a popular misconception, people with dyslexia do not see backwards, but they do process information differently. As a result, they may have difficulty in expressing themselves. Such difficulties may manifest in reading, writing, speaking their thoughts, or having difficulty following directions. However, this is not a result of lack of intelligence. But often, because of a wrong diagnosis, many children may be mislabeled as poor students or underachievers. In the event your child does display signs such as having difficulty reading or spelling words or exhibiting poor reading comprehension, delays in speaking, or other difficulties in expressing herself in writing or orally, you may seek further assessment as to whether she suffers from dyslexia. Also consider that dyslexia can be hereditary, so information from other family members might become useful in diagnosing this learning disability. In any event, as with other learning disabilities, early intervention is often the best remedy.

RESOURCES

The National Information Center for Children and Youth with Disabilities (NICHCY)
PO Box 1492
Washington, DC 20013-1492
(800) 695-0285
<http://www.nichcy.org>

Summary: The NICHCY is a national information and referral center that provides information on disabilities and disability-related issues for families, educators and professionals, including several free resources on dyslexia. Its focus is children and youths.

National Institute of Neurological Disorders and Stroke (NINDS)
National Institutes of Health
PO Box 5801
Bethesda, MD 20842
(301) 496-5751
<http://www.ninds.nih.gov/patients/disorder/dyslexia/dyslexia.htm>

Summary: NINDA is a component of the National Institutes of Health and is a leading supporter of research on disorders of the brain and nervous system.

The International Dyslexia Association (IDA)
The Chester Building, Suite 382
8600 LaSalle Road
Baltimore, MD 21286-2044
(410) 296-0232
<http://www.interdys.org/>

Summary: The International Dyslexia Association is a scientific and educational society dedicated to the study, treatment, and prevention of dyslexia. The society publishes a variety of educational materials for parents, educators, and physicians.

Autism

Autism and pervasive developmental disorder (PDD) are developmental disabilities that share many of the same characteristics. Usually evident by age three, autism and PDD are neurological disorders that affect a child's ability to communicate, understand language, play, and relate to others.

The causes of autism and PDD are unknown. Currently, researchers are investigating areas such as neurological damage and biochemical imbalance in the brain. These disorders are not caused by psychological factors.

Autistic disorder is one of the disabilities specifically defined in IDEA, the federal legislation under which children and youth with disabilities receive special education and related services. IDEA, which uses the term *autism,* defines the disorder as "a developmental disability significantly affecting verbal and nonverbal communication and social interaction, usually evident before the age of three, that adversely affects a child's educational activities and stereotyped movements, resistance to environmental change or change in daily routines, and unusual responses to sensory experiences."

Owing to the similarity of behaviors associated with autism and PDD, use of the term *pervasive developmental disorder* has caused some confusion among parents and professionals. However, the treatment and educational needs are similar for both diagnoses.

Some or all of the following characteristics may be observed in mild to severe forms:

- Communication problems (for example, using and understanding language)
- Difficulty in relating to people, objects, and events
- Unusual play with toys and other objects
- Difficulty with changes in routine or familiar surroundings
- Repetitive body movements or behavior patterns

Early diagnosis and appropriate educational programs are very important to children with autism or PDD. From the age of three, children with autism and PDD are eligible for an educational program appropriate to their individual needs. Educational programs for students with autism or PDD focus on improving communication, social, academic, behavioral, and daily living skills. Behavior and communication problems that interfere with learning sometimes require the assistance of a knowledgeable professional in the autism field who develops and helps to implement a plan which can be carried out at home and school.

RESOURCES

Autism National Committee (AUTCOM)
635 Ardmore Avenue
Ardmore, PA 19003-1831
<http://www.autcom.org>

Summary: AUTCOM is an advocacy organization dedicated to protecting the civil rights of all people with autism.

The Autism Society of America (ASA)
7910 Woodmont Avenue, Suite 300
Bethesda, MD 20814-3015
(301) 657-0881
<http://www.autism-society.org/asa_home.html>

Summary: The Autism Society of America maintains 220 chapters in forty-eight states. It is a leading source of information and referral on autism.

The ASA is dedicated to increasing public awareness about autism and the day-to-day issues faced by individuals with autism, their families, and the professionals with whom they interact. The society and its chapters provide information and education, support research, and advocate for programs and services for the autistic population.

College Planning

Preparation for Success

Most parents want the best for their children, which often encompasses a desire that their kids go to college. This is not surprising in an economy fueled by the philosophy that "what you earn depends on what you've learned," a maxim supported by a barrage of statistics showing, among other things, the following:

- College graduates typically earn $600,000 more over the course of their lifetimes than those who have only a high school diploma.
- Of the twenty-five occupations with the largest and fastest employment growth, high pay, and low unemployment, eighteen require at least a bachelor's degree.
- Occupations that require a bachelor's degree are projected to grow most quickly, nearly twice as quickly as the average for all occupations. All of the twenty occupations with the highest earnings require at least a bachelor's degree.

INSIGHT

The U.S. Bureau of Labor Statistics' *Occupational Outlook Handbook* provides a wealth of information on job growth, pay scales, educational requirements, and related matters. (See page 156 for the Web site address for the U.S. Department of Labor.)

Statistics aside, the reality is that not all kids are cut out for the standard four-year college track. If your child happens to be one of them, don't despair. Although higher education increases your child's chances of obtaining a high-paying job, many occupations—for example, registered nurses, blue-collar supervisors, electrical and electronic technicians/technologists, automotive mechanics, and carpenters—may not require a college degree yet offer higher-than-average earnings.

Whether your children are headed to college or are more interested in pursuing a technical or vocational line of work, they should be encouraged and challenged in accordance with their capabilities. Although your involvement in planning your child's educational future is important, don't feel as though you have to do it alone. Guidance counselors, before- and after-school programs, and mentoring programs may be available to offer your child additional guidance. Working in conjunction with any of these entities, you can help your child to figure out the most appropriate educational track for him or her.

RESOURCES

Bureau of Labor Statistics
<http://stats.bls.gov/opbhome.htm>

Summary: The Bureau of Labor Statistics is an agency within the U.S. Department of Labor offering a wide range of data and information related to labor statistics, including career information for students in grades K–12.

Types of Colleges

The two basic types of postsecondary education institutions are community colleges, including junior and technical colleges and four-year colleges and universities.

Community colleges are public, two-year colleges that mostly serve people from nearby communities and offer academic, technical, and continuing education courses. Junior colleges, generally, are two-year private educational institutions. Also, some junior colleges offer room and board and are attended by students outside of the neighboring area.

Technical colleges generally have a special emphasis on education and training in a technical field and may be private or public.

Some programs at two-year colleges lead to an A.S. or A.A. degree in an academic discipline, whereas others offer technical or occupational training. Depending on the curriculum and the degree received, the two-year degree may be transferable to a four-year school and credited toward a B.A. or B.S. degree.

Four-year colleges are postsecondary schools that provide full educational programs in the arts and sciences and confer bachelor's degrees. Universities are postsecondary schools that include a college of arts or sciences, one or more programs of graduate studies, and one or more professional schools. Universities confer not only bachelor's degrees but graduate and professional degrees as well.

Standardized Tests

Regardless of the school ultimately chosen, the preparation for getting accepted should be the same — plan on taking the SAT (Scholastic Aptitude Test) or ACT Exam. The SAT measures verbal and mathematical reasoning abilities, and the ACT measures English, mathematics, reading, and scientific reasoning abilities. Which test your child should take may depend on geography; generally, the SAT is used by colleges in the East and West, and the ACT is used by colleges in the South and Midwest.

Both the SAT and the ACT can be taken in the junior and senior years of high school and can be taken more than once in the hopes of raising the score. Besides repeating the exam, scores can be improved with some advance preparation utilizing the many resources and study guides available in bookstores and libraries. Also, private preparation companies offer courses for a fee that help students prepare for these exams.

Another preparatory aid is taking the Preliminary Scholastic Aptitude Test/National Merit Scholarship Qualifying Test (PSAT/NMSQT). The PSAT is usually administered to tenth- or eleventh-grade students. In addition to this test being good practice for the SATs, a good score on the PSAT, along with several academic performance criteria, may qualify your child for the National Merit Scholarship Program.

With regard to all of these issues and preparation for life beyond high school in general, the best starting point may be talking to your child's guidance counselor.

RESOURCES

The Princeton Review
(800)-2REVIEW
<http://www.review.com>

Summary: This comprehensive Web site is sponsored by the Princeton Review, a test prep company, and provides information about college standardized tests. Other features offered on this site include a listing of all colleges and information about scholarships and aid.

College Board On-Line
<http://www.collegeboard.com>

Summary: This Web site offers a number of services including registering for the SATs and searching for colleges.

U.S. Department of Education
<http://www.ed.gov/pubs/parents/index.html>

Summary: A number of publications are available on-line through the U.S. Department of Education pertaining to preparing your child for college.

Choosing a College

Considering the hundreds of college choices available, it can be difficult to narrow the list down to the one most suitable to your child's unique talents, personality, strengths, and weaknesses. In addition to affordability, you and your child should identify several important attributes of a well-suited college to make the task more manageable. Hopefully, your child is not placing too much emphasis on a prospective college's ranking as a party school, the relative numbers of the opposite sex there, the state's drinking age, or where the boyfriend/girlfriend/many friends may be going. Although such items may get some consideration, also establish whether it's preferable to go away or stay home; to be in or near a city or on a suburban campus; and to attend a small, intimate school or one with a large student body and sprawling campus. You should also determine if a specific program or course of study is being sought or if a more general liberal arts program is the preference at this time. When you throw in SAT scores, activities, other kids you already have in college or are heading there, and the fact that you're dealing with a teenager, the number of variables to consider in making such an important choice can become paralyzing. But after settling on several key points, the number of college choices can become less daunting. And regardless of where you are in your analysis, many resources can help you calculate and project costs; examine a school's courses, size, and student body; and rank virtually every other one of its attributes (including its party ranking). The following on-line resources will assist you and your child in making a choice.

RESOURCES

U.S. News On-Line
U.S. News and World Report
<http://www.usnews.com/usnews/edu>

Summary: This site includes college rankings from the periodical's annual survey. Other features include information on financial aid and planning worksheets.

Peterson's CollegeQuest
<http://www.collegequest.com>

Summary: This site was created in association with the National Association of Student Financial Aid Administrators (NASFAA). A guide to colleges is included, as well as financial aid and application services.

INSIGHT

Almost all colleges have or will have their own Web sites that provide relevant information. In fact, your child can apply on-line to many colleges.

Vocational Education

Young people who don't plan to attend college likely will find entering the job market more challenging than it once was. This is due, in large part, to technological advances and the globalization of manufacturing, which have greatly reduced the availability of entry-level positions in semiskilled, high-wage manufacturing occupations. Most jobs today require a combination of critical thinking and manual capabilities and the ongoing development of new skills.

Despite the need for new workers with increasingly sophisticated and flexible skills, according to the U.S. Department of Labor, about 75 percent of those now entering the U.S. workforce have limited verbal and computational skills.

Vocational education is aimed at filling this gap by helping non-college-bound students to obtain career-oriented, self-sustaining jobs after high school. Studies have shown that high school graduates who complete a log-ical sequence of vocational courses are more likely to find training-related jobs and to earn more in these jobs (7 to 8 percent more per month). Also, they are less likely to be unemployed over time than those with a more general educational background.

An increasingly popular approach in vocational education is the school-to-work program, which is based on the concept that education works best and is most useful for future careers when students apply what they learn to real-life, real-work situations. The core elements of a school-to-work program are

1. School-based learning—classroom instruction based on high academic and business-defined occupational skill standards
2. Work-based learning—career exploration, work experience, structured training, and mentoring at job sites
3. Connecting activities—courses integrating classroom and on-the-job instruction, matching students with participating employers, training of mentors, and the building of other bridges between school and work

If your child is on a vocational track, check with a school counselor or your local school district to inquire about relevant programs. In the absence of a formal program, your child still can benefit from talking with a guidance counselor about suitable high school courses to prepare him or her for postsecondary education at a community, junior, or technical college. Likewise, a guidance counselor can assist in finding local businesses or school-to-work councils that can provide your child with such opportunities.

Click on <http://www.Boomerbasics.com> for more information on school-to-work and other programs and resources related to vocational education.

RESOURCES

National School-to-Work Learning and Information Center
(800) 251-7236
<http://www.stw.ed.gov>

Summary: The School-to-Work Opportunities Act of 1999 provides federal seed money to states and local partnerships of business, government, education, and community groups to develop school-to-work programs.

Activities outside School

Family Travel

If planning a trip that will appeal to the entire family does not relieve more stress than it causes, forces you to dip into your retirement savings to finance it, and seems like more work than the job you're trying to leave behind for a week or two, just forget everything and go surfing—on the Net, that is! Get your feet wet with the following sites for help in planning your family vacation:

<http://family.go.com/Categories/Travel> (Deals to help families afford their dream vacation)

<http://havechildrenwilltravel.com> (Fun, active, learning adventures that are enriching for the whole family)

<http://www.familytravelforum.com> (With the mantra "Have kids, still travel," this site provides informed advice and practical tips for adults and children who journey together—but note that there are membership fees)

<http://www.gorp.com/gorp/eclectic/family.htm> (Great Outdoor Recreation Pages: An excellent resource on attractions, activities, locations, books, gear, and tours for outdoor travelers)

<http://www.backroads.com/experience/family.html> (Backroads Active Travel: Custom itineraries created with the family in mind)

Youth and Teen Travel

Whether your little cherubs are venturing off to their first day camp with crayons and lunchbox in tow or cramming their duffel bags with monogrammed T-shirts and underwear for six weeks of summer camp or trying to figure out how they'll possibly be able to carry everything on their back during an eight-week chaperoned tour of Costa Rica, you'll likely be taking a little trip of your own on a raft of mixed emotions—excitement, pride, worry, longing. As hard as it might be for some parents to separate from their kids for days or weeks at a time, various camps and travel programs offer tremendous learning and growth opportunities for preteens and adolescents.

Click on <http://www.Boomerbasics.com> to get you started, and then check out the following sites for more services and support:

<http://www.campfinders.com/student.htm> (Camp Finders: Free service to parents of kids from seven to seventeen years of age; works with parents to find an appropriate camp for their child)

<http://www.hiayh.org/> (Hostelling International/American Youth Hostels homepage)

<http://www.istc.org/p_ho.asp> (International Student Travel Confederation: A group of student travel organizations around the world whose focus is to develop, promote, and facilitate travel among young people and students; provides information on flights, other transportation, student and youth cards, travel insurance, work exchange programs and more)

Volunteer Opportunities

Volunteering is a great way for children of all ages not only to contribute to their communities but also to enrich their own lives. Helping others can provide children with broader cultural, social, environmental, political, educational, and economic perspectives and, more than that, can help them feel good about themselves. There's an additional bonus for students who are planning to continue their education after high school, as colleges typically look favorably on applications evidencing community service activities.

Many communities have a local center where people interested in volunteering can go to be assigned to an agency based on their interests and available opportunities. Girl Scouts and Boy Scouts can volunteer through their scouting organizations. Volunteers also can contact directly those organizations in which they're interested. The opportunities are limitless, and many are structured according to age-appropriate criteria. Some possibilities include hospitals and nursing homes, animal shelters, museums, schools, summer camps, wildlife refuges and nature centers, and senior centers. Specific organizations include the following:

- Americorps <http://www.cns.gov/americorps/index.html>
- Youth Volunteer Corps <http://www.reeusda.gov/pavnet/ye/Yeyouth.htm> (School-community partnerships to implement community-based, service-learning activities for middle and high school students—for example, tutoring/coaching kids, weatherizing homes for low-income families, helping to operate summer camps,

producing plays for youth centers, and planning activities for the elderly or disabled)

- Do Something <http://www.dosomething.org> (Inspires young people to believe that change is possible; trains, funds, and mobilizes them to be leaders who measurably strengthen their communities)
- Red Cross <http://www.redcross-cmd.org/Chapter/Volunteer/youth .html> (Assist at blood drives; help with special projects such as hospital teddy bear campaigns; assemble first-time blood donor kits; assist in fund-raising)
- Habitat for Humanity <http://www.habitat.org/>
- Big Brothers/Big Sisters <http://www.bbbsa.org/>

Sports

Numerous studies have shown that the more kids are involved in sports and physical fitness activities, the less likely they are to fall prey to academic troubles, substance abuse, and so on. Although participation in sports can help to build children's confidence and self-esteem and help them to learn important values like cooperation and teamwork, respect, discipline, responsibility, and sportsmanship, children still need their parents' guidance to learn these life lessons.

Unfortunately, when it comes to sports, some parents can do more harm than good by focusing on their children's minutes of playing time and win-loss records rather than on their effort and improvement. Those of you who decide to coach your children's teams should be particularly vigilant in examining your motivations for wanting to do so—are you truly interested in furthering the development of every team member (including your own children) and ensuring that they have a rewarding athletic experience, or are you primarily trying to live vicariously through your young superstars and are more concerned about how much playing time they get?

Whatever your level of involvement—as chauffeur, spectator, mentor, or coach—numerous resources are available to help make your children's sports experiences positive and rewarding . . . for them *and* for you.

Click on <http://www.Boomerbasics.com> or one of the following URLs for some excellent information on skills development, nutrition for young athletes, sports injuries, equipment, and psychological considerations as well as numerous tips for parents.

<http://sportsparents.com/index.html> (*Sports Parents* magazine: Offers information and advice to help parents enrich—and survive!—their children's sports activities)

<http://www.chre.vt.edu/cys> (*Coaching Youth Sports:* An electronic newsletter whose purpose is to present information about learning and performing sports skills)

<http://www.ysn.com> (*Youth Sports Network:* Stories about youth sports, a directory of sports camps, and an excellent instructional area with tips for players and coaches)

<http://ed-web3.educ.msn.edu/ysi> (*Institute for the Study of Youth Sports* [YSI] at Michigan State University: Founded to research the benefits and detriments of participation in youth sports; produces educational material and provides educational programs for parents, coaches, officials, and administrators)

<http://www.naysi.com> (*North American Youth Sports Institute:* Articles and information designed to help teachers, coaches, parents, and other youth leaders become more effective in their interactions with children in sports)

<http://www.specialolympics.org> (*Special Olympics:* Begun in 1968 to demonstrate that people with mental retardation are capable of remarkable achievements in sports and beyond)

Children and the Internet

As parents, we expect that as our children become teenagers and young adults, they will become knowledgeable—perhaps more knowledgeable than we are in certain areas. We, at least most of us, can handle this. What we are not prepared for, however, is when our younger children demonstrate superior knowledge, such as our pre-adolescent computer whiz (notice we use *whiz* and not *geek* because none of our children are geeks). The ultimate in parental ineptness is when your six-year-old can perform multiple simultaneous applications on the family computer and you haven't yet figured out where the on/off switch is.

Simply stated, our children are being raised in a computer-driven world, a very different world than the one we grew up in. We have a choice to join our kids in cyberspace or to just be plain lost in space.

For those of you who opt to travel in cyberspace with your children, you need to develop and hone your computer skills. Fortunately, many on-line resources can help you become and remain computer literate and will also provide information regarding parental control features to ensure that your child is using the Internet in a safe and appropriate manner.

RESOURCES

Computing Central
<http://www.computingcentral.com>

Summary: Self-described as an "information marketplace," the goal of this Microsoft product is to educate people who use computers at work and home. Excellent content is provided on this site for computer users of all kinds, from beginners to techies.

The Children's Partnership
<http://www.childrenspartnership.org>

Summary: Click on "Parent's Guide to the Information Highway."

The following Internet search engines, and many others, offer excellent educational information.

AltaVista
<http://www.altavista.com>

Summary: Click on the topic titled "Computers and Internet."

Lycos
<http://www.lycos.com>

Summary: This search engine also has a section titled "Computers and Internet."

Excite.com
<http://www.excite.com>

Summary: Click on "Computers."

INSIGHT

It seems that with every new day, purchasing a computer or software and contracting for Internet access is less costly. If you cannot afford a computer, you should check to see if you and your children could have free or minimal-cost access to a computer at your child's school, local library, or college. Another option is to lease, rather than buy, a computer and related accessories.

Now that you know how to use the computer, you can begin to experience why your children like to play and work on it. Yes, work! Many sites offer assistance with school work, including tutorials and research capabilities.

The quickest and easiest way to review Web sites dedicated to children and observe the range of the types of activities offered is to log on to the sites our kids visit. The following are a few examples.

RESOURCES

(Enjoy the colorful graphics on these and similar sites!)

> **Yahooligans: The Web Guide for Kids**
> Yahoo!
> <http://www.yahooligans.com>

Summary: Yahoo!'s site for children has the following channels: Around the World, Art and Entertainment, Computers and Games, School Bell, Science and Nature, and Sports and Recreation. Other features include Parents' Guide, Teacher's Guide, Almanac, and News.

> **KidZone**
> Netscape
> <http://www.netscape.com>

Summary: KidZone offers a variety of activities ranging from Cool Stuff to Do and New This Week to Places to Go. Your children will love to ask "Jeeves" questions or get help with their homework.

> **Lycos Zone**
> Lycos
> <http://www.lycoszone.lycos.com>

Summary: In addition to a parent's and teacher's section, this site features the following three areas: a Fun and Games Zone, Homework Zone, and a New Cool Zone. If your child likes the scary and grotesque, he or she will want to visit Club Yucky, "the yuckiest site on the Internet."

In addition to these sites that can be found on the search engines just mentioned, thousands of other educational and family sites can provide valuable information and resources to parents. Here are some great examples.

The Library of Congress
<http://www.kweb.loc.gov>

Summary: Excellent content. You and your family will enjoy the section titled "American Memory."

FamilyEducation.com
<http://www.familyeducation.com>

Summary: Consistent with its stated objective to help parents help their children succeed, this site provides comprehensive information and resources.

The Internet Public Library Reference Center
<http://ipl.org/ref>

Summary: A variety of worthwhile information is available on this site, including a special teen and youth collection.

American Library Association
<http://www.ala.org>

Summary: You will find 700 great sites for parents, caregivers, teachers, and others who care about kids.

KidSource.com
<http://www.kidsource.com>

Summary: This site provides comprehensive education and health information of interest to parents and their children.

ParentsPlace.com
<http://www.parentsplace.com>

Summary: Parentsplace.com is self-described as a one-of-a-kind environment where parents of all types connect, communicate, and celebrate the adventures of child rearing.

INSIGHT

This is by no means a comprehensive list. It is just a start. Whether you look up other sites directly from a search engine, speak with other parents about sites their kids are on, ask your kids which sites they like, or link to new sites from other sites, always remember new and exciting sites are just a click away. Also remember to always ensure that your children are visiting only age-appropriate sites.

Now that we've dealt with sites for the family and our young and adolescent children, we should also expose you to sites visited by our teenagers and young adults. Bolt.com is an example of a popular Web site hangout for high school and college students worldwide. On the Bolt site, members have access to fellow members of the Bolt community and information on a variety of topics, such as activism, jobs and money, sex, dieting, entertainment, and sports.

Also popular among young adults and those of teenage years are music and video sites, such as the MTV Web site <http://www.mtv.com>. Further, as noted in our college planning section on page 155 as well as in the "Personal" section of Part One, "Ourselves," on page 13, many excellent Web sites will help your children select a college or find a job.

In addition to the availability of thousands of sites, our children use the computer to communicate with their friends via e-mail, be it on an individual or group basis—a communication process that for some can begin when they wake up in the morning and that continues until they go to sleep at night. Their only break from e-mail may be when they are in school, although they can and do discuss past and future e-mails with their friends and confirm their respective e-mail addresses, which for some kids can change even more quickly than the latest fashion. By the way, do you know your child's e-mail address (AKA screen name) or password?

Fortunately, we boomers, too, can enjoy the ubiquity and community of e-mail. In fact, an argument could be made that e-mail is the new glue that can keep family members in touch with each other. For example, we can communicate with our children when they are away from home at places like college, summer sleep-away camp, or even a sleep-over at a friend's house. Further, e-mail is intergenerational. Grandparents who live far away can send letters, pictures, and family recipes for chicken soup via e-mail.

Special Issues Affecting Preteens and Teens

Peer Pressure and Fitting In

To the extent that we're all subject to others' opinions and influence, peer pressure is a pervasive influence throughout our lives, but its impact is no greater than during adolescence. As teenagers struggle to establish a sense of identity, they naturally challenge family, school, and often community rules and values. In seeking to establish their individuality, they defy the dictates of authority figures and turn instead to their peers for guidance and support.

No matter how inappropriate your children's peer groups might seem to you, the fact is that they likely boost your children's self-image, offering them a place where they're accepted and can feel good about themselves. They provide a support system of others who are in the same situation or experiencing similar problems.

"But I've always been there for my kids," you might say. That's exactly the point—on some level they know they've got to make it in this world by relying on themselves because you won't always be there, and adolescence is all about figuring out how to do that. That's one reason the teenage years can be so maddening, particularly for those parents who, for example, have been highly involved in their children's lives and have raised them with strict moral and ethical standards. It's important to remember, however, that it's not necessarily the standards themselves your kids are rebelling against— it's the fact that they're *your* standards. Your kids might need to shelve them temporarily as they try out others, but take comfort in the fact that old values taught from the cradle tend to be deep-seated and likely will return as your children negotiate their way into adulthood.

Although most adolescents are affected by peer pressure, those who are most negatively influenced tend to have low self-esteem, a feeling of not belonging, and poorly developed interpersonal, communication, and judgment skills. Although these skills can be taught at any age, obviously the earlier they're taught, the better. You're off to a good start if you share activities with your children, maintain reasonable expectations about their abilities (that is, let them be who they want to be rather than molding them to your vision for them), avoid comparing them with other children, encourage and reward efforts more than outcomes, and listen to their concerns.

Smoking and Substance Abuse

Probably one of the most common consequences of peer pressure is experimentation with tobacco, alcohol, and illegal drugs. Statistics indicate that 70 percent of all children try cigarettes, 40 percent of them before they get to high school. Approximately 4.6 million teenagers have a drinking problem, and alcohol-related accidents are the leading cause of death among those fifteen to twenty-four years old. More than half of all students have used an illicit drug (marijuana in the majority of cases) by the time they reach their senior year in high school.

Adolescents typically experiment with smoking, drinking, or drug use in order to fit in, to feel cool, or because they think it makes them more adultlike. Although some decide it's not for them, others may quickly become addicted, relying on tobacco, alcohol, or drugs as coping mechanisms.

Click on <http://www.Boomerbasics.com> or one of the following URLs for information concerning common characteristics of adolescents who are addicted to tobacco, alcohol, or drugs as well as intervention and treatment options.

<http://www.health.org/pubs/qdocs/index.htm> (National Clearing-house of Alcohol and Drug Information, a service of the Substance Abuse and Mental Health Services Administration: Statistics, tip sheets, treatment programs; a section is devoted to youth and teens)

<http://www.mninter.net/~publish/parent3.htm> (Indications that your child might be doing drugs)

<http://drugfreeamerica.org> (Partnership for a Drug Free America: offers valuable information, including a description and effects of drugs and a section titled "Help for Parents")

Many parents are reluctant to discuss tobacco, alcohol, and drug use with their children, perhaps because they don't believe their children would use illegal substances, they don't know what to say or how to say it, or they're afraid of being asked what they've tried in the past. No matter how difficult such a discussion might be, it's far easier to address in preventive terms rather than bringing it up after discovering your child has a problem. Many adolescents in treatment programs acknowledge having used alcohol and other drugs for at least two years before their parents found out. Given that young people who use alcohol, tobacco, and other drugs typically begin before leaving the ninth grade, you should talk with your children early on and continue to keep the lines of communication open. (See "Family Issues: Communicating with Your Children" for more tips on how to do that.)

In communicating with your children, remember that actions speak louder than words. Although what you tell them is important, it'll make a more lasting impression if you practice what you preach. This might be tough for smokers who, though addicted themselves, don't want their kids to start smoking. In that case, pointing out the power of addiction, as well as the physical and social implications of smoking, can be a strong deterrent.

Parents also might find it difficult to lecture about the dangers of alcohol given that alcohol is legal and that many parents drink. But talking with your kids about avoiding alcohol doesn't mean you can't have your usual glass of wine with dinner. Teenagers also need to understand the importance of moderation and the distinction that adults are old enough to drink *legally.*

Finally, if you did your share of experimenting with drugs as a young adult, you may feel a bit hypocritical in admonishing your kids not to do the same thing. The key is that you're practicing what you preach *now.* We've all made mistakes and, with the benefit of hindsight, we're in a much better position to help others from heading down the same path. Although you're not obliged to tell your kids about your own experimentation, most experts believe you shouldn't lie to them if they ask. Your honesty likely will impress them more than your ability to always make the right choices. You can tell them why you experimented and what you learned, and you can let them know you'd like to see them avoid making the same mistakes. You can also point out that drugs are much more potent today than they were thirty years ago and that a lot more is known now about their long-term effects.

In any event, open communication with your kids will let them know you care and that you were once in their shoes—considerably greater motivation for abstaining from alcohol and drug use than "because I said so."

Sex

Teens today are bombarded with sexual pressures at every turn—from the radio, television, movies, friends, and peers. The prevalence of sexual activity in the media sends the message that "everybody does it" with no harmful results. Add to the mix adolescents' natural curiosity about sex, their raging hormones, and their ongoing struggle to feel more grown-up, and it's no wonder that more than half of all teenagers have had sexual intercourse before they reach the age of twenty.

The sheer magnitude of daily exposure to sexual messages might lead you to think that your teenagers already know everything they need to know about sex. Despite any claims they might make about knowing it all, teens today need information about sex more than ever, and you are still the best source for that information. Start talking with them early and frankly about sex.

Click on <http://www.Boomerbasics.com> and review "Health: Puberty" later in this book for more information on what and when to tell your children about sex, contraception, and sexually transmitted diseases as well as for tips on how to talk with them about what many perceive as a difficult subject.

Independence/Responsibility

It's amazing how parents go from knowing it all to knowing nothing—at least in their children's eyes! Try not to take being knocked from your pedestal personally. Your teenagers are simply beginning a process of separating from you that will ultimately enable them to function as independent, healthy adults (assuming you don't strangle them first!).

Part of that process involves testing established boundaries and negotiating new ones. It's a delicate balancing act between affording your teenagers a certain amount of autonomy while maintaining your right (and responsibility) as a concerned parent to monitor their activities. With the proper guidance, your teenagers ideally will reach the age of emancipation (eighteen in most states) in one piece.

Fiscal Responsibility

If your children seem to think that money grows on trees, either they're flunking science or it's time to give them a few lessons on finances and budgeting. By including your children in discussions about family finances, you can help them to understand where the family's income is going, what they're getting from it (for example, food, shelter, clothing, and so on), and what it costs to maintain a basic standard of living.

By the time your children are teenagers, they're likely making most of their own decisions about clothing, music, entertainment, and the like. As much as you'd like to help your teens fit in with their peers, you might be wondering how long you can continue shelling out $120 for athletic sneakers or $65 for a pair of designer jeans.

Enter . . . the teen budget! First, figure out what you're willing to spend on each specific item for your teenagers (for example, $80 for sneakers, $40 for jeans, and so on) and then figure monthly totals by category ($100 for clothing, $40 for entertainment, $25 for school supplies). Once you've figured these expenses, deposit that amount each month into a checking account for each child. Consider setting up joint accounts with your children, with you and each child as signatories, to teach your teens how to manage a checking account and balance a checkbook. Explain about overdrafts and that your children will be responsible for paying the fees on any bounced checks. (This discussion is a particularly important preventive measure, because you will be legally responsible for the account as long as your children are minors.)

Once you've established a budget and set up a checking account, allow your teens to decide how they want to spend their allotted funds for the month. If your son decides to spend $80 on a Starter jacket and finds he needs $40 for a new pair of jeans in a given month, don't add to his clothing budget. He can decide to use his entertainment allotment to pay for the jeans, wait until next month's clothing allotment is deposited to get the jeans, or earn the balance of the money on his own, either by saving his allowance or by working at a job outside the home. By standing firm, you'll help your teens to realize the importance of making and sticking to a budget.

Driving

Johnny's been chomping at the bit for the last year to get his license, and although the thought is a bit terrifying, part of you can't wait to personally escort him to the Department of Motor Vehicles just so he'll stop pestering you! But before you hand over the car keys, it's important for you to instill in Johnny that driving is not only a privilege but an enormous responsibility—one that few teenagers are equipped to handle without parental guidance.

Consider the facts: Traffic accidents are the leading cause of death for teens and young adults—more than five thousand young people die each year in car crashes, and thousands more are injured. Teens are more likely to be involved in a car crash because of their driving inexperience and their tendency to take risks while driving.

You can combat these factors by establishing certain rules about driving even before your children obtain a license. Such rules might include the following: always wear a safety belt; no speeding or reckless driving; no tobacco, alcohol, or other drug use; no eating while driving; and no talking on the cell phone while driving. (You can set a good example by observing these rules yourself.) Be sure to discuss beforehand the consequences (such as revocation of driving privileges) associated with breaking the rules and be consistent in applying them. If your children complain, remind them that the rules are in place to ensure their safety.

Parents also can help by requiring that their children maintain good grades in school to continue their driving privileges. Also, check with your auto insurance company to see if any "good student" discounts are available.

In addition to the rules you establish, many states have laws governing teenaged drivers. Graduated licensing laws, for example, mandate that learning to drive be spread over three stages rather than the customary two (learner's permit and full license). Teen drivers must meet certain requirements for at least six months in each stage before moving to the next one. Driver's education classes, which typically include thirty hours of classroom teaching and six hours of behind-the-wheel training, would be expanded to encompass more complex decision-making and skills training at each stage. Although only twelve states currently have some form of graduated licensing laws, parents need not wait for a law to pass before implementing their own graduated licensing program. By slowly increasing your teenagers' driving privileges, you can help them to acquire the experience needed to drive safely and responsibly.

Family Issues

Communicating with Your Children

Many parents view communicating with their children primarily as a means of imparting information to them. Although that's an important aspect of parent-child communication, it's only part of the equation. Listening is equally important. If you feel like your communications with your children have stalled or that you've hit a dead end and don't know where to turn, you may want to consider the following suggestions, based on the SHARE concept:

1. **Schedule** talking and listening time with your children every day. It's easy to get caught up in the whirlwind of work, school, meetings, lessons, sports, socializing, and so on, but making time to actively communicate with your children is essential. Even just fifteen minutes a day lets them know you love them and are there for them. With younger children, spend extra time to talk with them when putting them to bed. With older kids, take advantage of time while driving together to catch up. Dinnertime offers a prime opportunity to connect with children of all ages.

2. **Hear** what your children have to say. Doing so requires that you give your children your undivided attention when they're talking; that you listen without interrupting, judging, or formulating your response before they've finished speaking; and that you tune into their body language and facial expressions to pick up on feelings they might not be articulating.

3. **Ask** your children if your understanding of what they've told you is correct. Rephrase what they've said, or ask them to "break it down" to help you understand. You both need to be on the same wavelength to communicate effectively.

4. **Respond** with empathy. Even if you don't agree with your children, empathizing lets them know you respect and appreciate what they are feeling. Try not to offer advice in response to everything your children say. Sometimes they just need you to listen. Finally, couch your responses in "I"

terms, such as "I'm concerned about . . ." or "I can see you're having a difficult time with . . . ." Your children likely will be more receptive to this kind of response, as opposed to one that begins, "You should . . . ," "If I were you, . . ." or "When I was your age, . . . ," which tends to signify that a lecture is on the way.

5. **Encourage** your children to come to you whenever they need to talk. Let them know that, no matter how busy you might seem, you'll always make time for them.

Sibling Rivalry

"MOM! Bobby hit me!"

"She hit me first!"

Sound familiar? The refrains of sibling rivalry are as old as humankind. You'd think someone would have come up with a solution by now! The fact is, there's no way to avoid it. Young children want all your attention all the time, and that naturally entails competition. Kids fight and tattle to get each other in trouble, thinking they'll look like angels in Mommy and Daddy's eyes if the finger is pointed at a brother or sister.

Although you can't eliminate sibling rivalry, you can minimize it by not taking sides (HINT: "Who started it?" is a no-no) and by giving all your children equal amounts of love, attention, and support. While avoiding the referee role, you can intervene to help your children resolve their differences through negotiation and cooperation.

RESOURCES

Parentsoup.com

<http://www.parentsoup.com>

Summary: Parentsoup.com is a part of the iVillage network of sites and offers information on many parenting topics. From its homepage, you can type in "sibling rivalry," and the search engine will provide updated information.

Effective Discipline

Most parents can relate to each other when talking about the sometimes annoying, sometimes exasperating, and sometimes even dangerous behaviors of their children. But when the discussion turns to how to deal with these behaviors, it typically sends parents scurrying to their respective corners, ready to duke it out with anyone who tries to tell them the best way to discipline *their* children.

Discipline is such a hot button for parents because, more than any other factor reflecting their effectiveness as parents, discipline is most on display. Although parental involvement and communication are arguably as important in raising happy, healthy, well-adjusted kids, they're typically more "preventive," behind-the-scenes measures. Discipline, in its standard sense, is a more reactive response to your children's sometimes unrelenting, in-your-face aggravation that, fairly or not, is often the benchmark by which others judge your abilities as parents. (Think about your own reactions when witnessing a parent who deals with a screaming toddler in a different way than you would—most people can't help passing judgment based on their own style of doing things.)

Your parenting style—whether you're permissive, authoritarian, or authoritative—has a lot to do with how you discipline your children. Permissive parents tend to focus on providing warmth and support and to neglect setting limits and supervision. Authoritarian parents are the opposite—more emphasis on limits and discipline and less on warmth and encouragement. Authoritative parents fall somewhere in between—while being warm and responsive, they're also able to establish and enforce standards for their children's behavior, monitor conduct, and encourage communication. Studies have shown that this latter parenting style is associated with fewer disciplinary, academic, and interpersonal problems among children.

Click on <http://www.Boomerbasics.com> for more information on the attributes and effects of various parenting styles.

Notwithstanding your parenting style, effective discipline starts with teaching children how to do the right thing and to avoid similar missteps in the future, rather than simply punishing them for misbehaving. Keep the following points in mind:

1. Begin by clearly defining with your children, in advance, reasonable expectations for their behavior, and discipline only when they don't meet these expectations. Be specific when outlining these expectations. Explain what the rules are and the reasons for them. Discuss the consequences of breaking the rules: what the punishment will be, how it will be carried out, how much time will be involved, and what the punishment is supposed to achieve.

2. Whatever style of discipline you choose, be consistent in applying it. Avoid merely threatening punishment without following through and avoid adding consequences different from those originally discussed; children need to know that X behavior means Y result. Also, keep discipline consistent in all circumstances. Children whose misbehavior is treated differently in public or when relatives are visiting learn that discipline is conditional—based on a particular situation rather than on their conduct.

3. If your children aren't meeting your expectations, perhaps the rules, rather than your children, need to change. Periodically review your expectations, with your children's input, concerning whether the rules are fair and the consequences appropriate.

4. Finally, remember that shame, rejection, silence, withdrawal of affection, or preferential treatment of one child over another have no place in discipline.

Part of effective discipline is being a good role model of the behavior you expect from your children. If you expect your children not to lie and then ask them, for example, to tell a telemarketer that you're not home, your actions suggest that dishonesty is okay in some circumstances. Similarly, if you tell your children that screaming is not an acceptable way to express anger and then blow your stack when they've pushed you to the edge, you're sending conflicting messages.

Finally, discipline tends to focus on correcting what your children are doing wrong. Don't forget the value of praising them for what they do right! Both are equally important in helping your children to distinguish right from wrong and to develop the self-esteem and confidence they'll need to make their own judgments in the future.

Click on <http://www.Boomerbasics.com> for additional perspectives on character development and discipline, including age-appropriate discipline guidelines, views on spanking and corporal punishment, and strategies on dealing with anger.

Separation/Divorce

If you're contemplating or going through a separation or divorce, you undoubtedly are concerned about the effect on your children. Although you might be tempted to shield them from the emotional fallout by avoiding the issue, they need to know what's going on—instead of protection, they need support and reassurance. Only by talking with them can you help to alleviate the stress they inevitably will feel based on so many impending changes.

Although most children have trouble accepting their parents' separation or divorce, their reactions will vary depending on various factors, including, among other things, their age, sex, inner strength, circumstances prior to the separation or divorce, parents' ability to cope with separation or divorce, economic concerns, and the degree of family love and support they feel. Moving, changing schools, and a parent's remarriage can cause additional stress.

Children's biggest concerns relate to changes in their home routines and responsibilities, loss of contact with the familiar (for example, parents, siblings, pets, or possessions), abandonment or feelings that they've somehow caused the split, hostility between parents, and money ("Are we going to be poor?").

Click on <http://www.Boomerbasics.com> for more information on how your children may respond to divorce or separation, including age-specific reactions and the impact of the factors previously mentioned in addition to others.

As tough as the separation or divorce is for you, it's probably more difficult for your children. One way you can help is by telling your children it's okay to be upset or angry. Encourage them to talk openly about their feelings. Also, let them know about any changes the divorce or separation will bring in their routines or responsibilities (for example, how they might have to take on additional chores when you go back to work, or who will pick them up from soccer practice after school) but avoid shouldering them with adult responsibilities by saying things such as "You're the man of the house now."

Avoid using your children as pawns in any disagreements or legal battles you might have with your expartner. You inevitably will disagree on issues related to the terms of the divorce or separation and the parenting of your children, among others, but it's important not to subject your children to such disagreements or force them to take sides. To the extent that you both are responsible for raising your children, try to keep the lines of communication open with your expartner and be willing to compromise. Respect your children's relationship with their other parent. No matter how much animosity you might feel toward your ex, don't make your children feel guilty or disloyal for wanting to spend time with him or her and avoid criticizing the other parent in your children's presence.

Click on <http://www.Boomerbasics.com> for additional suggestions to help both you and your children cope with the stresses of a divorce or separation.

Determining a custody and visitation arrangement that works for both you and your expartner and that causes the least disruption for your children is important. Numerous options are available concerning both physical custody (where the children live) and legal custody (parents' rights to make decisions about such matters as their children's schooling and medical treatment). Whereas children of divorced parents typically have lived with their mother, parents going through a divorce today increasingly are opting for joint physical custody, which allows children to live with both parents, usually by splitting their time between both homes. This can be done in a number of ways, depending in part on the proximity of the parents. For example, children may live half-time with each parent or weekdays with one and weekends with another or the school year with one and vacation with the other.

Click on <http://www.Boomerbasics.com> for additional information on custody arrangements and child support.

RESOURCES

> **Split-up.com**
> Family Law Software, Inc.
> 831 Beacon St., Suite 2900
> Newton Center, MA 02459
> (877) 477-5488
> <http://www.split-up.com>

Summary: Split-up.com provides a wide range of information and assistance on topics related to divorce and separation.

Remarriage and Blended Families

Somewhere between Cinderella's oppression by her evil stepmother and stepsisters on the one hand and the idyllic, happy-go-lucky portrait of family life with Mike and Carol Brady on the other lies the real-world truth of stepfamily relations. Most stepfamilies (often called *blended families*) have their share of tension, especially in the beginning as everyone is adjusting to each other, new routines, new rules, and so on.

One of the biggest areas of conflict is the struggle for authority—any resentment children might have about answering to their own parents is magnified tenfold when a nonbiological parent tries to tell them what to do. Disciplinary issues can also lead to conflict between parents, who might believe their spouse gives preferential treatment to his or her own kids. A host of other issues can arise, depending on myriad factors such as the ages and sex of the children, the nature of relationships among parents and children in the biological family, custody arrangements with the expartner, and so on.

Despite these challenges, however, many blended families go on to become cohesive, loving family units. The key is time. Just as it took you time to develop a loving, trusting relationship with your new spouse, it'll take your children time as well. Don't rush the process. Some experts say it can take as long as three years to develop stable relationships among blended family members, so be patient!

Click on <http://www.Boomerbasics.com> or one of the following URLs for additional information concerning the common problems blended families encounter and guidelines for coping.

<http://www.cyberparent.com/step/index.html> (The StepParent's Web. Its goal is to eliminate the myths surrounding stepparents and to help stepparents stay realistic while coping with the stresses of stepfamily relationships.)

<http://www.stepfamily.org> (Stepfamily Foundation. Provides training, information, and counseling to avoid pitfalls that stress stepfamily relationships. Offers tips and advice to stepparents in its "Free Information" section.)

<http://www.tsconnection.org> (The Stepparenting Connection. Its goal is to help improve relationships in the blended family. Features advice for stepkids, a therapist's corner, and articles on stepfamilies.)

FINANCIAL ~~~~~~~~

What is the cost of raising a child? It's probably best not to know! But if you insist, the most current estimates are that it costs $6,600 to $10,000 per year for middle- and upper-class families to raise a child. This figure includes housing, food, transportation, clothing, health care, education, and child care. It doesn't include the seemingly astronomical cost of a college education, which, assuming inflation has some effect, is likely to cost from $40,000 to $60,000 per year by the time a child born as of this writing reaches the age of eighteen. Given this disturbing trend, you may be concerned that you'll have to declare bankruptcy to help your children further their education or just say no to paying for college at all. This section looks at meeting the cost of raising a child from birth to high school, including the cost of education, through savings programs, gifts, and insurance. The benefits and programs available to assist with the costs of raising children with disabilities will also be explored.

Insurance

Life Insurance

Probably the first reason you buy life insurance is to provide a safety net for your spouse and your children in the event you predecease them, particularly when your children are younger. At this stage it is often difficult to accumulate any significant savings for long-term goals, and in the event of a death, it would be virtually impossible to cover such costs. Life insurance can fill this void in your savings plan.

The factors that you would need to consider in terms of what might be adequate coverage would include not only such obvious expenses as the amount of an outstanding mortgage or the cost of education for your children but also potential lost wages if you are working outside the home or, if you are not working outside the home, the cost of in-home care for younger children. Additionally, you might need to consider certain investment and estate planning aspects (see Part One, "Ourselves").

Depending on your objectives, purchasing life insurance can be a complicated process, given the ultimate tax, investment, and practical implications. (Regardless of your objectives, purchasing life insurance is rarely a stimulating process.) Nonetheless, many people purchase policies without learning in advance what they need to know to accomplish their objectives. Consequently, they often don't know or understand what kind of insurance they have. Before you buy, think about your resources and needs and then what types of insurance will meet those needs in the most affordable manner. Also, consider working with a life insurance agent to help you identify your needs or at least help you find the right policy for your situation and budget. Granted, some agents may latch on like a pitbull, but there are many professional, well-qualified agents as well. Ask for references, training, background and which company(-ies) they work for. You may pay a little more in premiums, but you won't be left figuring this out for yourselves.

The following are brief descriptions of the available types of life insurance, things to keep in mind when contemplating how much insurance to buy, and tips on how to name the beneficiaries.

Policy Types

The most common types of life insurance are term life, whole life, and universal life. Additionally, each is available with variations.

Term-life insurance provides coverage for a term, or specified period of time, as decided by you and the insurance carrier. This is the least expensive form of coverage on a short-term basis. If you die within that period, your beneficiary receives the insurance. If you are still alive at the end of the term, that's the good news because you get nothing back from the insurance company—there is no cash value for the premiums you have paid. Term-life policies are renewable for specified periods: one, five, ten, or even twenty years. Term-life policies can also be convertible—changed to a form of permanent insurance at a later date without a medical examination—or nonconvertible, which terminate at the end of the specified period without being exchanged. For a relatively low premium payment, you can get a large amount of coverage under a term-life policy. It is a good option for a young family whose income and savings are low but whose debts and liabilities are considerable, especially where mortgage payments on a home are involved.

INSIGHT

Many people purchase mortgage insurance, particularly through a bank, at time of closing so that the surviving spouse would not have to worry about mortgage payments. For many families, it makes more sense to purchase a term policy for the same or a slightly higher premium that would provide the cash equivalent of the outstanding mortgage debt. The surviving spouse then has the option either to pay off the mortgage or use the money for other expenses while still having ample funds to stay in the house for many years if that is what he or she chooses to do. If the interest rate on the mortgage is lower than what you can earn investing, continuing the monthly payments may make more financial sense. Having a fully paid-off house that you cannot maintain or no longer want is not the same as having enough money available to do what you want in the time frame that best serves your family.

Whole-life insurance is the basic type of permanent life insurance. It is permanent in that you never need to requalify your health status to keep this coverage in force as long as you continue to pay your premiums. It provides a death benefit in the face amount of the policy when you die. There is no term limit. You pay a set premium each year for your lifetime. This money is used to fund the death benefit; any amount in excess of the face amount and expenses goes into the carrier's investment portfolio and earns dividends for you. You may also receive dividends (excess earnings from the insurance carrier's investments), which you can use to purchase more insurance or reduce premium costs each year.

There are several policy variations on whole life: straight life, modified premium, and combination term–whole life. *Straight-life* premiums do not change throughout the period of coverage. *Modified premiums* allow you to start out with whole-life coverage with low premiums. After a specified period, the payments dramatically increase. This may be a good option if you have little cash now but anticipate some hefty raises in the future. With a *combination term–whole life* policy, the premiums initially cover term insurance, and upon expiration of the term, the coverage changes to whole life.

Universal life and *variable universal life* provide whole-life insurance protection with more investment options for added flexibility.

Click on <http://www.Boomerbasics.com> for a list of resources that provides detailed analysis of different types of life insurance. Also see the discussion on life insurance in Part One, "Ourselves."

Policy Costs

The costs for life insurance will vary dramatically based on your age, the amount of coverage, and the type of insurance. Costs for a $100,000 policy may range from less than $200 to as much as several thousand dollars per year. A term-life policy is generally cheaper than any other type of policy for any given year, but the cost increases as you get older. If you plan to maintain insurance for a significant period of time (more than five years), you should certainly do a cost comparison between the cost of a term policy for a set period of time versus an ordinary or whole-life policy for the same period. Cost comparisons for life insurance policies, unlike disability or health policies, are relatively straightforward. The only determining factor as to whether a benefit will be paid is whether you are alive or dead.

To make sure that you are paying an appropriate premium for your insurance, you should compare costs from several different companies and review the benefits that their contracts may have in the event that you are looking at something other than a straight-life policy. In many parts of the country, price quotes are available through toll-free numbers, and many Web sites offer price quotes and comparisons from major insurance companies. Also, savings banks offer savings bank life insurance (SBLI), which can prove to be a good value. When analyzing the cost, be realistic about the amount of coverage that you really need (which will influence the cost) and also the amount of time for which you will need coverage. For many of us, the amount of coverage needed will decrease as retirement funds build, children's college funds are increased, and mortgage liability decreases. These factors should have a direct impact on reducing costs for insurance.

INSIGHT

Insurance is easy to understand in general: You buy it and when you die, someone gets a large sum of money. But for each situation, insurance is complicated. It has great benefits, but there is a lot to know. Before you commit,

become well informed. Do some comparative shopping, find a strong reliable insurer, work with an experienced professional, and be wary of high-pressure sales tactics.

Click on <http://www.Boomerbasics.com> for a list of publications on purchasing insurance and a checklist for choosing the right insurance company.

Amount of Benefit

To decide how much insurance you need, you must consider your spending habits, your financial plan, how much you need to save for retirement for you and your spouse (see Part One, "Ourselves," and Part Three, "Our Parents," for considerations surrounding saving for retirement), how much you need for your children's college education (discussed later), and the amount of the anticipated shortfall between your family's expenses and their income in the event of your death.

You also should allow for some flexibility in your calculations. It's probably no secret that your life is in a constant state of change, so earmarking funds now that you won't need until much later may be difficult. Your perceived needs at the age of thirty, when you might have young children, a spouse taking care of the children at home, loans from college(s), and a large mortgage, are likely to be quite different from those when you are fifty-five, with the children out of the house, the mortgage paid off or almost there, and both you and your spouse working outside the home (or with the children having moved back into the house, a second mortgage started, and you wanting to retire soon).

Beneficiaries

Although neither the amount of insurance you can take out on yourself nor who you select as beneficiary are limited by law, individual insurance companies do set limits on how much they will pay out to a single individual and who can be a beneficiary. Choosing a beneficiary for your life insurance is as significant as deciding on the amount of your insurance policy. If you name your estate as the beneficiary, the benefits are controlled by your will (or if you don't have one, intestacy) and thus subject to probate—something you may want to avoid. If your primary goal is to provide a safety net for your family in the event of your death, you don't want to diminish that with additional expense or delay. Naming your spouse as the beneficiary is a simple option. If your children are minors, naming them may not be the most practical choice because a guardian of their property will have to be appointed for their funds. Such a guardian may then be limited in his or her choice of investments for your children. Alternatively, proceeds may be left in trust for your children's benefit to avoid having them directly receive a large sum of money upon reaching the age of majority (eighteen or twenty-one, depending on the state you're in). If the children are adults, they may be appropriate beneficiaries unless there is a concern about creditors or financial maturity.

Another beneficiary option is a life insurance trust, which offers estate tax savings and flexibility over how and how long the proceeds are distributed to the beneficiaries of the trust.

RESOURCES

Insurance Online
<http://www.insweb.com/>

Summary: This Web site is maintained by Ins Web Services, a licensed insurance agent. It serves as an insurance marketplace, providing quotes from participating companies, but also provides a lot of free insurance information. From the main screen, click on "Insurance 101" for a thorough explanation of often bewildering insurance terms.

Tips on Purchasing Life Insurance
<http://www.newyorklife.com/viewer/wsh-nyl/pfstchtp.html>

Summary: This Web site is maintained by an insurance carrier but provides a great deal of free information on what to do prior to purchasing insurance as well as how to select a reputable agent.

Consumer Insurance Guide
<http://www.insure.com/>

Summary: Insure.com, which does not sell life insurance, maintains this independent education site. From the main screen, click on "Life" to access a complete array of life insurance information, including valuable consumer information tips.

> **Life Insurance Trusts for Child Beneficiaries**
> <http://www.insure.com/life/trusts.html>

Summary: This section within the Insure.com Web site explains why a parent may wish to consider setting up a trust with life insurance.

Disability Insurance

Although it is difficult to think about our mortality, it is even more difficult to imagine ourselves stricken by a catastrophic or chronic illness or a devastating injury. Given the likelihood that more of us will be injured and sidelined from work for three months or more than will die before we retire, you should consider insuring one of your more important assets—your ability to earn an income. Several types of disability insurance are available to counter this risk. In reviewing disability insurance policies, you need to consider several factors so that you are clear about exactly what is protected in the unfortunate event you need to make a claim.

First, look at how *disability* is defined in the policy. You will want the definition to take into account your education, experience, and past earnings in determining what you as the insured can reasonably be expected to do. Some policies today provide an "own occupation" definition of disability, which provides for payment of benefits if you are unable to work in your specialty (for example, an orthopedic surgeon who breaks his wrist or a salesman who loses his voice).

Second, determine whether partial or residual disability is covered. Ascertain whether benefits are provided when the impairment allows you to perform only a portion of your duties. For example, if your disability permits you to perform your work at only 50 percent of your prior capacity, does this jeopardize or reduce payments from your disability insurance policy? Sometimes the policy may require a period of total disability at first before benefits kick in. Basically, the wording of the contract is very important.

Third, check the amount of benefit paid and update the benefit as your circumstances (such as living expenses) change. It is important to understand that long-term disability companies will not insure you for 100 percent of your compensation; in fact, most will not insure for more than 55 to 60 percent of an individual's salary because they do not want to give anyone an incentive not to recover and go back to work. The obvious downside is

that in the event that you are totally disabled, you will suffer not only physical discomforts and limitations but also significant adverse economic repercussions, no matter how well you are insured. Although this is not an ideal
situation, clearly some insurance is better than none at all.

The taxation of benefits received under a disability policy may also have
a significant impact. Basically, if your employer has paid the premiums for
your disability insurance with pretax funds, then any benefit you may
receive under the policy would be considered taxable income. If, however,
you pay for the premium with after-tax funds, then in the event of a disability, the benefit you receive would be received tax free.

Fourth, check to be sure that the waiting period (also referred to as the
elimination period) is appropriate for your circumstances. Commonly available periods before benefits begin after a disabling incident include thirty
days, sixty days, ninety days, six months, and one year. Naturally, the longer
the waiting period, the lower your premiums. However, price should not be
the sole determining factor. You should also consider your and your family's
needs, your cash reserves, and your income sources in deciding how long
you can afford to wait before the disability payments commence.

Fifth, think about how long you want the insurance to be effective.
Because a long-term medical disability can be financially devastating, you
should select a long-term benefit where possible. Most companies offer coverage to age sixty-five; some offer lifetime benefit periods.

INSIGHT

**Several specialized policies are available to businesspeople, including ones
that cover business overhead expenses, the cost of loss of a key employee, and
a disability buyout, which funds a buy-sell agreement for a disabled shareholder, executive or professional.**

RESOURCES

Disability Insurance Basics
<http://www.insuremarket.com/basics/disability/disbasics.htm>

Summary: This Web site is maintained by Quicken Insure Market, which is
comprised of participant insurance carriers. A lot of good information is

contained here, including coverage term explanations and advice on selecting appropriate levels of coverage.

> **Disability Insurance: How It Works**
> <http://www.insure.com/health/disability.html>

Summary: Insure.com, which does not sell insurance, maintains this Web site providing information on disability insurance options.

Click on <http://www.Boomerbasics.com> for a list of resources that can provide you with detailed information on how to choose the best disability insurance policy for you.

Casualty, Liability, and Property Insurance

Casualty, liability, and property insurance originally covered real and personal property loss, but today, casualty insurance is considered difficult to define because it can encompass many different types of insurance and risks. Use of the term *casualty* as it refers to property is waning, increasingly being replaced by the more understandable term *property insurance*. Casualty insurance, with its uncertain definition, can include the following types of coverage: health and accident insurance; automobile insurance; liability insurance; workers' compensation insurance; boiler explosion insurance; plate glass insurance; burglary, robbery, and theft insurance; credit insurance; and title insurance.

Most of these types of coverage can fall under the categories of either property or liability. Additionally, some of these, such as health and auto, have become their own separate categories of insurance because of the complexity of what each covers. The most common insurance, a homeowner's policy, is a combination of all these types, covering fire, theft, and personal liability. Depending on the type of coverage you choose and the company that provides it, your plan may be more comprehensive. In any event, assess the risks to your property and family and make sure that you are adequately covered.

Social Security Benefits for Children

In addition to life insurance, another source of replacement income for children in the event of a parent's death may be through the Social Security program. Benefits may also be available for disabled children. A child may be eligible for Social Security benefits in one of three ways:

1. Disabled children under the age of eighteen, who either come from homes with limited income and resources or have limited income and resources themselves, are eligible for Social Security insurance (SSI) benefits.

2. If a child under the age of eighteen without a disability has a parent who is collecting retirement or disability benefits, then that child is eligible for Social Security dependent benefits. Survivor benefits are available for children under eighteen whose parents have died, regardless of whether a parent received benefits. A child receiving dependent or survivor benefits receives them until the age of nineteen if he or she is a full-time student in elementary or high school.

3. A disabled child receiving dependent or survivor benefits will continue to receive Social Security dependent benefits past the age of eighteen (or nineteen if the child is a full-time student). There are two qualifications: First, the child must be the son or daughter of an individual receiving retirement or disability or of someone who has died; second, the child's disability must have begun before the age of twenty-two.

In all three circumstances, the child must meet an income requirement and, other than for dependent benefits, qualify under the Social Security Administration's definition of *disabled*. In addition, a parent's income is considered in determining a child's eligibility until he or she turns eighteen.

The Social Security Office determines if the financial requirements are met, while a state office, usually called the Disability Determination Service (DDS), decides if the child meets the disability requirements by having a doctor and a disability evaluation specialist examine all documents relating to the child. If there is not enough information about the child's alleged disability, the DDS may require that the child see a doctor, which visit is paid for by Social Security. According to the Social Security Administration, a disability is a condition or a physical or mental impairment that keeps an individual from doing any substantial work for at least one year. The Social

Security Administration considers a job that pays $500 or more per month "substantial" work. The Social Security Administration also considers someone disabled if they are expected to die as a result of their condition.

Because children usually do not have jobs that would meet the $500-per-month requirement, the law treats them differently. For a child, the disability must impair him or her from doing activities that other children of the same age are able to do. When determining if a child is disabled, the DDS evaluation specialist first looks to a list of impairments that the Social Security Administration considers as disabilities. If the child's condition is listed, the child is considered disabled. If the child's condition is not listed, the specialist will make a determination.

INSIGHT

To apply for benefits, you must fill out an application form at a local Social Security office. Bring the child's Social Security number and birth certificate as well as proof of resources and assets of both the child and the parents.

RESOURCES

Social Security Disability Insurance
<http://www.kidsource.com/nfpa/social.html>

Summary: This Web site is maintained by the national Foster Parents Association and provides basic information to parents on how to navigate the SSDI application process.

Benefits for Children with Disabilities
SSA Office of Public Inquiries
6401 Security Blvd.
Room 4-C-5 Annex
Baltimore, MD 21235-6401
<http://www.ssa.gov/pubs/10026.html>

Summary: This site is maintained by the Social Security Administration. Comprehensive information is provided here, including Social Security benefit application rules for disabled children, for adults who have been disabled since childhood, and for minor children of disabled or deceased workers.

Supplemental Needs Trust

A *supplemental needs trust* (SNT) is a legal document that allows certain financial resources to be used to improve life for your disabled child without jeopardizing the child's eligibility for governmental assistance. Simply put, it supplements the benefits otherwise received from governmental programs rather than replaces such benefits. Generally, to qualify for government programs such as Medicaid and SSI, your child must be below certain income and resource levels. If you were to give or bequeath money directly to your child, he or she would immediately exceed the income and resource levels and thus become ineligible for benefits until such funds are spent. Conversely, money held in a supplemental needs trust is typically not considered as a resource for these purposes. Under federal and state laws, an SNT can be funded with money from you or another family member (known as a *third-party SNT*) or with the funds of the disabled person. The trustee of the trust can be an individual, or you may want to consider appointing certain qualified not-for-profit organizations. There are certain benefits to using a not-for-profit—not only is it likely to have the expertise for handling the trust, but, because of its corporate nature, it would also continue to exist in perpetuity, whereas an individual trustee may not always to able to serve.

The SNT can be either a lifetime trust or a testamentary trust (created through a will). The laws regarding SNTs are relatively new and fairly complicated. If you think your child would benefit from an SNT, you should consult a lawyer about the technical aspects of creating the trust. This is not a do-it-yourself job because of the constantly changing laws in this area that, if not considered, could jeopardize your disabled child's future standard of living.

RESOURCES

Supplemental Needs Trusts
<http://www.seniorlaw.com/snt.htm>

Summary: A comprehensive article on SNT creation, legal requirements, and history.

Special Needs Advocate for Parents (SNAP)
1801 Avenue of the Stars #401
Century City, CA 90067
(888) 310-9889
<http://www.snapinfo.org/news/docs/398a.htm>

Summary: This is a basic article in the "Special Needs Advocate for Parents" newsletter that describes special needs trusts. SNAP is a not-for-profit education and support group for parents of disabled children.

Teen Employment Issues

Supplying savings and income to your children may seem like an endless one-sided obligation (and for some it is, unfortunately), but eventually the children themselves can help lessen your outflow of funds for their needs. Many teens are eager to earn some money of their own, and most parents are eager for this phase of their child's life to arrive. But regardless of how motivated your child may be to work, there are some rules for both of you to know.

The Fair Labor Standards Act is the primary federal law governing the employment of teenage children. This law generally requires employers to comply with minimum standards of employment conditions, including the age at which an employer may employ a teen, the type of work that an employer may require a teen to perform, and the time of day an employer may schedule a teen for work. If a parent has a question concerning whether or not the employer of his or her teen is complying with the Fair Labor Standards Act, the parent may contact a local office of the U.S. Department of Labor.

RESOURCES

U.S. Department of Labor
Fair Labor Standards Act (FLSA) Advisor
Wage and Hour Division
<http://www.dol.gov/elaws/Flsa.htm>

Summary: The FSLA Advisor provides employers and employees with on-line information regarding federal minimum wage, overtime, child labor, and record-keeping requirements.

Legal Work Age

The Fair Labor Standards Act places limits on the number of hours that fourteen- and fifteen-year-olds may work. On a school day, fourteen- and fifteen-year-olds may work no more than three hours, and these three hours must be after school hours. During a school week, fourteen- and fifteen-year-olds may work no more than a total of eighteen hours. On nonschool days and nonschool weeks, however, fourteen- and fifteen-year-olds may work eight hours a day and up to forty hours per week. In addition, the Fair Labor Standards Act stipulates that fourteen- and fifteen-year-olds may not begin work before 7:00 A.M. and may work no later than 7:00 P.M. From June 1 through Labor Day, however, fourteen- and fifteen-year-olds may work until 9:00 P.M. The job must be in nonmanufacturing, nonmining, nonhazardous jobs. The rules on agricultural jobs vary from state to state.

The Fair Labor Standards Act imposes less stringent requirements on employers as regards sixteen- and seventeen-year-old employees. They may work any number of hours they wish on school and nonschool days up to a maximum of forty-four hours per week, and they may do so at any time of the day.

Minimum Wage

The Fair Labor Standards Act generally requires employers to pay employees who are under twenty years of age a minimum wage of $4.25 per hour for the first ninety calendar days of employment. After these ninety days, employers must pay teenage employees a minimum wage of $5.15 per hour, subject to certain exceptions. For example, employers are not required to pay a minimum wage for employees holding seasonal or recreational jobs such as a teenager working for the summer at an amusement park or swimming pool.

Internships—Work-Study Programs

Internships are generally designed to give teenagers an introduction to the workplace and a more realistic view and assessment of a possible career. In many instances, they are either not paid for their work or are paid less than might be generally available in the area for comparable work. The idea of the internship is to provide the intern with knowledge and experience rather than financial compensation.

Internships fall into two categories: general internships and field-specific internships. A *general internship* is designed to introduce the individual to a large potential field of employment. For example, your teenager may serve an internship in an office or a retail establishment to determine whether the world of business is something that she would like to pursue. In addition to some job-specific knowledge, the internship programs are designed to also teach members skills that are generally considered useful in the workplace, such as punctuality, working effectively with other people, and responsibility. *Field-specific internships* are designed to give the applicant a firsthand look at the type of work and work environment that they could expect if they were to pursue that career. For example, internships are fairly common in medical labs, veterinary offices, and architect's offices. With these and similar occupations, the individual is introduced to specific challenges and responsibilities that a particular occupation would entail.

Apprentice Programs

Apprentice programs, today just as during the Middle Ages, are designed to introduce individuals to a specific trade or skill. The idea is for the individual to learn that craft or skill from someone who has achieved a high level of proficiency in the trade by starting at the most elementary level and working his or her way up.

Many of these programs are still used in the building trades and shipbuilding. Of course, in many states the medieval guilds have been replaced by unions. For those occupations that generally do not require a formal education process or for which formal education is not enough, a good apprentice program can be an invaluable experience.

College Costs

The costs of secondary and college education can add up quickly, particularly if you have more than one child and private schools are your choice. You already know that the costs are high, but to help quantify those costs further, the table provided in this section can provide a starting point. Naturally, your specific costs will vary depending on your overall spending plan and where you want to focus your resources.

Deciding where your children will go to college and how much you can afford to pay and filing all the financial aid paperwork isn't rocket science, but it can appear to rival NASA's planning (and budget) for launching a satellite into orbit. Some parents solve this problem by delegating the financial responsibility to their children. Others offer more help. For the great majority who intend to pay for all or part of a child's college, advance planning (before senior year) is crucial. You should consider the following:

- What amount of your child's college costs are you willing to provide?
- Is postgraduate education part of the plan?
- How much cash can you invest (or save) per month?
- Do you have any savings already accumulated?
- Are there any other possible financial source(s) to consider?
- Is there an investment in which you are particularly interested or of which you are especially wary?
- Are there any special circumstances that could affect your saving plan?

Table 5.1 tracks the increase in tuition and fees in private schools for the last three decades, up to the year 2000.

Over the last decade, when one looks at the cost of room and board as well as tuition and fees, the total cost is very significant, whether for private (Table 5.2) or public (Table 5.3) colleges.

Costs will also vary significantly by region. For example, the tuition and fees for a four-year, private institution will range from $11,275 in the Southwest to $20,171 in New England.[1]

---

[1] <http://www.collegeboard.org>, Trends in College Pricing, p. 6 (1999).

Table 5.1   *Tuition and Fees at Private Institutions*

Years	Four-Year Institutions ($)	Two-Year Institutions ($)
1971–1972	1,820	1,172
1981–1982	4,113	2,605
1991–1992	10,017	5,290
1999–2000	15,380	7,182

Source: <http://www.collegeboard.org>, *Trends in College Pricing, p. 7 (1999).*

Table 5.2   *Tuition, Fees, and Room and Board at Private Institutions*

Years	Four-Year Institutions ($)	Two-Year Institutions ($)
1990–1991	13,544	8,484
1994–1995	16,685	10,551
1999–2000	21,339	11,765

Source: <http://www.collegeboard.org>, *Trends in College Pricing, p. 8 (1999).*

Table 5.3   *Tuition, Fees, and Room and Board at Public Institutions*

Years	Four-Year Institutions ($)	Two-Year Institutions ($)*
1990–1991	4,970	884
1994–1995	6,512	1,298
1999–2000	8,086	1,627

*Tuition and fees only; no room and board charges.

Source: <http://www.collegeboard.org>, *Trends in College Pricing, p. 8 (1999).*

Because tuition costs likely will continue to outpace inflation, you should overestimate when trying to anticipate the amount that you will need for your child to attend school. Costs to consider include tuition, fees, and room and board as well as books, travel expenses, medical coverage (if not provided by your own insurance), and miscellaneous expenditures. Most college catalogs give a list of typical expenses.

RESOURCES

U.S. News Online
<http://www.usnews.com/usnews>

Summary: Lists and ranks colleges by regions of the country. Provides homepages on nearly every college and university in the United States. There are many worksheets, calculators, and tools to assist in college planning as well.

Why have costs been rising at an annual rate greater than inflation for twenty years? It costs a lot to replace faculty, to make up for reduced public funding, and to maintain, repair, and upgrade facilities and equipment that in many instances have been used continuously by teenagers since first put in place in the 1960s to handle the baby boom's invasion of higher education. What will keep costs climbing for certain is the ever-growing burden of financial aid.

As more people need assistance to meet the cost of higher education, financial aid budgets must grow. What accounted for less than 5 percent of a college budget in 1970 is generally more than 20 percent of the pie today.

There are millions of young people in college today, so prepare to do the following: 1) gulp, 2) get in line, and 3) get a plan.

How to Pay for College

There are basically four ways to pay for college.

1. *Save.* The more time you have before college, the more successful a savings plan can be. Start savings when the kids are young, the younger the better. Don't worry about how much you save, at least not at first.

The objective is to establish a regular savings pattern. You can increase the amount as comfort and circumstances permit, and besides regular savings, there are opportunity savings, too (a holiday gift, tax refund, bonus, and so on). How you save is also important. Keep in mind that the cost of college is going up faster than regular inflation, so make certain that your plan is shaped to outpace college inflation, 5 percent per year or more.

2. *Borrow.* When rewriting the Higher Education Act in the early 1990s, the federal government tried to eliminate the issue of paying for college. If

you can't do it on your own, the government will lend you the difference between financial aid and the cost of the college where your child enrolls, up to certain dollar limits. Great! But be careful, or Willard Scott may have to call you at work to wish you a happy birthday. The key to borrowing is to keep the debt load under control. First you must file the FAFSA (Free Application for Federal Assistance) form to apply for financial aid. Private colleges may require additional information or forms, but almost every lending source will ask for the FAFSA information.

In addition to institutionally provided aid, there are two primary, federally backed loan programs: the Stafford loan, which the student must pay back (a great way to share the responsibility for college costs), and the PLUS (Parents Loans to Undergraduate Students) loan, which goes to parents (see "Baby Boomer Resources").

Home equity loans from a line of credit may be an appealing alternative given the combination of prevailing rates and tax deductibility of interest. Borrowing from retirement plans may also be possible, but that should not be the first choice (see the section on retirement plans in Part Three, "Our Parents," and on Roth IRAs in Part One, "Ourselves").

3. Pay as you go. It would be nice if the cost of education could fit in your regular budget, right alongside groceries and cable TV. In some ways it will. Keep in mind that as the parent of a teenager, you have been paying bills all along. Part of the college cost is simply paying someone else to shelter and feed your child. In many cases, your young scholar can work over the summer and on holidays to help with costs. Most colleges bill twice per year or before the start of each term. There are usually alternative ways to pay, the most common being on a ten-month schedule that the college arranges through a payment company. These companies provide an excellent service for a modest fee, generally less than $100 per year.

4. Someone else pays. If there is a favorite way to pay for education, this is it. Scholarships (money that does not have to be paid back) are what we all like the most. As college approaches, have your teenager apply for every scholarship you can uncover. In addition to the schools themselves, companies, benevolent associations, private foundations, and other organizations offer awards. Additional awards may be available from a particular college, either through academic competition or participation in various programs within the school. Also, many local organizations offer small amounts of money for educational costs. Your child's high school guidance office is a good starting point for information about scholarships; you can find out even more by following up on your own.

INSIGHT

Be careful about using services or referral agencies that charge a fee for finding scholarships. Using information you could uncover yourself, some such agencies will point your child and thousands of others to the same group of scholarships.

Once scholarships were awarded primarily on the basis of need, offering what assistance a family required to make the college financially within reach. Although that is still true at many of the most competitive institutions, other colleges use financial aid as an incentive to get the candidates they want to enroll. This is known as *merit-based financial aid* (the kind once reserved for athletes and other special students, now parceled out more broadly to meet enrollment goals).

To see what aid is available, you must first apply, at least by filling out the basic FAFSA form. In general, the better your child's credentials stack up against other applicants to the college of choice, the more likely it is that aid will be offered as an incentive to enroll. If aid is important to the decision where to enroll, apply to several similar institutions and then compare financial aid offers. If your first choice does not offer as much as a comparable institution, ask for a review before making the enrollment choice. If the first choice college has the best financial package, you know you have a good match.

In addition to institutionally based scholarships, keep in mind that many private scholarships may be available. Ask the school guidance counselor or check "Baby Boomers Resources" for Web sites that provide comprehensive listings for scholarships.

Each of the four ways to pay for college differs in approach. For most people, some part of each will come into play.

The following are some commonly asked questions about how to prepare financially for your children's college education. Then, beginning on page 204, there is a listing of several excellent on-line resources to help you prepare further.

1. *How much should I save?* As much as you can, starting as soon as you can, is the quick answer. Better still, think about a practical commitment to

your children's education, whether that means planning to cover tuition at the state university or all expenses at an elite private college. (Click on <http://www.Boomerbasics.com> to project college costs for your family.)

The shortage of money saved will come from borrowing, current income, and financial aid. Keep in mind that college costs are spread over at least four years, so all the money doesn't have to be on hand when the first bill comes in the mail.

2. *If I save, will it cost me more in the long run because I won't get any financial aid?* Apart from some federal loan programs, financial aid is not an entitlement. In most instances, colleges first look at the family's ability to pay. Also, keep in mind that *financial aid* is a general term that covers both grants that don't have to be paid back and loans that do. For most applicants, the aid package contains more loans than grants. Therefore, the real question to be asked is, would you rather have bills paid out of savings on hand or from loans to be repaid when the children are done with college and retirement savings should be your financial focus?

3. *In whose name should I save?* In many instances, funds earmarked for college should be in the parents' name. It is an issue of control and being able to use the money as necessary when education costs begin. For example, what if one of your children pays the full amount at an elite university, while another wins a merit scholarship at a specialty college? Their financial requirements would be very different, and you should retain the flexibility to use savings as needed. A custodial account (as described under the Uniform Gifts to Minors Act [UGMA] or [Uniform Transfers to Minors Act]) is the child's money. If you have one of these accounts already, you can deplete it by spending on behalf of the child for other needs, for example, for music lessons, a computer, or sports camp. Also keep in mind that if need-based financial aid is possible, assets in the child's name will weigh more heavily against you in the family contribution formula, thus possibly reducing your chance for assistance.

4. *Can college costs keep going up?* Yes they can, and yes they will. Faculty originally recruited to teach the baby boom generation are now retiring, and the cost to replace them is significant. In addition, government-sponsored assistance for higher education hasn't kept pace since the early 1980s. Also keep in mind that campus facilities were expanded broadly in the 1960s

to accommodate baby boomers. Refurbishing and replacement needs today are expensive. The infrastructure and tools needed for the technology age are very new and very costly indeed. Also, to help people meet the rising cost of educating their children, a lot more financial aid is available than in the past. Think of the cost of education as a user fee: If you can pay it at all, you may be asked to do just that. More and more people find that difficult to do, so financial assistance programs are expanding to help more families, which keeps costs high and stretches out the payments.

The government is trying to help, too. The Hope Scholarship and the Lifetime Learning Credit created in the 1997 Tax Act provide some relief for those who fall within the income guidelines.

RESOURCES

U.S. Department of Education
400 Maryland Avenue SW
Washington, DC 20202
(800) USA-LEARN
<http://www.ed.gov>

Summary: The U.S. Department of Education publishes information for teachers, parents, students, researchers, and policy makers having a stake in education. Many of its publications are available in full on their Web site.

5. *What about College Savings Plans?* Since the late 1980s, state governments have tried to find ways to help families pay for college. In the early plans, a state would guarantee that in return for a certain sum invested when the child was young, tuition at the state university would be covered, no matter what happened in the investment markets or to college costs in the intervening years. These plans provide a very modest actual rate of return in exchange for the guarantee. (Click on <http://www.Boomer basics.com> for details on your state.)

A more recent development is the so-called 529 Plan, in which parents invest in a state-backed program that offers no guaranteed rate of return but provides some tax incentives for participants. The limited investment growth potential in most of these plans must be weighed against the tax advantages. But because no investment guarantee is required, these plans are becoming widely available. These plans can be very appealing to high-income earners because no limitations are placed on who can participate. Often, it makes sense for families to combine a state-sponsored program with their own investing to round out a college savings plan.

6. *What about U.S. savings bonds and the Education IRA?* Using U.S. savings bonds in a college savings plan was the federal government's first effort to help families save in a tax-advantaged way. There are two problems: Assuming the bonds were registered correctly when purchased, they still pay only the prevailing savings bond rate, which doesn't help much if you want to gain on the rate of college inflation. Also, be sure you will fall within the income standards for using savings bonds tax free. If your income at the time of use is greater than the plan permits, you will not receive the funds tax free.

The Education IRA has limited practicality because of its restrictions, primarily the $500-per-year contribution limitation and what the effect of using it may be on the Hope Scholarship and Lifetime learning credits that might be more useful to your family. For most people, these vehicles would not be the first place to turn to for education savings.

7. *What loans are available for college?* Since the early 1990s, federally backed loans have been made available to almost every family to meet the costs of education. The most common are the previously mentioned Stafford and PLUS loans.

A Stafford loan is a federal loan available to students who apply and qualify for financial aid. Stafford loans come in two types, subsidized and unsubsidized, depending on the income of the family. Subsidized loans guarantee that the government will pay for the interest on the loan while your child is in school. For partly or wholly unsubsidized loans, some students choose to pay off the interest while attending school, whereas others defer the payments until they have finished school. Repayment of Stafford loans must start six months after your child leaves school—even if he or she hasn't graduated. The payment start date can be delayed by going on to another school or to graduate school.

A PLUS loan is a federal loan that allows parents to borrow enough money to cover the cost of their child's education, with an interest rate that cannot exceed 9 percent. These loans are available through a bank or a private lender.

When you are shopping for financial assistance for college costs, begin with the federally subsidized programs, then check into state loan programs, and finally look at private financing. Examine the many details of the lender's offer. Compare among banks and companies because interest rates, fees, and caps vary. The sooner you can repay the loan, the better. See if the lender offers any incentives for on-time payments or directs payments from your child's bank account. Check the state where your child is attending college, as the programs may differ from those in your state of residence; states offer reduced interest rates for residents who attend school in state.

Another major source of loans is the college or university itself, and such loans sometimes come with a provision that some or all of the loan will be forgiven if the graduate works in certain "social benefit" careers. The base of all loans is the FAFSA form, which must be filed so that families can receive the nearly automatic certification to borrow from the government.

As a practical matter it may be preferable to borrow against the equity of a home. Because outside approval is required, be sure to have the line of credit in hand before tuition payment time gets too close. Borrowing from a 401(k) or 403(b) retirement program through work may also be an option for many, but doing so is generally less desirable given the impact it can have on the growth of retirement savings.

8. *Can others help with costs?* Paying education costs may be of interest to grandparents or other relatives, and some special opportunities may make it more appealing. First, there is no $10,000-per-year per-person limitation on gifting if the funds are used directly for education costs. Also, this does not enter into the financial aid equation if the gift is made payable directly to the college as a tuition payment rather than to the family of the student. One especially attractive opportunity in the years ahead is gifting of funds that have been accumulated in a Roth IRA, where no penalty is levied on funds used. The government may be of help also with special programs like the Montgomery GI Bill or Americorps.

9. *Where can I find out more?* Just about every secondary school guidance office and every local library and bookstore has reference material on higher education. Click on <http://www.Boomerbasics.com> for Web sites that focus on financial aid and loans for higher education.

10. *Will needing financial assistance hurt my child's admissions chances?* Unfortunately, the answer can be yes, especially at some of the nation's best colleges,

where the competition for admissions is great. At one time the admissions process and financial aid were separate. Now, with budgets tight and demand high, the ability to pay may be one factor in the admissions decision. This rarely happens when the applicant stands out from the competition. But even at the best schools, where most of the applicants are outstanding, the ability to pay may be one of the considerations in the admissions process.

Paying for college is a challenge for all parents, and it is felt acutely by members of the baby boom generation who were the first to benefit from the widespread belief that higher education was good for almost everyone. Now it's our turn to pay. Planning is the key, and an early start helps. Keep in mind that if you plan correctly and intelligently, your children will have the same or better opportunities that you had, and you will be free to focus on other issues that are also part of your long-term agenda.

RESOURCES

Council of Better Business Bureau
4200 Wilson Boulevard, Suite 800
Arlington, VA 22203-1838
<http://www.bbb.org/library/finaid.html>

Summary: The Better Business Bureau provides free information on government programs and companies that offer help in securing scholarships, loans, and financial aid.

The College Board
45 Columbus Avenue
New York, NY 10023-6992
(800) 626-9795
<http://www.collegeboard.org>

Summary: Grant and scholarship information, among numerous other college-related topics, is provided at this Web site.

Financial Aid Search
<http://www.fastweb.com>

Summary: This site provides a large database of scholarships.

Financial Aid for College
<http://www.finaid.org>

Summary: Covers all types of aid, from loans and scholarships to military aid, and allows you to ask specific financial aid questions on-line.

U.S. Department of Education
(800) 433-3243
<http://www.ed.gov>

Summary: Provides information on student loans through its Federal Student Aid Information Center.

Free Federal Application for Student Aid
(800) 801-0576
<http://www.fafsa.ed.gov>

Summary: Provides free application for federal student aid.

Nelliemae
(800) 367-8848
<http://www.nelliemae.org>

Salliemae
(800) 239-4269
<http://www.salliemae.com>

Summary: These resources provide information on student loans, including prequalifying and applying for loans on-line.

Investment Tools

In recent years, inflation has continued to rise at the rate of about 3 percent annually, while the cost of college has increased 5 percent per year or more. Today's low market returns for traditional investments, such as certificates of deposit and zero coupon bonds, make it difficult to prepare for college expenses without taking some risks.

Short-term investments are effective when your children are within a few years of beginning college and you prefer to make a lower risk investment. For a longer investment period, the best rates of return historically come from investing in stocks, which have outperformed all traditional investments for the past fifty years. Mutual funds, which make it possible for you to acquire a stock portfolio, provide liquidity, flexibility, and reduced risks, making them a natural and attractive alternative to other forms of savings. By adjusting your mutual fund allotment, you can take advantage of aggressive growth funds when your children are young and gradually shift into more conservative funds as they approach college age. Deciding which type of funds are best for your planning may be easier if you seek help from a professional, but some preliminary advice is offered in Part One, "Ourselves," and some can also be found here to ease you into the strategic maze.

RESOURCES

Alliance for Investor Education
<http://www.investoreducation.org/>

Summary: The Alliance for Investor Education is a not-for-profit organization that provides a broad array of objective investment information.

The American Association of Individual Investors (AAII)
625 N. Michigan Ave.
Chicago, IL 60611
(800) 428-2244
<http://www.aaii.com/>

Summary: AAII is a not-for-profit investor education and research organization.

The American Stock Exchange
<http://www.amex.com/>

Summary: The NASDAQ stock market Web site provides market information (with an approximately twenty-minute delay). From the homepage, click on "investor services" for a great deal of basic investment information.

Deloitte & Touche LLP
Center of Excellence
700 Walnut Street
Cincinnati, OH 45202
<http://www.dtonline.com/>

Summary: This is a comprehensive guide to personal finance produced by Deloitte & Touche LLP.

> **Fortune**
> <http://www.fortuneinvestor.com/>

Summary: This Web site is maintained by *Fortune* magazine. Many investment services are provided here, such as a financial news wire service, professional analysis of hundreds of mutual funds, and a market tracker. This is a subscription-based Web site, but the first thirty days are free. Much free information is still offered after you subscribe.

> **Financial Web**
> <http://www.financialWeb.com/>

Summary: This Web site provides free stock quotes, mutual fund information, sophisticated technical analysis, and market research.

Mutual Funds

With mutual funds, the investment company pools the money of its shareholders to invest in diversified stocks, bonds, and other securities. The diversification within the fund reduces your investment risk. The typical fund is composed of dozens of distinct investments, and because your investment dollar is spread in such a manner, the potential for catastrophic loss stemming from any individual investment is minimized.

Professional managers or management teams control the investment strategy. Fund managers keep watch over market fluctuations and investment climates and can sell off poorly performing stocks quickly. Fund managers have different styles and investment objectives; some are willing to accept more risk than others. These objectives are set forth in the mutual fund's prospectus.

In general, risk and return are inversely proportional. The more risk attached to your investment, the more chance your return will be higher. Diversification, or following the old adage "Don't put all your eggs in one basket," reduces risk but does not eliminate it. Although mutual funds are preferred over many types of securities as a good way to spread your investment dollars, they do not guarantee positive returns. Therefore, it's important to look at the objective of the fund and the track record of the fund's manager(s) when selecting from among the more than eight thousand funds available currently. For more about mutual funds and other investment strategies, consult Part One, "Ourselves," and Part Three, "Our Parents."

Savings Bonds

For qualifying investors, savings bonds, which are direct obligations of the United States, can be used in your education planning. With these popular investments, it is important to understand their actual rate of return, which is subject to special rules regarding income taxation and use of the cashed mature bond for tuition purposes.

Series EE Bonds

Series EE bonds are purchased for one-half their face value, and the increase in redemption value is taxable as interest. When held five years or longer, EE bonds become eligible to receive a market-based rate that is retroactive to the first day of the month of issue. The interest earned from these bonds may be deferred until the year they are cashed in or the year in which the bond matures. Additionally, you may exclude from your income part or all of the interest if the bond is cashed in and used for tuition expenses as long as you meet certain criteria, including that the bonds be issued in your name and not your child's.

RESOURCES

Bureau of Public Debt
<http://www.publicdebt.treas.gov>

Summary: This bureau provides answers to virtually any question you may have about savings bonds, T-bills, and T-notes, including calculators to determine values of bonds you may own.

Gifts to Minors

Key factors to consider when deciding whether and how to make major gift contributions to children include the child's age and the possible tax consequences. The child's age is important because children under the age of eighteen (under twenty-one in some states) are legally restricted or prohibited from taking care of their own property or holdings. Special rules apply to gifts as regards estate taxes, generation-skipping transfer (GST) taxes, and income taxes. (See the "Financial" section of Part One, "Ourselves.") The IRS allows you to give each family member (or anyone else) gifts totaling up to $10,000 a year without incurring any gift taxes. If the minor is a grandchild or great-grandchild, any gift up to $10,000 may also be excluded from the GST tax. The following sections describe some ways of giving property, money, stocks, or other gifts to a minor.

RESOURCES

Northern Trust Financial Services
Tax-Wise Ways to Make Financial Gifts to Minors
<http://www.ntrs.com>

Summary: Comprehensive discussion on gifting assets to minors including references to relevant Internal Revenue Code provisions. This site is maintained by Northern Trust Financial Services.

Direct Gifts

A supposedly simple direct transfer to a child will often cause problems precisely because the gift is to a child. It's plain to see how a young adult might mismanage a substantial financial gift if given free rein to use it as he or she pleases. Until the child reaches the age of eighteen or twenty-one (the age of majority depends on the state of residence), the court might need to appoint a guardian, to be legally responsible for managing the minor's property. Although parents are legally described as the natural guardians of their children, the court will want to ensure that any property (and property always includes money in legal terms) owned by a minor is used for his or her best interests. The guardian must request court permission to make expenditures and must account to the court on a regular basis. Once the child reaches the age of majority, he or she has full control of the gift.

Click on <http://www.Boomerbasics.com> to determine the age of majority in each state.

In-Trust-For Bank Accounts

In-trust-for accounts, commonly called Totten trusts, are revocable accounts owned by the donor for the benefit of the minor (or any other named beneficiary) for whom the funds are in trust. Because the donor retains complete control of the funds in a Totten trust account, all income (that is, interest) earned on the account during the donor's lifetime will be charged to the donor's yearly taxable income, and the account can be attached by the donor's creditors.

At the donor's death, the accounts will be included in the donor's taxable estate, but the money in the account becomes the property of the minor. If the individual is still a minor when the donor dies, the funds will be subject to the same rules as apply to direct gifts to children, which means that some type of guardian will need to be appointed.

INSIGHT

A better way to make this same gift could be to make the bequest in a will or testamentary trust. The money will be available at the same time, and a will can contain conditions regarding when the money will be distributed and who will be the guardian of it.

Uniform Gifts to Minors Act/Uniform Transfers to Minors Act

To avoid the hassles created through direct gifts to minors wherein a guardian is required, you can make a gift through the Uniform Gifts to Minors Act (UGMA) or the Uniform Transfers to Minors Act (UTMA), depending on where you live. Under both laws, a named custodian monitors the minor's gift until he or she reaches the age of majority. Unlike a guardian, a custodian is not subject to the control of the court. Under UGMA and UTMA, the money can be used for the child regardless of the parents' assets or liabilities. You should not, as the gift giver, name yourself as custodian if you have a taxable estate because if you should die before the custodianship ends, the money will be taxed to your estate. Instead, name another adult, a bank, or a trust company. Under both acts, gifts under $10,000, like any such gift, are excluded from gift taxation. The most common arrangement is to have one spouse make the gift and have the other spouse be named the custodian. This keeps the arrangement very simple and within the family, and yet in the event of premature death of one spouse, it does not compound estate complexity.

INSIGHT

Because the transfer under UGMA or UTMA is in fact a gift, it is only appropriate that the person receiving the gift pay income tax on the interest or dividends earned. In order to accomplish this, make sure that your child's Social Security number is the first one listed, as financial institutions will report the income based on the first Social Security number. Tax rules vary when your child is fourteen or older, but in almost all family situations, the child's income bracket will initially be lower than the parents'.

RESOURCES

Gifts under the Uniform Gifts to Minors Act

<http://www.reports-unlimited.com/giftstominorsact.htm>

Summary: Sample legal form for a UGMA transfer for the benefit of a minor child.

Uniform Gifts to Minors Act

<http://www.invest-faq.com/articles/tax-ugma.html>

Summary: This investment FAQ Web site is maintained by Christopher Lott and contains a complete guide on how and why one opens a UGMA account.

Trust Gifts

A trust allows you to transfer legal title to property to a trustee who manages the property for the beneficiary—namely, your child. The trustee, not the child, retains control over the assets in the trust. The trust's terms can also specify the purposes for the money. As a practical matter, because of the cost of creating and administering a trust, it usually does not make economic sense to create a trust for your child's education with less than approximately $75,000. The major advantage of a trust is that you have control over the assets so that they are spent in the form and manner that you feel is best for your child. For example, the money in trust goes for college education and not for the new Corvette. The second advantage is your ability to control the time when your children have access to a potentially large amount of money. For example, if you had dedicated $100,000 to $150,000 toward your child's education and you had the good fortune for that child to receive a full scholarship (or the potentially bad fortune that the child was not college material), the child may have full access to a large amount of money in his or her UGMA account, totally unfettered, upon reaching the age of majority. However, very few parents would think that putting that much temptation into the hands of a newly minted adult would be the best course of action.

Income Trust

With an income trust, the trustee oversees the funds and pays out the income yearly to the trust's beneficiaries. Unless there are stated limits in the trust agreement, the trustee can use the base or principal amount of the trust, as well as the yearly interest, to benefit the minor or individual. You can set age limits on when the gift is disbursed—for instance, you might divide the principal amount into halves, quarters, or eighths and designate that a portion of the original amount be paid to the beneficiary at specified dates (ages twenty-five, thirty, and thirty-five, for example).

An income trust does not qualify for the $10,000 annual exclusion for gifts (which is given only for so-called present interest gifts). The amounts that a person receives at later dates, if the principal is broken down, will not get the benefit of the $10,000 exclusion. A GST tax may apply if the minor to whom you are giving is a grandchild or otherwise in another, younger generation where tax can be as high as 55 percent for gifts over $1 million. Needless to say, an arrangement such as this involves several income, gift, and estate tax considerations; therefore, this is not one you want to try at home on your own. At the very least, discuss the tax and control issues with an attorney.

Age Twenty-One Extension Trust

With an age twenty-one extension trust, which terminates when the beneficiary reaches that age, the trustee usually is given a great deal of power to use any part of the principal (corpus) or interest for the benefit of the minor. If the minor or beneficiary dies before she or he turns twenty-one, the gift then becomes part of his or her estate.

This type of trust is eligible for the $10,000 annual exclusion, and the GST tax does not apply. The major disadvantage to this type of trust is that the entire gift becomes the sole property of the beneficiary at age twenty-one—an age not typically associated with sound financial decision making. However, if drafted correctly, there is a loophole for donors who are concerned about the trust funds being squandered: The beneficiary has thirty days after turning twenty-one to assert his or her ownership of the trust and to remove it from control of the trustee. If the beneficiary fails to do so, after being notified by the trustee of this right, the trust is extended automatically until a predetermined age or several ages, but in the name of the beneficiary, not the original gift giver, as donor. In practice, donors usually explain to their minor donees that if they choose to not extend the trust and instead withdraw the money when they turn twenty-one, they could get written out of their inheritance. This explanation is often easily grasped by the minor donee and thus the trust is extended for a further term of years.

Direct Payment of Tuition or Medical Expenses

One way to avoid the potentially messy tax problems associated with gifts is to pay the cost of your child's college tuition (or medical) expenses directly to the institution. Current tax law treats this kind of payment as a freebie. It is extremely important that the payments be made directly to the institution and not to the minor or a guardian first.

No gift tax applies to this type of gift because the tax law considers it a nongift; therefore, you can still make an additional $10,000 annual gift to your child without any gift tax consequences. Furthermore, the GST tax does not apply if the payments are made on behalf of a grandchild or other lower generation member. A GST tax can also be avoided if the money is put into a trust and the trustees make payments directly to the educational institutions or medical providers. However, other gift or estate taxes may apply to this type of trust.

HEALTH ~~~~~~~~

When parents bring their newborn infant home for the first time, they are faced with many questions about how to care for their new child. How will they feed the baby? When can the baby go outside? What should they do if the baby gets a cold? What do they do if their child gets sick? They've embarked on a new, ongoing, and seemingly eternal journey in which the answers to these questions will be followed by another series of questions. As the parent of the teenager said to the parent of the infant, "The challenges get harder as they get older."

General Health Care Organizations/Web Sites Dedicated to Children's Health Issues

Several health-related organizations provide parents with comprehensive information, products, or services. When your child is confronted with a disease, illness, or other health problem or issue, these organizations may also be able to inform you about resources that could help you and your child successfully address those challenges.

RESOURCES

> **KidsHealth.org**
> <http://www.kidshealth.org>

Summary: KidsHealth.org is a Web site created by the Nemours Foundation Center for Children's Health Media, a nonprofit organization. This site contains hundreds of articles on pediatric health for parents, teenagers, and children. Topics of interest cover a broad spectrum of physical and social health problems affecting children and teens. The site features health tips, which are updated daily, as well as interactive learning tools on health for kids.

**National Information Center for Children and Youth
  with Disabilities (NICHCY)**
PO Box 1492
Washington, DC 20013
(800) 695-0285
<http://www.nichcy.org>

Summary: The NICHCY is a national information and referral center providing several services pertaining to disabilities and related issues, including a list of a wide range of publications, referrals to other disability organizations, and information searches of their databases and libraries. The NICHCY does provide responses to individual questions or concerns via e-mail and phone. This site can also be viewed in Spanish.

The American Academy of Pediatrics
National Headquarters:
141 Northwest Point Boulevard
Elk Grove Village, IL 60007-1098
(847) 228-5005
(847) 228-5097 (Fax)
Washington, DC, Office:
Department of Federal Affairs
601 13th Street NW
Suite 400 North
Washington, DC 20005
(202) 347-8600
(202) 393-6137 (Fax)
<http://www.aap.org>

Summary: The American Academy of Pediatrics is a membership organization for pediatricians and pediatric medical specialists. The Web site for the AAP provides current information on pediatric health for health care professionals and parents. Features of interest to parents include publications on child health and safety, immunization information, a pediatrician referral service, and questions and answers for families on managed care as well as links to other children's health sites on the Internet. A special feature on this site, "A Minute for Kids," provides audiofiles on children's health care topics that can be downloaded and listened to.

PEDINFO
<http://www.pedinfo.org>

Summary: PEDINFO is a Web site providing an index of on-line information on pediatric health and related issues for health care professionals and resources for parents. Although the criteria for resources included on this site require the information to be of use to pediatricians, there are many links for parents that direct them to other Web pages and on-line discussion groups for specific diseases or problems. There are also links to pediatric health organizations, government organizations, publications, and educational resources.

kidsDoctor
<www.kidsdoctor.com>

Summary: kidsDoctor is an on-line reference on children's health issues, safety, and parenting topics. The topic list is extensive, ranging from specific conditions to preventive health information. There is also a question-and-answer section that includes responses to e-mails written by Dr. Lewis A. Coffin III, M.D. This site has received numerous awards for its contents and usefulness.

The American Academy of Child and Adolescent Psychiatry (AACAP)
3615 Wisconsin Ave. NW
Washington, DC 20016-3007
(202) 966-7300
(202) 966-2891 (Fax)
<http://www.aacap.org>

Summary: The American Academy of Child and Adolescent Psychiatry is the national organization for medical professionals that provides services and information for medical professionals as well as parents with children afflicted with mental, behavioral, or developmental disorders. The Web site contains pertinent information on publications, organizations, and other resources relating to emotional, behavioral, and developmental disorders. There is also a national referral guide, organized by state, to finding a child or adolescent psychiatrist.

INSIGHT

Many of the comprehensive health organizations and Web sites listed in Part One, "Ourselves," also provide information related to the health and well-being of our children.

Well-Child Care, Including Immunizations and Accident Prevention

Well-child care has become part and parcel of good parenting. It is vital to the development of the infant and child. Regular well-child checkups help to monitor a child's growth and development so that measures can be taken where necessary to prevent or to correct potentially lifelong problems.

Well-child care includes regularly scheduled visits to the pediatrician, proper nutrition, and the appropriate immunizations. The recommended primary schedule of preventive immunization begins in infancy and is completed in early childhood (with the exception of boosters). The physician will administer these immunizations on the recommended schedule and provide the parents with a record, which they will be required to present when the child begins school. Well-child care also includes visits to the dentist.

Safety is critical to the well-being of our children. Accidents are not only the largest single cause of death in children but also the leading cause of permanent or temporary disabilities in children over the age of one. Accidents kill more children than the five leading fatal diseases combined. A parent's worst nightmare will become reality if their child is seriously disabled or killed as a result of a preventable accident. For the sake of your children reduce and, if possible, eliminate those elements that pose a serious safety risk for your children.

The following is a list of routine activities or occurrences that may place your children at risk for injury if safety precautions and common sense are not applied:

- *Bicycle riding.* Did you know that 900 bicycle riders are killed in the U.S. every year and that 75 percent of them die from head injuries? Do you need any other reason for making your child wear a helmet?
- *Swimming.* Did you know drowning is the second leading cause of injury-related death for children up to the age of four?
- *Riding in a car.* Did you know that for children up to the age of fourteen, injuries resulting from motor vehicle crashes are the leading cause of death?
- *Playing with or near fire.* Bad things happen when children are allowed to play with matches.
- *Faulty playground equipment.*
- *Unsafe toys and products.* The Consumer Products Commission is forever identifying toys and products specifically made for children that present serious dangers to children.
- *Failure to childproof the home.* There are many hazards within the home. Isn't it amazing children still fall out of windows?
- *Clothing with strings that can cause strangulation in infants and young children.* Clothing can be harmful to a child's health!
- *Unlocked firearms.* Did you know that firearms were involved in 29 percent of adolescent deaths in 1995?

To provide your child with a safe environment, the U.S. government suggests that all parents comply with the following safety guidelines.

Safety Guidelines Checklist—All Ages

_____Use smoke detectors in your home. Change the batteries every year and check once a month to see that they work.

_____If you have a gun in your home, make sure that the gun and ammunition are locked up separately and kept out of children's reach.

_____Never drive after drinking alcoholic beverages.

_____Use car safety belts at all times.

_____Teach your child traffic safety. Children under nine years of age need supervision when crossing streets.

_____Teach your children how and when to call 911.

_____Learn basic life-saving skills (cardiopulmonary resuscitation, or CPR).

_____Keep a bottle of syrup of ipecac at home to treat poisoning. Talk with a doctor or the local poison control center before using it. Post the number of the local poison control center near your telephone (and write it in the space under "Important Information"). Also, be sure to check the expiration date on the bottle of ipecac to make sure it is still good.

Safety Guidelines Checklist—Infants and Young Children

_____Use a car safety seat at all times until your child weighs at least forty pounds.

_____Car seats must be properly secured in the back seat, preferably in the middle.

_____Keep medicines, cleaning solutions, and other dangerous substances in childproof containers, locked up and out of reach of children.

_____Use safety gates across stairways (top and bottom) and guards on windows above the first floor.

_____Keep hot water heater temperatures below 120 degrees Fahrenheit.

_____Keep unused electrical outlets covered with plastic guards.

_____Provide constant supervision for babies using a baby walker. Block access to stairways and to objects that can fall (such as lamps) or cause burns (such as stoves).

_____Keep objects and foods that can cause choking away from your child, such as coins, balloons, small toy parts, hot dogs (unmashed), peanuts, and hard candies.

_____Use fences that go all the way around pools and keep gates to pools locked.

Safety Guidelines Checklist—Older Children

_____Until children are tall enough so that the lap belt stays on their hips and the shoulder belt crosses their shoulder, they should use a car booster seat.

_____Make sure your child wears a helmet while riding on a bicycle or motorcycle.

_____Make sure your child uses protective equipment for rollerblading and skateboarding (helmet, wrist, and knee pads).

_____Warn your child of the dangers of using alcohol and drugs. Many driving- and sports-related injuries are caused by the use of alcohol and drugs.

RESOURCES

The National SAFE KIDS Campaign
1301 Pennsylvania Ave. NW, Suite 1000
Washington, DC 20004-1707
(202) 662-0600
(202) 393-2072 (Fax)
<http://www.safekids.org>

Summary: The National Safe Kids Campaign is the first and only national organization dedicated solely to the prevention of unintentional injury— the number one killer of children ages fourteen and under.

U.S. Consumer Product Safety Commission (CPSC)
Washington, DC 20207
(800) 638-2772
<http://www.cpsc.gov>

Summary: The U.S. Consumer Product Safety Commission is a federal regulatory agency that provides information on general safety concerns, including information on safety risks from consumer products. One feature on the Web site is "Kidd Safety," an interactive learning tool that helps children learn about safety concerns related to the home, playing sports, and using consumer products through game playing. Other features on the site include resources for additional safety information and a reporting system for unsafe products.

American Burn Association
National Headquarters Office
625 N. Michigan Avenue, Suite 1530
Chicago, IL 60611
<http://www.ameriburn.org/home.htm>

Summary: The American Burn Association is a national association of professionals providing information, research, and education on all aspects of burns and related care. The Web site provides resources for publications, on-line discussions, and links to related sites pertaining to child safety issues such as safe sleepwear and the safe use of fireworks.

> **Bicycle Helmet Safety Institute**
> 4611 Seventh Street South
> Arlington, VA 22204-1419
> (703) 486-0100
> (703) 486-0576 (Fax)
> <http://www.helmets.org>

Summary: The Bicycle Helmet Safety Institute is a nonprofit helmet advocacy program affiliated with the Washington Area Bicyclist Association. The Web site provides information on how to buy a bicycle helmet, helmet and injury statistics, and a newsletter with updates on helmet information and related safety issues.

> **National Center for Injury Prevention and Control (NCIPC)**
> Mailstop K65
> 4770 Buford Highway NE
> Atlanta, GA 30341-3724
> (770) 488-1506
> (770) 488-1667 (Fax)
> <http://www.cdc.gov/ncipc/ncipchm.htm>

Summary: The National Center for Injury Prevention and Control is a program established by the Centers for Disease Control and Prevention. The primary purpose of the NCIPC is to reduce injury and its associated costs outside the workplace. The Web site offers national statistics on injuries and resources on prevention. Fact sheets on such issues as youth violence in the United States and playground safety are very helpful.

Click on <http://www.Boomerbasics.com> for safety precautions you should take around infants and children. Use the checklist of important safety precautions to measure how safety conscious you are!

Poison Control

Childhood poisoning is yet another example of deleterious and often tragic events that could have been prevented with simple precautions. For example, lead poisoning is entirely avoidable, yet according to the CDC, nearly one million children living in the United Sates have lead levels in their blood that are high enough to cause irreversible damage to their health.

Your child can be poisoned in many other ways, including taking unprescribed medication, eating household plants, and drinking poisonous household products. When you suspect that your child has ingested a poisonous substance, you should immediately contact your local poison control center.

RESOURCES

American Association of Poison Control Centers
<http://www.aapcc.org>

Summary: The American Association of Poison Control Centers is a membership organization that provides information on poison control and related topics. Nonmembers can access the closest poison control center by using the map provided, using the directory, or entering a ZIP code. This site is not intended to provide treatment for poisoning. It has a very comprehensive list of links to other related sites that may be helpful in non-emergency situations.

Medical History

It is very important for parents to have readily available their children's medical history, which will provide doctors and other health care professionals the information that they will need to properly diagnose and treat any health problems. In an emergency situation, for example, where your child needs immediate medical care, it is important for the doctor to know if your child has allergies, asthma, epilepsy, diabetes or other medical conditions that will adversely or positively impact on your child's treatment and recovery. Even in a situation that is not an emergency, information about your child's medical history will ensure that your child receives proper care. The medical provider will need to know if your child has received up-to-date vaccinations and any medications he or she is taking. You also need to include information about your child's family medical history, which will indicate if the child is especially prone to certain illnesses or conditions.

Moreover, you need to be sure that you inform any child care provider or babysitter about your child's medical needs and what steps need to be taken if a health-related problem develops. According to the CDC, you should provide your child care provider with the health history and immunization information, including, but not limited to, the following:

- Where parents can be reached—full names and work and home phone numbers and addresses.
- At least two people to contact if parents can't be reached—phone numbers and addresses.
- The child's regular health care providers—names, addresses, and phone numbers.
- The hospital that the child's family uses—name, address, and phone number.
- Any special health problems or medical conditions that a child may have and procedures to follow to deal with these conditions. Examples of conditions needing special procedures are allergies, asthma, diabetes, epilepsy, and sickle-cell anemia. These conditions can cause sudden attacks that may require immediate action. You should explain 1) what happens to the child during a crisis related to the condition, 2) how to prevent a crisis, 3) how to deal with a crisis, and 4) whether the child care provider or babysitter needs training in a particular emergency procedure.
- The child's vaccination status.
- Whether the child has been evaluated with a tuberculosis (TB) skin test (using the tuberculin-purified protein derivative [PPD]).

Medical First Aid Kit

There is no substitute for preparation. It is inevitable that your child will experience scrapes and bruises and other injuries, hopefully none too serious, that will require first aid.

You should always have readily available a fully stocked medical first aid kit in case of a medical emergency. Click on http://www.Boomerbasics .com for what items should be included in such a kit.

Medical Conditions Affecting Our Children

Be it the common cold or potentially deadly diseases such as AIDS, our children are susceptible to challenges to their health and well-being. In this section, we provide you with basic health information and related resources regarding AIDS, the common cold, conjunctivitis (pink eye), ear infections, allergies, asthma, and juvenile diabetes.

INSIGHT

Look to <http://www.Boomerbasics.com> and the Web sites listed throughout this section as well as the comprehensive health care sites listed in Part One, "Ourselves," for more information about these and other medical issues confronting our children.

After our discussion on these medical conditions, we will shift our focus to the onset of puberty. In addition to attitude, puberty brings with it a host of potentially serious health issues that we must be prepared to deal with as parents.

INSIGHT

Think of your child's puberty as a second bite of the apple—in other words, see if you can help your teenagers avoid or minimize the problems you encountered when hormones took control of *your* body.

AIDS

According to the CDC, in 1997 there were over eight thousand reported cases of acquired immune deficiency syndrome (AIDS) in children younger than thirteen years of age and over three thousand adolescents with AIDS; the CDC's statistics reveal that over 90 percent of the AIDS cases reported for children under the age of thirteen resulted from prenatal transmission of the HIV virus. Given the dramatic decline in the percentage of deaths caused by AIDS for people of all ages, there is optimism among health care professionals that many infants and children with AIDS may also be treated effectively with medication recently approved by the FDA.

Parents and health care professionals must face the difficult issue of how much information to disclose to a child with AIDS. In a policy statement titled "Disclosure of Illness Status to Children and Adolescents with the HIV Infection," published in January 1999, the American Academy of Pediatrics generally recommends disclosure consistent with a variety of factors including age, cognitive ability and clinical status.

RESOURCES

The Elizabeth Glaser Pediatric AIDS Foundation
2950 31st Street
Santa Monica, CA 90405
(310) 314-1459
<http://www.pedaids.org>

Summary: This is an excellent site. In addition to providing useful information, the foundation's goal is to identify, fund, and conduct critical AIDS research that will lead to the prevention and treatment of HIV infection in infants and children.

National Pediatric and Family HIV Resource Center
University of Medicine and Dentistry of New Jersey
30 Bergen Street—ADMC #4
Newark, NJ 07103
(973) 972-0410
(800) 362-0071
(973) 972-0399 (Fax)
<http://www. Pedhivaids.org>

Summary: The National Pediatric and Family HIV Resource Center is a nonprofit organization that serves professionals who care for children, adolescents, and families dealing with HIV infection and AIDS. This site provides factual, statistical, and treatment information regarding pediatric AIDS.

American Academy of Pediatrics
National Headquarters
141 Northwest Point Boulevard
Elk Grove Village, IL 60007-1098
(847) 228-5005
(847) 228-5097 (Fax)
<http://www.aap.org>

Summary: The American Academy of Pediatrics provides numerous resources on pediatric HIV and related illnesses. This site's links include an Internet Resource Guide that contains information on HIV education and teenagers, AIDS prevention, and detection and support services.

Common Cold

The *common cold* is a term used to describe an inflammation of the respiratory tract caused by various viruses. Symptoms may include nasal congestion, runny nose, cough, fever, fatigue, irritability, and decreased appetite. Because colds are generally viral, they usually do not respond to antibiotics. However, bacterial ear infections or bronchitis may follow, and these diseases *do* require antibiotics. Treatment is generally symptomatic and takes such forms as drinking more fluids, resting, and taking medications. Because colds are spread through person-to-person contact of respiratory secretions, it may be a good idea to keep contact with others to a minimum and to wash your hands often.

Conjunctivitis (Pink Eye)

Conjunctivitis, or *pink eye,* is an infection on the inside of the eyelid that gets its name from its visual appearance. Symptoms of pink eye include redness, irritation, burning, itching, and drainage from the affected eye. It is contagious, and thorough hand washing is most important in preventing occurrence in the unaffected eye and spreading this condition to others.

Conjunctivitis can be caused by bacteria or viruses as well as allergies or chemicals. Treatment depends on the causative agent and may range from alleviating the symptoms to a regimen of antibiotics.

Ear Infections

Infections of the middle ear, otherwise known as *otitis media,* are very common in children. In fact, recent data indicates that ear infections represent almost 30 percent of visits to the pediatrician, and at least 66 percent of children will have one ear infection by the age of three. Many parents watch helplessly while their child suffers in pain, tugging at his or her ears, or just becomes very irritable. Once told of an ear infection, parents often worry if it will become a chronic problem and portends surgery in their child's future.

Manifestations of ear infections may include but are not limited to pain, rubbing or tugging at the ear, irritability, fluid draining from the ear, nasal congestion, fever, and sometimes loss of appetite. However, signs and symptoms vary from child to child, and some children have minimal signs until the pain is severe.

Ear infections are generally treated with antibiotics in acute stages and as a preventive measure. There are also surgical procedures that involve draining the fluid from the ear and then placing tubes inside the ear to continue the draining process.

Some of the long-term effects from chronic ear infections include hearing loss and speech and language problems.

RESOURCES

American Academy of Audiology
8300 Greensboro Dr., Suite 750
McLean, VA 22102
(703) 790-8466
(703) 790-8631 (Fax)
<http://www.audiology.com>

Summary: The American Academy of Audiology is dedicated to improving the quality of hearing services by providing information, education, and research for the profession as well as increasing the public's awareness of hearing problems and services available. The Web site contains a consumer section that provides information about hearing loss in infants and children. The site also offers tips on locating an audiologist in your area.

> **American Society of Pediatric Otolaryngologists (ASPO)**
> <http://www.entnet.org/aspo>

Summary: The American Society of Pediatric Otolaryngologists is dedicated to improving the care of children with hearing disorders. Although it is primarily geared to medical professionals, there are links on its site to other resources and institutions that parents may find helpful.

Allergies

Many children (and adults) have one or more allergies. You can be allergic to food, animals, hair, health and beauty products, molds, dust, pollen, plants, insect bites, medication, and so on. Tests can be performed to determine if you have allergies and, if so, to what substance or substances.

When you come in contact with a substance that gets on your skin or that you inhale or swallow and to which you are allergic, you will usually have an allergic reaction. The intensity, frequency, and duration of the reaction will vary based on a variety of factors. Allergic reactions can be mild to deadly. Such reactions will manifest themselves in ways such as wheezing, cough, redness or tearing of the eyes, stuffed or runny nose, sore throat, and the like.

Although no magical cure exists for the elimination of allergies, some children will outgrow them. Allergies can be controlled as well with medication, allergy shots, diets, and a number of other treatment options.

RESOURCES

> **National Institute of Allergies and Infectious Diseases (NIAID)**
> National Institutes of Health
> NIAID Office of Communication and Public Liaison
> Building 31, Room 7A-50
> 31 Center Drive MSC 2520
> Bethesda, MD 20892-2520
> <http://www.NIAID.gov>

Summary: This government site provides research information and links to other sites.

> **Asthma and Allergy Foundation of America (AAFA)**
> 1125 Fifteenth Street NW, Suite 502
> Washington, DC 20005
> (800) 7-ASTHMA

Summary: The AAFA is a not-for-profit organization dedicated to finding a cure for controlling asthma and allergic diseases. The AAFA sponsors chapters and support groups, provides educational materials, and also offers products and materials for sale.

> **American Academy of Allergy, Asthma and Immunology**
> 61 East Wells Street
> Milwaukee, WI 53202
> (414) 272-6071
> <http://www.aaaai.org>

Summary: This organization is dedicated to the study and treatment of allergy diseases through education, research, and cooperation. It offers many other services, including a physical referral directory and a patient/public resource center.

Asthma

Asthma is one of the leading childhood afflictions. More than one of every ten children suffers the misery of asthma attacks, which are characterized by constriction or spasms of the airways. This tightening is accompanied by swelling and the formation of mucus plugs, which leave less room for air to pass through. The result is the familiar asthmatic wheeze, which is actually the sound of air trying to pass through the narrowed opening. On top of the physical discomfort, the feeling of suffocating can terrify a child.

Most asthma starts within a child's first two years, and almost all asthmatics' problems begin before the age of five. Some causes for asthma appear hereditary. One study showed that 90 percent of asthmatic children have at least one parent with airway hyperactivity, which is a characteristic of asthma. A genetic inclination for asthma can become the real thing upon exposure to certain triggers, the more common of which include colds and infections; exercise; allergies to molds, pollens, animals, and certain foods; wind, rain, cold air, or other dramatic changes in the weather; medications; and such irritants as aerosol sprays, odors, smoke, dust, air pollution, paint fumes, and perfume.

The good news about asthma is that it may not last. About 50 percent of children with asthma are symptom free as adults, and another 25 percent grow up to have mild symptoms; only 25 percent of those who were asthmatic in childhood have severe symptoms as adults. In a typical case, asthma develops at some point during childhood and may even be severe throughout the growing years. As adolescence approaches, it usually lessens and often seems to disappear completely. Although there may be no active symptoms, airways still remain hypersensitive or hyperactive. In most instances, the abatement appears permanent, but unfortunately, sometimes the symptoms will reappear during adulthood, often at the end of a respiratory infection.

RESOURCES

National Heart, Lung and Blood Institute (NHLBI)
<http://www.nhlbi.gov>

Summary: The National Heart, Lung and Blood Institute (NHLBI) is a part of the National Institutes of Health (NIH). This site includes the "Asthma Management Model System," which provides users with information regarding asthma assessment, education, and research.

American Lung Association
<http://www.lungusa.org>

Summary: The American Lung Association is dedicated to fighting lung disease through education, community service, advocacy, and research. It has an excellent Web site that is dedicated in part to issues involving asthma.

Click on <http://www.Boomerbasics.com> for a list of national organizations that can guide you on the subject of asthma.

Juvenile Diabetes

Diabetes ranks third in chronic illnesses among school-aged children, peaking between the ages of ten and fourteen. The two major forms of diabetes are type 1 and type 2. Type 1, or insulin-dependent diabetes mellitus (IDDM), is characterized by a lack of insulin production and a tendency to develop *ketoacidosis,* a condition characterized by increased body acid. Most children with diabetes have this form. Type 2 diabetes (adult-onset diabetes) is strongly associated with obesity. In the rare instances when type 2 diabetes occurs in children, they are usually obese, and weight reduction is the primary treatment. Type 2 diabetes is characterized by a lack of responsiveness rather than a lack of production of insulin.

Early diagnosis of diabetes allows it to be controlled more easily and prevents potentially serious metabolic complications; therefore, understanding the disease and being able to recognize its symptoms are key. When insulin levels are decreased, the blood sugar level increases. This increased sugar spills into the urine, causing the kidneys to produce large volumes of urine. To compensate for the increased loss of fluids, the child gets very thirsty and drinks excessively. Because a diabetic cannot metabolize food properly, the child will eat excessively but will lose weight. In an effort to supply energy, the body will break down fats and produce an increased amount of acid.

As noted, the newly diabetic child will urinate, drink, and eat excessively but will lose weight. She may begin to wet the bed because of the excessive need to urinate. The child will also complain of excessive fatigue because of lower energy levels stemming from a malfunctioning metabolism.

The treatment for juvenile diabetes involves replacing the insulin the child is unable to produce naturally along with monitoring diet and encouraging exercise. These measures will help to regulate glucose (blood sugar) production and thus contribute to the child's normal physical and psychological development.

Most children with diabetes can control their condition with two to four injections of insulin a day. The precise dose of insulin will vary among children and is determined by the blood glucose level after the peak effect of the insulin has occurred. Glucose kits and machines are available to allow the child or family to measure blood glucose levels at home. By testing their own blood, children and parents are able to change the insulin regimen on their own according to guidelines set up by their physician.

Nutritional needs of diabetic children are no different than those of healthy children except that concentrated sugars must be omitted. Children with diabetes require no special foods or supplements. The distribution of carbohydrates, proteins, and fats for a diabetic child is similar to that for a healthy child—approximately 50 percent of the daily calories should be carbohydrates; 30 percent, fat; and 20 percent, protein. Approximately 70 percent of the carbohydrate content should be derived from complex carbohydrates such as pasta, whole grains, breads, and cereals, while highly refined sugars and concentrated sweets should be limited or avoided.

Exercise should be included as part of diabetes management. In general, the diabetic child is never restricted from participating in any sport. Insulin injections can be timed appropriately and diet can be adjusted to accommodate an exercise plan. Besides providing a feeling of well-being, regular exercise enhances the body's ability to metabolize food and may even decrease insulin requirements. Activities that require a lot of energy could lead to lower blood sugar levels; these, too, can be accommodated by providing the child with extra snacks before, or if prolonged, during the activity.

Even a well-monitored diabetic child may experience mild symptoms of hypoglycemia (low blood sugar). Prompt recognition of the signs and symptoms of hypoglycemia is essential. The most common causes are bursts of physical activity without additional food; delayed, omitted, or incompletely consumed meals; or too much insulin. The initial symptoms of mild hypoglycemia are hunger, weakness, lack of energy, and irritability. This is treated by eating a simple sugar, followed by a complex carbohydrate or protein. If a large and sudden drop in blood sugar occurs, the child may experience sweating, dizziness, nausea, vomiting, shakiness, and a rapid pulse. Recognition of these signs and symptoms is imperative to prevent coma or brain damage. This latter condition is treated by administering glucose immediately, followed by a meal of carbohydrates and protein.

Click on <http://www.Boomerbasics.com> for a list of national organizations that can guide you on the subject of juvenile diabetes.

Puberty—Gateway to Adulthood

"My little baby's growing up. . . ." Common words among parents—spoken with equal parts wistfulness, pride, and trepidation—as they witness their children starting out on the road to adulthood via that sometimes funny, sometimes torturous, always challenging route called puberty.

It's at once an exciting and a confusing time for adolescents and, conse-quently, for their parents. Teens may be thrilled about their bodily changes at the same time they're embarrassed by them, and they may struggle with adapting to an array of new and often conflicting feelings such as being self-conscious, angry, frightened, excited, or out of control. In other words, a girl may look like a woman but not feel like one, and a boy may feel like a man but not look like one. No wonder teenagers can feel so ambivalent about whether they really do want to grow up!

Parents can help to ease the transition by talking with their children ahead of time about the kinds of changes they can expect during puberty. Let them know how they will be developing physically and that they'll probably feel at times as though they're on an emotional roller coaster. It's also important to remind your children that kids go through puberty at dif-ferent ages, so they shouldn't feel weird or different if they're developing at a slower or faster rate than their peers.

Click on <http://www.Boomerbasics.com> for a wealth of informa-tion on talking with your kids about puberty. Resources include specifics on the types of physical and emotional changes they can expect, timelines for development, possible implications associated with precocious (early) puberty, how to talk with your children about their periods or wet dreams, and tips for helping adolescents (and parents) cope with these changes. The following Web sites might also offer you some guidance:

<http://www.plannedparenthood.org/teenissues/teenmainhtm/teenwire
    .com/index.asp.html> (A Planned Parenthood site with a good over-
    view for prepubescents on the types of physical changes that will occur
    in puberty)
<http://www.sexualitybytes.ninemsn.com.au/adult/growingup/puberty.
    html> (A good sampling of questions likely to arise in children's minds
    as they go through puberty)
<http://www.kotex.com/girlspace/> (Information for girls about the
    female body, feminine health, and menstruation)

Sexuality

You need to talk to your children about sex long before puberty. Many experts believe that six years of age isn't too early; some suggest you should begin to talk with your children about sex when they first start asking pertinent questions (for example, "Where do babies come from?"), which can happen at age three or four. If you put off talking with your kids about sex, they likely will go elsewhere for information, which may turn out to be incomplete, romanticized, or just plain wrong.

Click on <http://www.Boomerbasics.com> for tips on how to talk with your kids about difficult subjects. The following Web sites can also help:

<http://www.talkingwithkids.org/first.html> (Talking With Kids, a national campaign by Children Now and the Kaiser Family Foundation, provides helpful parent materials (a free booklet), national and community resources, and other readings for parents and children.)

<http://www.pta.org/programs/knottext.htm> (An edited transcript from a chat session on talking with your kids about sex)

Whatever age you decide is appropriate for talking with your children about sex, both boys and girls should already know certain things well before they reach their teens, including the names and functions of male and female sex organs, the purpose and meaning of puberty, the function of the menstrual cycle, what sexual intercourse is, and how women become pregnant.

When you explain things to your kids, use direct language. As difficult as it might be, call a penis a penis, a vagina a vagina. Relying on euphemistic "birds and bees" terminology will only confuse your children. In addition, if they see that you can talk about sex openly and honestly without being embarrassed, they're more likely to ask questions, which is exactly what you want!

The "how things work" lesson is only the beginning. As your children enter adolescence, your talks about sex should shift to the social and emotional aspects of sex. Acknowledge your teenagers' (perfectly natural) curiosity about sex and let them know they can talk with you about dating and relationships. These discussions will be a lot easier if you've opened the door to talking openly about sex with your children when they were younger.

INSIGHT

When your teenagers ask you questions about sex, you should answer in terms of your own values, even if you think they're old-fashioned by today's standards. If you strongly oppose sex before marriage, for example, you should tell your teenagers that, along with your reasons for feeling that way (being careful not to lecture or moralize). The fact that you have strong beliefs supported by sound reasoning will leave an impression on your teenagers and increase the likelihood that they'll adopt your values.

Before dating begins, ask your teenagers how they feel about dating, setting limits, and engaging in sexual activity. Find out what they know about sex and try to answer their questions directly and clearly. Ask them if they've thought about whether they're ready to have sex and what it signifies to them. Let them know it could be one of the most important decisions they'll ever make; tell them you want to ensure they've thought about all the implications so that they won't have any regrets later.

Setting limits is one thing; adhering to them is something else. Talk with your teens about the role of peer pressure. Help them to recognize that no one but them should determine when they're ready to have sex and that even if it *seems* as though all their friends are doing it, many teenagers are, in fact, deciding to delay sexual involvement. Discuss the dangers of acquaintance (date) rape, which are often heightened when teens are under the influence of drugs or alcohol. Explain to both your daughters *and* sons that no means no.

Any discussion with your adolescents about sex should address birth control and sexually transmitted diseases (STDs). Even if you've made your wishes clear about not wanting your children to have sex, the choice is ultimately theirs, and it should at least be an informed one to prevent an unwanted pregnancy. (Contraception, STDs, and teen pregnancy are all discussed later in this section.)

Whew! After all that, you're likely an old hand by now on talking with your kids about sex. But wait . . . you're not off the hook yet. Two of the most difficult subjects for many parents to address with their children are masturbation and forms of sexuality (that is, heterosexuality, homosexuality, and bisexuality). Both subjects have long been associated with a great deal of shame, leading many teenagers to feel that any thoughts or actions along these lines are abnormal or sick.

Masturbation is a normal and healthy part of human sexuality, as are questions about sexual orientation. Young people often wonder whether they're gay or lesbian when they find themselves attracted to a friend or teacher of the same sex. Such attractions are normal and do not necessarily mean your teenagers are gay, lesbian, or bisexual. Or that might be exactly what they mean.

INSIGHT

Many parents have a hard time accepting that their teenagers are gay, thinking they must have done something wrong in raising their children. Even if you don't understand your children's gay or lesbian orientation, try to accept it. At the very least, let your teenagers know you won't reject them if they discover that they are, in fact, gay, lesbian, or bisexual.

Click on <http://www.Boomerbasics.com> or go to one of the Web sites listed below for information to help parents both accept *and* understand their gay, lesbian, or bisexual children.

<http://www.pflag.org/pflag.html> (Parents and Friends of Lesbians and Gays [PFLAG] homepage)
<http://www.dynapolis.com/PFLAG/understand.html> (Pamphlets and brochures recommended by PFLAG)
<http://www.gaywired.com/gaybooks/parenting.html> (Recommended books for parents of gay or lesbian children)

Teen Pregnancy

The good news is that teenage pregnancy rates have declined 19 percent in the last two decades and that more and more teens are using contraceptives the first time they have sex (presumably because of greater knowledge about sexually transmitted diseases and unwanted pregnancies). The bad news is that the numbers are still too high. Each year, one in nine young women between the ages of fifteen and nineteen will become pregnant, 90 percent of whom are unmarried and had no intention of becoming pregnant.

Unfortunately, no amount of education can guarantee your daughter won't become pregnant if she does decide to have sex. The best you can do as a parent is to provide her with the proper guidance and then hope she makes the right decision.

In addition to the risk of an unwanted pregnancy, sex increases teenagers' risk of exposure to STDs including but not limited to AIDS (HIV), chlamydia, genital warts, gonorrhea, hepatitis B, herpes, and syphilis. Approximately 86 percent of all STDs occur in people between the ages of fifteen and twenty-five. The only sure way to prevent STDs is not to have sex. If your teens do not postpone having sexual intercourse, they can minimize (though not entirely eliminate) their risk of contracting an STD by regular and proper use of latex condoms and limiting their sexual involvement to one partner.

Let your teens know about other types of birth control as well but be sure to emphasize that such methods will not prevent HIV infection or other STDs. Other types of contraception (and their relative effectiveness) include abstinence (100 percent); oral contraceptives such as birth control pills (99 to 100 percent when used properly); injectable synthetic hormones such as Depo-Provera (more than 99 percent); implantable hormone systems such as Norplant (97 to 99 percent); female condoms (95 to 96 percent); barrier methods such as the diaphragm and cervical cap (97 to 98 percent when used properly; high user failure makes them only 75 to 80 percent effective); intrauterine devices (IUDs) (95 to 98 percent); foams, creams, jellies, films, and suppositories (78 percent if used alone; 99 percent if used with condoms); fertility awareness methods (65 to 85 percent); sterilization (99.6 percent); and withdrawal (coitus interruptus) (75 to 85 percent).

Click on <http://www.Boomerbasics.com> or visit one of the following Web sites for more in-depth information on the different methods of birth control, including overviews of the advantages and disadvantages of each method.

RESOURCES

Planned Parenthood
(800) 230-PLAN
<http://www.plannedparenthood.org/BIRTH-CONTROL/Index
   .htm>

Summary: Planned Parenthood is a nonprofit international organization that believes it is every person's right to make an informed choice on having children. The site features information regarding birth control with a specific site for birth control for teenagers. The homepage has links to information on sexually transmitted diseases and a site for teens to talk about relationships and sexuality.

> **Sexuality Information and Education Council of the United States (SIECUS)**
> 130 West 42nd St., Suite 350
> New York, NY 10036
> <http://www.siecus.org>

Summary: The Sexuality Information and Education Council of the United States is a nonprofit national organization that promotes education and provides information and resources on sexuality. There is a specific section devoted to parents with many materials on how to educate your children on sexuality and birth control. The site also provides resources such as publications and reviews of videos to enhance education of children.

After talking with your teens how *not* to become pregnant, you should discuss with them what they would do if they in fact became pregnant. Ask them how they think a baby would change their lives, whether they think they're ready to have a child, and how they would manage financially. Such thought-provoking questions can be real eye-openers, and helping your teens to understand the implications ahead of time may prevent them from taking unnecessary risks.

Acne

Acne—otherwise known as the bane of almost every teenager's existence. The fact that 85 percent of people between the ages of twelve and twenty-five develop acne is small comfort to most adolescents, who rarely can see beyond the zit at the end of their nose to notice others' blemishes.

Although no one knows for sure exactly what causes acne, researchers do know that it usually starts in adolescence (probably brought on by hormonal changes) and that heredity plays a big role (one more thing your teens can blame you for!). Stress also has been targeted as a contributing factor (witness the zit that pops up right before a big date).

Most teens can handle the occasional pimple, but severe acne can cause physical scarring and leave teens feeling insecure and inferior. Lest you've forgotten the angst of dealing with acne when you were a teen (unless, of course, you were one of the fortunate few blessed with a clear complexion), remember that acne outbreaks are usually a *big deal* to teenagers.

You can help not only by empathizing but also by offering suggestions to help them combat those "unsightly blemishes." Because there's nothing they can do about their genes, have them focus on those areas they can control. Help them to determine if outbreaks occur at particular times or after eating certain foods. Although it's not been proven that foods such as chocolate, nuts, cola drinks, potato chips, french fries, and other junk foods cause or exacerbate acne, it can't hurt for your children to cut down on or eliminate certain foods if they notice an outbreak shortly after eating them.

If your teenagers have a mild case of acne that doesn't clear up after they wash their face once or twice daily, they could try an over-the-counter, topical acne medication. A dermatologist can prescribe drugs for more severe cases.

Eating Disorders

Many of us are all too familiar with this health issue. In fact, the American Anorexia Bulimia Association states that over five million Americans—including 1 percent of U.S. teenagers—suffer from some type of eating disorder. Teenagers, particularly high school girls, are very concerned about their appearance and sometimes take very drastic steps to lose weight because they perceive themselves as fat. Drastic dieting coupled with strenuous exercise programs and poor self-image and thus poor self-esteem can lead to serious health problems, even death, if not noticed and treated properly.

There are several types of eating disorders. *Anorexia nervosa* is a condition whereby the individual is preoccupied with thoughts of being fat and therefore eats very little. Some of the signs to look for are loss of weight with continued dieting because of still feeling fat, preoccupation with food and nutrition, anxiety, depression, irregular menstrual cycles, weakness, heart tremors, and fainting spells.

Bulimia is a condition in which an individual eats a lot of food at one time and then purges the food, either by manually triggering vomiting or using some type of medication to induce vomiting. The signs of this condition differ from anorexia in that the individual may not be underweight—in fact, he or she may be overweight. Symptoms of this disorder include uncontrolled eating habits, going to the bathroom right after a meal, depression, irregular menstrual cycles, and a feeling of being out of control.

If anorexia or bulimia is suspected, psychological help should be obtained as soon as possible, along with medical evaluation of the individual's physical condition. Often, these disorders affect an entire family, and family counseling may be recommended.

RESOURCES

American Anorexia Bulimia Association, Inc.
165 West 46th Street, Suite 1108
New York, NY 10036
(212) 575-6200
<http://www.aabainc.org/>

Summary: The American Anorexia Bulimia Association is a nonprofit organization that provides information to the public and professionals on eating disorders, including prevention and treatment. The Web site offers excellent information about specific disorders and resources for additional information. There is also a link for families and friends who want help in understanding eating disorders.

KidsHealth.org
<http://kidshealth.org/teen/bodymind/eat_disorder.html>

Summary: KidsHealth.org offers a section devoted to teens and eating disorders that provides a list of warning signs of anorexia and bulimia as well as a list of resources that teens can access for more information.

The American Academy of Child and Adolescent Psychiatry (AACAP)
3615 Wisconsin Ave. NW
Washington, DC 20016-3007
(202) 966-7300
(202) 966-2891 (Fax)
<http://www.aacap.org>

Summary: The American Academy of Child and Adolescent Psychiatry contains numerous articles and publications on eating disorders for both teens and their families. There are also clinical practice guidelines for professionals that provide assessment and treatment options that may provide more information regarding eating disorders for the public.

Paying for Your Child's Health Care

If you do not have health insurance or if your health insurance is inadequate, your out-of-pocket health care expenses can be substantial. You need to be familiar with your health insurance options and determine if you or your family is entitled to government assistance to help you pay for health care.

Click on <http://www.Boomerbasics.com> for information regarding health insurance.

RESOURCES

Health Care Financing Agency (HCFA)
Children's Health Insurance Program (CHIP)
7500 Security Blvd.
Baltimore, MD 21244-1850
(410) 786-3000
<http://www.hcfa.gov>

OUR PARENTS

With a combination of love, commitment, frustration, obligation, guilt, and sense of responsibility, we rearrange our schedules to drive them to their appointments—and if they are out without us, we worry that they'll get home okay; we disagree over what they are and are not capable of doing but want to respect their independence; we get used to being challenged or corrected when we are not even wrong, or at least we don't think we're wrong; we are alerted to any cough, sneeze, or sniffle, hoping it's not the start of something worse; we have to suggest things in such a way that they think the idea was theirs; we sometimes see ourselves when we look into their faces, ever more so with every passing day; we find ourselves doing things that annoyed us when they did it and sometimes still does; we still hate to admit that we enjoy their bragging about us to their friends; and most of all, we find it difficult to watch them move through the aging process. Loving a parent is not always easy.

To many of us, our parents, along with our children and spouses, are the bedrock of our most precious and meaningful relationships. So for whatever faults, habits, or characteristics they may have, acquire, or amplify in older age, we hope that we have our parents available to participate in our lives and our children's lives for as many years as possible.

Confronting the fact that our parents are aging is not easy. (It's hard enough confronting our own aging.) Between our busy schedules, their equally busy schedules, and the unpopular nature of some issues relevant to their aging, it is easy to continue to not address the matter. But to reduce the potential financial and emotional costs, it must be addressed—and hopefully early on and together, because some of the potential burden and uncertainty about the future can be lessened through sound planning. Although planning can't erase the fear of illness, the burden of care, and the sorrow of death, it can lighten some of the load that accompanies such potentially difficult times.

Having a better understanding of the diverse issues that our parents face as they enter the latter phases of their lives will not only allow us to be a greater resource for them but will also give us a view of what we might expect for ourselves. Also, being more sensitive to these matters will enable us to formulate and ask questions that our parents may not raise on their own. Too often our parents are accepting of the status quo or answers given by doctors, lawyers, and other professionals and institutions, because their assumption has been that any answer they receive from such sources is correct, and they trust that it is definitive. Having been raised in more skeptical times, we do not necessarily accept everything at face value, or we recognize that often there are alternatives to one professional's advice. Most qualified professionals are not offended by constructive advocacy, so we can often help our parents reach a more satisfactory resolution. Even if it is the same as the original one, we can make them more comfortable in understanding how the answer was reached.

The following section explores many issues relevant to our parents that can both enhance our relationship with and facilitate our assistance to them. Whether the discussions are initiated while golfing with our parents, picking our kids up after our parents have watched them, or sitting down with them and a professional advisor, this material can help them get the process started. Alternatively, if the discussions are initiated because a parent is in the early stages of Alzheimer's disease, a debilitating illness, or death, the following section can minimize some of the confusion, misinformation, and anxiety surrounding the situation. Either way, we should be ready, willing, and more able to reprioritize our lives as necessary to become the resource our parents now need or will need in the not-too-distant future.

Regardless of whether we appreciate our parents because they made us talented, successful, thoughtful, hardworking, athletic, or caring or only because they simply made us, and although their interaction with us may not always be beneficial or welcomed, we ultimately want to be a resource for them to the fullest extent possible.

PERSONAL ~~~~~~~~

Implications of Aging

For some, the physical changes and the loss of sex appeal (real or imagined) may be the most challenging aspects of aging. "Mirror, mirror on the wall, who's the . . ." Oh well, never mind! For others, being forced to retire, the fear of debilitating illnesses, the nightmare of Alzheimer's disease, the inevitable death of oneself and one's spouse, indeed, the whole array of losses and endings presents a daunting emotional challenge in print, never mind in real life! And believe it, the concerns are there, whether your parents express them or gloss over them. Being sympathetic, or at least cognizant, of these changes can enhance our relationship with our parents as well as make us a better resource for them if need be.

Longevity

The life expectancy of our parents exceeds the life expectancy had by their parents. We can expect to have a life expectancy longer than our parents', and in all likelihood our children's life expectancy will far exceed ours. As we all live longer, we must consider the opportunities and challenges that will confront our parents as well as ourselves in the latter part of our lives.

Increased Life Expectancy and Its Implications

The following statistics were reported in *A Profile of Older Americans: 1998,* a brochure prepared by the Program Resources Department, American Association of Retired Persons (AARP), and the Administration on Aging (AOA), U.S. Department of Health and Human Services (Washington, DC; 1998):

- The older population (people sixty-five years of age or older) numbered 34.1 million in 1997.
- By 2030, there will be about seventy million older people, more than twice their number in 1997.
- In 1997, people reaching the age of sixty-five had an average life expectancy of an additional 17.6 years. In other words, if your parents live to the age of sixty-five, their life expectancy increases to almost eighty-three and a half years.
- A child born in 1997 could expect to live seventy-six and a half years, about twenty-nine years longer than a child born in 1900.

These statistics clearly show that our parents, our children, and ourselves can expect (and hope for) long lives. However, a longer life expectancy does not necessarily ensure a healthy, fulfilling, and prosperous life, especially in the later years, as noted in the following statistics compiled by AOA and AARP in that same brochure:

- Most older persons have at least one chronic condition and may have multiple conditions. The most frequently occurring conditions per 100 elderly in 1994 were arthritis (50), hypertension (36), heart disease (32), hearing impairments (29), cataracts (17), orthopedic impairments (16), sinusitis (15), and diabetes (10).
- Older people accounted for 40 percent of all hospital stays and 49 percent of all days of care in hospitals in 1995.
- Although a small number (1.4 million) and percentage (4 percent) of the population over the age of sixty-five lived in nursing homes in 1995, the percentage increased dramatically with age, ranging from 1 percent for people sixty-five to seventy-four to 5 percent for people seventy-five to eighty-four and 15 percent for people eighty-five and older.

The following data from the Alzheimer's Association and the National Center for Health Statistics point to other implications of aging:

- According to the Alzheimer's Association, approximately four million Americans have Alzheimer's disease, including one in ten people over the age of sixty-five and nearly half of those over eighty-five.
- The data collected in the 1995 National Health Interview Survey conducted by the National Center for Health Statistics further illustrated the correlation between aging and chronic health conditions. For example, individuals sixty-five years of age and older had a significantly greater incidence of many chronic conditions, including but not limited to arthritis; vision impairment, including cataracts and glaucoma; hearing impairments; gastritis; diabetes; anemia; kidney trouble; bladder disorders; prostate disease; heart disease; hypertension (high blood pressure); cerebrovascular disease; hardening of the arteries; and emphysema.

Although chronic health problems will arise more frequently as our parents (and we) get older, it is important to note that not all older people will be affected by them, at least not to a degree that would severely hamper their independence. In an AOA study conducted in 1996, it was reported that twenty-two million individuals ages sixty-five to eighty-four (more than three-fourths of the population in that age group) have neither mobility nor self-care limitations, compared with five million in the same age group who do.

Not only will most of our parents live into their seventies and eighties, but the majority of them will also remain at home. According to the AARP/AOA study:

- Eighty percent of older men and 57 percent of older women lived either with their spouses, children, siblings, or other relatives.
- Approximately 31 percent of all noninstitutionalized older persons in 1997 lived alone; this figure represents approximately 41 percent of older women and 17 percent of older men. Living alone correlates with advanced age and, given that women tend to outlive men, it is not surprising that a greater percentage of older persons living alone are women.
- The need for nursing facility care increases with age.

This brief statistical analysis demonstrates some of the details of the phenomenon of aging that our parents and ourselves will undergo. We can also conclude from it that we will all age in our own unique way. We must simultaneously be mindful of the aging process while at the same time encouraging our parents' independence and quality of life.

RESOURCES

Several on-line and off-line government resources can provide statistical information about our parents, our children, and ourselves. If you like statistics, you can get as much information from these sources as you need to satisfy your quantitative appetite.

Administration on Aging
National Aging Information Center
330 Independence Ave. SW
Washington, DC 20201
<http://www.AOA.gov/stats/statpage.html>

Summary: This site offers a potpourri of statistical information on older persons.

Fedstats
<http://www.FEDSTATS.gov>

Summary: The Federal Interagency Council on Statistical Policy maintains this site to allow for easy access to the full range of statistics and information provided by over seventy federal agencies.

INSIGHT

Although statistics help us understand ourselves and our loved ones and help us plan for the future, we are all unique human beings and we should, we must, always respect and cherish how precious we are as individuals, not as numbers.

Changes in Physical Appearance

Remember the ads for Geritol that featured two gray-haired adults on motorcycles riding off into the sunset? That picture of old age is as stereotypical in its own way as that of Granny in her rocker with her hand cupped to her ear— "the better to hear you with, my dear." Individuals age differently. Although certain changes in appearance are an inevitable consequence of aging, genetics can greatly affect the rate at which such changes occur. Certain seventy-year-olds can look younger and have more energy than some forty-year-olds, perhaps because their skin retains its elasticity longer, their immune systems stay stronger longer, and their nervous systems retain the ability to maintain bodily integration and to prevent bodily deterioration.

Whenever these physical changes occur, however, they more often than not have a profound emotional impact. As with most things, our parents cope with the entire aging process—graying hair, wrinkles, bifocals, canes, difficulty in hearing—in different ways. Some seek the fountain of youth through cosmetic surgery; others accept changes more or less gracefully. Not being able to do the things they once could is likely to be an ongoing source of frustration as each new limitation manifests itself.

RESOURCES

Note: Refer to the "Ourselves" section, "Physical Changes in Appearance and Performance" (pages 6–8), for additional information and resources.

Fit for Life
181-I Nantucket Road
Clarksville, TN 37040
(888) 479-9355
<http://www.iamfitforlife.com>

Summary: Created by a physical therapist, this Web site offers inspirational stories, tips, and exercise products that are appropriate for the mature exerciser.

Cosmetic Surgery Network
Plastic Surgery Network
3 Via Pasa
San Clemente, CA 92673
<http://www.cosmetic-surgery.net/home.html>

Summary: This referral source for participating plastic surgeons provides consumers with comprehensive information on individual procedures, fees, and insurance coverage data.

Loss of Autonomy

Our parents may fear the loss of autonomy that comes with age more than the physical signs of its advent. For some who are afflicted with a mental or physical disease, the loss of self-sufficiency can be quick and painful. For others, it may be more gradual but insidious nonetheless.

Perhaps the most acute loss of autonomy is that caused by a catastrophic stroke, which can leave its victim paralyzed, without speech, and depending on its severity, cognitively impaired as well. Within minutes, a stroke can rob a wholly functional person of his or her independence.

The more gradual decline associated with aging presents its own challenges as routines that once were the norm become difficult or impossible. Driving an automobile is a classic example. In some of our parents' circles, the most important criteria for someone looking for a new spouse is whether the gentleman or lady can drive at night! When driving is no longer safe, the person has lost the capacity to travel independently. The license to drive that many teenagers long for becomes forbidden to the adult.

Click on <http://www.Boomerbasics.com> for resources that can help seniors to determine whether it is still safe for them to drive and to cope with the loss of the privilege. Also see "Housing and Support Services for Parents Living at Home" later in this book, which discusses transportation issues for older people.

Sex

Although sex seems to be on everyone's mind—from radio and TV talk shows to fashion and Madison Avenue ads—the elderly are generally not represented in this sexual sideshow. Given the physical and often cognitive decline that accompanies aging, it may be difficult to think of our parents as sexual beings. Because we probably had difficulty imagining our parents as sexually active in their youth, contemplating them having sex as they get older will surely make some of us blush.

Nevertheless, like all human beings, the elderly are capable of expressing their sexuality. As medical advances allow aging people to enjoy good health longer, many of us will thrive over the course of our long lives and continue to enjoy sex. Although some may face physiological obstacles to intimacy or a lack of privacy, sex remains a natural part of life for the elderly. For the physiological obstacles, such as impotency, medical treatments may help. And, of course, there's the miracle of Viagra. And that's good news for us, isn't it? Remember, we're not getting any younger either.

RESOURCES

> **Seniors-Site.com**
> c/o Walter J. Cheney
> 5443 Stag Mt. Road
> Weed, CA 96094
> (916) 938-3163
> <http://seniors-site.com/sex/index.html>

Summary: Provides resources and information designed to increase the sexual sophistication of older adults. Offers useful suggestions and recommendations for making adaptations to compensate for physiological changes experienced by many seniors.

> **Sexuality Later in Life**
> National Institute on Aging
> NIA Information Center
> PO Box 8057
> Gaithersburg, MD 20898-8057
> (800) 222-2225
> <http://www.aoa.dhhs.gov/aoa/pages/agepages/sexualty.html>

Summary: (Note that *sexuality* within the Web address is intentionally spelled incorrectly.) Fact sheet compiled by the National Institute on Aging that describes changes in sexual function caused by age, surgery, alcohol, and illness.

Mobility and Coordination

Aging affects mobility and coordination. To the extent that coordination involves the sensory organs to take in information, the nervous system to relay that information to the brain, the brain to decide on the appropriate action, and the muscles to perform that action, a loss of coordination could result from age-related changes to any of these systems.

Whether due to arthritis, failing eyesight, or dizziness stemming from chronic illness, high blood pressure, a reaction to medication, or some other factor, older people are much more prone than younger people to injury from falls. Common causes of falls include tripping or stumbling over something in the home; failing to successfully negotiate curbs, ramps, or stairs; and getting up and down from a bed, toilet, tub, and so on.

Click on <http://www.Boomerbasics.com> and review "Housing and Support Services for Parents Living at Home" later in this book for suggestions about home modifications to help prevent accidents and to facilitate independent living for older people. Also see "Health" later in this book for more information on the conditions that might increase your parents' susceptibility to injury from falls (for example, osteoporosis).

Whatever the cause, the result is an impaired ability to get around. If your parents have trouble walking long distances, standing for long periods of time, or maintaining their balance when doing either, they might benefit from a number of adaptive devices, including canes, walkers, wheelchairs, and motorized carts, to name a few. They also might consider obtaining a permit through the Department of Motor Vehicles to allow them to park in spots reserved for people with disabilities.

Despite the various aids available, the biggest hurdle might be getting your parents to admit they need assistance, particularly if they've been accustomed to leading an active life. Although the emotional adjustment might take some time, the physical adjustment likely will be easier than it used to be, thanks to the greater access afforded by passage of the Americans with Disabilities Act (ADA) in 1992.

The ADA requires public accommodations such as stores, restaurants, banks, and so on to provide people with disabilities equal access to the accommodation's goods and services, either by removing certain barriers or by making the goods and services accessible in another manner. For people with mobility impairments, reasonable accommodations might include installing automatic door openers, installing elevators or chair lifts, installing raised toilet seats and grab bars in restrooms, widening doors, lowering drinking fountains, creating accessible parking spaces, and making curb cuts in sidewalks and entrances.

RESOURCES

Americans with Disabilities Act Information
<http://www.usdoj.gov/crt/ada/>

Summary: This Web site, maintained by the U.S. Department of Justice, lists enforcement mechanisms for ADA violations in the areas of employment, housing, and public and commercial accommodations. For general ADA information, free ADA materials, or information about filing a complaint, call (800) 514-0301.

Entering Retirement

Current low levels of unemployment and the strong economy may give us cause to believe (or at least to hope) that the days of massive downsizing have passed. Although job security may never be what it was thirty years ago, the declining number of younger workers and the so-called graying of America might just lead employers to recognize the advantages of retaining their more experienced and knowledgeable senior employees to serve more or less as mentors to the younger workers who will eventually replace them.

Arrangements such as phased-in retirement, part-time employment, job sharing, and flexible workplace assignments can benefit everyone involved. If your parents are nearing retirement but want to continue working, encourage them to discuss such alternative work arrangements not only with their employer but with each other as well.

Click on <http://www.Boomerbasics.com> for additional information on alternative work arrangements, including the financial ramifications.

RESOURCES

Third Age Work
Third Age Media
585 Howard Street, 1st Floor
San Francisco, CA 94105-3001
<http://www.thirdage.com/work/>

Summary: Provides tips, strategies, and advice for the senior job hunter.

> **Employment and Older Americans: A Winning Partnership**
> Administration on Aging
> 330 Independence Ave. SW
> Washington, DC 20201
> (202) 619-0724
> <http://www.aoa.dhhs.gov/factsheets/employment.html>

Summary: The Administration on Aging maintains this fact sheet that describes trends in senior employment and lists federally funded senior employment opportunities.

The U.S. Department of Labor administers the Senior Community Service Employment Program (SCSEP) through state job service offices. The SCSEP is a program for low-income persons age fifty-five or over and can be reached at (202) 219-5904 or at <http://www.wdsc.org>.

Forced Retirement

For those of us who have worked most of our adult lives, the idea of not working simply never crosses our minds. For those whose eye is always on the next rung up the ladder, the end is never in sight. Even if work plays second fiddle to many other things, lots of us can't imagine not having that job and the accompanying paycheck. So close your eyes and imagine . . . no more work, no more titles, no more job routine, the retirement dinner is over, and everyone is back to work but you.

For many of our parents, forced retirement is a cruel joke. One minute they are in the catbird seat, with all the knowledge and experience of a lifetime of work, and the next minute they are yesterday's news, and someone younger is filling their shoes. Their days seem aimless, and time hangs heavily on them because all the important things are happening at the office. The emotional blow can pack the wallop of a physical punch. To many older people, everything looks as though life can only go downhill from there. Depending on the circumstances, however, they may have some rights to either keep their job or, at least, make the departure more beneficial for all of you.

Click on <http://www.Boomerbasics.com> for resources on age and employment discrimination in the workplace.

RESOURCES

Facts About Age Discrimination
<http://www.eeoc.gov/facts/age.html>

Summary: In this Web site, the Equal Employment Opportunity Commission explains the Age Discrimination in Employment Act, which protects individuals over the age of forty from workplace discrimination based on age. (User note: At the end of this site, click on "return to home page": once at the homepage, click on "filing a charge" for initial guidance on filing a complaint against an employer.) The Equal Employment Opportunity Commission may be reached at U.S.E.E.O.C., 1801 L Street NW, Washington, DC 20507, (202) 663-4900.

Employment Discrimination: An Overview
Legal Information Institute
Cornell Law School
Myron Taylor Hall
Ithaca, NY 14853
(607) 255-7193
<http://www.law.cornell.edu/topics/employment%5Fdiscrimination
%2ehtml>

Summary: This site is provided by the Legal Information Institute, which was created by Cornell University for the purpose of sharing university resources with interested individuals. Contained herein are recent court decisions as well as current statutes and regulations on age discrimination.

Factors Affecting the Adaptation to Retirement

Because retirement involves considerable planning and (usually) anticipation, being forced into it is akin to being thrown into the deep end of a swimming pool without knowing how to swim. Your parents probably will flounder and sputter for a while and might even feel as though they're drowning, but they'll eventually make it poolside by dog-paddling furiously, floating calmly, or getting back to dry land with the help of someone else. The same anxiety could result if they think they're ready and jump in only to find out it's not what they expected.

Although most people might think they'd have no trouble getting used to a life of not working, retirement is nonetheless a major life event that requires a period of adaptation. How your parents adapt will depend on whether retirement was forced or voluntary, how well they are prepared financially and emotionally, and how closely the reality of retirement mirrors their conception of what retirement would be like.

The beginning of retirement is often marked by a honeymoon phase, in which retirees try to do all the things they never had time for before (unless, of course, they aren't financially prepared for retirement, in which case they can't afford a honeymoon). This very active period may be followed by an "R and R" stage of low activity, when retirees relish the thought of just taking it easy. After sufficient rest and relaxation, most will begin to get restless and will resume a normal, more balanced level of activity. There might also be a period of disenchantment when the retiree discovers that retirement isn't all it's cracked up to be. Getting beyond this feeling usually requires retirees to realign their expectations and be more realistic.

Adapting to retirement is a process not only for retirees but also for their families. If, for example, your father retires first, he might drive your mother crazy in any number of ways. If Dad decides to help with the laundry and cooking, Mom might become a little upset upon discovering he washed a load of light reds in hot water or left the kitchen looking like a tornado zone after making dinner. Alternatively, Dad might decide that after so many years of working, he deserves a little leisure time, rationalizing, for example, that the lawn can go another week before it needs to be mowed. Or even though he is retired, your mom might not want to completely abandon her interests and activities all of a sudden.

If both parents retire at the same time, the result could be very good or very bad. They might revel in finally getting the chance to travel or to build the retirement home they've always dreamed of, or they might recoil from spending every waking moment together. They might decide to move further away to a warmer climate or closer so that they can see you and their grandchildren more often. Either way, it's likely to affect your relationship with them in some way.

If your parent is widowed, retirement may bring newfound loneliness that your mom or dad was able to avoid through working. The result might be withdrawal and depression or a greater reliance on you and your siblings for emotional support.

In all of the previous scenarios, it is likely your input will neither be sought nor welcomed, but with a heightened awareness you can be a greater resource in areas where your help will be needed now or later.

INSIGHT

You should suggest that your parents not make radical life changes soon after retirement. The benefits of moving far away, for example, even if it's to a better climate, must be balanced against substantially fewer visits and accessibility to loved ones such as children and grandchildren. The cold reality of barriers created by distance often eliminates the comforts of the warmer climate.

Legal Issues Involving Voluntary and Mandatory Retirement

With retirement comes a host of legal issues ranging from health insurance coverage as mandated by the Consolidated Omnibus Budget and Reconciliation Act (COBRA), pension and other financial benefits that may be triggered upon retirement, unemployment insurance, and the legality of mandatory retirement rules (and exceptions) to tacit and explicit age discrimination. You need to be aware of these and other related issues as they apply to your particular situation.

Click on <http://www.Boomerbasics.com> for further discussion and available resources concerning these matters.

Retooling—Pursuit of Second Careers

Some researchers predict that the trend of the last forty-five years toward early retirement may be reversing, as changes in the age of eligibility for Social Security retirement benefits, Medicare, and private pensions, along with a decline in personal savings, lead more older workers to remain in or reenter the workforce.

Whether your parent went kicking and screaming into retirement or whether the passage was a bit calmer, the decision to pursue a second career may be motivated by financial need, a desire to continue learning or to stay busy, or an identity crisis (if your parent's life has been defined largely by his or her primary occupation), among other factors.

Whatever the reasons for reentering the workforce, similar challenges face most older workers: Despite a lifetime of experience, expertise, and skills, they spend, on average, about twice as long as younger workers in seeking new employment, and they frequently are offered considerably lower salaries in their new jobs; some become so discouraged as to stop looking for work altogether. In addition, the shift from a heavy industry and manufacturing economy to one that emphasizes high technology and a service orientation necessitates that many older workers be retrained to enter these new areas of job growth.

Such issues will also have implications for you if these trends continue. Even if the percentage of older workers who remain in the workforce declines slightly, the hordes of baby boomers will increase the number of people in the labor force who are fifty-five or older by 6.7 million. This increase is twice that projected for the total labor force!

Click on <http://www.Boomerbasics.com> for organizations that deal with employment issues as they relate to older workers.

Activities

The type and level of activities in which your parents engage are based not only on the availability of more free time (for example, because of retirement or the kids leaving home) but also on any physical, age-related limitations and a change in living situation (for example, moving to a retirement community or a nursing home).

You also might find that they're likely to spend most of their leisure time doing more of the things they've always done rather than trying lots of new activities (something you might find particularly comforting the next time you pick up your son from soccer practice and drop him off for his piano lesson, arrange for your daughter to ride home with her friend after rehearsing for the school play [reminding her to bring her violin home to practice], drive back to school to pick up the books your kids forgot, meet your spouse at the driving range to work on those pesky short irons, and have dinner in several shifts, all before hooking up with your reading group to discuss R.U. Ovkilter's *Finding Balance in 24 Hours,* while all you can handle by that time is a pop-up book).

Your parents will probably have no trouble keeping busy and, in fact, will likely be busier than ever before. Assuming that they can fit more into their schedules, numerous activities, organizations, and experiences are available to make retirement that much more enjoyable. The following will give you a head start in exploring several alternatives.

RESOURCES

The Older Americans Act Program may be reached through the Eldercare Locator at (800) 677-1116 or through an area agency on the aging.

The National Senior Service Corps oversees many senior volunteer programs including the Foster Grandparent program, the Senior Companion Program, and the Retired and Senior Volunteer Program (RSVP). It may be reached at (800) 424-8867.

The Service Corps of Retired Executives (SCORE) provides management counseling and training to first-time entrepreneurs and small business owners. The National Senior Service Corps or your local city or state aging agency can connect you to the nearest SCORE chapter.

Click on <http://www.Boomerbasics.com> to learn of other activities that may be of interest to your parent(s).

Advance Directives

Advance directives are written documents that serve as an individual's instructions regarding health care or property management. Authorized in virtually all states, they permit your parent to appoint you, another family member, a friend, or some other third party to act on your parent's behalf if your parent should subsequently become incapacitated.

Sometimes advance directives permit your parents to spell out in writing their wishes regarding medical treatment. Sometimes they address only either property management or health care. Sometimes both topics are covered in one document. In the absence of an advance directive, should one of your parents become incapacitated, you may need to have a guardian appointed by the court—an expensive and lengthy proceeding that can embroil the family in a legal nightmare at precisely the time you are looking for some measure of crisis control!

INSIGHT

Take steps to encourage your parents to execute these legal documents while they have the capacity to understand them, to ensure that their wishes will be honored.

INSIGHT

The names, types, and availability of advance directives vary from state to state, so it is important that you and your parents familiarize yourselves with the requirements in your state. **If your parents spend time in more than one state (perhaps they are so-called snowbirds who might live in New York but spend winters in Florida), they should consider executing documents consistent with each state's laws.**

Financial Decision Making—Powers of Attorney

Although many of our parents probably are reluctant to discuss their financial situations, they should be aware that problems may arise if they suffer a temporary or permanent loss of capacity. Who will step in to handle their financial matters? Who can endorse the pension or annuity check? Sign the deed for the house? Sell the stock? Designate a beneficiary? Banks and other financial institutions generally won't wink at a forged signature, and neither are they legally permitted to authorize the requests of a loving spouse, child, or other well-meaning person who does not possess written legal authority to act on behalf of the incapacitated person.

A *power of attorney* is a legal document, signed by your parents, that gives a third party the authority to make certain property, financial, and other legal decisions on your parents' behalf. When your parents execute a power of attorney, they give the agent access to and control over their assets. It is vital for you and your parents to understand the legal implications of this key to the bank, as it were. Although blank power-of-attorney forms can be purchased at stationery and legal supplies stores, your parents would do well to consult an attorney who can advise them on how best to limit or expand the authority of the agent to meet their needs and serve their best interests.

A *general power of attorney* often is used to handle one-time transactions or to manage money for a short time. If, for example, your parents spend the winter in Florida, at some time they may need to handle a banking transaction back home in Chicago. If they execute a power of attorney naming you as their agent, you can take care of the banking for them. Your parents can revoke such a power of attorney at any time. The agent's authority becomes effective immediately but will automatically terminate if your parents die or become mentally incapacitated.

When a parent is a victim of a catastrophic illness or disability, someone must still pay his or her rent or mortgage, medical bills, utilities, and credit cards. The general power of attorney is useless in such a circumstance because it is precisely when you need it—when your parent becomes incapacitated—that it fails.

Fortunately, your parent has the option to use a power of attorney that remains or becomes effective if they become disabled. A *durable power of attorney* gives your parent's agent immediate authority to act, and that authority continues even if your parent becomes incapacitated, which is why this power of attorney is called durable. Many states have a statutory durable power of attorney form that sets forth the powers that your parents can choose for their agents.

A *springing durable power of attorney* becomes effective upon the occurrence of a later event—typically a diagnosis by a physician of incapacity. Many people are comforted by the thought that the agent does not have any immediate authority. In other words, the agent can't act unless and until a determination of incapacity is made.

RESOURCES

> **CBS Marketwatch**
> <http://www.cbs.marketwatch.com>

Summary: This Web site offers a personal finance library which includes estate planning articles on topics such as powers of attorney.

INSIGHT

All powers of attorney die when the principal dies. If, for example, your mother (the principal) appoints you to act as her agent (attorney-in-fact), your authority ends upon her death.

Click on <http://www.Boomerbasics.com> for samples of selected state statutorily approved powers of attorney.

Health Care Decision Making

If your parents become incapacitated and unable to decide the course of their medical treatment, someone will have to make these decisions for them. Hospitals, nursing homes, and managed care organizations will look for someone who clearly has the authority to make such decisions. In many states a spouse, child, or other loved one will not be deemed to have legal authority to make such decisions unless your parent(s) has executed an advance directive. Such advance directives may include health care proxies and living wills.

Each state has its own laws as to how, when, and by whom health care decisions are made on behalf of an incapacitated person. You need to know the laws of the state where your parent resides. For example, will your state honor a health care proxy, living will, or both?

RESOURCES

Before I Die
The Robert Wood Johnson Foundation
Route 1 and College Road East
PO Box 2316
Princeton, NJ 08543-2316
(609) 452-8701
<http://www.pbs.org/wnet/bid>

Summary: This excellent site provides a full transcript of *Before I Die,* the PBS program sponsored by the Robert Wood Johnson Foundation. Several expert panelists exchange thoughts and insights on end-of-life issues.

10 Legal Myths about Advance Directives
<http://www.abanet.org/elderly/myths.html>

Summary: The American Bar Association has prepared responses to commonly held misconceptions relating to advance directives. The information is thorough and is entirely appropriate for lay people.

The American Bar Association also offers advance directive forms for each state and may be contacted at

American Bar Association
740 15th St. NW
Washington, DC 20005-1022
(202) 662-8690

Advance Directives Can Be a Gift to Loved Ones
<http://www.ktv-i.com/news/nf04_09_97b.html>

Summary: An article contained in the interactive health Web site Kaleidoscope that illustrates the importance of advance directives through a personal story.

Choice in Dying Advance Directives
Choice in Dying
1035 30th Street NW
Washington, DC 20007
(202) 338-9790
<http://www.choices.org/ad.htm>

Summary: This Web site is maintained by the not-for-profit organization Choice in Dying. The information provided is thorough. All end-of-life decisions are covered, and links to individual state statutes are provided. The user should be advised, however, that this group advocates full personal choice in all end-of-life matters, including euthanasia.

Health Care Advance Directives
<http://www.ama-assn.org>

Summary: The American Medical Association maintains this on-line booklet describing health care proxy and living will requirements and powers.

State-specific guidebooks about advance directives can be obtained from the following source:

Legal Counsel for the Elderly
AARP
PO Box 96474
Washington, DC 20090-6474
<http://www.aarp.org>

Health Care Proxy

A *health care proxy* allows your parents to appoint a third person to make health care decisions in the event your parents become incapacitated and unable to make them. Like durable powers of attorney, health care proxies are not just for seniors—you should have one, too.

The health care proxy generally applies to all health care decision making unless limited by the person signing the proxy. The health care proxy has the power to make decisions only when it has been medically determined by your parent's attending physician that he or she is incapable of making health care decisions. The more detailed your parents' instructions, the easier it will be for the proxy to make these decisions on their behalf. In discussing with your parents the scope of the proxy (assuming you are the appointed agent), be sure to ask them about their wishes and beliefs (religious and moral) regarding the extent of medical treatment they would desire in particular medical circumstances. You should also discuss their wishes concerning artificial nutrition and hydration (tube feeding).

INSIGHT

Your parents should keep the proxy with all other important papers. One copy should be kept in a wallet or purse; one should be given to you or whoever is the agent, and one should be given to your parent's doctor(s).

If your parents reside in a different state for part of the year, they should execute health care advance directives according to the laws of that state as well.

INSIGHT

You want to be sure that the proxy is legally effective. In New York, for example, the proxy must be signed by two independent witnesses; the agent may not be a witness. If the proxy is filled out incorrectly, it will be deemed defective.

Generally, any adult over the age of eighteen—a family member, a close friend, or another trusted person—can serve as the health care proxy. If your parents want to appoint their doctor, check the applicable state rules to determine whether any guidelines or limitations govern such an appointment.

If your parents live in a nursing home or other facility, also check to see whether special rules govern the appointment of an employee of the facility. Generally, only one person can be appointed as agent. However, if the law of the state where your parents reside permits the appointment of a successor or alternate agent, encourage your parents to do so in case the person originally appointed is unable, unwilling, or unavailable to act.

Generally, attorney assistance is not necessary to complete a proxy. If your parents have appointed each other and one of them becomes ill or incapacitated or dies, the health care proxy should be redone and a new agent appointed unless a successor agent was listed in the proxy form. If the health care agent is a spouse and your parents subsequently get separated or divorced, the proxy should be terminated and a new one executed that lists the new agent.

Living Will

A *living will* contains a person's written instructions regarding such issues as the withholding or withdrawal of life-sustaining treatment in certain medical situations. Your parents, for example, may want to refuse unwanted medical treatment, such as the administration of artificial food and water (or tube feeding), if faced with a terminal condition, permanent unconsciousness, or irreversible brain damage with no reasonable expectation of recovery. On the other hand, they may want to use the living will to declare their desire for any available life-sustaining treatment regardless of their medical condition.

Again, consult the laws of the state where your parents live to know what special limitations apply to living wills in that state. Some states, such as New York, do not have living will statutes, although both states provide for the appointment of a health care proxy. In these states, it is important that your parent's proxy know their wishes regarding artificial nutrition and hydration. Additionally, in states without a living will statute, if your parents sign a written document expressing their wishes regarding life-sustaining treatment, it may be considered substantial evidence of their wishes if the matter is subsequently reviewed by a court or a health care facility's ethics committee.

Guardianship

A *guardianship* is a legal relationship in which a court appoints you or another family member, friend, or independent third party, such as an attorney, to make certain personal or financial decisions for your parents because they can no longer make those decisions for themselves.

INSIGHT

The term for the court-appointed guardian may vary from state to state (for example, some states may refer to *conservators* or *committees*).

Click on <http://www.Boomerbasics.com> for selected state guardianship statutes.

Your parents may need a guardian if they become physically or mentally incapacitated because of an accident or disease or merely through the natural process of aging. This incapacity must pose a risk of harm to your parents that they do not understand. In that event, a guardianship would be necessary if your parents have not completed a durable power of attorney or a health care proxy.

INSIGHT

The appointment of a guardian is an intervention of last resort. For example, many states will not authorize the appointment of a guardian for an individual who has properly executed financial and health care advance directives and the agent is acting responsibly. For example, New York specifically provides that the court should not revoke a previously executed power of attorney or health care proxy unless it was executed while the person was incapacitated.

The appointment of a guardian is governed by state law, and each state's requirements will vary. Generally, however, a family member can ask the court to appoint a guardian. If you commence a guardianship proceeding, the court typically will appoint an impartial evaluator to interview your parent and you, other family members, and service providers and to make recommendations to the court. The court hears from all interested parties, especially the person who allegedly needs a guardian if that person is able to communicate his or her wishes. The court makes a final determination as to whether a guardianship is necessary only after a hearing is held, at which you (or whoever petitioned the court), the evaluator, the person alleged to be incapacitated, and his or her attorney (if he or she has one) are all present and heard.

The court typically will appoint a family member as guardian unless a material conflict appears to exist between that family member and the allegedly incapacitated person. The scope of the guardian's authority to make decisions is determined by the court. This authority might include the power to manage the monthly income and expenses of the incapacitated person, sell real or personal property, hire home health aides, apply for government benefits, or make health care treatment decisions. The guardian is a court-appointed fiduciary and, as such, his or her most important responsibility is to the incapacitated person. The guardian must protect the incapacitated person within the scope of the authority the court has granted the guardian.

Typically, the guardian's other responsibilities include providing the court with a yearly report on the status of the incapacitated person and his or her recommendation about whether the guardianship should continue. If the incapacitated person becomes able to make decisions for himself or herself, the guardianship can be terminated. The recovered incapacitated person, the guardian, or anyone who could have sought the appointment of a guardian can apply to the court to have the guardianship ended.

When the guardian is appointed, the court generally fixes the fee that will be paid to the guardian for his or her services, and this fee is paid from the incapacitated person's assets. Guardianship can be an expensive and time-consuming process.

RESOURCES

American Bar Association
750 N. Lake Shore Drive
Chicago, IL 60611
(312) 988-5000
<http://www.abanet.org/media/factbooks/eldq13.html>

Summary: The ABA's Division of Media Relations and Public Affairs provides broad background information on guardianship proceedings.

National Guardianship Association
1604 North Country Club Rd.
Tucson, AZ 85716
<http://www.guardianship.org>

Summary: This site is maintained by a fee-for-membership organization that offers education training and networking opportunities for professional guardians. However, the information provided here will also be of use to families.

Grandparents' Rights

The relationship between our parents and our children finds us once again sandwiched in the middle. You may be delighted that your parents are forming attachments with their grandchildren, or you may view their presence as disruptive. Your marital status may be a contributing factor in how everyone is getting along. Divorce often affects the ability of grandparents to form a relationship with their grandchildren. If you are divorced, in a second or third marriage, or just plain unhappy with the multiple grandparents in your children's lives, you may be debating whether and how often grandparents can visit your children.

Although the rules about grandparent visitation are not uniform, grandparents appear to have the right in every state to seek some form of visitation. Although grandparents do not have an automatic right to visit their grandchildren, the various laws governing such visits mark a departure from the traditional view that parents alone have the authority to determine who can visit with the child.

In some instances, your parents' involvement with their grandchildren may extend beyond mere visitation. Increasingly, more and more grandparents find themselves raising a grandchild or two because of the parents' death, catastrophic illness, divorce, or alcohol or substance abuse.

Whatever the circumstances, grandparents who have assumed parental roles with their grandchildren (known popularly as "kinship care") more often than not will find it even more challenging the second time around for many reasons—not the least of which is that their rights to make decisions on their grandchildren's behalf may not always be clear in the absence of a formalized legal relationship to the children established through guardianship, legal custody, or teen adoption. For example, enrolling the child in school, consenting to medical treatment, obtaining medical insurance, and even obtaining government benefits may be an uphill and, in some situations, an unsuccessful battle.

RESOURCES

Grandparent Visitation Rights
<http://www.grandtime.com/visit/html>

Summary: This is a general source of information on the subject with referrals to grassroots organizations that may be able to assist grandparents with custody problems.

Grands Place
c/o Pixie Wescott
PO Box 132
Wanchese, NC 27981
<http://www.grandsplace.com>

Summary: Grands Place is an organization that offers support, resources, and information to paying members on the subject of grandparents raising children.

Grandparent Caregiver: A National Guide
IGC
6741 Eastern Ave., Suite 200
Takoma Park, MD 20912
(202) 588-5070
<http://www.igc.org/justice/cjc/lspc/manual/cover.html>

Summary: This is an excellent source of information, referrals, and success stories by and for grandparent caregivers.

The Foundation for Grandparenting
7 Avenida Vista Grande, Suite B7-160
Santa Fe, NM 87505
<http://www.grandparenting.org>

Summary: This is an excellent education source for families that emphasizes the special role and evolving rights of grandparents.

Grand Parent Again
<http://www.grandparentagain.com/>

Summary: This is an interactive organization that attempts to offer support and referrals to grandparents who because of death, imprisonment, or substance abuse, are raising their children's children.

Housing and Support Services for Parents Living at Home

Although shelter is a basic human need, it involves a lot more than just having a roof overhead. A critical consideration for older people in choosing a place to live, whether they stay at home or move, is the extent to which they can remain independent.

> **INSIGHT**
>
> **As long as your parents have capacity, it is their decision as to whether or not they can live safely and independently at home. Most parents, however, will welcome your input, especially after they have experienced a traumatic life event, such as the loss of a spouse or a medical emergency.**

Consequently, any decision your parents make about housing options should take into account, in addition to their personal preferences, their physical needs (for example, as might be dictated by mobility impairments), transportation needs, access to quality medical care, their in-home support network (including their proximity to you or other family members), community and social resources, climate, safety concerns, and of course, finances.

Housing options for seniors generally can be divided into three categories: (1) living at home (either independently or with a caregiver), (2) living in a supportive residential environment that accommodates the special needs of older persons (such as retirement communities, adult homes, congregate care facilities, and assisted living programs), or (3) living in a nursing home or similar medically oriented facility that provides around-the-clock care and support.

Living at Home

"Be it ever so humble, there's no place like home." Most seniors couldn't agree more. Besides representing independence and the security that often accompanies a sense of the familiar, our parents' homes likely are filled with years of memories (both literally and figuratively!) and an incalculable amount of "sweat equity."

Even so, the fact is that most single-family homes are not designed with the elderly or disabled in mind. As homeowners, our parents must at least be able to care for themselves, drive, shop, cook, pay their bills, and do household chores. Although independent living might become more challenging for our parents, given the physical, mental, emotional, financial, and social changes that can accompany aging, it's nonetheless entirely possible through a variety of arrangements such as those discussed in this section.

RESOURCES

American Association of Homes and Services for the Aging (AAHSA)

901 E Street NW, Suite 500

Washington, DC 20004

(202) 783-2242

<http://www.aahsa.org>

Summary: The American Association of Homes and Services for the Aging represents not-for-profit organizations dedicated to providing high-quality health care, housing, and services to the nation's elderly. The AAHSA Web site offers information on all types of housing and health care arrangements for the elderly: click on "Consumer Tips: Home and Community Based Services."

Home Modifications

In home-care terms, the ability to perform activities of daily living (ADLs) equates with independence. Walking, toileting, or climbing stairs are performable with the assistance of ramps, special bathroom fixtures, and railings or stair glides. An occupational therapist can evaluate difficulties with certain activities such as preparing food, dressing, or feeding. If the problems relate to functional mobility—such as bed mobility, coming to a sitting or standing position, or ambulation (that is, walking)—a physical therapist can provide an evaluation.

It's also important to have a physical therapist evaluate your parents' home for safety. Given that the consequences of a fall usually are disastrous for the elderly, a little foresight and effort can dramatically increase your parents' chances for sustained independence. An essential feature of any elderly person's home should be a bedroom and a large bathroom on the main floor. The bathroom should have a shower or tub and special fixtures for the elderly. With our own golden years just around the corner, you may want to consider making some of these changes now. Medicare and Medicaid pay for some adaptive equipment, such as a walker or a special cane, but not much else. The American Association of Retired Persons (AARP) publishes materials on home remodeling, and there are books on the market that can be of assistance.

Some of the ways in which a home can be modified include the following: installing railings, ramps, lifts, bathing bars, seats, single-lever faucets, and roll-out shelves in cabinets; lowering cabinets and thresholds; replacing knobs with levers; widening doorways for wheelchairs; and adding additional lighting and adaptive equipment such as trolley carts to serve food and step stools with railings. Simple adaptations such as reworking for proper lighting, wearing nonskid shoes, and removing scatter rugs and excess furniture can help to prevent falls.

Limited Resources

Even with modifications such as those just discussed to accommodate your parents' physical limitations, the cost of remaining at home may be prohibitive. However, several options may make it more feasible to continue living in their home even if their financial resources are limited.

Shared Housing

Sharing a home can provide a source of income. Nonprofit organizations in many communities match elder homeowners with those needing a place to live. Some organizations work only with the elderly; others attempt to match older homeowners with younger people who can provide some degree of security and financial and household assistance.

Sale/Leaseback Option

In a *sale/leaseback,* your parents would sell their home to a third party, who would then lease the property back to your parents. Such an arrangement could create a stream of income for your parents, but because they continue to pay to live in the home, they should consider the projected net benefit before entering into a sale/leaseback. Also, consult with an attorney about the legal and tax implications of such an option, especially if the sale is being arranged between parents and children and whether or not your parent receives or expects to receive government assistance in the near future.

Reverse Equity Mortgages

As discussed on page 323, your parents can enter into a reverse mortgage that may provide them with available resources to make required home improvements. However, such an arrangement would change their ownership interest in their residence.

Click on <http://www.Boomerbasics.com> for further information regarding reverse mortgages.

Community Services

Many of our parents may need only limited support to continue to function independently in their own homes. Many community services are offered by public and private agencies to facilitate your parents' continued autonomy. The fees for these various services will depend on the agencies involved. Public agencies often provide the service for free or at a minimal cost. Private agencies may operate on a sliding-fee scale or have established rates for particular services. Any initial inquiry should include a question about fees.

INSIGHT

You or your parents should call a local area agency on aging to identify services available in your parents' community. An excellent starting place to get the information you need is the ElderCare Locator, a public service of the Administration on Aging of the U.S. Department of Health and Human Services. You can find information regarding community assistance in your area by calling (800) 677-1116 or by going on-line at <http://www.aoa.gov /elderpage/locator.html>.

The following are examples of community services.

Visitor Services

Community agencies and volunteer organizations provide elderly people living alone with telephone calls and home visits for social interaction and reassurance.

Personal Emergency System

Your parent can be provided with a personal alarm device that links him or her with local emergency and health agencies. When the device is activated, it summons help immediately. There may be a one-time cost (which may be payable in installments) for the purchase of the equipment. A monthly fee also may be assessed.

Household Services

Public and private agencies often offer services that include light house-keeping, laundry, and food shopping and preparation. Heavier chores such as floor or window washing, yard work, and repairs can often be arranged as well.

Transportation Services

Public and private transportation companies can provide access to community shopping, banks, physicians' offices, and other business establishments. Wheelchair-accessible vehicles are also available in most communities. Some providers may require that appointments be scheduled in advance, and certain restrictions may apply to cancellations.

INSIGHT

You or your parents should notify the transportation company if your parents will need assistance with getting in and out of the vehicle; some carriers may not provide this service. Check also with your parents' local senior center for information on its transportation services.

Nutrition Services

Many community senior centers, churches, and schools provide hot meals to elderly persons. Meals are nutritionally balanced and served in a social setting. Programs such as Meals on Wheels provide hot midday and evening meals in your parents' home. Some dietitians provide individual counseling to elderly persons and their families where specific health concerns exist.

Click on <http://www.Boomerbasics.com> for selected national and state organizations that provide meals to elderly persons.

Social Services

Most communities have a senior center that can serve as the main source of social, recreational, health, and other programs for older adults. The center may be part of a not-for-profit community organization, or it may be associated with a religious organization. The programs offered will depend on the organization, but they frequently involve daily leisure, educational, and cultural events. Other services may include counseling support groups, employment services, and legal and financial planning services. Some centers may provide transportation or arrange rides with volunteers.

Adult Day Care

Some health care facilities offer structured day programs that provide nursing, rehabilitation, and personal services. The extent of such services will vary, as will the cost and payors of such programs.

Home Health Services

The fact that your parents may require a certain level of medical care does not preclude them from remaining at home. In addition to adult day care, where nursing or rehabilitation can be provided in the community, home health care services are available to assist those who are recovering from acute medical conditions or suffering from chronic conditions and those who are frail or functionally impaired.

Home care services are provided by both public and private agencies as well as by some health care facilities. Fees will depend on the type of agency, and Medicare or Medicaid reimbursement may be available in some states. Private insurance may also provide coverage under certain conditions. Private agencies will have a broad range of prices, and some may use a sliding-fee scale. You should investigate several agencies before entering into a service agreement.

Services may include skilled nursing care, physical or occupational therapy, health monitoring and medication administration, health evaluations and preadmission evaluations for nursing home placement, psychological counseling, and education for individuals or family caregivers relating to ongoing care.

Home health care agencies may also provide home attendants or personal care aides. These workers provide assistance with bathing, feeding, toileting, walking, and other personal activities. The workers are required to have specialized training or certification in attendant care and are normally supervised by a registered nurse, but regulations may vary from state to state.

Other Implications of Living at Home

Apart from financial, security, and health considerations, isolation is another issue that must be weighed in deciding whether parents with diminished capacity should remain at home. Isolation is an important factor because it may lead to loneliness and victimization by the unscrupulous. Incidents of elder abuse and fraud by people preying on vulnerable older adults is on the rise. Telemarketing scams are often targeted at elderly people living alone. Promises to provide care and services in exchange for a transfer of property or granting a power of attorney are another scam that allows thieves to steal significant assets of the elderly person or to sell the house and keep the proceeds.

INSIGHT

If your parents have the necessary funds, neither you nor they should compromise on securing safe and appropriate care.

Respite Care

Respite care is designed to provide family caregivers with free time away from their caregiving responsibilities. Provided both in house and on a short-term residential basis in adult homes, assisted living facilities, and nursing homes, this service takes care of all the elderly individual's needs in the absence of the family caregiver.

Click on <http://www.Boomerbasics.com> for information regarding respite care.

Hospice

For individuals who are terminally ill, hospice care can provide a less restrictive alternative to traditional long-term care. Hospice care emphasizes the quality of the patient's remaining life rather than attempting to cure the illness. Patients are encouraged to have as much control over the remaining weeks and months as possible. Hospice care can be provided in the home or in a residential facility depending on the individual program and desires of the patient.

Aggressive pain management and control of other symptoms is provided in accordance with a patient's wishes and philosophy. Most hospice programs provide counseling and social services to help with an array of end-of-life issues. When selecting a hospice care provider, one may ask whether the program offers grief counseling services to the family.

Coverage for hospice care can be provided by Medicare, Medicaid, or private insurance. To qualify for Medicare coverage, two conditions must be met: The patient must be certified by a physician as terminally ill, which is defined as having a life expectancy of six months or less, and the hospice care provider must be approved by Medicare to provide these services. This is true even though the organization might be approved by Medicare to provide other health services.

Hospice programs are often affiliated with religious organizations. Care should be paid to whether the program is rooted in the doctrine of a particular religion and, if so, whether this is compatible with the patient's philosophy. Whenever possible, it is important to involve the patient in these decisions. Even though an individual may not have participated in an organized religion in many years, he or she may have a need to discuss some end-of-life issues with clergy. Clergy can often perform an important role in the hospice care by helping the patient to work through feelings of anger, fear, and confusion.

Click on <http://www.Boomerbasics.com> for information regarding hospice care.

The Important Role of Geriatric Care Managers and Other Concerned Professionals

The graying of America has spawned a dizzying array of programs and services geared toward the elderly that only continues to expand. You want to help your parents figure out the best options for them, given their unique circumstances, but where do you begin? A geriatric care manager (GCM), who is an advisor on the availability and quality of services to the elderly, might be your answer.

Responsible for the practical, day-to-day aspects of the care plan, geriatric care managers usually are trained as nurses or social workers. They often have trained themselves on the coverage, advantages, and disadvantages of local public, fee-for-service, and philanthropic programs for the elderly. Sometimes insurance companies use GCMs or other trained personnel as case managers who create and supervise comprehensive plans for the care of an elderly or disabled person.

RESOURCES

National Association of Professional Geriatric Care Managers
North Country Club Road
Tucson, AZ 85716
(520) 881-8008
<http://www.caremanager.org>

Summary: This organization's site gives assistance in finding a care manager and offers care management resources.

Family Caregivers

If the time comes when your parents need help to remain at home, they likely will turn to you or other family members for assistance. And chances are that you'll want to help—not only because of some obligation you might feel but also because now might seem like a good time to give back to them some of the support and guidance they provided you on the rocky road to adulthood.

The type of assistance your parents require will be dictated by numerous factors, including their needs and wishes, their financial situation, and their proximity to you or other family members, among others. The following scenarios involving family caregivers are typical:

- An adult child, sibling, or other relative who lives nearby occasionally helps parents with grocery shopping, household repairs, transportation, and so on.

- An adult child, sibling, or other relative moves into the parents' house to provide regular assistance with many of the usual activities of daily living such as cooking, housecleaning, paying bills, and so forth.
- The parents move into the home of an adult child, sibling, or other relative.

Despite your good intentions, such arrangements can lead to all kinds of conflict, stemming primarily from trying to juggle the demands of caring for your parents with the responsibilities and expectations associated with caring for your own family and, more often than not, working outside the home.

A variety of community and home health services (discussed in the following sections) can help your parents to maintain some degree of independence and provide you with support and respite. Nonetheless, as a caregiver, you must not overlook the importance of taking care of yourself with the same diligence you afford your parents.

Make sure you have a personal support network of family and friends—people you know you can always turn to. The support of other caregivers can also be invaluable.

Involve other family members to the greatest extent possible. Even if they can't help out with day-to-day tasks because they live far away, they might be able to provide emotional or financial support. When others do offer assistance, take them up on it and don't be shy about asking others for help. Start with small, specific requests (such as "Would you mind running to the grocery store for a few items?"), and you might just be surprised at how people are willing to lend a hand.

If your caregiving responsibilities conflict with the demands of your daily job, discuss the possibility of alternative work arrangements (for example, flextime, job sharing, telecommuting, and rearranging your schedule) with your boss to help minimize your stress.

Try to think ahead to develop possible contingency plans in case circumstances change. Be sure to involve your parents in discussions about their care and any decisions that need to be made. It's also important for you to let them know your limits (which assumes you've figured them out for yourself first!) and to ask that they respect them. Finally, don't forget to reward yourself—go to lunch, play a round of golf, take a bubble bath—whatever will help you to recharge.

Click on <http://www.Boomerbasics.com> for additional valuable information for caregivers.

RESOURCES

Geocities
<http://www.geocities.com>; then search under "Elderly" to find
  several relevant sites

Summary: Caregiver support and referral organization for families dealing with issues that affect the elderly. Geocities describes itself as the largest free on-line community on the Web. It features many member homepages that provide a place for those who care for and about the elderly to share information. Click on <http://www.geocities.com/cgi-bin/search/search>.

Tad Publishing Co.
PO Box 224
Park Ridge, IL 60068
(847) 823-0639
<http://www.caregiving.com>

Summary: This site contains information of interest to caregivers of the elderly. Features include discussion and support groups, referrals, and articles of interest.

American Association of Retired Persons (AARP)
601 E. St. NW
Washington, DC 20049
(800) 424-3410
<http://www.aarp.org/caregive/1-care.html>

Summary: AARP maintains this Web site, which features on-line support groups, financing information, and comparison service referrals.

How to Assist Parents after They've Been Hospitalized

While still not yet recovered from the need for hospitalization, the patient and patient's family must begin to deal with when, how, and where the patient will be discharged. As health-care discharge planners will tell you, discharge begins upon admission. Prior to being released from the hospital, patients have a legally protected right to discharge planning. The discharge-planning process generally begins with a consultation between the hospital discharge planner or social worker and the attending physician. When the hospital team decides that inpatient care is no longer warranted, the discharge planner should help coordinate services that the patient will need in the community after discharge. The discharge plan may include some combination of nursing home care, home care, hospice care, adult day care, private duty nursing, transportation services, meal services, and telephone reassurance programs.

The discharge planner can be helpful in navigating the often confusing payment and coverage policies and procedures necessary to obtain needed care. The patient and family should take advantage of the free hospital discharge-planning process prior to investigating costly community case management services. However, if you or your parents have financial resources, you should not hesitate to hire an independent professional if you feel the hospital is more concerned with getting your parent out of the hospital immediately than planning and coordinating a safe and appropriate discharge.

The goal of any discharge plan should be to help the patient make a smooth transition to his or her postdischarge environment. Ideally the plan will provide for regular postdischarge follow-up visits to ensure that care needs are being met.

Sometimes a patient may feel that the hospital discharge is premature. To appeal a hospital discharge notice, the patient should telephone the peer review organization or any other independent professional entity authorized by law to review hospital discharges. This call generally must be immediately followed up by the patient's written appeal request. It is recommended that a health law or elder law attorney be consulted at this juncture.

Click on <http://www.Boomerbasics.com> for more information regarding hospital discharges and available laws and resources to assist you.

Supportive Residential Environments

Selecting a Residential Facility

Because your parents' home can represent a comforting source of continuity, particularly in the face of continual change (such as declining health, relocation of family, and the death of friends), moving can be a very unsettling and stressful experience for them.

You can ease the burden of such a major transition by helping them to explore the various residential alternatives in light of their needs and resources. The more your parents can define what features of a new home are important to them, the better their chances of finding the right environment—one whose offerings complement their objectives and that meets their needs without being overly restrictive.

In assessing their needs, your parents should consider health concerns and access to medical care, home maintenance responsibilities, transportation needs and options, meals, social and recreational opportunities, and privacy and safety concerns, among others. They should compare the services available among the various types of residences, always being on the lookout for additional or hidden charges.

Finally, your parents should visit each facility they are considering for answers to questions that no brochure can provide related to the facility itself (for example, questions about cleanliness, accessibility, and safety mechanisms), staffing and level of care (questions about the attentiveness and friendliness of staff, quality of food, and scope of activities), and administrative concerns (questions about fee structures and billing practices, transportation services, and therapeutic and social services).

RESOURCES

Senior Alternatives for Living
An On-line Service
(800) 350-0770
<http://www.senioralternatives.com>

Summary: This site discusses a wide range of senior lifestyle options and provides a state-by-state national directory. This site also includes checklists to use when evaluating residential facilities.

Senior Residence and Adult Homes

If your parents are able to function independently with limited support and assistance, they may choose to live in senior housing complexes, adult homes, or assisted living communities. Such settings provide the security of communal living with the privacy of independent living.

Some settings offer support services such as meals as well as social, recreational, and transportation services. Others provide personal care in varying degrees. Although some settings accommodate personal furniture and effects, your parents should find out about any restrictions before entering into a residence agreement. Similarly, they should consider the quality and integrity of the care and support services provided.

INSIGHT

As you and your parents tour various settings, be alert to cleanliness, orderliness, and the appearance of other residents. Speak with both residents and staff about the facility and its services and its ability to meet the terms of its service agreement.

Many communities, especially in larger cities, have rental apartments that have been architecturally modified for the needs of the elderly. Although these complexes offer residential security, they do not offer the types of personal services found in other settings.

Adult homes provide limited personal care services to elderly residents as well as meals, laundry and housekeeping services, and social and recreational activities. Private and semiprivate rooms are available, with either a private or shared bath. Medical and social services are coordinated for residents by the home's staff, as are arrangements for transportation, shopping, and help in managing personal finances where requested.

Assisted Living

Assisted living facilities are similar to adult homes, but they offer more extensive personal care. Nursing and personal care are provided on a twenty-four-hour basis, and individual plans of care are developed for each resident by a professional clinical staff. Routine services include meals, housekeeping, laundry, social and recreational programs, and where requested, management of personal finances.

RESOURCES

The National Center for Assisted Living (ACAL)
1201 L Street NW
Washington, DC 20005
(202) 842-4444
<http://www.ncal.org>

Summary: The National Center for Assisted Living was formed by The American Health Care Association, an organization representing long-term care providers. ACAL's Web site contains information on assisted living facilities, with a very good checklist for choosing a facility.

> **American Health Care Association (AHCA)**
> 1201 L Street NW
> Washington, DC 20005
> (202) 842-4444
> <http://www.ahca.org>

Summary: The AHCA is a professional organization representing long-term care providers. On AHCA's Web site under "Consumer Information," see "Consumer Guide to Assisted Living and Residential Care Facilities."

> **Assisted Living Federation of America (ALFA)**
> 10300 Eaton Place, Suite 400
> Fairfax, VA 22030
> (703) 691-8100
> <http://www.alfa.org>

Summary: ALFA is a nonprofit trade association devoted to the assisted living industry and the consumers it serves. ALFA's Web site provides information for consumers interested in assisted living, including an overview, a checklist for choosing a facility, and a directory for locating facilities.

Continuing Care Retirement Communities

Known alternatively as life care communities, continuing care retirement communities (CCRCs) are becoming increasingly popular. They are designed to accommodate a person through the various stages of aging by offering a wide range of services. So, for example, your parent might start off by living in an apartment on his or her own with as much autonomy as possible for as long as possible. Personal and health care services would be available; CCRCs can have a number of special features, including walking trails, pools, lakes, and golf courses for the elderly who wish to remain physically active. If your parent becomes less able to handle everyday tasks, he or she would transfer to an assisted living apartment where staff members help with daily tasks, including meal preparation and bathing. If your parent's health deteriorated, he or she would transfer to a nursing home facility on the premises for around-the-clock care. Many CCRCs also require that if a serious medical condition should occur or worsen, the resident must relocate to another facility.

These types of living arrangements may vary from state to state as they are typically heavily regulated by individual states. The regulation is usually carried out through the insurance department. The financial arrangements are usually provided in the contract, which calls for a single lump-sum payment that would cover all services for life. Other communities offer a variation: a lump-sum entry fee plus monthly payments for various services for the residents. Such services may range from basic delivery of meals on up to nursing and personal care services. In all cases, however, it will be helpful to assist our parents in reviewing what is included in the entry and monthly fees if our parents are considering a CCRC. Among the important questions to ask of the CCRC and its sponsors are the following:

Are the units already built? If not, are there a completion schedule and penalties for delay?

What kinds of services are provided under the contract?

Are services available that are not part of the basic contract and for which an extra charge is imposed?

Do residents have an equity interest in their living units?

What is the amount of the entry fee and continuing monthly fees (if any)?

What are the refund provisions?

What is the policy on fee increases?

Who are the project's sponsors, and what is their track record?

Are adequate financial records provided for review?

What is the project's income/expense history (usual state requirement: disclosure of balance sheet and income statement for five years or existence of project, if shorter than five years)? Are there reserve funds? Are assets pledged as collateral?

What is the actuarial and financial soundness of the assumptions behind the financial records (for example, will a nursing home bed be available when needed)?

What remedies do dissatisfied residents have?

RESOURCES

American Association of Homes and Services for the Aging (AAHSA)
901 E Street NW, Suite 500
Washington, DC 20004
(202) 783-2242
<http://www.aahsa.org>

Summary: The AAHSA is a national association of not-for-profit organizations dedicated to providing quality housing, health, community, and related services to older people. The AAHSA Web site contains useful information on selecting a CCRC.

Nursing Homes

Today's nursing homes are a far cry from the old age homes of fifty years ago. Unfortunately, our parents' perceptions of nursing homes are often influenced by the abuse-ridden warehouses of yesteryear—as well as the few such awful institutions that continue to exist today.

Now, convalescents of all ages can expect to receive quality long-term care in a setting that fosters independence and autonomy and focuses on rehabilitation whenever possible.

Nursing home care may appropriately be considered when an individual has any combination of the following care needs:

- Skilled nursing and/or medical requirements
- Personal care needs such as dressing, eating, toileting, and walking

The nursing home decision-making process should begin with a determination as to whether needed care may appropriately be delivered in a less intrusive manner such as through home care, adult day care, or assisted living arrangements. Only when an individual cannot reasonably be expected to make use of home- and community-based care alternatives should the nursing home selection process begin.

Finding the right facility is of paramount importance to a loved one's physical, social, and spiritual well-being. Ideally, the patient, together with family and a social worker or hospital discharge planner, should participate in the search. When comparing facilities, the following checklist will help begin the process of identifying whether the home meets the needs, preferences, and desires of the patient.

_____Is the facility clean and free from unpleasant odors?

_____Is the use of restraining devices minimal and resorted to only when every alternative has been explored?

_____Are staff and volunteers sensitive to patient needs for dignity and privacy?

_____Does the facility have a written description of patient rights and responsibilities?

_____Are patients and families involved in developing their own care plan?

_____Are staffing levels adequate to meet patient needs? (It is often recommended to visit a facility during evenings and weekends to get an accurate assessment.)

_____Are staff members courteous to patients and other staff?

_____Does staff show a genuine interest in and respect for individual patients?

_____Does the facility have a current license from the state?

_____Is the latest state survey available for review?

_____If needed by the individual, is the facility certified to provide Medicare or Medicaid coverage?

_____Does the facility have an arrangement with a nearby hospital?

_____Are accommodations made for holding beds when patients are hospitalized?

_____Is a physician available in an emergency?

_____Are medical records and plans of care kept?

_____Are patients and families involved in treatment plans?

_____Does the facility periodically report to the patient's personal physician?

_____Are physical therapy services available?

_____Are group and individual activities encouraged?

_____Is the dining area attractive and inviting?

_____Does a dietician plan menus for patients on special diets?

_____Is a nurse call bell by each bed?

_____Are patients encouraged to decorate rooms with personal items such as pictures, crafts, and furniture?

INSIGHT

If possible, observe a meal and recreational activities at the nursing home and take time to ask the residents how they feel about the facility and the services and programs provided. Note the residents' appearances and level of social interaction and the way in which the staff respond to resident questions and requests for assistance.

To the extent that a patient is able to participate in the selection process, he or she will be less traumatized by the transition. Prospective patients and families will no doubt find comfort in the fact that nursing homes are among the most regulated industries in our nation.

INSIGHT

Information is readily available from both federal and state agencies regarding the compliance of nursing homes with government regulations. If you desire the information, you should contact the Department of Health in your state or the Health Care Financing Agency (HCFA) of the U.S. Department of Health and Human Services in Washington, D.C. You can also request survey information directly from the nursing home.

Once a home has been selected, the focus shifts to paying for care. With some monthly rates approaching $10,000, even substantial nest eggs can be quickly eaten away. Although there has been a tremendous increase in the purchase of long-term care insurance policies, the overwhelming percentage of nursing facility residents do not have private insurance that will pay the cost of nursing home care. It is therefore not surprising that most people eventually rely on Medicaid to cover these expenses.

Nursing home administrators should be available to discuss financial conditions in great detail. It is extremely important that all payment agreements be in writing. Be aware that nursing facilities are prohibited from requiring the waiver of Medicare or Medicaid coverage. It is also unlawful for a nursing facility to require a third party such as yourself to guarantee payment as a condition of admission.

RESOURCES

Health Care Financing Administration (HCFA)

7500 Security Blvd.

Baltimore, MD 21224

(410) 786-3000

<http://www.medicare.gov/nursing>

<http://www.HCFA.gov>

Summary: The HCFA provides both valuable on-line and off-line information about nursing homes and the availability of Medicare and Medicaid benefits to pay for nursing home care.

National Citizens Coalition for Nursing Home Reformation (NCCNHR)

1424 16th Street NW, Suite 202

Washington, DC 20036-2211

(202) 332-2275

<http://www.ncchnhr.org>

Summary: The mission of the NCCNHR, an organization of consumers and advocates, is to define and achieve quality for people with long-term care needs.

Careguide.com

1160 Battery, 4th Floor

San Francisco, CA 94111

(415) 474-1278

<http://www.careguide.com>

Summary: This site provides information about nursing homes throughout the country.

Elder Abuse and Fraud

Elder abuse refers to the maltreatment or neglect of older persons by caregivers in a domestic or institutional setting. Whether the problem itself has intensified or incidents of abuse are being reported more often is unclear. Whatever the case, elder abuse is a very real concern.

The National Elder Abuse Incidence Study prepared for the U.S. Administration on Aging (AOA) in September 1998 by the National Center on Elder Abuse at the American Public Human Services Association estimates that at least half a million older people in domestic settings were abused or neglected (by others or themselves) in 1996. These figures, which indicate a 150 percent rise nationwide in state-reported elder abuse cases between 1986 and 1996, likely are just the tip of the iceberg, given the secrecy that often surrounds elder abuse and neglect. In fact, the AOA study suggests that for every reported incident of elder abuse or neglect, about five go unreported. (For a copy of the full report, click on <http://www.aoa.gov/abuse/report>.)

RESOURCES

National Center on Elder Abuse
<http://www.gwjapan.com/NCEA/index.html>

Summary: Provides articles of interest and elder abuse resource referrals as well as a state-by-state listing of numbers to call to report elder abuse.

Dealing with Death—The Loss of Loved Ones and Our Own Mortality

For many of us, the involvement in our parents' affairs may be unnecessary or unwelcomed during their lifetimes. Invariably, this changes upon their death when we may be called upon to provide such things as caregiving, comfort, and making funeral arrangements. The loss of a loved one, a spouse, and friends is a fact of life that confronts older people routinely. The reactions of the survivors vary. For some, the loss of longstanding relationships with siblings, spouse, and friends often intensifies their sense of loneliness and isolation and the vulnerability that comes with recognizing one's own mortality. The sense of loss may be profound and lead to deep depression. For others, the reaction is less intense. They remain active in personal, social, family, and community activities, or they may seek the company of others to relieve the pain. Still others ride a perpetual roller coaster between peaks of hope and valleys of despair.

Particular circumstances may affect the mourning process. When a spouse dies, for example, the surviving spouse may be living and sleeping alone for the first time in many years. The absence of the other spouse may lead to fears about safety at home and in the community. When a special friend dies, the surviving friend loses a meaningful companionship and may lose access to regular social activities such as card playing, tennis, or vacationing. The cumulative impact of a series of deaths close in time may add to the feelings of pain and sadness.

Click on <http://www.Boomerbasics.com> for a list of publications on the grieving process and a list of organizations that can provide support and advice on bereavement.

INSIGHT

Remember how voraciously we devoured the works of Doctor Spock and all those other baby books that helped guide us through our children's infancy and early years? Take some time to read about the aging process and what it does to our parents. Although knowledge gathered from such resources may not make the aging of our parents less challenging, it might make us more understanding about life and death issues.

RESOURCES

Coping with Grief and Loss
The American Association of Retired Persons (AARP)
601 E St. NW
Washington, DC 20049
(800) 424-3410
<http://www.aarp.org/griefandloss>

Summary: The AARP's site contains articles of interest to the widowed as well as information for adult children and professionals.

GriefNet
PO Box 3272
Ann Arbor, MI 48106-3272
<http://www.rivendell.org>

Summary: This Web site, which is maintained by a clinical psychologist, provides support to individuals working through pain and loss.

Grieving Process Booklet
<http://www.add.ca/grieving.htm>

Summary: This site was created by the organization Against Drunk Driving, but it provides helpful information for anyone grieving over the loss of a loved one.

Grief and Bereavement
<http://www.growthhouse.org/death.html>

Summary: This interactive site provides chat rooms for discussing grief and referrals for bereaved families.

Widownet
<http://www.fortnet.org/WidowNet/>

Summary: This educational resource guide was created by and for the widowed. Includes helpful tips and articles of interest such as "Getting Through the Holidays."

What to Do When a Parent Dies

A parent's death can leave you emotionally drained and vulnerable. Although it may sound morbid, knowing what needs to be done and, where appropriate, planning ahead will ease the burden of decision making during the grieving process. Knowing your parents' wishes, even though they may not be legally binding, and carrying them out will hopefully provide some comfort during your mourning.

Funeral Options

Deciding whether to have a burial, a memorial service, or a cremation can be less burdensome if you know what your parent would want. Finding out if he or she would want to donate organs also is important.

Click on <http://www.Boomerbasics.com> regarding making an organ donation plan.

If these decisions haven't been made prior to death, the decision becomes yours to make. You need to determine whether to donate organs or to bequeath the body to a learning institution, whether to hold a service and what kind, whether to choose cremation or burial, whether you would like an open- or closed-casket service, whether you will have a viewing or visitation of the body, and how much money you are willing to spend. You don't have to spend the most to get the very best—many inexpensive choices can offer the same degree of dignity as more expensive alternatives. Knowledge of the options and planning ahead will help you to avoid over-spending at a time of great vulnerability.

RESOURCES

Funeralnet
<http://www.funeralnet.com>

Summary: A national directory of 20,000 funeral homes. This site provides useful suggestions and contains excellent links to funeral service suggestions, veterans' death issues, and cremation information.

Funeral and Memorial Planning
<http://www.growthhouse.org/funeral.html>

Summary: Guide of general use in navigating the many funeral and memorial planning options.

National Funeral Directors Association
13625 Bishop's Drive
Brookfield, WI 53005
(800) 228-6332
<http://www.nfda.org/about/#info>

Summary: This trade organization provides education for its member funeral directors as well as the public. Its Web site describes trends in funeral services and maintains a referral service.

Burial

Burial is the most expensive type of disposition. It usually involves paying a funeral home to take care of all the details. An average funeral costs about $4,100 and includes a casket, preparation, and a memorial service. This price can jump to more than $10,000 depending on the type of casket, the degree of embalming desired, and other extras. The funeral home typically will provide the following services: embalm the body (replacing the body fluids with a chemical preservative) and prepare it for viewing; provide the casket you have chosen; provide facilities for the funeral service; coordinate the service, including music, pallbearers, florists, and other items you may require; provide memorial cards and register books; refer you to the cemetery and give you advice on purchasing a plot, headstone, and grave liner or vault; and provide a funeral procession to the gravesite as well as a committal service.

To keep the price modest on a traditional funeral and earth burial, ask the funeral director if you can view more inexpensive caskets. The law requires that inexpensive models be displayed along with expensive ones. The cost of caskets can range from $250 for a plain, respectable pine coffin to over $10,000 for mahogany and other more elaborate woods and finishes. The relatively new use of plastic caskets is also an inexpensive alternative you should investigate.

INSIGHT

Keep in mind your needs and financial limitations. Stick to your original budget and don't be swayed by the appearance of the caskets and the funeral director's suggestions. Review the contract of the funeral home carefully for hidden costs or details that are not covered. Bring someone along who can help make the decisions.

Inquire whether embalming is necessary. The law does not require it except in certain circumstances such as if the body must travel for a long distance on a train or plane or otherwise be stored for a period of time or if death occurred from a communicable disease. The funeral director may require it for an open-casket service.

Other costs associated with burial involve notices, honoraria for clergy, opening and closing the grave, the cemetery plot, the headstone or memorial plaque, transportation, and use of the funeral home. This list may include other items depending on the choices you make for the burial.

You may choose to bury your parent without any type of service, with a memorial service and burial, or with a funeral service and burial. If you choose to have no service, you may still have a committal service at the burial site. This can be just for the immediate family and can be nonreligious. If you choose to have a memorial service, the service is conducted without the presence of the body, and the burial can occur before or after. The third choice is to have a funeral service at the funeral home or church, followed by a burial. This is the most traditional and most expensive option.

The Wake or Shivah and Other Religious or Spiritual Practices and Traditions

Whether you choose a burial or cremation, if you have services you will need to consider whether to have a viewing, or wake. The details of the wake are dictated by personal preference: location, length of time, open or closed casket, clothing for the deceased, music, and eulogies. You may choose not to have a wake and only a funeral service. Or your great-aunt Katherine may have told you before she died that she wanted to be laid out in an open casket, arrayed in her best Sunday dress with her pearls during a two-day wake with afternoon and evening hours to be followed by a full funeral service at church with an organ and a soloist. If you love Aunt Katherine and fear meeting her in the hereafter, you know what your choice is!

Your family may instead follow the Jewish tradition of sitting Shivah, which involves an initial period of deep mourning that generally lasts from one week to the next Sabbath. During that period, every evening you hold a prayer service at the home of the closest relative (for example, the spouse). Then for the next twelve months, the mourners attend religious services on a regular basis and wear a black ribbon that has been torn to symbolize their mourning.

Other spiritual practices and traditions exist as well, and the best choice is one that balances what Aunt Katherine wanted (or what you think she would have wanted) with what is financially and emotionally practicable.

Funeral Service

The level of formality of the funeral service is also your decision. You'll need to consider the choice of pallbearers and whether you will need a limousine for the ride to the service and gravesite. The funeral director can offer advice and assistance in these matters. Some families choose to have a small reception after the burial at their home or some other location. That decision and the scope of the reception depends on what you think is appropriate under the circumstances.

Prepaid Funerals

Planning ahead is a good idea, but buying ahead may not be. Prepaid funeral or cemetery plans (so-called preneed arrangements) allow a person to plan the details of his or her funeral and pay for the funeral or interment before he or she dies. The intended goal is to allow you to make known your wishes and to lock in a price for a funeral at today's cost.

Although planning ahead has the benefit of letting everyone know what you desire for your funeral, paying ahead—whether a in a lump sum or installments—should be approached cautiously. Government oversight of preneed arrangements generally varies widely. Although some states require that any money paid in advance be put in a trust fund, much like the security deposit for renting a house or apartment, other states do not require the funeral director to establish these funds. It may be hard to get your money back if you move or cancel the plan or if the funeral home goes out of business, or you may have to pay additional money at the time of death if you change the casket or some other feature of the funeral or if the funeral costs exceed your contractual amount. If you put your money in a bank or money market account, you can achieve the same goal without the potential hassles of the prepaid plan.

Sorting through Documents

After the service and burial, you will need to sort through your parent's belongings. Put aside important legal documents: bank records, bills, birth certificates, credit cards, insurance records, loan papers, house and property records, marriage certificates, military papers, pension records, safety deposit records, savings bonds, Social Security card and information, stocks and bonds records, vehicle titles and registrations, and will (if one exists, make sure it is the latest one). There may be insurance policies to cash in and medical insurance to cancel. Credit card and charge accounts and memberships may need to be canceled, too.

The Boomer Basic Crisis Information Checklist in the appendix is an effective way of working through the organization of these documents. Charting this information while your parents are still alive will help them to stay on top of things, and it will benefit you to have all this information in one place when you need to sort through their things after they die.

INSIGHT

You should seek the assistance of an attorney for technical matters. If your parent had a will, the attorney who prepared it may be the most helpful in terms of having the necessary information. If your parent did not have a will, you should still consult an attorney to determine the proper procedure for dealing with your parent's assets.

Administration of a Parent's Estate

You should be aware of how to handle the assets and debts your parent leaves behind. If your parent made a will, then the terms of the will may govern the distribution of the property in the probate estate.

INSIGHT

Not all property passes through the probate estate. Some property passes by operation of law. See the discussion on estate planning in Part One, "Ourselves."

If the decedent did not have a will, then some or all of the assets are distributed in intestacy, meaning that they are distributed in accordance with state laws for such matters. In other words, if you don't have a plan for distributing your assets, the government will decide who gets them.

Click on <http://www.Boomerbasics.com> for the specific state statutes regarding the distribution of assets in intestacy.

If your parent dies with a will, he or she generally will have named an executor or personal representative to carry out the legal proceedings relating to the will and to act on his or her behalf after death. If your parent dies without a will, any interested person can seek to be appointed as the administrator or personal representative of your parent's estate. Either appointment is made by petitioning the court that oversees estates in your parent's state. Generally, this court is known as the probate or surrogate's court. Once this court receives the petition, it notifies all interested parties—family members, persons named in the will (if there is one), and all individuals legally entitled to notice.

Assuming that the will is not challenged or if there is no will, the court then appoints the legal representative and authorizes him or her to act, gather assets, get an appraisal of the assets, pay bills and calculate taxes, and distribute remaining assets in accordance with the terms of the will or as required by law in the absence of one. The personal representative will need certain documents to conduct his or her business: certified copies of the letters of administration (obtained from the court); certified copies of the death certificate (obtained from the funeral director or city hall); and, in many states, tax waivers to take possession of the deceased's assets. The personal representative must also notify the IRS of his or her appointment.

Click on <http://www.Boomerbasics.com> for the forms needed from the IRS and telephone numbers for getting them.

Additionally, the personal representative may have to

- Terminate any leases and collect security deposits
- Notify the Social Security Administration of the death
- Transfer all bank accounts to an estate account
- Transfer all CDs to an estate account (being careful to avoid early withdrawal penalties)
- Collect the contents of any safe-deposit boxes
- Collect debts owed to the deceased
- Take possession of all real estate and collect all rents

The personal representative may also have to sell a business owned by the deceased.

All in all, administering an estate can be a complex job. As the executor, you probably should consider consulting an attorney for advice on how to meet the requirements of the state where the estate is being administered.

For assets valued approximately at less than $25,000, a less formal procedure for administering the estate may be available. If your parent's estate falls into that category, check with your local probate court for the forms and procedures to follow. Usually, you will not need an attorney in such a case.

RESOURCES

Legal Information Institute
Cornell Law School
Myron Taylor Hall
Ithaca, NY 14853
(607) 255-7193
<http://www.law.cornell.edu/uniform/probate.html>

Summary: Provides state-specific statutes on probate and administration proceedings.

INSIGHT

Click on <http://www.Boomerbasics.com> for additional tips on estate administration, tax issues, and related matters.

FINANCIAL ~~~~~~~~

Notwithstanding that approximately $10.4 trillion will pass from our parents to us, their baby boomer children, we can offer no particular guarantee about what our respective parents will do with their money now and upon their death. Many of us will be monetary beneficiaries of our parents' estates; others will be left only with memories. Hopefully, your case includes some of the former and not just the latter. But if you're looking for ways to enhance your inheritance, you won't find them here. This discussion offers ways for you to help your parents develop a plan to manage their assets in a manner that is consistent with their wishes and desires even in the event of incapacity. For some people this may mean leaving a substantial financial gift to their children and grandchildren. For others it may mean spending it now. Most seek to find a balance between these two extremes. Regardless of your parents' objectives, good asset management, both during life, whether healthy or ill, and upon death will help them maximize their goals with a minimum of cost, delay, and stress.

INSIGHT

As just mentioned, the good news is that over $10 trillion will pass to the baby boom generation from parents and grandparents. The bad news is that unless you come from or marry into a wealthy family, you're probably not going to participate in this windfall.

Depression-Era Mentality

Not surprisingly, many of our parents' attitudes about money are as diverse as our own. Some who live month to month, relying heavily on their Social Security check, believe they are rich. Some are millionaires and think they'll never have enough money. Many of our parents lived through the Great Depression—a time when they, their families, and others they knew may have lost all or a substantial part of their finances and property. Because they always want to be prepared for the proverbial rainy day, they live on less than their available income and never, absent a catastrophe, touch their savings—even on a rainy day.

No matter what your parents' attitudes, focusing on their financial management and estate plan will benefit them with both monetary and emotional rewards. But getting them to initially include us in the process or, at least, letting us know that such planning is in place is not always a simple matter.

Where Do We Fit In? How Can We Help?

Parents do not usually look to their children for advice regarding their money. All of their lives they have made major decisions without your input, and this includes financial decisions. But as your parents get older, many unique issues and considerations arise that you might like to discuss with them, ranging from financial and estate planning and long-term care to funeral arrangements. Your intent should not necessarily be to counsel your parents or steer them in a certain direction but simply to know that they have at least addressed the issues in some way. However, initiating such a discussion is awkward for most of us. None of these topics are great conversation starters. In fact, there are not many things from which to segue when trying to raise these issues for discussion without sounding morbid, greedy, or both. With the wrong approach, your question can be interpreted as "I'm nearing retirement myself soon but haven't saved anything; will that be a problem? and, by the way, how's your health, Dad?" We also discourage the "one last chance" approach, in which you tell your parents that their one last chance to correct all their failures as parents would be to give a sizeable lifetime gift or leave a large inheritance to you, their loving, caring, and sensitive child. To avoid such scenarios, raise the issues in broad-based terms, stating that the details of their plans do not have to be shared but that you are concerned that they not ignore or overlook ways to simplify matters in the event of sickness or death. Basically, you would like to know that a plan exists. And that plan should include a will or some other way to carry out their wishes in the event of death; it should include the appointment of someone to act on their behalf for financial and medical decisions in the event of incapacity; it should encompass living and caregiving arrangements if one or both parents requires nursing care; and it should be updated to take into account changes in their health, where they live, tax laws, and beneficiary designations.

Chances are good that they will be glad the subject has been raised because they are equally uncomfortable discussing their death or other depressing issues. Often, once the issue has been broached, parents are happy not only to acknowledge that they have planned but also to either share many of the details or ask for assistance in finding professionals to steer them through the issues if their planning has been incomplete.

We can gladly report to you that in the thousands of matters the authors have been involved with, most parents not only consult with their adult children but also take great pleasure and comfort from their children's concern and love. After all, if your parents cannot count on you, who can they count on?

Some of you more squeamish boomers may not be able to muster the courage or nerve to raise these difficult and emotional issues with your parents. If this is the case, you can either tell your siblings they should do it or simply give this chapter to your parents to read.

INSIGHT

The issue is not what your parents plan to do but rather whether they have developed a plan that will ensure their wishes and desires are articulated and fulfilled.

Assuming that you are assisting your parents with their planning, the Boomer Basics Crisis Information Checklist in the appendix of this book is an effective way for you and your parents to organize and access all the information needed to make appropriate decisions. It will also help to have all this information in one place to prevent panic in a crisis. Use the Boomer Basics Crisis Information Checklist as you go through the next several parts of this discussion of financial issues with your parents.

Planning Ahead: The True Cost of Retirement

The transition from worker to retiree can be difficult for many people. Despite longing for the phase of life where there's no more heading off to work every day, once that phase arrives, much uncertainty comes with it. For some, the uncertainty is over how they'll fill their newfound spare time. For others, anxiety grows over whether their savings, pensions, and the like will be sufficient for life. For many, it's both.

Too often, our parents commence retirement and immediately begin looking for mail-in rebates, senior discounts, and early-bird specials, and it's not because they need the one-dollar rebate checks or suddenly feel like eating dinner at 4:30 P.M. Usually, the motivating factor is the concern that their retirement funds will run out before they do. Although it is always good to save where possible, consideration should also be given to whether it is absolutely critical to meet their planning objectives. But until they actually review their resources, circumstances, and goals, they may continue to judge activities not so much on the experience itself but rather on the amount of free food and discounts that come with it. Perhaps you can help them raise issues and reach some sound conclusions in their planning.

A number of considerations will be taken into account as our parents begin to quantify and implement their retirement plan. In most cases, however, those many considerations usually comprise a basic universal retirement planning objective in that they want to unite lifetime and postdeath planning, using their income and assets to provide a comfortable postretirement lifestyle (including medical and custodial care as needed), whether or not capacity is retained. The following considerations can help you work with your parents (and yourself, for future reference) to formulate a way to achieve that objective.

The day of their retirement is approaching or already here, so retirement planning is a current, major issue, not a minor, future issue that can be put off for another day. Consider the following:

- Your parents probably do not have minor children, so support of children is not a leading consideration.
- A surviving spouse will probably not be capable of earning any sort of income, so greater reserves may be needed.
- Dealing with actual or potential incapacity is a critical planning concern.

- Ensuring the availability of acute medical care—and custodial care for chronic conditions—is a vital planning objective; so is securing payment mechanisms for the care.
- In general, public benefits (for example, Social Security, Medicare, and Medicaid) assume an important part in the planning process.
- Their living situation may change because of preferences or needs.
- Trusts may become a more important planning tool.
- Their insurance portfolio should be reviewed to provide for changed circumstances and different coverages.
- Often, planning for receiving a lump sum must be anticipated.
- Their investment needs may change.
- Their spending patterns will likely change.
- The plan must be even more fully documented than a financial plan for someone younger so that others can step in if necessary.

After reviewing the many subjective considerations that will help establish the amount of income needed through retirement, you can work on actual numbers. Click on <http://www.Boomerbasics.com> for assistance in calculating cash needs now and in the future. Alternatively, your parents may prefer the following low-tech method.

First, in two columns estimate their current costs and those that are expected to lower when they retire. In another column, project costs that might increase when they retire. A review of these figures will give you their estimated annual retirement expenses. For estimating purposes, keep the following in mind:

- You can expect total monthly retirement expenses to be approximately 70 percent of their current income.
- You don't need to adjust their expenses for inflation. Instead, think about how their expenses will change at retirement and then reallocate the dollars accordingly. For example, they may not spend as much on clothing and personal care, but they may spend more on recreation and travel.

Assets

Assets consist of financial holdings such as bank accounts, stocks, bonds, real properties, mutual funds, and so on. Your parents should know the extent of their assets and how they hold title to their property. They may be surprised to learn that they have miscalculated the value of their assets, finding out that they have more than they thought or, unfortunately, that they have less. Knowing how much they have can help ensure that they will have sufficient funds to meet their ongoing obligations and to maintain their current lifestyles. If your parents have substantial assets, they may wish to consider the estate, gift, and income tax consequences of different investments and insurance options and possible gifting programs. They particularly need to know the extent of their assets in case they eventually need to pursue government benefits, such as Medicaid, for help in paying for health care.

To accurately assess your parents' current financial situation and thus help with their planning, it is important that you and they understand their net worth. Together with them, write their information on paper to determine the current value of their assets and liabilities. After subtracting liabilities from assets (hopefully it's a positive number), they can estimate their total net worth.

For assistance in identifying asset classes and types of liabilities and calculating net worth, click on <http://www.Boomerbasics.com>.

Modalities of Ownership and Their Legal Significance

Your parents (and you and your spouse, too) need to know what each owns individually and what they own jointly. They should also review the way title is listed on their assets in regard to rights, effective during their lives or upon their demise, that they may have granted, intentionally or otherwise, to others.

Joint Accounts

Assets held jointly generally are those assets to which each of the joint owners has complete access and when one dies, the total interest passes to the surviving owner. For example, let's assume Mike is a seventy-seven-year-old widower with $100,000 dollars in a bank account. His son, Greg, is a joint tenant on the account. Because this is a joint account, Greg has complete access to these funds, and the entire amount will pass by operation of law to Greg upon Mike's death. Peter, Bobby, Marcia, Jan, and Cindy—Mike's other children and beneficiaries under their father's will—generally will not be entitled to these funds because they will bypass the estate and pass directly to Greg. Their father might not be pleased when he discovers that this is the case.

In some states, assets held by two people may look like a joint account but may actually be a *convenience account,* which means that the owner of the account put a second person's name on the account for convenience to the owner. For example, Mike put Greg's name on the account so that Greg could pay Mike's bills out of the account. If it is a convenience account, the money in the account at Mike's death goes into his estate, and Greg and his siblings share in it as provided by their father's will. For obvious reasons, it is vital that the intent and the title of the accounts are coordinated.

An alternative to a joint or convenience account would be to have the parent keep the account in his or her own name and then execute a power of attorney in favor of a child (children). As an agent under a power of attorney, the child (children) is a fiduciary, not an automatic beneficiary.

Click on <http://www.Boomerbasics.com> for selected state laws regarding joint and convenience accounts.

Tenants in Common

Assets held by tenants in common are held in equal parts. At the death of one of the parties, the share belonging to the deceased person passes to the deceased's estate rather than to the surviving owners. So, for example, if your father and you held a piece of real estate as tenants in common, you do not automatically become the owner of the property upon your father's death, as Greg did in the previous example of the bank account. Your father's share goes into his estate and, depending on the terms of his will, may go to the beneficiaries under the will or may be treated as property governed by the laws of intestacy (the laws that govern property distribution when a person dies without a will).

Tenants by the Entirety

Property held as tenants by the entirety relates to real property held by a husband and wife. In that case, just as with joint tenants, each spouse has complete access to the entire asset, and when one dies, the total interest passes to the surviving spouse. Unless designated otherwise by your parents, real property held by your parents will generally be deemed as a tenants-by-the-entirety account.

In-Trust-For Accounts (Totten Trusts)

Named after the famous Totten family case, a Totten, or in-trust-for, account lists a beneficiary. For example, assume your mother has a bank savings account in which she names your sister as the beneficiary. Your sister will receive the funds in that bank account upon your mother's demise. So if, for the purpose of this example, your sister is an evil, horrible person who your mother cut out of her will, she still will likely get the money in this account when your mother dies.

> **INSIGHT**
>
> **Lawyers make a lot of money representing family members in legal battles to determine whether an account should pass to the surviving joint tenant or an in-trust-for beneficiary or be distributed according to the terms of the deceased parent's estate. Unless you or your parents wish to generate unnecessary and costly legal work, careful attention should be given to the manner in which assets are held and titled. In other words, poor planning or a failure to plan may result in your lawyer being an unintended beneficiary of your parent's estate.**

Click on <http://www.Boomerbasics.com> for a chart that outlines the different types of joint accounts and the corresponding legal implications of each.

Types of Income That Our Parents Receive

Your parents receive income from a variety of sources. Most parents receive Social Security benefits. They may also receive income from pension funds and Individual Retirement Accounts (IRAs) (deferred income that they have saved from their work and to which their former employers may have contributed). Other sources of income may be rental income, wages, reparation payments, and partnership interests. Additionally, they may receive income from their assets in such forms as interest, dividends, and capital gains distributions.

Wages

For many of our parents, wages become a less significant part of their total income package as they approach (or currently enjoy) retirement. Nevertheless, it is important to have an understanding of how traditional earned income interplays with the tax and benefit rules of Social Security and deferred income, because this phase of life has its own unique set of rules.

The subject of wages often comes up in a postretirement setting when a recent retiree decides that he or she wishes to go back to work on a full- or part-time basis, not necessarily for monetary reasons but just for something to do. Depending on the amount, this additional earned income may have an effect on the timing and taxability of Social Security benefits.

Another issue that arises is whether this earned income could be used to fund an IRA or Keogh plan, even though the individual earning the money is in fact retired.

The allure of employee benefits such as health insurance and the socialization of working with other people, rather than earned income, draws many seniors into part-time employment after they have officially retired. Therefore, it is imperative that a decision be made that is not just based on the taxability of Social Security or the job's impact on a tax bracket but also on the more intangible issues of self-esteem and interpersonal exchange that work provides to an individual.

Social Security

According to Social Security Administration statistics, over forty-four million people receive some form of Social Security benefit. Most recipients receive their benefit because they, a spouse, or a parent contributed to the Social Security system when they were gainfully employed. The amount of such contributions generally affects the amount of the benefit.

Most of our parents will start collecting retirement benefits from Social Security at age sixty five (which is considered the normal retirement age) if they have not already begun to do so. (Beginning in 1999, normal retirement age began to increase gradually; it shall reach the age of sixty-seven in 2022.) Alternatively, they can start collecting benefits at age sixty-two, but the benefits will be less. If they should choose to begin receiving benefits after age sixty-five, the checks would be greater. Naturally, the trade-off is that early retirement means more checks because they start earlier and with more certainty (less risk of dying before getting the first check), whereas late retirement means that each check will be greater.

The actual decrease or increase in the check is based on early retirement being reduced at the rate of five-ninths of 1 percent per month. If someone were to delay retirement, each month of delay after the normal retirement age would increase their check by one-third of 1 percent per month. For example, if your parent were to elect to receive Social Security at age sixty-two, that would be thirty-six months prior to normal retirement age, meaning that the checks would be reduced by 20 percent (36 × 5/9 of 1 percent).

How Work Affects the Benefits

Your parents can continue to work after they start receiving Social Security benefits. However, until they reach the age of seventy, the amount they receive from Social Security will be reduced if their income exceeds certain limits.

If your parent is between the ages of sixty-five and seventy, his or her benefits will be reduced by $1 for every $3 in excess earnings that they have. For 2000, "excess earnings" are earnings above $17,000.

If your parent is under sixty-five, then excess earnings result in a reduction in benefits of $1 for every $2 of excess earnings. For 2000 in this category, excess earnings are those above $10,080 per year.

If your parent is seventy or older, they receive full benefits regardless of when they may have retired and regardless of how much in wages they may earn per year.

The caveat in all of this is that your parents should consider whether taking a part-time job would be worthwhile financially. It is quite possible that taking on such a job could increase their wages to the point where they actually lose money because income and payroll taxes and a decrease in Social Security benefits result in less net income than if they had not worked. Could there be a more thankless job?

Table 8.1, which was prepared by the Social Security Administration, illustrates how much in the way of Social Security benefits your parent would receive for one year based on monthly benefits and estimated monthly earnings.

Table 8.1   Social Security Benefits by Age and Income Level for 1999

For People under Age Sixty-Five

If Your Monthly Social Security Benefit is ($)	And You Earn ($)	You Will Receive Yearly Benefits of ($)
400	9,600 or less	4,800
400	15,000	2,100
600	9,600 or less	7,200
600	15,000	4,500
600	20,000	2,000
800	9,600 or less	9,600
800	15,000	6,900
800	20,000	4,400

For People Age Sixty-Five through Sixty-Nine

If Your Monthly Social Security Benefit Is ($)	And You Earn ($)	You Will Receive Yearly Benefits of ($)
400	15,500 or less	4,800
400	20,000	3,300
600	15,500 or less	7,200
600	20,000	5,700
600	30,000	2,367
800	15,500 or less	9,600
800	20,000	8,100
800	30,000	4,833

Source: Social Security Administration Publication No. 05-10069, February 1999, ICN 467005.

Derivative Benefits

Derivative benefits may be paid to a disabled child, minor children of a deceased Social Security recipient, or a spouse.

In addition to the worker receiving benefits based on his or her earnings history, other family members may also be entitled to benefits based on that person's earnings history. A spouse is entitled to receive up to 50 percent of the insured worker's benefit as long as he or she is sixty-two or older or cares for the worker's minor child.

Further benefits, up to a maximum of 50 percent of the insured worker's benefit, may be available for a divorced spouse. In order to receive this money, the ex-spouse must meet several qualifications, including being sixty-two years old or older, not having remarried at the time of application for the benefits, and having been married to his or her previous spouse for at least ten years. This raises an interesting planning consideration. In the event the marriage is on the rocks after seven, eight, or nine years, it may be worthwhile just to hang on until year ten and receive this benefit. One final note is that this benefit to a divorced spouse may be paid even if the insured worker is eligible but not yet retired.

A surviving spouse or surviving divorced spouse is also entitled to a benefit based on the deceased spouse's earnings history. In this case, the maximum benefit would be 100 percent of the insured worker's benefit, assuming that the surviving spouse was not otherwise entitled to receive benefits. The same worker can have both a widow/widower and surviving divorced spouse receiving benefits based on his or her earnings history. The surviving spouse must be over sixty or over fifty and disabled, and generally, the surviving spouse must not be married at the time of application for this derivative benefit.

Death of First Spouse

When both spouses have worked and earned their Social Security benefits, each will receive his or her respective benefit, that is, two checks will arrive in their mailbox every month. However, when the first spouse dies, the survivor will receive one check—generally the greater of the two checks formerly received by the spouses.

As an example, say that the husband received $1,200 a month before he died and the wife received $800 a month. Upon the husband's death, the wife will receive approximately $1,200 a month.

At the risk of stating the obvious, for couples with limited means who rely on their respective Social Security checks, the death of the first spouse may also result in financial hardship to the survivor.

INSIGHT

If you have paid into the Social Security system, you have a right to expect not only that you will receive this benefit when you become eligible but also that your benefit should be the maximum allowable amount pursuant to applicable law.

RESOURCES

Social Security Administration (SSA)
6401 Security Boulevard
Baltimore, MD 21235
(800) 772-1213
<http://www.ssa.gov>

Summary: The SSA is a huge federal agency. It has prepared and distributes many booklets on Social Security matters that you can order on-line or by calling its toll-free number. The SSA has created an excellent state-of-the-art Web site that provides valuable information in addition to many special features. For example, Social Security applicants can apply for benefits on-line as well as make inquiries about benefits or future eligibility.

Social Security Advisory Service (SSAS)
271 Miller Avenue
Mill Valley, CA 94941-2862
(800) 440-4780
<http://www.ssas.com>

Summary: The SSAS is a private organization that provides information to Social Security recipients and their advocates. Its Web site provides numerous helpful links.

National Organization of Social Security
   Claimants' Representatives (NOSSCR)
6 Prospect Street
Midland Park, NJ 07432-1634
(800) 431-2804
<http://www.nosscr.org>

Summary: The National Organization of Social Security Claimants' Representatives is an association of over three thousand three hundred attorneys who represent Social Security and supplemental security income claimants. It offers an attorney referral service.

Americans Discuss Social Security (ADSS)
2001 Pennsylvania Avenue NW, Suite 825
Washington, DC
(202) 955-9000
<http://www.americansdiscuss.org>

Summary: The ADSS is a nonpartisan effort funded by the Pew Charitable Trust.

Electronic Text Retrieval Systems, Inc.
Robert C. Danes, Publisher
(800) 910-0910
<http://adss.org>

Summary: This site lists applicable Social Security laws and provides links to other Social Security–related sites as well as a state-by-state list of attorneys and nonattorneys who represent claimants before the Social Security Administration.

Interest and Dividends: Taxable and Nontaxable Income

Two of the cornerstones of retirement income are interest and dividends.

Interest is composed of traditional payments from a bank or certificate of deposit as well as from corporate, treasury, and municipal bonds and income funds of many mutual funds.

One of the crucial things for your parents to consider about their investments is whether interest payments they receive from them should be taxable or nontaxable. Although everybody's first reaction is to choose the nontaxable option, remember that there is no such thing as a free lunch. The municipalities that provide nontaxable interest income also pay a lower rate of interest.

Aside from any philosophical or moral commitment to not paying taxes, this decision is best made by addressing the issue of how much money your parents actually receive after taxes. To do this, one must have a firm grasp on the tax bracket that the individual is in. Once that is determined, the net benefit to the person can easily be determined, and whatever puts the most in one's pocket is obviously the way to go.

For example, if you had the opportunity to purchase a $10,000 bond for one year that paid either 8 percent taxable or 6 percent tax free, you cannot make the determination on what will be the best benefit to you unless you know what tax bracket you are in. Thus, if you are in the 28 percent tax bracket, you are actually better off receiving the 6 percent interest (5.7 versus 6 percent). If you are in the 15 percent tax bracket, you are better off paying taxes on the 8 percent than receiving 6 percent tax free (6.8 versus 6 percent).

Dividends are paid by private corporations and may be paid quarterly, semiannually, annually, or not at all. They are always taxable. It is not unusual for seniors to have purchased stock during their working years, particularly from their employer, and directed that the dividends be reinvested to purchase additional shares of stock. Over a period of years, this can accumulate to a substantial amount of principal. However, if no one has directed the dividend reinvestments to be paid to your parents, they may not be receiving the cash benefit of owning these stocks. Some seniors have hundreds of thousands of dollars of stock but remain concerned about their month-to-month cash flow simply because the dividends being paid out by the stock were directed to purchase additional stock twenty or thirty years ago. It may be time to change from an accumulation phase to a spending one.

Individual Retirement Accounts and Other Deferred Income

A full description of IRAs and other forms of deferred income is contained in Part One, "Ourselves." This section focuses on what these things mean to someone who has retired.

We have historically been encouraged to save for retirement or the future through savings vehicles that allow us to defer income tax in special situations. *Deferral* means simply that no income tax is due until funds that are saved are withdrawn at some future time, usually after retirement. Probably, you are more familiar with deferred income than you may realize. The following examples illustrate this point.

Your mother worked as a teacher and, through her union, she had a fixed amount placed in her pension every year. She is now sixty-five years old and ready to retire. During her working years, the money placed in her pension and the income it accrued was not taxed. Now that she is ready to take distributions from this retirement account, they will be subject to income tax.

Your parents funded their IRA accounts every year. Depending on the year and the circumstances in which they made their IRA contributions, the funds they placed in the IRA may not have been subject to income tax. Regardless, the income earned on the funds in the IRA accounts were not subject to income tax because the tax was deferred. However, now they have reached retirement age and wish to take distributions, so these funds will be subject to income tax as they are withdrawn from their IRAs.

Your parents may also have established annuities in which they are paid an income—often a fixed amount over a set number of years.

Your parents have collected U.S. Savings bonds over the years. Each month for twenty years, they purchased a $25 bond. When these bonds are cashed in, the income earned on the bonds may be subject to federal income tax.

As you can see, the first step is determining what kinds of income your parents have. After that, a series of issues need to be considered:

1. When must your parents take mandatory distributions of these retirement accounts? In other words, when must they withdraw the money?

2. How much must they take in distributions each year?

3. What are the tax consequences of the distributions?

4. Must your parent or parents elect a beneficiary on these deferred retirement accounts?

5. If a beneficiary is required, must it be a spouse? What if the spouse is deceased or prefers not to be the beneficiary?

6. If the parent who owns the deferred account dies, what happens to the funds?

7. Does the estate of the deceased pay the income tax? What if the spouse is the beneficiary?

The answers to these questions are often complex, and the applicable laws frequently change. A competent attorney, financial planner, or accountant can provide you with answers.

If you want to learn more about deferred income and tax consequences, you should refer to one or more of the following resources.

RESOURCES

CBS Marketwatch
<http://www.cbs.marketwatch.com>

The Vanguard Group
PO Box 2600
Valley Forge, PA 19482-2600
(800) 871-3879
<http://www.vanguard.com>

Roth Ira Website Homepage
<http://www.rothira.com>

Strong On-Line
<http://www.strong-funds.com/strong/retirement98/roth/rothind>

Smith Barney Investment Update
<http://www.salomonsmithbarney.com>

The Investment FAQ
<http://www.invest-faq.com/articles>

401(k) Forum
625 Third St.
San Francisco, CA 94107
(415) 547-1120
<http://www.401kforum.com>

Benefits Link
1014 E. Robinson St.
Orlando, FL 32801
(407) 841-3717
<http://www.benefitslink.com>

Quicken
<http://www.quicken.com>

Small Business Advisor
Information International
Great Falls, VA 22066
(703) 450-7049
<http://isquare.com/retire.htm>

Summary: Each of these sites discusses various aspects of deferred income plans, including IRAs, Roth IRAs, 401(k), 403(b), and other pension alternatives.

Pension Options/Elections

One momentous decision can be made at pension election time: whether to take the entire pension in one lump sum or in some form of periodic or lifetime payout.

In the event that your parents have already made some form of annuity election, chances are good that their decision is irrevocable. Nevertheless, it is still of great importance to determine what election they did make because the death of the retiree in most instances will have a significant impact on the planning of the surviving spouse's pension income.

The surviving spouse may continue to receive the exact same amount of monthly benefit or may receive some reduced percentage of the monthly benefit or, in some cases, may receive no pension payment whatsoever after the death of the retiree. If you are in the position of being able to assist your parents in their long-range planning, clearly it is of vital importance to know what financial impact the death of a retiree would have on the surviving spouse.

Click on <http://www.Boomerbasics.com> for more information on pension options and elections.

Reparation Payments

Many Holocaust survivors, as well as heirs of survivors, who reside in the United States already have received or may at some time in the future receive reparation payments. At this point, it is unclear whether federal and state governments will subject these payments to income tax, but they have begun to at least consider the issue. During the 105th Congress, senators and representatives introduced legislation that would exclude from gross income any monies received by Holocaust survivors as reparation payments. The Senate and the House referred the legislation to the Finance Committee and the Ways and Means Committee, respectively, but took no further action. On the state level, Pennsylvania has taken the lead on this matter by declaring that as a general rule it will not subject reparation payments to its personal income tax or inheritance tax.

Income from Foreign Countries or Entities

It probably does not come as a surprise to read that the United States generally taxes all income regardless of whether the income is earned inside or outside of the United States. For example, the United States taxes, at regular individual tax rates, all income received from foreign sources by a U.S. citizen. A qualifying individual may offset individual income tax liability by claiming the foreign income tax exclusion and the exclusion for excess housing expenses. As a practical matter, however, these exclusions are available only in limited circumstances because to qualify for the exclusions, an individual must either be physically present in a foreign country for 330 days out of the past twelve months or a bona fide resident of a foreign country for a full tax year. In addition, a taxpayer with foreign earned income may reduce individual income tax liability either by deducting the amount of any foreign taxes paid or accrued during the tax year or by claiming a credit against income earned from sources within the United States.

Income from Family Residence

Although the principal residence is very often the largest asset that many seniors own, it is almost never viewed as an income-producing asset. If anything, it is seen as a cash drain owing to outstanding mortgage debt, taxes, and costs associated with maintaining the home. However, the principal residence can be a source of income.

Rent

Some seniors (but not too many) have decided that one way to help with the cost and maintenance of their large and largely unused homes is to rent some space to a tenant. Depending on the nature of the community that you live in, this may present distinct and perhaps insurmountable zoning problems. Aside from that, the senior is often looking not only for an additional source of income but also for some degree of companionship or caregiving from the tenant. And unless the house was built to accommodate two families or has some other type of separate living arrangement, the tenant is not going to be an indistinguishable name on a rent roll; chances are that he or she will become an integral part of your parent's day-to-day life. This can bring a number of concerns, and it is therefore important that you take an active interest in the type of tenant to whom your parent may be renting. It is also advisable, particularly where there is no division of the premises, such as in a two-family house, that duties and obligations beyond financial arrangements be spelled out in a formal agreement. Arrangements for cooking, cleaning, shopping, modifying the living premises, and doing yard work can serve as a boon for your parents or be a source of constant irritation for which there is no relief.

Reverse Equity Mortgage

Unlike a standard mortgage, a *reverse equity mortgage* offers a monthly payment by the lender to the homeowner for either a term of years or for the life of the homeowner. Some seniors have found this an effective way to utilize the equity in their home without actually giving up their home. As with any large financial transaction, your parents should fully understand all of the ramifications of the mortgage documents and the fees involved. Also, they should be sure that the amount of money that they would be receiving, whether it takes the form of a lump-sum payment, a monthly payment, or a line of credit, is adequate for the purposes they had in mind.

The large dangers inherent in these transactions are 1) the senior may not understand or properly calculate the amount of money that he or she requires, 2) a fixed-period loan may present thorny problems if they live beyond the fixed period yet want to remain in their home, and 3) an unhealthy financial institution may be unable to make the lifetime payment.

Income Tax Issues Confronting Our Parents

Not only are there variations from our planning in the types of income that our parents may receive, but there are several income tax considerations unique to them as well.

Standard Deduction

Elderly (over the age of sixty-five) or blind taxpayers are entitled to an additional standard deduction on their income tax returns, and your parents should avail themselves of this option if they can. Multiple additional standard deductions can be claimed in the event they are both elderly *and* blind. Also, the additional standard deduction(s) can be claimed whether or not the parent qualifies as a dependent of yourself or another taxpayer. However, if your parent is eligible as a dependent, a special calculation must be used to limit the ordinary standard deduction.

Credit for the Elderly and Disabled

People who are disabled or aged sixty-five and older are entitled to a tax credit. Although limitations are set on the credit based on income, savings may be available to you in offsetting someone's tax liability by virtue of this credit.

Deductibility of Medical Expenses

If your parents are spending substantial amounts of money on medical bills, they should consider whether the amount they spend is sufficient to deduct from their taxes. Medical expenses are deductible to the extent they exceed 7.5 percent of adjusted gross income but only if they are not reimbursed by someone else, for example, Medicare or medical insurance. Some additional deductions may be taken for the full cost if your parent is in a nursing home receiving skilled nursing care. Please note, however, that if your parent is in an adult home or assisted living arrangement, then only those costs associated with medical care may qualify for this deduction. In either case (nursing home or assisted living), while they may be incurring large capital gains from the sale of assets in order to pay for care, they might be able to claim substantial deductions to offset those gains, or any other income, on their tax returns.

Tax Implications of Sale of a Home

Much confusion previously existed over the use of a once-in-a-lifetime exemption of tax on the capital gain realized on the sale of a home when the seller is over the age of fifty-five. The rules have now been simplified to allow an exclusion of up to $500,000 per couple ($250,000 for an individual) in the event they should sell their principal residence, regardless of their age. Additionally, this may be done multiple times provided they are selling a home that has been their principal residence for two of the last five years. Although this creates an enormous opportunity for savings on income tax, you must be careful, as many families transfer a house to their children. If your parents want to do so, remind them that they are transferring it to someone who may sell the house eventually, but it may not be their principal residence at the time of the sale. Therefore, they will not get the benefit of this income tax break, and the family will instead realize a capital gain that it might not have had to otherwise declare.

The second income tax issue to consider with regard to the home is the *tax basis,* which is the cost of the home plus subsequent improvements. Upon selling a home, the sale price minus the tax basis amounts to the capital gain realized from the sale. If your parents were to give their house to you, your basis would remain the same as their basis (that is, their purchase price plus the cost of improvements). However, if they should leave the house to you upon their death, then the IRS provides a benefit in that your basis is stepped up to equal the fair market value of the home as of the date of their death, which is probably more than they paid for it. This creates a valuable planning opportunity; it may be wise to leave the house in your parents' name until death, thereby eliminating or reducing any capital gains. This is the rule regardless of whether it is a principal residence or not.

(This rule also applies to other appreciated assets such as stocks as well.) In cases where it is the principal residence, capital gain may not be an issue as previously discussed. If the family owns a second home or a vacation home, this may represent a very real tax savings for them.

> **INSIGHT**
>
> **Whether your parents consider gifting, selling, or disposing of real property, they must also consider applicable gift, estate, or income taxes.**

Taxation of Pensions and IRAs

The basic rule regarding pensions and IRAs is that funds that have not already been taxed are fully taxable at ordinary income tax rates when they are withdrawn. In cases where after-tax contributions to pension plans or IRAs may have been made, these will not be taxed a second time. However, the money received from the pension plans or IRAs usually has never been taxed before. Thus, it is usually wise to use IRAs as late as possible, as the invested funds will continue to grow on a tax-deferred basis. Eventually, your parents will have to withdraw money from their IRAs (after reaching the age of seventy and one-half years), but as long as they are getting sufficient income from other sources, it may be best to defer the withdrawals for as long as possible.

> **INSIGHT**
>
> **Remember, as discussed and distinguished in the "Financial" section of Part One, "Ourselves," there will be tax due on withdrawals from a traditional IRA but not from a Roth IRA. In a Roth IRA, the funds are subject to tax prior to setting it up.**

Claiming a Parent as a Dependent

It is not unusual for a parent to move in with a son or daughter and receive room, board, and medical care at their expense. In some cases, you may claim your parent on your income tax return as a dependent. However, five conditions must be met before the IRS will allow you to do so:

1. The taxpayer must be the child or in-law of the elderly person, or the elder person must be a member of the taxpayer's household.

2. The dependent's gross income must not exceed the amount of the personal exemption. Social Security benefits are *not* counted for this purpose.
3. The dependent must not file a joint tax return.
4. The dependent must be a U.S. citizen or lawful resident.
5. The dependent must get at least half of his or her support from the taxpayer, or a multiple-support agreement must be in effect, under which the dependency deduction is available by agreement to a person furnishing more than 10 percent of the elderly person's support. Besides cash payments, IRS regulations also count in-kind support such as providing food and lodging.

Satisfying all five requirements is difficult, but if you do meet each requirement, you can then claim an additional dependency exemption on your tax return for your parent.

Your parent probably has income higher than the standard deduction amount, so a dependency exemption cannot be taken. However, you can take a deduction for medical expenses that you are covering for your parent.

If your parent is incapable of caring for him- or herself and lives with you, then you may be entitled to claim a dependent-care income tax credit for expenses relating to taking care of your parent while you work.

RESOURCES

The Internal Revenue Service, U.S. Department of Treasury
<http://www.irs.ustreas.gov/prod/cover.html>

Summary: The IRS operates a Web site titled "The Digital Daily" that contains news, frequently asked tax questions, general tax information, forms, and on-line publications.

SmartMoney.com—The Wall Street Journal magazine
<http://www.smartmoney.com>

Summary: A good Web site from *SmartMoney* magazine with information on a large number of tax issues and estate planning.

Click on <http://www.Boomerbasics.com> for more information on income tax issues.

Investment Philosophy
Historically Embraced by Our Parents

At or during retirement, your parent may, for the first time, be confronted with having to articulate an investment philosophy. It is not at all unlikely that your parents may have gone through their entire working lives without having to make investment selections, as those were made for them by virtue of employer stock plans, pension plans, trustees, or the Social Security Administration. Unlike many of the pension plans we have today at our jobs, employees didn't have much input with earlier retirement savings plans. And as discussed previously, your parents may often be confronted with a large lump-sum payment of some type. Again, this may come from a life insurance payment, proceeds from the sale of their home, or a lump-sum distribution from a pension plan. It is because of these large sums coming into their hands that they often seek advice from children or professional advisors. Because they may come to you for advice or input, a valuable service can be provided in helping them consider what their investment needs might be.

Investing for the Long Term

In the not-too-distant past, our parents' investment philosophy was that after retirement they would live off of their pension income for a short time and then pass away within five to ten years. Their view was usually based on friends and relatives who considered that "long term" might mean ten years. Back then, a long-term investment strategy was not as important as it is today, when parents are living twenty, twenty-five, thirty, or more years beyond the date that they retire. In many cases, retirement lasts longer than the working years. Therefore, it is important that they understand the need to invest for more than just income and to protect against inflation. As discussed in the following section, a number of alternatives will allow for growth over the long term. However, impressing the need to invest for the long term to our parents is often a difficult task.

Investments

Our parents tend to become more conservative at this stage of life, preparing themselves to live comfortably without their accustomed paycheck.

They typically reduce debt such as credit card and home equity balances and make their final payment on a first mortgage. Their investment philosophy also tends to turn more conservative, reflecting this new stage of life.

Typical investment objectives include capital preservation, some continued growth, and an increased emphasis on income. These are prudent goals given both the need for stability and expected long-term use of the funds. A number of different investments can provide the results needed to achieve each of these goals:

1. Conservative Investments
    a. Some things don't change at all after retirement. Retirees still want the convenience of plenty of money on hand and easy to tap without red tape, any time, at a moment's notice. Liquid savings assume a more active role in the retiree's lifestyle; they're not just an emergency fund anymore. Typically they keep about 20 percent of their savings in a money market account that offers checking and relatively good potential returns. Other popular choices available: Treasury notes, bonds or bills, and CDs.
2. Growth and Income Potential Investments
    a. Not all moderate-income, moderate-risk investments are alike. Some offer a higher-than-average level of security that makes them especially attractive for retirees.
        i. Mutual funds, growth funds that seek long-term growth, or balanced funds that seek to preserve initial principal and provide current income and long-term growth
        ii. Unit investment trusts promise fixed income and payment of full face value at maturity, with tax advantages.
        iii. Blue-chip stocks, known historically for their quality and ability to earn profits and pay regular dividends
        iv. Corporate bonds
3. High-Growth Potential Investments
    a. Retired investors need to balance their tolerance for risk against the need for some growth to fight inflation and perhaps keep some investments in stocks and aggressively managed mutual funds.

b. All stocks are said to be high risk, but some stocks are much less risky than others. Blue chips or large company stocks were once unknowns. Finding tomorrow's blue chips is not easy, but it's not impossible, either. Taking the time to do the research can become a fascinating hobby or can be done through an investment advisor.

4. Quick and Easy Strategy

a. Put a portion of your assets in a conservative asset allocation fund, which includes a conservative mix of stocks, bonds, and cash equivalents.

For more information about the various types of investments your parents can make, see Part One, "Ourselves," under "Financial."

RESOURCES

Financial Engines
<http://www.financialengines.com>

MSN Money Central
<http://www.moneycentral.com>

Financenter
<http://www.financenter.com>

Charles Schwab & Co.
<http://www.schwab.com>

Quicken
<http://www.quicken.com>

Summary: These commercial sites all offer free services to assist in investment planning, including crunching numbers and calculating projections from retirement, education costs, taxes, and the like.

Forbes.com
<http://www.forbes.com/funds>

Fund Alarm
<http://www.fundalarm.com>

Index Funds.com
<http://indexfunds.com>

Mutual Fund Education Alliance
<http://www.mfea.com>

Financial Web
<http://www.financialweb.com>

Summary: Each of these sites provides information and research on thousands of mutual funds, and many offer links to mutual fund family sites.

Estate Planning

The typical estate plan for our parents (and probably for ourselves, too) usually came about once they had children. The plan is usually as basic as leaving everything to the surviving spouse, and if both should die, then their assets would be left to the children outright or in trust. At later stages in life, your parents often want, or need, to amend this plan. Now that the children are probably grown up, they may wish to leave bequests in a different manner. For example, depending on the financial, health, or emotional status of the children, it may make more sense to leave money in trust rather than giving it outright to them where it might be subject to their creditors, disqualify them from governmental benefits, or simply be misspent by them. Conversely, where a trust might have once been appropriate to their circumstances simply because they were minors, it may no longer be necessary. In some instances, it may make more economic sense to simply bypass the children and make gifts directly to grandchildren so as to avoid a generation of estate tax.

Another consideration comes about if your parent is widowed. Not only do issues of second-estate circumstances arise (that is, additional income and estate tax burdens or bequests to second families in the event of a subsequent marriage), but the parent must also update his or her beneficiary designations on life insurance, pension plans, IRAs, and the like to conform to the overall plan. Typically, years ago, each spouse named the other as beneficiary on all such designations without giving much thought to a contingency plan. Now, a contingency plan is needed to avoid unnecessary costs or delays upon death. Also, in the case of a widow or widower, inherited assets may make Medicaid planning difficult or impossible because the goal is to spend down and give away assets, not add to them.

Another variation that may impact an estate plan considerably is if a parent becomes, or already is, incapacitated. In this situation, the simple "all to each other" estate plan may not only result in financial disaster if the well spouse were to predecease the incapacitated one but also leave the family with very little ability to implement an appropriate estate plan for the surviving spouse.

The final consideration is that in any event, the impact of estate taxes must be taken into account.

INSIGHT

Estate planning done haphazardly or incorrectly can result in an estate catastrophe in which the wishes of your parents are not realized. If your parents have an estate worth planning, they could probably well afford to seek the counsel of a competent estate attorney.

For a complete discussion on estate planning, wills, trusts, and estate taxes, see Part One, "Ourselves," or click on <http://www.Boomerbasics .com> for more information.

Gifts

Among the many estate-planning techniques, the most common and perhaps easiest to implement is gift giving. Parents make gifts for a variety of reasons, whether it be to help finance a new home, help with the cost of college education, buy a new car, help start a business, support a charity, or reduce an estate. Regardless of whether they are motivated by tax or nontax reasons, it is important to note that for a gift to be legally complete, the donor must not only intend to make a gift but actually give up control as well. If your parents say, "You can have all of my silver, china, and crystal, but I want to keep it in my house until I die," they are not making a complete gift. Therefore, upon their passing, those items fall into their estate and are controlled by their will or trust. The IRS also follows this rule in calculating the decedent's gross estate. In other words, if you retain any control or have any strings attached to property that you were intending to give, then the IRS considers it to be yours at the time of your death. For example, your mother might add your name to her checking account that she intends to use until her death, at which time it becomes yours as the joint holder. This is not a completed gift. Conversely, if she puts it in your name alone and gives up control, then that item is no longer part of her gross estate.

INSIGHT

A completed gift is something you give away that you can't get back even if you change your mind.

Gifting as Part of the Estate Plan

In considering whether to make lifetime gifts as a part of an estate plan, your parents must identify their estate-planning objectives. Depending on the amount of control, access, and flexibility over the assets they wish to keep, your parents may not want to give things outright but instead examine various restricted ways to make gifts to others. For example, if your father would like to leave a substantial amount of money to your children but still needs the interest and dividends from those funds while he is alive, he may wish to establish a trust. This may not be a completed gift under the legal definition, but it still accomplishes the avoidance of probate and allows your father to maintain his retirement lifestyle. In other situations, your parents may wish to make gifts to their children or grandchildren but only for particular purposes such as buying a home or paying for college tuition. Again, a trust arrangement may allow them to make the gift but retain some control over when the funds are released to them. In other cases, they may desire to have no access or control over the funds, so outright gifts would accomplish this goal. Through each of these scenarios, the form of the gift giving is a matter of preference by the donor. As to the tax consequences, those may vary considerably based on the access and control retained by the donor.

INSIGHT

You need to consider whether the recipient of the gift is in a position to accept the gift in the manner in which you intended. If the recipient has credit (or other) problems, it may not be prudent to make an unconditional gift.

Tax Implications of Gifts

Lifetime Gifts

The federal unified gift and estate tax system potentially taxes each item of property you transfer to someone else. This is the case whether the transfer is made while you are alive or upon your death. However, for lifetime gifts, an annual federal gift tax exclusion allows each individual to transfer up to $10,000 to any donee free of gift tax. Additionally, there is no limit as to the number of donees to which a person may make such $10,000 gifts each year. If your parent has $100,000 they wish to give to their ten grandchildren in one year, they may do so without any gift tax consequences. (This $10,000 gift tax annual exclusion is indexed annually by increases to the cost of living based on 1997 but rounded to the next lowest multiple of $1,000. Given the recent low cost of living increases, there will be no adjustment during 2000.)

An additional feature of the annual exclusion is that a married individual may make a $20,000 gift and split the gift tax exclusion with a spouse. Even if one spouse has all of the funds from which the gift is made, both spouses can use their $10,000 annual exclusions to that donee so as to make a larger tax-free gift, up to $20,000. For example, your parents may wish to help you and your spouse purchase a new home that requires a $40,000 down payment, and your mother is willing to use $40,000 she has in a bank account. With your father consenting to the use of his annual exclusion, your mother could give $20,000 to you and $20,000 to your spouse this year, thus transferring $40,000 without incurring any gift tax.

Also note that for the annual gift tax exclusion to be applied, the gift must be the gift of a present interest. Therefore, gifts with any strings attached, such as gifts to trusts, would not receive this annual gift tax exclusion treatment because they are gifts of a future interest.

In addition to the $10,000 annual gift exclusion, you may also make tax-exempt payments for educational bills, nursing home bills, and medical bills as long as you pay such bills directly to the university, nursing home, or doctors on behalf of the donee. In addition to avoiding gift tax, there may be some income tax benefits by way of itemized deductions gained by this strategy as well.

One additional reminder is that as with the estate tax, an unlimited amount of funds may be transferred to spouses with no gift or estate tax credits.

Lifetime gifts are thus a very easy and inexpensive way to execute part of an estate plan. However, there are disadvantages aside from losing access and control over the gifted property. Chief among the disadvantages is the issue of a step-up in basis if appreciated property is the subject of the gift, especially if the donee intends to sell the appreciated property in the near future. Conversely, if there are no plans to sell the property in the near future, the disadvantage may not be a real drawback. To illustrate the effect of a loss of a stepped-up basis, assume that your parents want to give you some stock that they purchased when they were married forty years ago. At that time, the stock was purchased for $10 per share. Today it is worth $1,000 per share. In making a lifetime gift of the stock, you retain their cost basis ($10 per share). Upon your subsequent sale of the stock, you therefore have a gain of $990 per share ($1,000 sales price less $10 basis) and are therefore subject to income tax on a capital gain of $990. Conversely, had your parents retained that stock until death and passed it on to you through their will, your basis would be equal to the fair market value of the stock at the date of their death. In IRS terms, your basis is stepped up. In other words, assuming the stock was worth $1,000 at the date of their death, your basis would be $1,000. Upon your subsequent sale of the stock, you would realize no capital gain ($1,000 sales price less $1,000 stepped-up cost basis). Many people get so concerned about the costs of property transfers at death that they may overlook some very large income tax pitfalls in rushing ahead.

Charitable Gifts

For many of our aging parents, charitable giving has become a more important part of their estate plan than when they were younger and had fewer assets. Such gifts may provide a number of income, gift, and estate tax benefits in addition to the personal satisfaction they may receive in making such gifts. However, charitable gifts, unlike other lifetime gifts, rarely result in no net decrease in the family's wealth, so it is important that the person be charitably inclined to proceed with such planning. With regard to income tax benefits, a number of complex limitations are placed on how much people may deduct on their taxes for a gift in relation to their income in any given year. Generally, the deductible amount is equal to the fair market value of the property gifted to the charity. The same holds true for gifts upon death.

And when choosing which assets to use for charitable donations, look to the highly appreciated ones first rather then simply donating cash. The benefit is that you avoid tax on capital gains, so there is more for the charity. For example, if you have stock worth $1,000 that you bought for $100 and then sold, you would have about $600 to $700 left after taxes for the charity. If you instead gave the stock to the charity, it would receive the full $1,000 while you enjoy a $1,000 tax deduction. In many cases, however, your parents may not be in a position to part with the full value of the property and may instead wish to consider split-interest charitable transfers. Such transfers can combine both lifetime and estate-planning objectives in that they can remove large sums from their estate while providing themselves with additional income during their lifetimes.

If you want to retain some control over the asset by keeping a lifetime interest, it can be done, but certain IRS rules must be followed to qualify for the charitable deduction. In following such rules, such split-interest gifts to charities usually take one of two forms—as a charitable lead trust or charitable remainder trust. Briefly, a *charitable lead trust* allows income to the designated charity, and the remainder interest goes to the donor or some other noncharity, such as children or grandchildren. A *charitable remainder trust* is the reverse in that your parents or another noncharity receive the income and upon death the remainder would pass on to the charity. Granted, this is a simplification of the split-interest rules, as several other provisions must be followed to receive the full tax benefits. But it may be a good way for your parents to accomplish their charitable intentions while providing themselves or other beneficiaries with a portion of the gifted property.

Click on <http://www.Boomerbasics.com> for more information regarding charitable gifts.

Impact on Potential Eligibility for Governmental Assistance

Often, our parents make gifts to children and grandchildren in furtherance of their overall estate plan. However, depending on their health, they must be mindful of the consequences with regard to eligibility for Medicaid, which is the joint federal and state program designed to cover the cost of certain medical expenses, such as nursing home care. However, to qualify for Medicaid, a person must meet asset and income requirements and not violate the transfer penalty rules. Because the program is based on financial need, the transfer penalty rules are in place to prevent someone from simply giving all of their money away one day and saying they are financially needy the next. Therefore, in the event your parents are making any large gifts, they must be certain to have sufficient assets and income to cover any penalty period that they may incur by virtue of those gifts. Naturally, if they are healthy, the likelihood of such gifts having an impact on eventual Medicaid eligibility is unlikely. And if there should be an unexpected change in health, gifts may be returned in part if necessary to gain Medicaid eligibility. In any event, the transfer penalty rules can be confusing and are calculated differently not only from state to state but also from county to county. Therefore, it is important to find out the local law when coordinating a gift-giving program with any Medicaid planning your parents may be implementing.

Gifting the Primary Residence

Life Estate

For many parents, their residence is the primary asset in their estate and thus is the focal point of their estate plan. Although they would like to keep the home in the family or at least have the proceeds from a sale go on to children some day, they still want to remain living there. What many people hastily do is simply deed the property to their children. This does keep it in the family, but it is often a costly way to do it in the long run. An outright transfer typically results in a very large tax burden to the family at some point in the future when the house is sold because the opportunity for a step-up in basis is lost. Alternatively, the family should consider transferring the house by way of a deed with a retained life estate.

A *life estate* is essentially a limited interest in real property. A life estate holder does not have full title to the property but has the use of the property for his or her lifetime. Upon death, the property passes to what are known as the *remaindermen*. While the life tenant is alive, he or she is responsible for the typical costs of upkeep, maintenance, and carrying the home. Such costs only shift to the remaindermen upon death of the life tenant. For most families, this is exactly in line with what their intentions would be: Their parents would live in the home for their lifetimes and would transfer to the next generation immediately upon their death.

Tax Consequences

Capital Gain

As previously mentioned, capital gain can be a problem when a home is simply deeded to someone else in that the recipient receives the same basis that the donor had. For example, if your parents purchased their home for $50,000 and it is now worth $100,000 and they deed it to you, your cost basis remains the same as their $50,000 purchase price. Therefore, upon a subsequent sale by you, you would realize a capital gain of $50,000 ($100,000 sales price less $50,000 basis). And because it is a capital gain on the sale of a home that would normally receive some capital gain exclusion, remember it is not the sale of your principal residence. Therefore, you do not get this special tax benefit and would thus pay tax on the capital gain.

Now contrast the outright transfer to the transfer by deed with a life estate. In the life estate situation, your parents transfer the $100,000 house to you and retain the right to live there for the remainder of their lives. Because this is not a complete gift in accordance with the IRS rules, it remains a part of their gross estate. However, they will still be obligated to report this as a taxable gift. Upon their death, the value of the house ($100,000) is a part of their gross estate, but if the survivor has less than a $675,000 estate, there is no estate tax. Furthermore, the date-of-death value becomes your cost basis. Assuming that you sell the home shortly after your parents have passed away, the sale price is not likely to be much higher than date-of-death value (that is, your stepped-up basis amount). In most cases, this results in virtually no capital gain at all, thereby saving the family substantial income taxes.

Possible Loss of Senior Citizen, Veteran, and Other Tax Exemptions

Many of our parents receive various exemptions through state or local municipalities with regard to their real property taxes. These benefits may come about by virtue of their being senior citizens, veterans of the armed forces, or otherwise qualified for other state and local programs relevant to senior homeowners. It is for this reason that our parents are often reluctant to consider transferring their home whether outright or with a deed with a life estate because they do not want their property taxes to go up. As the technique of using the deed with life estate has become more readily used, most municipalities do not view the life estate as an outright transfer and do acknowledge that your parents remain the occupants and legal owners of the property for their lifetimes, so the benefits remain in force. If the situation should arise where their exemptions cease or taxes go up, it would be advisable to contact the municipality's assessor's office to explain to him or her before you make the transfer that your parents will remain on the deed as life tenants and will in fact remain residents of the property. Typically, they will not deem the transfer as a change in ownership that adversely affects your parents' tax exemption status.

> *Impact on Medicaid Eligibility If a Transfer*
> *Is Not a Permissible Medicaid Transfer under Federal Law*

As with any other gift of property, Medicaid does look at the transfer to determine whether it violates the transfer penalty rules when considering Medicaid eligibility. When transferring a property by deed with a life estate, the value of the gift is not equal to the full fair market value of the house but instead is equal to the value of the remainder interest. In other words, the value of the gift is determined by what the remainderman will ultimately receive in the future. The local Department of Social Services will calculate the value of a life estate and remainder interest based on the current fair market value of the property and the age of the donor. A life estate with a remainder interest table is published by the Federal Health Care Financing Administration in its annual *Medicaid Manual*. Click on <http://www.Boomerbasics.com> for a copy of this table.

Gifting Program

When your parents are deciding to make major gift contributions to their children, many factors need to be considered. Some of the ways to give property, money, stocks, or other gifts to a minor are discussed in Part Two, "Our Children," under "Financial."

RESOURCES

> **Deloitte & Touche Estate Planning Guide**
> <http://www.dtonline.com/estate/cover.htm>

Summary: This on-line guide is produced and maintained by Deloitte & Touche LLP, a professional services firm. The Estate Planning Guide contains planning worksheets and helpful tips and strategies for financial planning.

Insurance

Life Insurance

As our parents age, the traditional needs for life insurance (mortgage satisfaction, providing for young children, payment of college tuition) seem to fade into the background. This does not mean that your parents should not review and quite possibly continue to maintain life insurance.

First, it is important to have a basic understanding of the two major types of life insurance: term insurance and whole-life or cash-value insurance (see also the section on insurance in Part One, "Ourselves"). Term-life insurance becomes either cost prohibitive or simply not available as we age. Many policies stop coverage at age sixty-five, seventy, or seventy-two, regardless of whether or not an individual is able to pay the premium. Once the term is up, no death benefit and no residual value remain in a term-life insurance policy.

It is not unusual for our parents to have purchased the whole-life or cash-value life insurance. For many of that generation, a life insurance policy was considered an investment and a supplement to their retirement. It was a policy that had a fixed premium for life based on the age when they took out the policy. Often, the dividends that these policies paid were used to pay the premiums or to pay for additional insurance.

Cash Value

The cash value of a policy and the option selected for the dividend payments are available from the insurance company. (Of course, they have their own forms to fill out, but it is usually worth the effort.)

It is fairly common for seniors to have a life insurance policy in which the cash value is almost equal to the death benefit. Depending on the economic circumstances and desires of your parents, it may be wise to cancel the policy and have them receive the cash value for their use and enjoyment while they are alive as opposed to waiting for the beneficiary to receive what may be only a slightly higher death benefit in a postmortem situation.

Many veterans have what is commonly called NSLI (National Service Life Insurance), which they acquired as a result of their military service. Once again, such policies are usually very low profile, and your parents must make known to other family members that the policy exists; otherwise, the benefit will often go uncovered.

Use in Income Planning

Occasionally life insurance is purchased in the later years to work in conjunction with the election of a retirement plan option. Under this plan, a significant life insurance policy is purchased on the retiree, with the surviving spouse or some other family member named as beneficiary. The retiree collects a single-life-only payout from his or her retirement plan, which maximizes the monthly benefit he or she receives while alive. Once the retiree passes away, the life insurance proceeds are used to replace the lost pension benefit. If the spouse or other family member that the policy was intended to benefit predeceased the retiree, the retiree could then be free to cancel the insurance policy and thus receive the maximum benefit without also having to pay for the insurance premium.

In order for this plan to work, the after-tax single-life annuity payment (less insurance premiums for the new insurance policy) must exceed the reduced annuity payment that would cover a surviving spouse or other family member.

Policy Ownership

The owner of a life insurance policy is not necessarily the same person as the policy's insured and typically not the same as the beneficiary. Normally, when policies are taken out, the owner is the one insured, and the beneficiary is usually the spouse and then the children. For our parents, the ownership of a life insurance policy does not constitute an asset that has a large intrinsic value while they are alive (with the exception of the cash surrender value). Therefore, for estate-planning purposes, the transfer of the ownership of the policy, not the change of the beneficiary, very often permits a reduction in estate taxes without imposing any real hardship on the owner of the policy. The transfer of the ownership of a policy is a relatively simple procedure that may be initiated, after you have considered the estate and gift tax ramifications, by contacting the insurance company and requesting the necessary forms.

A discussion of the various types of life insurance is contained in Part One, "Ourselves," under "Financial."

RESOURCES

Insurance News Network
<http://www.insure.com>

Summary: Insure.com is the Insurance News Network, an independent news site that does not sell insurance. This Web site contains information and guidance for consumers on different types of insurance, including life insurance, with worksheets for calculating your insurance needs.

Commercial Union Life Insurance Company's Life Insurance Basics
<http://www.culife.com/lif>

Summary: This site has helpful information on the different types of policies and calculators to help determine life insurance needs and costs for insurance.

Health Insurance

Medicare

Health insurance is one of the many things that significantly change as our parents get older. The traditional health insurance coverage that they had for their working and younger years will be replaced, usually at age sixty-five, by Medicare. For almost all seniors, Medicare becomes their primary health insurance, with other insurance policies or HMO benefits becoming secondary.

Medicare is the federal health insurance program for the aged and disabled established by Congress in 1965. It is administered by the Health Care Financing Administration, commonly referred to as the HCFA.

Medicare beneficiaries are eligible for benefits regardless of income or assets. Medicare is not a need-based program like Medicaid, the jointly administered federal and state health insurance program for low-income people.

The Medicare program is divided into Part A and Part B. Part A (hospital insurance) primarily covers inpatient hospital, skilled nursing facility, and home health and hospice services. Part A is premium free for those who have earned forty credits or more as determined by the Social Security Administration. In 1999 you earn one credit for each $740 of wages or self-employment income you earn—up to four credits each year. Part B (supplemental medical insurance) covers almost all reasonable and necessary medical services, including physician's services, outpatient hospital care, therapy, laboratory tests, X rays, mental health services, ambulance services, and durable medical equipment. Part B is purchased for a monthly premium ($45.50 to $80 in 1999).

The traditional Fee-for-Service Medicare coverage takes care of most reasonable and necessary health care services but does not cover most outpatient prescription drugs, preventative care, dental services, custodial or long-term nursing home care, or experimental procedures.

Under this government program, although the bulk of the covered costs are paid for by Medicare, your parents must still contend with significant deductibles ($768 annual deductible in 1999 for hospital care). For nursing home coverage, which Medicare will pay up to a maximum of 100 days for qualified beneficiaries, the patient must pay a coinsurance amount of almost one hundred dollars a day from day 21 to day 100.

As with other government programs, a lot of public information is available to help you and your parents learn about your rights and responsibilities under the Medicare program (see the Resources listings following this section on page 345).

INSIGHT

It is imperative that you and your parents understand that Medicare, at best, generally covers a minimum amount of long-term nursing home care or home care.

Many seniors are used to having Medicare cover most of their medical costs, and when they find out it covers only a small portion of nursing home care, they are both shocked and trapped, because very often there is no option for them other than financial ruin.

Medigap Insurance

To reduce many of these previously mentioned out-of-pocket expenses and to help pay for things that are not covered by standard Medicare policies such as excess doctor charges or at-home recovery assistance, most Medicare beneficiaries buy a Medicare supplemental insurance (Medigap) policy or have a retiree policy from a former employer or union.

One of the largest advantages that Fee-for-Service Medicare provides is that beneficiaries have a great deal of control over their medical care; they can choose their doctors, including specialists, as well as other health care providers and facilities. They may also choose among the full array of available medical treatments and receive treatment anywhere in the United States.

The biggest disadvantage is cost, whether arising from deductibles and copayments or from the premiums for the Medigap policies. However, if a parent became the victim of a serious acute or chronic disease, the actual cost of care will substantially exceed the costs of supplemental insurance. Medigap policies come in a range of ten standardized plans, labeled Plan A through Plan J, from which your parents may choose.

> **INSIGHT**
>
> **None of these Medigap policies cover long-term custodial care at home or in a nursing facility, unlimited prescription drugs, hearing aids, or eye care.**

The basic benefits contained in Plan A and each of the other plans includes coverage of all hospital co-insurance, an additional 365 days in the hospital, 20 percent co-insurance for Part B services, and the first three pints of blood. Plans B through J include plan A's basic benefits plus a combination of additional benefits. (Click on <http://www.Boomerbasics.com> for a comparison chart of Medigap benefits from Plans A through J.)

The annual cost for these policies ranges from $900 for a basic policy to more than $2,000 for a more comprehensive policy. Premiums for a policy may vary among the insurance companies and from state to state.

Medicare HMOs

Medicare Managed Care (Medicare HMOs) has been available for Medicare beneficiaries since 1982. In 1997 approximately 13 percent of the Medicare population was enrolled in Medicare HMOs. Generally, the HMO contracts with the federal government to provide Medicare beneficiaries the full range of services that would otherwise be available to them under the Fee-for-Service Medicare program. HMOs will also provide additional services not covered under the traditional Medicare plan.

INSIGHT

Enrollees in these types of plans will generally be covered only for services received from health care providers in the HMO's network, except for emergency and urgent care services. A careful analysis of the various coverages (and potential medical problems of your parents) must be done when selecting whether or not the Medicare HMO makes sense, no matter how alluring the advertising may be.

Medicare HMO costs and related charges vary by plan. Members continue to pay their Part B premium and may be charged some additional premium by the HMO (although the popular plans have no premium.) Profits of the HMO over a certain threshold must be returned to enrollees through lower premiums, lower copayments, or additional benefits. As a result, most Medicare HMOs do not charge premiums, have copayment (usually ranging from $2 to $20 for each service), or offer additional benefits, which includes free eyeglasses or generic drug coverage. Most HMO members must choose a primary care physician. This is a significant difference from the Fee-for-Service concept. The primary care physician, in consultation with the medical director or other administrator, generally decides which specialist the beneficiary will see, if any, and which treatments or other medical services are medically necessary for the beneficiary.

RESOURCES

Health Insurance Association of America (HIAA)
<http://www.hiaa.com>

Summary: This Web site contains a very good consumer-oriented guide to health insurance.

Health Care Financing Agency
7500 Security Blvd.
Baltimore, MD 21244
(410) 786-3000
<http://www.hcfa.gov>
<http://www.medicare.gov>

Summary: The HCFA is a federal agency that administers several government programs, including Medicare and Medicaid. The HCFA provides the public with a variety of on-line and off-line services that include, but are not limited to, Web sites and publications, including the following:

1. *Medicare and You*
2. *1999 Guide to Health Insurance for People with Medicare*
3. *Understanding Your Medicare Choice*
4. *Guide to Choosing a Nursing Home*
5. *Advance Directives*
6. *Guide to Medicare Savings Accounts*

You can order these and other publications by calling Medicare's toll free hotline number at (800) 318-2596. These publications can also be viewed and, in some cases, downloaded from the Internet.

The HCFA's Web sites, which are linked to each other, provide valuable information to Medicare beneficiaries and other interested persons. In addition to providing an overview about the Medicare program, eligibility requirements, premiums, and copayments, these Web sites provide information on many related issues.

Medicare Rights Center
1460 Broadway
New York, NY 10036
(212) 869-3850
<http://www.medicarerights.org>

Summary: The Medicare Rights Center is a national not-for-profit organization devoted to ensuring that seniors have access to affordable health care.

Medicaid

Medicaid is an entitlement program for individuals who meet financial and medical eligibility requirements. Approximately thirty-six million people receive Medicaid benefits.

Elderly individuals who have minimal incomes and resources may be eligible for Medicaid, which covers almost all health care expenses including, in some cases, Medicare premiums, deductibles, and coinsurance. Medicaid covers a much broader range of services than Medicare, including preventive care, eye care, prescription drugs, and custodial care in a nursing home. However, the particular services included will differ somewhat from state to state because Medicaid is a state-administered program whereas Medicare is a federal program.

For residents in nursing facilities, Medicaid is or quickly becomes what pays for their care. The cost of nursing facility care is substantial, and few people have the resources on their own to pay for it over an extended period of time. In New York, for example, monthly nursing facility care can cost over $10,000 in certain facilities. Moreover, the Medicaid programs have been designed to allow applicants to qualify for benefits through sophisticated planning as long as such planning conforms with applicable requirements. Hence, it can be argued that Medicaid is a form of national long-term care insurance.

Click on <http://www.Boomerbasics.com> for more information on the Medicaid program as well as a review of the legal techniques to plan for Medicaid eligibility.

Long-Term Care Insurance

As noted in the introduction to the "Personal" section of this part, as our parents age, the likelihood that they will require long-term care services, whether in their home, in a skilled nursing facility, or in some other in-patient setting, increases.

Given the exorbitant cost of long-term care, our parents, as well as ourselves, should consider the option of purchasing long-term care insurance. Such insurance may be costly, but if your parents require long-term care coverage and have an appropriate policy, they can protect their assets.

Over the past several years, the availability of quality long-term care products has increased substantially. Many of these products provide coverage for services that can be provided in your parents' home or in an in-patient facility, such as a nursing home.

You and your parents should be aware of several areas of importance when reviewing a long-term care policy, particularly the following ones:

- *Age.* Are your parents too old to qualify for a policy?
- *Levels of care.* Does the policy provide for different types of services your parents may require, including but not limited to home care and nursing home care?
- *Pre-existing medical conditions.* Will your parents be deemed ineligible or will the premiums be higher if they have pre-existing medical conditions?
- *Exclusions.* What services are not provided?
- *Length of benefit.* How long will they be eligible to receive the benefit?
- *Waiting period.* When will they begin to receive benefits?
- *Actual benefits.* What exactly are the benefits they will be receiving?

Although quality long-term care products now exist, it may not be in your parents' best interest to purchase such a policy. If, for example, your parents have limited income or assets, the cost of an appropriate policy may be prohibitive; depending on factors such as your parents' age and medical condition, such a policy could have an annual cost of several thousand dollars. Moreover, your parents may be eligible for other benefits, such as Medicaid (see the discussion on page 347).

Click on <http://www.Boomerbasics.com> for additional information regarding long-term insurance.

RESOURCES

Americans for Long Term Care Security (ALTCS)
1275 K St. NW, Suite 601
Washington, DC 20005
<http://www.ltcweb.org/>

Summary: The ALTCS is a coalition of organizations formed to educate policy makers, the media, and the general public about the need for long-term care security.

American Health Care Association (AHCA)
1201 L St. NW
Washington, DC 20005
(202) 842-4444
<http://www.ahca.org>

Summary: On the homepage, click on "Consumer Information" and then choose from the list "What Consumers Need To Know About Long Term Care Insurance."

HEALTH ~~~~~~~~

As noted in the section on longevity, the stereotypical view held by many that the elderly are frail and sick is inaccurate. There is no ironclad rule stating that when you reach a certain age, you will be stricken with a serious medical condition. However, as we get older, our susceptibility to chronic conditions, illnesses, or disabilities increases dramatically.

This section provides basic information about several common diseases and conditions affecting our parents, what to look for in terms of early warning signs, and resources available to assist our parents and ourselves in coping with these problems.

INSIGHT

Most of the resources listed in the "Health" section of "Ourselves" address many of the health issues that affect our parents.

Health Issues of Special Concern to Our Parents

Arthritis

Arthritis is the catchall term for more than one hundred diseases that affect the joints. Degenerative arthritis (osteoarthritis), which is characterized by the breakdown of the cartilage cushion within the joint, is the most common form, afflicting more than sixteen million Americans. More than half of those over the age of sixty-five have some evidence of osteoarthritis visible on an X ray. Degenerative arthritis of the knees and hands occurs more frequently in women; osteoarthritis in the hips affects women and men equally. Other joints commonly affected by the disease are in the back, neck, and toes.

Osteoarthritis can be caused or exacerbated by heredity, excess weight, joint injury or overuse, or lack of activity. If your parents experience any of the following symptoms that last for more than two weeks, they should talk with their doctor about the possible presence of osteoarthritis:

- Pain or stiffness in or near a joint
- Bony swelling in a joint
- Crackling noises (think Rice Krispies!) when moving a joint
- Inflammation (swelling, redness, and tenderness) in a joint

Although osteoarthritis can't be prevented or cured, its symptoms can be managed through a combination of weight loss, exercise, physical or occupational therapy, hot or cold packs, medication, and in severe cases, surgery.

RESOURCES

Arthritis Foundation
1330 West Peachtree Street
Atlanta, GA 30309
(404) 872-7100
<http://www.arthritis.org>

Summary: The Arthritis Foundation is dedicated to improving the quality of life for people who are affected by arthritis through research, advocacy, and other services.

Arthritis National Research Foundation
200 Oceangate, Suite 440
Long Beach, CA 90802
(800) 588-CURE
<http://www.curearthritis.org>

Summary: The Arthritis National Research Foundation is a nonprofit organization that provides funding for research for the prevention, treatment, and cure of arthritis and rheumatic diseases.

Diabetes

Adult-onset (type 2) diabetes affects more than fourteen million Americans, a figure that will only increase as the population ages because type 2 diabetes usually strikes after age forty.

Diabetes screening might be a good idea for your parents, even in the absence of symptoms, because early diagnosis of hypoglycemia (low blood sugar) may reduce subsequent complications of the disease. Your parents should see their doctor about screening if they are significantly overweight, have a parent or sibling with diabetes, have hypertension or high cholesterol levels, or belong to a high-risk ethnic group (African American, Hispanic, or Native American). If the test results are normal, your parents should be screened every three years.

Because the symptoms of type 2 diabetes tend to come about gradually, they may go unnoticed until problems develop. Your parents should see their doctor immediately for a diabetes screening if they exhibit any of the following: frequent urination; unusual thirst; extreme hunger; unexplained weight loss; extreme fatigue; blurred vision; irritability; tingling or numbness in the legs, feet, or hands; frequent infections of the skin, gums, vagina, or bladder; itchy skin; or slow healing of cuts and bruises.

Left untreated, diabetes can have serious long-term complications, including increased risk of high blood pressure, stroke, and heart disease; nerve damage; peripheral vascular disease (which, in severe cases, can lead to amputation); and increased risk of eye disorders such as cataracts, glaucoma, and even blindness. The duration of type 2 diabetes does not correlate with the likelihood of vascular complication. Therefore, screening is key.

RESOURCES

The National Diabetes Information Clearinghouse (NDIC)
1 Information Way
Bethesda, MD 20892-3560
(301) 654-3327
<http://www.niddk.nih.gov/health/diabetes/ndic.htm>

Summary: The NDIC is an information and referral service of the National Institute of Diabetes and Digestive and Kidney Diseases, which is a division of the National Institutes of Health.

The American Diabetes Association (ADA)
1660 Duke Street
Alexander, VA 22314

(703) 549-1500

<http://www.diabetes.org>

Summary: The ADA is a nonprofit health organization providing research, information, and advocacy concerning diabetes.

INSIGHT

For additional information regarding diabetes, refer to page 102 of Part One, "Ourselves."

Osteoporosis

Osteoporosis (defined as decreased bone density, which makes bones brittle and susceptible to fracture) affects twenty-eight million Americans, 80 percent of them women, and results in one and a half million fractures a year. As many as 25 percent of postmenopausal women have some degree of osteoporosis, and 89 percent of women over age seventy-five are affected. Around 40 percent of all U.S. women will fracture at least one bone before they reach the age of seventy. Besides gender and age, other risk factors include a family history of osteoporosis, ethnicity (the highest incidence is among Caucasians and Asians), having low bone mass, prolonged deficiency of estrogen (women) or testosterone (men), lifelong low calcium or vitamin D intake, inactivity, smoking, excessive alcohol and caffeine intake, and a smaller body size.

A broken bone (particularly in the vertebrae, hip, or wrist) is often the first sign of osteoporosis. If osteoporosis is present, everyday activities such as walking or standing or even strenuous coughing can cause a series of compression fractures, which can eventually lead to the loss of height and humpbacked appearance so common in many older women. Hip fractures, which are about half as common as spinal fractures, can be especially devastating because they often require long-term care or hospitalization. Almost one-third of women who live to the age of ninety likely will have a hip fracture related to osteoporosis.

If your parent has many of the risk factors for osteoporosis or has already experienced any symptoms of the disease (such as loss of height or a fracture from a mild fall), she or he should consult a doctor about the possibility of osteoporosis. Testing will involve a measurement of bone density and will be used to rule out other possible causes of low bone mass or low back pain, such as degenerative arthritis and disc disease.

Because there's no way to reverse the effects of osteoporosis, treatments usually focus on preventing further skeletal degeneration. Estrogen replacement therapy (ERT), which for years was used in the short term to relieve the symptoms of menopause, has more recently been administered over the long term to prevent osteoporosis and heart disease in women. ERT is controversial because of its side effects, which may include a greater risk of breast and uterine cancers. Given the variety of treatments available, the best course of action is for your mother to discuss these options with her doctor, who can make recommendations based on your mother's age, medical history, other risk factors, and so on.

RESOURCES

National Osteoporosis Foundation (NOF)
1232 22nd Street NW
Washington, DC 20037-1292
(202) 223-2226
<http://www.nof.org>

Summary: The National Osteoporosis Foundation is a nonprofit organization that provides information and resources on preventing and treating osteoporosis as well as education and training for health professionals and participates in research relating to osteoporosis. Membership is available for individuals and health professionals and includes such services as a newsletter and other publications.

Sexual Dysfunction

Sexual dysfunction in older men and women may appear as a lack of desire or as an inability to become excited or aroused. Whatever the cause, sexual dysfunction is not an inevitable part of aging. Despite the widely held belief that some people believe they're just too old to have sex, studies have shown that even men and women in their eighties can enjoy healthy sex lives.

INSIGHT

If you don't believe older men and women are having sex (and enjoying it!), you should study the statistics on older persons who suffer from sexually transmitted diseases, which demonstrate not only that older persons are having sex but also that, unfortunately, some have still not learned how to practice safe sex.

A lack of desire is the primary problem for about half the people who see doctors about sexual disorders, and the majority of those having this complaint are men. A low libido in both sexes can arise from any number of factors, including changes in health, lifestyle, or relationships. It is also characteristic of depression and may be a side effect of certain medications. In older women, a lack of desire for sex might stem from the hormonal changes of menopause; it also might be associated with painful intercourse as a result of vaginal atrophy and inadequate natural lubrication.

Treatments can be difficult to prescribe because of the myriad factors involved. Treating an underlying illness, switching medications, or discontinuing the one that caused the symptoms all may revive the libido. Lubrication problems in women can be treated with a topical vaginal estrogen cream and by using water-based lubricants such as K-Y Jelly. If the problem appears nonphysical, more positive sexual experiences, open communication with a partner, and exploring one's own needs through fantasy and so forth may help.

Problems with excitement or arousal in older women might also be due to the lack of natural vaginal lubrication, which can make intercourse painful. More often, however, the disorder likely is rooted in an underlying psychological cause such as depression, stress, or anger and hostility toward a partner.

Although older men typically take longer to achieve an erection, the inability to sustain an erection sufficient for sexual intercourse more than 25 percent of the time is called erectile dysfunction (commonly called impotence, though that term is falling out of favor because of its negative connotations). This condition can result as a side effect of certain medications and from disorders that interfere with the blood flow to the penis, such as heart disease, atherosclerosis, high blood pressure, diabetes, chronic alcoholism, liver failure, and an elevated cholesterol level. In addition, because smoking interferes with blood flow to the penis, it is considered the number one risk factor in erectile dysfunction. Other possible causes are low testosterone levels and neurological disorders such as spinal cord damage and multiple sclerosis. Psychological problems such as anxiety, depression, guilt, and low self-esteem can be both causes and effects of erectile dysfunction.

Treatment options for erectile dysfunction include oral drug therapy (witness the rise in Viagra use), vacuum constriction devices, penile injection therapy, intraurethral drug therapy, and surgery. Psychotherapy or marital therapy might be appropriate options for psychologically rooted problems.

RESOURCES

American Foundation for Urologic Disease (AFUD)
1126 N. Charles
Baltimore, MD 21201
(410) 468-1800
<http://www.afud.org>

Summary: AFUD is a nonprofit corporation dedicated to supporting research, education, and patient support services for those affected by a urologic disease or disorder.

Impotence World Association (IWA)
PO Box 410
Bowie, MD 20718-0410
<http://www.impotenceworld.org>

Summary: The Impotence World Association is a nonprofit organization offering information and educational resources on impotence, treatment, and information for partners of men who suffer from this condition. A membership program provides members with additional services such as a newsletter and access to medical professionals who can supply additional information.

National Kidney and Urologic Diseases Information Clearinghouse
  (NKUDIC)
3 Information Way
Bethesda, MD 20892-3580
<http://www.niddk.nih.gov/health/kidney/nkudic.htm>

Summary: The NKUDIC is an information and referral service of the National Institute of Diabetes and Digestive and Kidney Diseases, a division of the National Institutes of Health.

Click on <http://www.Boomerbasics.com> for more information on the causes of and treatments for sexual dysfunction in both men and women.

Sensory Impairment

Vision

For most older adults, the aging process leads to a slow but steady decrease in visual functioning. The degree of decline varies tremendously. What's important is how the visual impairment affects the individual's way of life. Rather than admitting their eyesight is worsening, the elderly may simply withdraw from activities they previously enjoyed because of their visual limitations. The best insurance against potentially catastrophic visual impairments is to schedule eye exams regularly.

Some changes in vision occur naturally as a result of the aging process. For example, the number of eyelashes decreases, leading to a greater risk of eye injury; there are fewer tears, physiologically speaking anyway (the tear production of an eighty-year-old is just 25 percent of a teenager's), which can increase eye irritation; the lens becomes more discolored, which can lessen color perception; and the muscle tissue surrounding the eye begins to lose its elasticity, which can contribute to increased blurring, worsening night vision, and a greater sensitivity to glare.

Many older adults complain of burning and itchy eyes. The eyelids become less elastic and sag. The elderly eye gradually loses the ability to focus when performing up-close tasks such as reading or sewing. Decreased peripheral vision and depth perception increase the risk for accidents and injuries. Floaters—flecks, spots, or brilliant crystals in the older person's field of vision—are common and a real source of frustration when they interfere with the simplest of visual activities, such as watching television.

Cataracts, a condition in which the lens of the eye becomes clouded, are common among the aged. Although just 5 percent of those between the ages of fifty-two and sixty-two develop cataracts, that figure jumps to 46 percent for people between the ages of seventy-five and eighty-five. Cataracts develop over time and lead to a painless loss of vision. Common symptoms include difficulty adjusting to bright light or glare and the need to change an eyeglass prescription frequently to accommodate deteriorating sight. When vision becomes severely affected, the cataract or lens must be surgically removed, and vision is then corrected by a surgically implanted lens, a contact lens, or cataract glasses.

Another common visual problem in the elderly is glaucoma, which is caused by increased fluid pressure in the eye that can damage the retina. Initially, peripheral vision is affected, and eventually blindness may occur. Because glaucoma has no obvious symptoms, anyone over the age of forty should receive regular eye exams, which can measure eye pressure simply and quickly. The excess fluid can then be drained before full-scale glaucoma sets in and the retina is damaged.

For those who already suffer visual limitations, encourage the use of large-print books, magazines, and newspapers; magnifying glasses; telephones with enlarged numbers and letters; large-number playing cards; and large-eye sewing needles. Proper lighting is essential for the visually impaired. The use of bright tape or paint on stairs will help to prevent accidents, especially at night. Silverware and things such as toothbrushes and hairbrushes that have bright handles will be easier to locate. Lastly, don't rearrange the furniture without showing those with visual impairments what you've done.

INSIGHT

Amazing and wonderful discoveries have been made that make possible surgical and nonsurgical intervention to improve or correct vision-related problems. For many with visual impairments, such intervention may prove to be the difference between day and night. There is no greater medicine for most

parents than to see the smile of their children and grandchildren; they need to know if and how they can maintain and improve their eyesight!

RESOURCES

American Foundation for the Blind
11 Penn Plaza, Suite 300
New York, NY 10001
(212) 502-7661
<http://www.afb.org>

Summary: The American Foundation for the Blind is a nonprofit organization. It is a leading national resource for people who are blind or visually impaired, the organizations that serve them, and the general public.

Glaucoma Research Foundation
200 Pine Street, Suite 200
San Francisco, CA 94104
(800) 826-6693
<http://www.glaucoma.org>

Summary: The Glaucoma Research Foundation is a charitable organization that provides research, public awareness, and patient education.

Hearing

Between 30 and 50 percent of people over the age of sixty-five and 90 percent of those over the age of eighty suffer from some type of hearing impairment. Hearing loss—which is most prevalent among men, individuals exposed to long-term job or environmentally related noise, or those with hereditary hearing disorders—affects many activities of daily life. Older individuals are often labeled as demented when they actually have a serious hearing loss, because many of the presenting symptoms are similar.

Hearing loss often leads to feelings of isolation, boredom, and low self-esteem. These individuals may have difficulty hearing everyday sounds such as the doorbell or telephone or warning signs such as a police or fire alarm or the horn of a car. An older adult's refusal to admit a hearing loss could lead to further social isolation. An audiological exam will determine the cause and nature of the hearing loss as well as whether a hearing aid will help the particular type of hearing loss. A hearing aid must be individually fitted and will cost between $350 and $1,000. Batteries must be changed frequently.

Communicating effectively with the elderly who are hearing impaired requires special consideration. When talking to anyone who has trouble hearing, try to do so in a quiet place to reduce surrounding noise and distractions. Speak slowly and enunciate clearly, perhaps using simpler words or writing more difficult words, to facilitate understanding. You can ask the individual to repeat what you've said to ensure he or she understands. Finally, make sure that hearing aids and batteries are in place and in proper working order. Allow the older individual who is hearing impaired every opportunity to fully comprehend what is being said.

RESOURCES

Self Help for Hard of Hearing People, Inc.
7910 Woodmont Avenue, Suite 1200
Bethesda, MD 20814
(301) 657-2248
<http://www.shhh.org>

Summary: SHHH is a nonprofit educational organization dedicated to the well-being of people of all ages who do not hear well.

American Academy of Audiology
8300 Greensboro Dr., Suite 750
McLean, VA 22102
(703) 790-8466
(703) 790-8631 (Fax)
<http://www.audiology.com>

Summary: The American Academy of Audiology is a professional organization of individuals dedicated to providing quality hearing care to the public.

INSIGHT

A hearing aid that lacks working batteries is nothing but an unnecessary ear ornament.

Coronary Heart Disease

Atherosclerotic cardiovascular disease encompasses a number of disorders involving the heart and its blood vessels, including coronary artery disease (CAD), which is the number one killer of both men and women in the United States. Risk factors include obesity, smoking, hypertension, diabetes, a sedentary lifestyle, a family history of heart disease, and high blood cholesterol. Males and postmenopausal females are at increased risk. Ethnicity also plays a part, as African Americans are at the highest risk.

Atherosclerosis results in cholesterol-laden plaque buildup in the coronary arteries that feed the heart. If one or more of the arteries leading to the heart narrows significantly from such plaque buildup, it limits the amount of oxygen the heart gets from the bloodstream. A clot at the site of the narrowing can completely block blood flow. Chest pain is the usual result, and if the total blockage lasts long enough, a heart attack ensues.

Symptoms of coronary disease may vary. A heart attack is usually characterized by severe, prolonged chest pain, often radiating to the arms and associated with sweating, nausea, or shortness of breath. Angina occurs when oxygen demand transiently exceeds supply, typically during times of emotional stress or after exercise or a large meal.

The severity of discomfort does not correlate with the severity of the disease. The pain may be a mild pressurelike sensation, and the location may be atypical—jaw, arms, lower chest, and so on.

If your parents have any of the symptoms, they should be evaluated.

Click on http://www.Boomerbasics.com for more information on the role of relevant risk factors.

There are three types of diagnostic test for coronary artery disease— exercise stress testing, myocardial perfusion imaging (MPI), and coronary angiography.

- *Stress testing* involves attaching electrodes to the arms, legs, and chest and monitoring electrocardiographic changes while the patient walks or jogs on a treadmill.
- In *MPI,* a small amount of radioactive material (thallium or cordiolite) is injected into a vein, and a scanner is used to detect the levels of

radiation emitted, which indicates the amount of blood that has reached the various parts of the heart. Images are obtained at rest and under stress and then compared. The more severe the disease, the greater the difference between stress and rest will be.

- *Coronary angiography,* or *cardiac catherization,* is the most accurate tool for evaluating the presence of CAD. In this procedure, a catheter is inserted into a coronary artery, and a special dye is injected through it to make blood visible on a moving X-ray camera, which takes detailed pictures of blood flow to the heart and points out any blockages in the arteries.

If testing reveals that your parent has coronary artery disease, treatment may involve medication, angioplasty, or surgery, along with an attempt to minimize or eliminate any risk factors. The approach selected will depend on your parent's age, general health, the severity of his or her symptoms, and the severity of the disease.

RESOURCES

American Heart Association
7272 Greenville Avenue
Dallas, TX 75231-4596
(214) 706-1220
<http://www.americanheart.org>

Summary: The AHA is a nonprofit health organization dedicated to the reduction of death and disability from cardiovascular diseases, including heart diseases and stroke.

National Heart, Lung and Blood Institute Information Center
PO Box 30105
Bethesda, MD 30105
(301) 251-1222
<http://www.nhlbi.nih.gov/nhlbi/infcntr/infocent.htm>

Summary: The NHLBI's Information Center provides information and answers inquiries on the prevention and treatment of heart, lung, and blood diseases.

Cerebrovascular Accident (Stroke)

Stroke, or cerebrovascular accident (CVA), is the third most common cause of death in the United States following heart disease and cancer. Strokes can occur at any age but are most common in individuals over the age of sixty-five. The likelihood of fatality following a stroke increases with age. Strokes occur more often in men than women, and African Americans are affected more than any other group. Even when not fatal, strokes are the leading cause of disability. Most strokes are related to arteriosclerosis, hypertension, diabetes, or a combination of these. Smoking, inactivity, and elevated cholesterol levels are also risk factors. The incidence of strokes has been declining over the past thirty years, in part as a result of improved control of hypertension and diabetes, increased diet consciousness and the decreased incidence of smoking.

Warning signs that often precede a stroke may include lightheadedness, headache, behavioral and memory changes, and a fall caused by the leg muscles becoming flaccid without a loss of consciousness. There may also be a transient loss of speech or hemiplegia (weakness in arm or leg on one side of the body) hours or days before a stroke. These warning signs should alert the individual to seek immediate medical attention.

A stroke is caused by a disturbance of the blood supply to the brain. Symptoms persist for more than twenty-four hours and are often permanent. Specific deficits depend on the exact location of the disturbance and the extent of the damage. A stroke that occurs on the right side of the brain may lead to weakness of the left arm or leg, an impaired sense of humor, visual and spatial problems, poor judgment, loss of impulse control, unawareness of the loss of neurological function, and inappropriate responses. A stroke on the left side of the brain may lead to weakness of the right arm or leg, language and speech disturbances, behavior changes, and mood changes with a tendency toward worry, depression, anger, and frustration. Some stroke victims recover completely, but most are left with some lingering deficits. Most improvement occurs within the first six months following a stroke; any deficits that linger longer than six months are more likely to be permanent.

Following a stroke, the individual may suffer from disturbances in body image, may have a distorted view of him- or herself, and may lack the awareness to use certain body parts. Injury, weakness, and lack of care may result from disuse of the affected limbs. For this reason, physical therapy to improve gross motor skills and occupational therapy to improve fine motor skills are essential. Depending on the extent of involvement, such therapy can take place in a rehabilitation facility, in a nursing home, or through home care.

RESOURCES

American Heart Association
7272 Greenville Avenue
Dallas, TX 75231-4596
(214) 706-1220
<http://www.americanheart.org>

Summary: The AHA is a nonprofit health agency whose mission is the reduction of death and disability from heart disease and stroke.

National Stroke Association (NSA)
(800) STROKES
<http://www.stroke.org>

Summary: The mission of the NSA is to reduce the incidence and impact of strokes. On its Web site, you will find information on a variety of related topics including the types and effects of strokes, prevention, recovery and rehabilitation, and recognizing symptoms.

National Heart, Lung and Blood Institute Information Center
PO Box 30105
Bethesda, MD 30105
(301) 251-1222
<http://www.nhlbi.nih.gov/nhlbi/infcntr/infocent.htm>

Summary: The NHLBI's Information Center provides information and answers inquiries on the prevention and treatment of heart, lung, and blood diseases.

Parkinson's Disease

One out of every 100 people over the age of fifty is diagnosed with Parkinson's disease. An estimated fifty thousand new cases are diagnosed each year. It is more common in men and most often presents in the fifth decade of life, continuing to progress for an average of ten years.

Symptoms appear gradually and vary widely. Parkinson's disease affects how the body controls movements and often initially manifests as a faint tremor on one side of the body, which progresses over a long period of time along with a general weakness, slowing down, and difficulty ambulating. As the disease progresses, tremors occur at rest, decrease with conscious movement, and are totally absent in sleep. When symptoms become severe, a total lack of body movement may occur, and a person may actually be frozen in one spot. What initially appears as a slight stiffness in one leg while walking may later turn into a shuffling gait with short steps.

In the advanced stages of the disease, a person may stand with his or her head, shoulders, and spine flexed forward, giving the appearance of a stooped posture. Drooling, difficulty swallowing, and slow or monotone speech may occur as a result of muscle rigidity and weakness. The face may take on a masklike appearance, and eye blinking becomes less frequent. These individuals are more likely to fall. Emotional instability and depression may be present.

Although various medications can relieve some of the symptoms of Parkinson's disease, they are not a cure. To help in coping with the physical ramifications of Parkinson's disease, those so afflicted should be taught techniques for enhancing voluntary movement through physical and occupational therapy.

If you have a parent with Parkinson's, you can help by encouraging him or her to perform range-of-motion exercises to prevent rigidity and contractures; to maintain correct posture; and to avoid flexing the neck, shoulders, and spine. Give your parent extra time to complete simple tasks such as dressing, bathing, and eating. Finally, home safety is critical. Remove all obstacles. Install grab bars in the bathroom and shower. Avoid hot liquids because tremors can cause your parent to spill these. Provide walking aids when needed.

RESOURCES

The National Parkinson's Foundation, Inc.
1501 NW 9th Avenue
Miami, FL 33136-1494
(800) 327-4545
<http://www.parkinson.org>

Summary: The National Parkinson's Foundation, Inc., supports medical research and provides educational and medical information for patients, families, neurologists, and general medicine practitioners.

The American Parkinson Disease Association, Inc.
1250 Hylan Boulevard, Suite 4-B
Staten Island, NY 10305-1946
(800) 223-2732
<http://www.apdaparkinson.com>

Summary: The American Parkinson Disease Association, Inc., provides research, patient and family support, and education about Parkinson's Disease.

Incontinence and Other Urinary Tract Problems

Although urinary incontinence—the inability to control urine flow—is relatively common among older persons, affecting at least 10 percent of those over the age of sixty-five, it is *not* an inevitable part of aging. What's more, it's often a treatable condition. The problem is that many people suffer in silence, too embarrassed to talk about it with their doctor.

Although television commercials and magazine advertisements for products such as Depends are a good start, they focus on managing the symptoms of the disorder rather than on treating the cause.

If you know or suspect that your parent has trouble with bladder control, you both should realize that numerous treatment options are available that can minimize or eliminate the problem altogether. The treatment will depend in large part on what causes the incontinence, which typically varies according to gender. However, some incontinence might stem from more serious disorders in both men and women, including cancer, diabetes, stroke, Parkinson's disease, or multiple sclerosis.

INSIGHT

The embarrassment that accompanies urinary tract problems is understandable; allowing the problem to persist without seeking a proper diagnosis and treatment is unfortunate. This is yet another example of a common problem that may be effectively dealt with by open communication and the use of available resources.

Women and Incontinence

Most bladder control problems in women are caused by weak pelvic muscles or an overactive bladder. The pelvic muscles can weaken as a result of stretching during pregnancy or childbirth or with the onset of menopause, when female hormone production stops. Weaker pelvic muscles can lead to stress incontinence—urine leakage that results from coughing, sneezing, laughing, or lifting something heavy.

An overactive bladder leads to a different kind of problem—*urgency incontinence,* characterized by strong, sudden urges to go to the bathroom, even if the bladder isn't full. Urgency incontinence can be caused by bladder infections, alcohol or caffeine consumption, or some medicines.

Other types of incontinence are *overflow incontinence,* in which the bladder continues to fill with urine because the woman can't or doesn't feel the need to go to the bathroom. Eventually, the bladder becomes so full that it overflows. *Functional incontinence,* rather than stemming from any physical abnormality of the urinary tract, has more to do with external factors, such as diuretics that increase a woman's need to urinate so much that it becomes difficult to control or physical disabilities such as arthritis that prevent a woman from getting to the bathroom quickly.

Whatever the cause, chances are your mother can benefit from one or more of the myriad treatments, which include pelvic muscle exercises, bladder training, weight loss, moderated intake of certain foods and drinks, electrical stimulation of the muscles surrounding the urethra, biofeedback, medicines, and surgery. Additionally, certain devices such as a pessary, urethral insert, or urine seal can help with bladder control. Medications that modulate bladder function may also help.

Men and Incontinence

One of the most common causes of incontinence in men is benign prostatic hyperplasia (BPH), or enlargement of the prostate gland. Prostate enlargement is a fact of life for most older men—more than 50 percent of men in their sixties and as many as 90 percent of men in their seventies and eighties have some symptoms of BPH.

INSIGHT

The bad news is that if you live long enough, you're likely to have a prostate problem. The good news is if a prostate problem is recognized and treated at an early stage, serious medical problems may be minimized or eliminated.

Given the prostate's location just below the bladder, it's easy to see how an enlargement would cause the gland to press against the urethra (the canal that carries urine out of the body). When that happens, urine backs up in the bladder, causing irritation there. The bladder eventually weakens and loses the ability to empty itself completely. Obstruction of the urethra and partial emptying of the bladder lead to many of the problems associated with BPH.

The most common symptoms of BPH are a hesitant, interrupted, weak urine stream; an urgent need to urinate; leaking or dribbling; and more frequent urination, especially at night. However, a man who doesn't have any of these symptoms may one day find he can't urinate at all. Known as *acute urinary retention,* this condition may be triggered by taking over-the-counter cold or allergy medicines or, where the urethra is partially obstructed, by alcohol, cold temperatures, or long periods of immobility. Left untreated, BPH can cause serious problems such as urinary tract infections, bladder or kidney damage, bladder or kidney stones, and total incontinence.

If your father is experiencing any of these symptoms, urge him to tell his doctor right away. If his doctor suspects BPH to be the culprit, he or she likely will refer him to a urologist for further testing. The urologist may use any of the following to determine whether medication can address the problem or if surgery is necessary: a rectal exam, ultrasound, a urine flow study, an X ray of the urinary tract (intravenous pyelogram), or cystoscopy.

RESOURCES

> **The National Association for Continence (NAFC)**
> PO Box 8310
> Spartanburg, SC 29305
> (800) 252-3337
> <http://www.nafc.org>

Summary: The NAFC is a nonprofit organization that provides education, advocacy, and support to the public and health professionals about causes, prevention, diagnosis, treatment, and management alternatives for incontinence.

> **The National Kidney and Urologic Diseases Information Clearing-**
> **house (NKUDIC)**
> 3 Information Way
> Bethesda, MD 20892-3580
> <http://www.niddk.nih.gov/health/kidney/nkudic.htm>

Summary: The NKUDIC is an information and referral service of the National Institute of Diabetes and Digestive and Kidney Diseases, a division of the National Institutes of Health.

Alzheimer's Disease

Alzheimer's disease, which is the most common form of dementia in people over the age of sixty-five, has no known cure. It affects approximately 10 to 15 percent of people over age sixty-five, 18 to 20 percent of people over age seventy-five, and 45 to 50 percent of people over age eighty-five.

Memory loss is the beginning stage of Alzheimer's. Family and friends, rather than the afflicted individual, are usually the first to recognize the symptoms, such as poor judgment or carelessness in work habits and in carrying out household chores. For example, the individual sufferer may look for clothing in the home that had been brought to the cleaners only the day before or may forget to complete a job he or she had started.

The Alzheimer's disease sufferer, in the early stages, may be unable to adapt to new challenges. Other common, early-stage symptoms include irritability, indifference, and suspicion of others. Attention span may shorten, and subtle personality changes may occur. The individual may realize something is wrong but may also be unable to identify his or her behavior and thus becomes anxious and scared.

As the disease progresses, confusion and disorientation increase. The person may have language disturbances, such as difficulty finding the right word or talking around a subject rather than about it. Spontaneous speech becomes difficult, and the person uses words in the wrong context. The person may have increased difficulty doing everyday activities such as brushing teeth or shaving.

Family may notice frequent pacing and wandering, especially at night, as well as rituals and repetitive behaviors. Wandering is a common and serious problem because Alzheimer's sufferers often do not know who or where they are. (The Alzheimer's Association has a Wanderer's Safety Program that registers people who are prone to wander and provides them with an ID bracelet. The association will notify police and other authorities when an Alzheimer's sufferer has wandered away and is lost.) Depression and irritability worsen, and delusions may start to appear. At this stage in the disease, the person may begin to have occasional incontinence.

In the final stage of Alzheimer's disease, all mental abilities are lost, including speech. The person basically loses all ability to care for him- or herself. Urinary and bowel incontinence is frequent, voluntary movement is minimal, and the person may become totally immobile.

Alzheimer's disease is emotionally difficult and frustrating for the individual suffering from the disease as well as for friends and families. As the disease progresses, we begin to grieve for the loss of the parent we used to know. Each decline in functioning is another source of grief. Normal family routines and relationships are lost. Not being recognized by a parent or spouse is extremely traumatic. We are suddenly dealing with a person we no longer know.

In spite of the effect that Alzheimer's has on loved ones, the afflicted individual needs their support and encouragement more than ever to help him or her in coping with the disease. Of utmost importance is the need to protect the sufferer's dignity despite the forgetfulness and unusual and often bizarre behaviors. Those with Alzheimer's disease often become extremely frustrated, which they may show by increasing motor activity such as pacing, waving their arms or fists, or raising their voices. You should try to pinpoint the source of the frustration and attempt to remove your parent from that situation. Memory loss may actually work as an advantage here because removing your parent from the situation may actually make him forget what was upsetting him.

The forgetfulness that is so prevalent with Alzheimer's makes safety an important concern. Hazards in the home must be eliminated by safeguarding electrical devices and outlets, removing toxic substances, supervising cooking, and providing adequate lighting. Your parent may even forget where the bathroom is. Nutritional problems also can arise as a result of forgetfulness. Sufferers may not feel hungry, may think they have eaten when they haven't, or may just forget to eat or drink. You must provide constant reminders to eat as well as provide meals at approximately the same times each day. Restrict fluids at night to help maintain urinary continence.

Reorientation and repetition are useful and help the individual to maintain autonomy as much as possible while increasing confidence and self-respect. The individual requires a great deal of encouragement and reminders along with a step-by-step approach to completing any task. Predictability and consistency are best provided by a limited number of caregivers and will help the individual sufferer to cope with the disease. Twenty-four-hour help lines are available to provide information, referrals, and support to family and caregivers.

Options such as adult day care allow individuals suffering from Alzheimer's to be cared for out of the home on a daily basis while continuing to live in their own homes. Home health aides are available to assist spouses or family members in caring for parents who have the disease. Respite care is another option that allows the caregivers and family a few hours or days of freedom to take care of errands or work or simply to get some needed relief from caring for a parent with Alzheimer's. Although employing such assistance can be difficult for those who see themselves as dutiful caregivers, it often becomes necessary to provide the afflicted individuals with optimal care and to allow family members to continue with their own lives.

RESOURCES

**Alzheimer's Disease Education and Referral (ADEAR) Center,
National Institute on Aging**
PO Box 8250
Silver Spring, MD 20907-8250
(800) 438-4380
<http://www.alzheimers.org>

Summary: The ADEAR center maintains and distributes information on current research efforts and provides referrals to resources, treatment centers, support groups, and family support services.

Alzheimer's Association
919 N. Michigan Avenue, Suite 1000
Chicago, IL 60611-1676
(800) 272-3900
<http://www.alz.org>

Summary: The Alzheimer's Association is a nonprofit organization founded to heighten public awareness of Alzheimer's. The Web site contains factual information on the disease and provides helpful resources for Alzheimer's patients and their families and caregivers.

The Alzheimer's Research Forum Foundation
c/o The Fidelity Foundation
82 Devonshore Street, S3
Boston, MA 02109
<http://www.alzforum.org>

Summary: The Alzheimer's Research Forum is a nonprofit organization. The forum's Web site was established to promote rapid scientific communication and creative thinking in the search for causes and treatments for Alzheimer's disease.

Depression

Depression is a catchall term for a variety of mental and emotional states, ranging from extreme sadness, apathy, and withdrawal to suicidal behavior. Estimates suggest that about 15 percent of people over the age of sixty-five suffer from depression, but that figure may be low because of older people who don't seek treatment for what they or their family members perceive as a passing mood or because it may be masked by other illnesses. In any event, we do know that depression affects nearly twice as many women as men in the United States and that it's much more prevalent among the elderly in hospitals and nursing homes.

Depression can develop in response to some event, such as a death in the family, or it may have no apparent cause. Whatever the cause, it's important to distinguish depression from the everyday blues most people experience or the normal grief following the loss of a loved one: Sadness or grief become depression when they last longer than they should or interfere with the ability to function normally over a period of time.

Warning Signs

Common feelings that accompany depression in older people include a persistent sadness lasting two weeks or more; feeling helpless, hopeless, worthless, or slowed down; and excessive worry about finances and health problems. Many older people with depression have trouble thinking, concentrating, remembering, and making decisions, and they may withdraw from their regular social activities. They may also pace and fidget more, have difficulty sleeping, or neglect their personal appearance. Physical symptoms include appetite changes with weight loss or gain, headaches, dizziness, inexplicable weeping or perpetually sad facial expressions, and psychosomatic disorders frequently involving pain or gastrointestinal distress.

Even if your parents don't feel or seem sad, the presence of any of these other symptoms might still indicate depression, or it could signify another problem. In any case, your parents should consult their doctor if they experience any of these symptoms for a prolonged time.

Risk Factors

In addition to genetics and any biochemical changes in the brain that might result from aging, the primary risk factor for depression among the elderly is the stress of coping with physical and social losses.

Stress generally stems from any event or situation that evokes frustration, anger, or anxiety. Because people respond differently, however, it's not always easy to pinpoint the cause of stress. The effects are more certain, as considerable evidence suggests a strong link between stress and health problems.

Classic research on the impact of various life events on health resulted in a scale of life stressors, among which the death of a spouse was listed as number one. Such a loss may be even more profound for our parents because it means losing a lifetime of shared experiences. Or if a number of their friends have passed away, our parents may feel surrounded by death and loneliness, perhaps believing their own time is limited. Although a period of bereavement is normal and even healthy, persistent grief, especially when accompanied by any of the symptoms listed previously, can be a sign of depression.

In addition to social loss, another common source of stress among older people stems from the physical and emotional consequences of dealing with a debilitating disease such as cancer, Parkinson's disease, heart disease, stroke, or Alzheimer's disease. The prolonged impact on your parent from cancer, for example, would be understandable. First, there's the emotional drain from learning he or she has cancer and, perhaps for the first time, staring his or her own mortality in the face. Then there's the physical stress on the body from the disease itself and the related treatment. Side effects from the treatment and additional medications may prolong the physical stress, while the fear of recurrence—no matter how successful the treatment—is undoubtedly always present as an emotional stressor.

Even in the absence of a serious illness, depression can crop up in older people who have trouble accepting the physical limitations and social changes that often accompany aging, such as a decline in vision, hearing, and mobility; retirement; moving from the family home; or changes in the neighborhood.

Treatment

Depression left untreated persists. The capacity to participate in life, to interact with others, to take pride in past accomplishments, and to initiate everyday tasks—the very means by which one maintains a sense of worth or value—seem lost forever in depression. Sadness becomes so pervasive that it overshadows any past achievement or success.

Depression can be treated effectively with medication and psychotherapy. The type of antidepressant (mood-elevating) medication prescribed is based on the patient's symptoms and his or her past responses to antidepressant medications. Antidepressant medications may take up to four weeks to alleviate the associated symptoms. They typically are prescribed for a period of six months to one year, followed by a closely supervised discontinuation process in which the dosage is gradually reduced over a period of several weeks or longer.

Common side effects of antidepressants include sedation, a fast heart rate (tachycardia), dry mouth, constipation, urinary retention, blurred vision, weight gain, and changes in sexual functioning. Some of the newer antidepressants (such as the serotonin receptacle inhibitors [SSRIs] Prozac, Paxil, Zoloft, and Celexa) have fewer side effects and often work more quickly to effectively relieve symptoms.

Psychotherapy can help the individual to see him- or herself in a realistic light. It helps to strengthen the individual's capacity to cope with problems that emerge. Psychotherapy may also help the individual who might be reluctant to take medication. Many forms of short-term therapy (ten to twenty weeks in duration) have proved effective for treating mild to moderate depression in the elderly.

In addition to these standard treatments, the benefits of interaction with others can't be overlooked. As many psychotherapists note, the self is shaped by its relationships with others, not in isolation. The social support that many depressed people shun has been documented time and again as an effective buffer against depression. If your parents are depressed, one of the ways you can most help them is to include them in family get-togethers and to encourage them to engage in regular social activities on their own.

Families can be extremely helpful and supportive if they are given the appropriate information and are allowed to take an active role in treatment.

RESOURCES

National Depressive and Manic-Depressive Association
730 N. Franklin Street, Suite 501
Chicago, IL 60610-3526
(800) 826-3632
(312) 642-0049
(312) 642-7243 (Fax)
<http://www.ndmda.org>

Summary: The National Depressive and Manic-Depressive Association is a nonprofit organization dedicated to providing education, information, and resources to people suffering with depression and their families and caregivers. There are many resources for professionals as well. The site provides several videos on depression that can be downloaded and watched on the computer. National and state support group information is also provided on this site.

Depression.com
<http://www.depression.com>

Summary: Depression.com is an Internet site providing information on depression, including types and causes of depression, available treatment and medications, and current news regarding depression that is updated regularly.

Medication Management

Many of us have noticed that our parents and grandparents tend to possess an arsenal of medication that they either use or collect on an ongoing basis. The intermittent use of such medications and the friendly exchanges that take place would almost be comical if not for the serious ramifications that may result from such drug use. This section is dedicated to the concern of the use of such drugs in an uncoordinated and unsupervised manner.

RESOURCES

Office of Consumer Affairs (OCA), U.S. Food and Drug Administration, U.S. Department of Health and Human Services
5600 Fishers Lane (HFE-88)
Rockville, MD 20857
(888) 463-6332
<http://www.fda.gov>

Summary: The OCA serves as a clearinghouse for FDA consumer publications and handles consumer inquiries.

Prescription Overuse

Because seniors tend to suffer not only from more chronic illnesses (for example, arthritis, diabetes, and heart disease) than younger people, but also from multiple conditions simultaneously, they very often take many different drugs at the same time. Even in the absence of a specific disease, the elderly might be relying on a multitude of remedies (both prescribed and over-the-counter) to relieve certain effects of aging.

Statistics reveal that although Americans over the age of sixty-five currently represent about 12 percent of the population, they take one-third of all prescription drugs and purchase 40 percent of all over-the-counter (OTC) medications. Some estimates indicate that the elderly take an average of 4.5 medications at any given time and are issued an average of thirteen to fifteen prescriptions a year.

The tendency toward excessive and unnecessary use of medications (called *polypharmacy*) stems from several factors: A patient who is seeing several specialists at once may not inform one what the other is doing; in our medicine-oriented society, both patients and doctors tend to overlook the potential value of alternative therapies before beginning a new medication; and physicians may fail to obtain a thorough drug history or, because the patient is elderly, may simply dismiss complaints such as depression or grogginess, which could be side effects of taking too many drugs. Whatever the cause, polypharmacy can lead to potentially dangerous drug interactions and adverse drug reactions.

We must address not only the use of drugs by our teenage children but also those taken by our parents and grandparents as well.

Adverse Drug Reactions

Older people are three times as likely as younger adults to experience an adverse drug reaction (ADR). In fact, 40 percent of those who suffer ADRs are over the age of sixty. Even these figures likely underestimate the problem, however, considering that ADRs often go unnoticed or are misdiagnosed in the elderly because older patients may not recognize a new symptom as an ADR and therefore do not report it to their doctor and because physicians may attribute patients' complaints to the "normal" effects of aging, the worsening of an existing condition, or the onset of a new health problem rather than to the effects of medications.

The symptoms of adverse drug reactions in the elderly can include fatigue, constipation or diarrhea, anorexia, confusion, incontinence, frequent falls, depression, weakness, tremors, excessive drowsiness or grogginess, hallucinations, agitation or anxiety, dizziness, lowered sex drive, and rash.

Part of the reason older people are more susceptible to ADRs is because of age-related physiological changes that affect the way drugs are processed in the body. Because drugs remain in an older person's body longer, doses appropriate for younger people may be too much for the elderly. Likewise, certain drugs should be avoided entirely because they are ineffective or generally more toxic than equally effective alternatives or, if effective, they may affect central nervous system functioning.

Another problem is that as many as 40 percent of elderly patients don't follow the prescribed regimen for taking their medications, perhaps because of the sheer number of medicines prescribed and the accompanying confusion of different dosing schedules, the expense of the drug, difficulty opening pill containers, forgetting to take the medication in the absence of symptoms, or discontinuing the treatment prematurely.

We should discuss with our parents the medications they are taking. For those parents who take a daily variety of medication, they should keep written

record of their medications as well as relevant information regarding their medical history and allergies. We, as concerned children, should be alert to changes in our parent's medical condition or behavior that may result from the use of medication.

Drug Interactions

In a drug interaction, any of the following might happen: One drug reduces or increases the effects of another, with harmful consequences; two drugs taken together produce a dangerous reaction; or two similar drugs taken together produce an effect greater than that expected from one drug.

"Drugs" include both prescription and OTC medicines. Drugs may interact with each other or with OTC medications; OTC medications also can interact with each other. Although prescription drugs are usually stronger and have more side effects than OTC medicines, many OTC preparations contain ingredients that, when taken in large quantities, can equal a dose normally available only by prescription. Decongestants, antacids, aspirin, antihistamines, laxatives, iron supplements, and vitamins can lead to serious problems if overused or taken in combination with certain other drugs. Taking certain drugs with alcohol, caffeine, illicit drugs, salt, spices, herbs, natural remedies, and other foods and beverages also can have dangerous consequences.

RESOURCES

For a free reprint (in large type) of "Food and Drug Interactions," originally published in the *FDA Consumer* magazine, send your request to FDA, HFE-88, 5600 Fishers Lane, Rockville, MD 20857.

Recommendations for Using Medications Safely

Many elderly patients are reluctant to question their physicians about their prescription regimen, believing that the doctor knows best. But information and communication are two of the most effective tools in preventing medication-related problems. Your parents can learn more about the nature of various drugs, their side effects, and contraindications by consulting any of the numerous medical guides on the market today.

The more your parents' physician knows about their medical history and current drug regimen, the less likely the potential for adverse drug reactions and interactions. Encourage your parents to tell their physician about all medicines (prescription and OTC) they currently take as well as any reactions to medications they've had in the past. When seeing the doctor for a new condition that might warrant a prescription, your parents should first discuss alternative therapies with their doctor.

If the doctor does write a new prescription, encourage your parents to ask questions before leaving the physician's office to ensure they understand the purpose of each prescription, how to take it, possible side effects, and so forth. If expense is a consideration, they should ask their physician about a generic equivalent. Additionally, they should let their doctor know about any symptoms that arise either immediately after beginning the new prescription or a few weeks later, as some medicines might cause a delayed reaction.

Other strategies for ensuring safe drug use include taking the medication as directed, taking it for as long as directed, taking the medicine in its original form (that is, don't crush a pill or open a capsule to make it easier to swallow unless a physician approves of doing so), keeping an up-to-date medication record and a daily dosage schedule, and using one pharmacy.

Some medication don'ts also apply. Your parents should not share medications, take medications without first checking the label, use medications that have expired, ask for unprescribed refills, or store medications where there's excessive light, heat, or humidity (for example, on a window sill, above the oven, or in the bathroom).

RESOURCES

Pharmaceutical Information Network
<http://www.pharminfo.com>

Summary: Pharmaceutical Information Network is an on-line drug information resource owned and operated by mediconsult.com, which describes itself as a consumer health marketing company specializing in using Internet tools to improve health outcomes and business performance. This site has an extensive glossary of drugs and medical conditions.

INSIGHT

"Using Your Medicines Wisely: A Guide for the Elderly" is a useful booklet published by the National Institute on Drug Abuse. For a free copy, write to Elder-Ed, PO Box 416, Kensington, MD 20740.

Organ and Tissue Donation

Your parents may wish to consider donating their organs or tissues after they die to help save the lives of others. Many of the more than fifty-eight thousand Americans on a national list to receive organ transplants die each year because the need for organs far outweighs the supply. In 1997, for example, fewer than five thousand five hundred organs were retrieved after donors had died.

Even those who opt to donate their organs may not qualify. Because the organs must be retrieved while the heart is still beating but after brain function has stopped, the only eligible donors typically are those kept alive with the aid of an artificial respirator. But most people can be tissue donors because tissues can be retrieved many hours after a donor's death.

Organs your parents can donate include kidneys, heart, liver, lungs, intestines, and pancreas. Tissues that can be donated include corneas, skin, bone, middle ear, bone marrow, connective tissues, heart valves, and blood vessels.

To become donors, your parents need only sign a donor card (or in some states, the back of their driver's license). Perhaps they already have! In any event, discussing their wishes with them is important because even if they have signed a donor card, their family will be asked to consent to the donation.

RESOURCES

Transweb: All about Transplantation and Donation
<http://www.transweb.org>

Summary: Transweb is an Internet site containing over ten thousand items pertaining to organ transplants and donations. This site contains resources, links to organizations, and information on organ transplants and donations as well as life experience articles written by people who have received or donated organs. One of the special features of this site is a multimedia guide to the organ transplant process.

APPENDIX

AccentHealth.com
2203 N. Lois Ave., Suite 1100
Tampa, FL 33607
(813) 349-7100
<http://www.accenthealth.com>
Page 93 Ourselves

Adam.com
90 Tehama St.
San Francisco, CA 94105
(415) 541-9164
<http://www.adam.com>
Page 93 Ourselves

**Administration for Children,
   Youth and Families**
U.S. Department of Health and Human
   Services
<http://www.acf.dhhs.gov/programs
   /acyf/>
Page 140 Our Children

Administration on Aging
National Aging Information Center
330 Independence Ave. SW
Washington, DC 20201
<http://www.AOA.gov>
Page 252 Our Parents

**Advance Directives Can Be a Gift
   to Loved Ones**
<http://www.ktv-i
   .com/news/nf04_09_97b.html>
Page 266 Our Parents

Alliance for Investor Education
<http://www.investoreducation.org>
Page 53 Ourselves
Page 209 Our Children

Alliance of American Insurers
3025 Highland Parkway, Suite 800
Downers Grove, IL 60515-1289
<http://www.allianceai.org>
Page 26 Ourselves

AltaVista
<http://www.altavista.com>
Page 165 Our Children

Always
<http://www.always.com>
Page 124 Ourselves

Alzheimer's Association
919 N. Michigan Avenue, Suite 1000
Chicago, IL 60611-1676
(800) 272-3900
<http://www.alz.org>
Page 372 Our Parents

**Alzheimer's Disease Education
    and Referral (ADEAR) Center,
    National Institute on Aging**
PO Box 8250
Silver Spring, MD 20907-8250
(800) 438-4380
<http://www.alzheimers.org>
Page 372 Our Parents

**The Alzheimer's Research Forum
    Foundation**
c/o The Fidelity Foundation
82 Devonshire Street, S3
Boston, MA 02109
<http://www.alzforum.org>
Page 372 Our Parents

AMA Health Insight
American Medical Association
515 North State St.
Chicago, IL 60610
(312) 464-5000
<http://www.ama-assn.org>
Page 94 Ourselves

AMA Health Insight–Nutrition Information
American Medical Association
515 North State St.
Chicago, IL 60610
(312) 464-5000
<http://www.ama-
    assn.org/insight/gen_hlth_nutrinfo/part3
    .htm>
Page 12 Ourselves

A.M. Best's Ratings
<http://www.ambest.com/ratings/access
    .html>
Page 83 Ourselves

**American Academy of Allergy, Asthma
    and Immunology**
61 East Wells Street
Milwaukee, WI 53202
(414) 272-6071
<http://www.aaaai.org>
Page 232 Our Children

American Academy of Audiology
8300 Greensboro Drive, Suite 750
McLean, VA 22102
(703) 790-8466
(703) 790-8631 (Fax)
<http://www.audiology.com>
Page 230 Our Children
Page 360 Our Parents

American Academy of Child and Adolescent Psychiatry (AACAP)
3615 Wisconsin Ave. NW
Washington, DC 20016-3007
(202) 966-7300
(202) 966-2891 (Fax)
<http://www.aacap.org>
Page 219 Our Children
Page 243 Our Children

American Academy of Facial Plastic and Reconstructive Surgery (AAFPRS)
310 S. Henry Street
Alexandria, VA 22314
(800) 332-FACE
<http://www.facial-plastic-surgery.org>
Page 7 Ourselves

American Academy of Pediatrics
National Headquarters
141 Northwest Point Boulevard
Elk Grove Village, IL 60007-1098
(847) 228-5005
(847) 228-5097 (Fax)
<http://www.aap.org>
Page 137 Our Children
Page 218 Our Children
Page 229 Our Children

American Anorexia Bulimia Association, Inc.
165 West 46th Street, Suite 1108
New York, NY 10036
(212) 575-6200
<http://www.aabainc.org>
Page 243 Our Children

American Association for Marriage and Family Therapy (AAMFT)
1133 15th Street NW, Suite 300
Washington, DC 20005-2710
(202) 452-0109
<http://www.aamft.org>
Page 19 Ourselves

American Association of Homes and Service for the Aging (AAHSA)
901 E Street NW, Suite 500
Washington, DC 20004
(202) 783-2242
<http://www.aahsa.org>
Page 275 Our Parents
Page 290 Our Parents

American Association of Individual Investors (AAII)
625 N. Michigan Ave.
Chicago, IL 60611
(800) 428-2244
<http://www.aaii.com>
Page 54 Ourselves
Page 209 Our Children

American Association of Poison Control Centers
<http://www.aapcc.org>
Page 225 Our Children

American Association of Retired Persons (AARP)
601 E. Street NW
Washington, DC 20049
(800) 424-3410
<http://www.aarp.org/caregive/1-care.html>
Page 284 Our Parents

American Bar Association
750 North Lake Shore Drive
Chicago, IL 60611
(312) 988-5000
<http://www.abanet.org>
Page 24 Ourselves

American Bar Association
750 North Lake Shore Drive
Chicago, IL 60611
(312) 988-5000
<http://www.abanet.org/media/factbooks
/eldq13.html>
Page 266 Our Parents
Page 271 Our Parents

American Burn Association
National Headquarters Office
625 N. Michigan Avenue, Suite 1530
Chicago, IL 60611
<http://www.ameriburn.org/home.htm>
Page 223 Our Children

American Cancer Society
(800) ACS-2345
<http://www.cancer.org>
Page 116 Ourselves

**American College of Sports Medicine
(ACSM)**
PO Box 1440
Indianapolis, IN 46202-3233
(317) 637-9200
<http://www.acsm.org>
Page 10 Ourselves

American Council on Exercise (ACE)
5820 Oberlin Drive, Suite 102
San Diego, CA 92121-3787
(619) 535-8227
<http://www.acefitness.org>
Page 10 Ourselves

American Dental Association
211 E. Chicago Avenue
Chicago, IL 60611
(312) 440-2500
<http://www.ada.org>
Page 24 Ourselves

American Diabetes Association (ADA)
1660 Duke Street
Alexander, VA 22314
(703) 549-1500
<http://www.diabetes.org>
Page 352 Our Parents

American Foundation for the Blind
11 Penn Plaza, Suite 300
New York, NY 10001
(212) 505-7661
<http://www.afb.org>
Page 359 Our Parents

**American Foundation for Urologic
Disease (AFUD)**
1126 N. Charles
Baltimore, MD 21201
(410) 468-1800
<http://www.afud.org>
Page 356 Our Parents

American Health Care Association
1201 L St. NW
Washington, DC 20005
(202) 842-4444
<http://www.ahca.org>
Page 288 Our Parents
Page 349 Our Parents

American Heart Association
National Center
7272 Greenville Avenue
Dallas, TX 75231-4596
(214) 706-1220
<http://www.americanheart.org>
Page 12 Ourselves
Page 362 Our Parents
Page 364 Our Parents

The American Institute of Certified Public Accountants
1211 Avenue of the Americas
New York, NY 10036
<http://www.aicpa.org>
Page 25 Ourselves

American Library Association
<http://www.ala.org>
Page 167 Our Children

American Lung Association
<http://www.lungusa.org>
Page 233 Our Children

American Medical Association
515 North State Street
Chicago, IL 60610
(312) 464-4818
<http://www.ama-assn.org>
Page 23 Ourselves

American Parkinson Disease Association, Inc.
1250 Hylan Boulevard, Suite 4-B
Staten Island, NY 10305-1946
(800) 223-2732
<http://www.apdaparkinson.com>
Page 366 Our Parents

American Psychiatric Association (APA)
1400 K St. NW
Washington, DC 20005
(202) 682-6000
<http://www.psych.org>
Page 94 Ourselves

American Sleep Disorders Association
<http://www.asda.org>
Page 121 Ourselves

American Society for Reproductive Medicine (ASRM)
1209 Montgomery Highway
Birmingham, AL 35216-2809
(205) 978-5000
<http://www.asrm.com>
Page 131 Our Children

American Society of Pediatric Otolaryngologists (ASPO)
<http://www.entnet.org/aspo>
Page 231 Our Children

American Stock Exchange
Investor Services/Nasdaq Web Site
1735 K Street NW
Washington, DC 20006
<http://www.amex.com>
Page 54 Ourselves
Page 209 Our Children

American Surrogacy Center, Inc.
638 Church Street
Marietta, GA 30067
(770) 426-1107
<http://www.surrogacy.com>
Page 131 Our Children

Americans Discuss Social Security
2001 Pennsylvania Avenue NW, Suite 825
Washington, DC
(202) 955-9000
<http://www.americansdiscuss.org>
Page 317 Our Parents

Americans for Long Term Care Security (ALTCS)
1275 K St. NW, Suite 601
Washington, DC 20005
<http://www.ltcweb.org>
Page 348 Our Parents

Americans with Disabilities Act Document Center
<http://janweb.icdi.wvu.edu/kinder>
Page 148 Our Children

Americans with Disabilities Act Information
<http://www.usdoj.gov/crt/ada/>
Page 257 Our Parents

AmericasDoctor.com
11403 Cronridge Dr., Suite 200
Owings Mills, MD 21117
(888) 88AMDOC
<http://www.americasdoctor.com>
Page 93 Ourselves

America's JobBank
U.S. Department of Labor
<http://www.ajb.dni.us/>
Page 13 Ourselves

Arthritis Foundation
1330 West Peachtree Street
Atlanta, GA 30309
(404) 872-7100
<http://www.arthritis.org>
Page 351 Our Parents

Arthritis National Research Foundation
200 Oceangate, Suite 440
Long Beach, CA 90802
(800) 588-CURE
<http://www.curearthritis.org>
Page 351 Our Parents

Ask the Headhunter
Nick Corcodilos
<http://www.asktheheadhunter.com>
Page 15 Ourselves

**Assisted Living Federation of America
(ALFA)**
10300 Eaton Place, Suite 400
Fairfax, VA 22030
(703) 691-8100
<http://www.alfa.org>
Page 288 Our Parents

**Asthma and Allergy Foundation
of America (AAFA)**
1125 Fifteenth Street NW, Suite 502
Washington, DC 20005
(800) 7-ASTHMA
Page 232 Our Children

Autism National Committee
635 Ardmore Avenue
Ardmore, PA 19003-1831
<http://www.autcom.org>
Page 154 Our Children

Autism Society of America
7910 Woodmont Avenue, Suite 300
Bethesda, MD 20814-3015
(301) 657-0881
<http://www.autism-society.org/asa_home
.html>
Page 154 Our Children

Bank America Corp.
<http://www.bankamerica.com>
Page 41 Ourselves

**Bankruptcy Laws: Free Information on
Chapter 7 or 13 Personal Bankruptcy
Laws**
<http://www.bankruptcyresource.com>
Page 89 Ourselves

Before I Die
The Robert Wood Johnson Foundation
Route 1 and College Road East
PO Box 2316
Princeton, NJ 08543-2316
(609) 452-8701
<http://www.pbs.org/wnet/bid>
Page 266 Our Parents

Benefits for Children with Disabilities
SSA Office of Public Inquiries
6401 Security Blvd.
Room 4-C-5 Annex
Baltimore, MD 21235-6401
<http://www.ssa.gov/pubs/10026.html>
Page 193 Our Children

Benefits Link
1014 E. Robinson St.
Orlando, FL 32801
(407) 841-3717
<http://www.benefitslink.com>
Page 45 Ourselves
Page 321 Our Parents

Bicycle Helmet Safety Institute
4611 Seventh Street South
Arlington, VA 22204-1419
(703) 486-0100
(703) 486-0576 (Fax)
<http://www.helmets.org>
Page 224 Our Children

Bonds OnLine
7251 W. Mercer Way
Mercer Island, WA 98040
<http://bondsonline.com>
Page 55 Ourselves

Budget Life
<http://www.budgetlife.com>
Page 82 Ourselves

Bureau of Labor Statistics
<http://stats.bls.gov/opbhome.htm>
Page 156 Our Children

Bureau of Public Debt
<http://www.publicdebt.treas.gov>
Page 211 Our Children

CBS Marketwatch
<http://www.cbs.marketwatch.com>
Page 265 Our Parents
Page 320 Our Parents

Career Advice
PO Box 24938
Denver, CO 80224
<http://www.careeradvice.com>
Page 15 Ourselves

CareerLab
William S. Frank
(303) 790-0505
<http://www.careerlab.com>
Page 14 Ourselves

Career Magazine
4775 Walnut St., Suite 2A
Boulder, CO 80301
(303) 440-5110
<http://www.careermag.com>
Page 14 Ourselves

Careerpath
523 West Sixth Street, Suite 515
Los Angeles, CA 90014
(213) 996-0200
<http://new.careerpath.com/>
Page 14 Ourselves

Careguide.com
1160 Battery, 4th Floor
San Francisco, CA 94111
(415) 474-1278
<http://www.careguide.com>
Page 141 Our Children
Page 293 Our Parents

The Center for Debt Management
199 Camp Sargent Road
Merrimack, NH 03054
<http://www.center4debtmanagement
   .com>
Page 35 Ourselves

**Centers for Disease Control
   and Prevention (CDC)**
1600 Clifton Rd. NE
Atlanta, GA 30333
(404) 639-3311 (CDC operator)
(800) 311-3435 (CDC public inquiries)
<http://www.cdc.gov>
Page 98 Ourselves

Charitable Choices
1804 S Street, NW
Washington, DC 20009
(888) 410-1999
<http://www.charitablechoices.org>
Page 80 Ourselves

Charitable Giving
Tips on Charitable Giving
<http://www.bbb.org/about/tipsgive.html>
Page 79 Ourselves

Charles Schwab
NY Operations Center
PO Box 179
Newark, NJ 07101-9671
<http://www.myschwab.com>
Page 32 Ourselves
Page 330 Our Parents

**Children and Adults with Attention
   Deficit/Hyperactivity Disorder
   (CHADD)**
8181 Professional Place, Suite 201
Landover, MD 20785
(301) 306-7070
<http://www.chadd.org>
Page 151 Our Children

Children's Partnership
<http://www.childrenspartnership.org>
Page 165 Our Children

Children's Rights Council
300 I Street NE, Suite 401
Washington, DC 20002
(202) 547-6227
<http://www.vix.com>
Page 20 Ourselves

Choice in Dying Advance Directives
Choice in Dying
1035 30th Street NW
Washington, DC 20007
(202) 338-9790
<http://www.choices.org/ad.htm>
Page 267 Our Parents

The College Board
45 Columbus Avenue
New York, NY 10023-6992
(800) 626-9795
<http://www.collegeboard.org>
Page 207 Our Children

College Board On-Line
<http://www.collegeboard.org>
Page 158 Our Children

College of William and Mary
Job Resources by U.S. Region
Williamsburg, VA 23187-3329
(757) 221-3240
<http://www.wm.edu/csrv/career/>
Page 14 Ourselves

**Commercial Union Life Insurance
   Company's Life Insurance Basics**
<http://www.culife.com/>
Page 342 Our Parents

Computing Central
<http://www.computingcentral.com>
Page 165 Our Children

Consumer Insurance Guide
<http://www.insure.com>
Page 82 Ourselves
Page 188 Our Children

Coping with Grief and Loss

The American Association
of Retired Persons (AARP)
601 E St. NW
Washington, DC 20049
(800) 424-3410
<http://www.aarp.org/griefandloss>
Page 295 Our Parents

Cosmetic Surgery Network

Plastic Surgery Network
3 Via Pasa
San Clemente, CA 92673
<http://www.cosmetic-surgery.net/home
.html>
Page 253 Our Parents

The Council for Exceptional Children (CEC)

1920 Association Drive
Reston, VA 20191-3660
<http://www.cec.sped.org>
Page 147 Our Children

Council of Better Business Bureau

4200 Wilson Boulevard, Suite 800
Arlington, VA 22203-1838
<http://www.bbb.org/library/finaid.html>
Page 207 Our Children

CyberDiet

<http://www.cyberdiet.com>
Page 12 Ourselves

Cyberinvest.com

3620 Third Ave., Suite 201
San Diego, CA 92103
(619) 295-5408
<http://www.cyberinvest.com>
Page 30 Ourselves

Debt Counselors of America

<http://www.dca.org>
Page 35 Ourselves

Debt Relief Counseling Service

234 Aquarius Drive, Suite 109
Birmingham, AL 35209
(888) 211-6144
<http://www.drcs.org>
Page 35 Ourselves

DEI New Age Web Works

PO Box 4032
Felton, CA 95018
<http://www.newageinfo.com/res
/welcome.htm>
Page 22 Ourselves

Deloitte & Touche LLP

Center of Excellence
700 Walnut Street
Cincinnati, OH 45202
<http://www.dtonline.com/>
Page 54 Ourselves
Page 209 Our Children

Deloitte & Touche Estate Planning Guide

<http://www.dtonline.com/estate/cover
.htm>
Page 340 Our Parents

Depression.com
<http://www.depression .com>
Page 376 Our Parents

Disability Insurance Basics
<http://www.insuremarket.com/basics
/disability/disbasics.htm>
Page 84 Ourselves
Page 190 Our Children

Disability Insurance: How It Works
<http://www.insure.com/health/disability
.html>
Page 84 Ourselves
Page 191 Our Children

**Disability Studies and Service Center
(DSSC)**
<http://dssc.org>
Page 148 Our Children

Divorcesource
<http://www.divorcesource.com>
Page 20 Ourselves

Do Something
<http://www.dosomething.org>
Page 163 Our Children

drkoop.com
7000 North Morac, Suite 400
Austin, TX 78731
(888) 795-0998
<http://www.drkoop.com>
Page 94 Ourselves

Drugstore.com
13920 SE Eastgate Way, Suite 300
Bellevue, WA 98005
(800) 378-4786
<http://www.drugstore.com>
Page 95 Ourselves

Electronic Text Retrieval Systems, Inc.
Robert C. Danes, Publisher
(800) 910-0910
<http://www.adss.org>
Page 317 Our Parents

**The Elizabeth Glaser Pediatric AIDS
Foundation**
2950 31st Street
Santa Monica, CA 90405
(310) 314-1459
<http://www.pedaids.org>
Page 228 Our Children

**Employment and Older Americans:
A Winning Partnership**
Administration on Aging
330 Independence Ave. SW
Washington, DC 20201
(202) 619-0724
<http://www.aoa.dhhs.gov/factsheets
/employment.html>
Page 258 Our Parents

Employment Discrimination: An Overview
Legal Information Institute
Cornell Law School
Myron Taylor Hall
Ithaca, NY 14853
(607) 255-7193
<http://www.law.cornell.edu/topics
    /employment%5Fdiscrimination%2ehtml/>
Page 259 Our Parents

Equifax, Inc.
PO Box 740241
Atlanta, GA 30374-0241
(800) 997-2493
<http://www.equifax.com>
Page 34 Ourselves

Excite.com
<http://www.excite.com>
Page 165 Our Children

Facts about Age Discrimination
<http://www.eeoc.gov/facts/age.html/>
Page 259 Our Parents

FamilyEducation.com
<http://www.familyeducation.com>
Page 167 Our Children

Fedstats
<http://www.FEDSTATS.gov>
Page 252 Our Parents

Financenter.com
1860 East River Road, Suite 200
Tucson, AZ 85718
(520) 299-9009
<http://financenter.com>
Page 31 Ourselves
Page 330 Our Parents

Financial Aid for College
<http://www.finaid.org>
Page 208 Our Children

Financial Aid Search
<http://www.fastweb.com/>
Page 207 Our Children

Financial Engines
<http://www.financialengines.com>
Page 330 Our Parents

Financial Web
<http://www.financialweb.com/>
Page 54 Ourselves
Page 210 Our Children
Page 331 Our Parents

Fit For Life
181-I Nantucket Rd.
Clarksville, TN 37040
(888) 479-9355
<http://www.iamfitforlife.com>
Page 253 Our Parents

Forbes.com
<http://www.forbes.com/funds>
Page 330 Our Parents

Fortune
<http://www.fortuneinvestor.com>
Page 54 Ourselves
Page 210 Our Children

Foundation for Grandparenting
7 Avenida Vista Grande, Suite B7-160
Santa Fe, NM 87505
<http://www.grandparenting.org>
Page 273 Our Parents

4Babynames.com
<http://www.4babynames.com>
Page 136 Our Children

401(K) Forum
625 Third St.
San Francisco, CA 94107
(415) 547-1120
<http://www.401kforum.com>
<http://www.kafe.com>
Page 45 Ourselves
Page 321 Our Parents

Free Federal Application for Student Aid
(800) 801-0576
<http://www.fafsa.ed.gov>
Page 208 Our Children

Fund Alarm
<http://www.fundalarm.com>
Page 330 Our Parents

Funeral and Memorial Planning
<http://www.growthhouse.org/funeral
    .html>
Page 297 Our Parents

Funeralnet
<http://www.funeralnet.com>
Page 297 Our Parents

Geocities
<http://www.geocities.com>; then search
    under "Elderly" to find several relevant
    sites.
Page 284 Our Parents

**Gifts Under the Uniform Gifts
    to Minors Act**
<http://www.reports-unlimited.com
    /giftstominorsact.htm>
Page 214 Our Children

Glaucoma Research Foundation
200 Pine Street, Suite 200
San Francisco, CA 94104
(800) 826-6693
<http://www.glaucoma.org>
Page 359 Our Parents

Grand Parent Again
<http://www.grandparentagain.com>
Page 273 Our Parents

Grandparent Caregiver: A National Guide
IGC
6741 Eastern Ave., Suite 200
Takoma Park, MD 20912
(202) 588-5070
<http://www.igc.org/justice/cjc/lspc
    /manual/cover.html>
Page 273 Our Parents

Grandparent Visitation Rights
<http://www.grandtimes.com/visit.html>
Page 272 Our Parents

Grands Place
c/o Pixie Wescott
PO Box 132
Wanchese, NC 27981
<http://www.grandsplace.com>
Page 273 Our Parents

Great Outdoor Recreation Pages
<http://www.gorp.com/gorp/eclectic
  /family.htm>
Page 161 Our Children

Grief and Bereavement
<http://www.growthhouse.org/death
  .html>
Page 296 Our Parents

GriefNet
PO Box 3272
Ann Arbor, MI 48106-3272
<http://www.rivendell.org>
Page 296 Our Parents

Grieving Process Booklet
<http://www.add.ca/grieving.htm>
Page 296 Our Parents

Healthatoz.com
66 Witherspoon St., Suite 345
Princeton, NJ 08542
(609) 409-8200
<http://www.healthatoz.com>
Page 95 Ourselves

Health Answers
Healthway Online, Inc.
10435 Burnet Rd., Suite 122
Austin, TX 78758
(800) 794-2088
<http://www.healthanswers.com>
Page 13 Ourselves

Health Care Advance Directives
<http://www.ama-assn.org>
Page 267 Our Parents

**Health Care Financing Administration
  (HCFA)**
7500 Security Blvd.
Baltimore, MD 21224
(410) 786-3000
<http://www.HCFA.gov>
<http://www.medicare.gov/nursing>
Page 293 Our Parents
Page 346 Our Parents

Health Care Financing Agency (HCFA)
Children's Health Insurance Program (CHIP)
7500 Security Blvd.
Baltimore, MD 21244-1850
(410) 786-3000
<http://www.hcfa.gov>
Page 244 Our Children
Page 346 Our Parents

Healthcenter.com
<http://healthcenter.com>
Page 139 Our Children

**Health Insurance Association
of America (HIAA)**
<http://www.hiaa.com>
Page 345 Our Parents

Healthfinder.org
Office of Disease Prevention
    and Health Promotion
Office of Public Health and Science
Office of the Secretary
U.S. Department of Health
    and Human Services
Washington, D.C.
<http://www.healthfinder.org>
Page 99 Ourselves

The Health Network
1440 Sepulveda Blvd.
Los Angeles, CA 90025
(310) 444-8123
<http://www.ahn.com>
Page 97 Ourselves

Health World Online
Fitness Center
<http://www.healthy.net/fitness/index
    .asp>
Page 10 Ourselves

HotJobs.com
24 West 40th Street, 14th Floor
New York, NY 10018
(212) 302-0060
(212) 944-8962 (Fax)
<http://www.hotjobs.com>
Page 15 Ourselves

IDEA
(800) 999-4332
<http://www.ideafit.com>
Page 10 Ourselves

Impotence
HealthGate Data Corp
25 Corporate Drive, Suite 310
Burlington, MA 01803
<http://www.bewell.com/hic/impotence/>
Page 124 Ourselves

Impotence Resource Center
American Foundation for Urologic Disease
    (AFUD)
(800) 433-4215
<http://www.impotence.org>
Page 124 Ourselves

Impotence World Association (IWA)
Impotence Institute of America
PO Box 410
Bowie, MD 20718-0410
(800) 669-1603
<http://www.impotenceworld.org>
Page 125 Ourselves
Page 356 Our Parents

Independent Charities of America
(800) 477-0733
<http://www.independentcharities.org>
Page 80 Ourselves

Index Funds.com
<http://www.indexfunds.com>
Page 331 Our Parents

Institute of Certified Financial Planners
3801 East Florida Avenue, Suite 708
Denver, CO 80210-2544
(303) 759-4900
<http://www.icfp.org>
Page 25 Ourselves

Insurance News Network
<http://www.insure.com>
Page 342 Our Parents

Insurance Online
<http://www.insweb.com>
Page 81 Ourselves
Page 188 Our Children

Intelihealth
(800) 244-4636
<http://www.Intelihealth.com>
Page 95 Ourselves

Internal Revenue Service, U.S. Department of Treasury
<http://www.irs.ustreas.gov/prod/cover.html>
Page 327 Our Parents

The Internet Public Library Reference Center
<http://www.ipl.org/ref>
Page 167 Our Children

The International Dyslexia Association (IDA)
The Chester Building, Suite 382
8600 LaSalle Road
Baltimore, MD 21286-2044
(410) 296-0232
<http://www.interdys.org/>
Page 153 Our Children

The Investment FAQ
<http://www.invest-faq.com/articles>
Page 44 Ourselves
Page 320 Our Parents

Keeping Cholesterol under Control
Food and Drug Administration
5600 Fishers Lane
Rockville, MD 20857
(800) INFO-FDA
<http://www.Fda.gov>
Page 115 Ourselves

kidsDoctor
<http://www.kidsdoctor.com>
Page 219 Our Children

KidsHealth.org
<http://www.kidshealth.org>
Page 217 Our Children

KidsHealth.org
<http://www.kidshealth.org/teen/bodymind/eat_disorder.html>
Page 243 Our Children

KidSource.com
<http://www.kidsource.com>
Page 167 Our Children

KidZone
Netscape
<http://www.netscape.com>
Page 166 Our Children

Lawrence Berkeley National Laboratory
University of California
<http://www.walkersurvey.org>
Page 10 Ourselves

Leave a Legacy
PO Box 12097
Berkeley, CA 94712-3097
(888) 747-0454
<http://www.leavealegacy.org>
Page 79 Ourselves

Legal Council for the Elderly
The American Association
   of Retired Persons (AARP)
PO Box 96474
Washington, DC 20090-6474
<http://www.aarp.org>
Page 267 Our Parents

Legal Information Institute
Cornell Law School
Myron Taylor Hall
Ithaca, NY 14853
(607) 255-7193
<http://www.law.cornell.edu/uniform
   /probate.html>
Page 303 Our Parents

The Library of Congress
<http://www.loc.gov>
Page 167 Our Children

Life Insurance
Insurance Company Ratings
<http://www.insure.com/ratings/index
   .html>
Page 83 Ourselves

**Life Insurance Trusts for Child
   Beneficiaries**
<http://www.insure.com/life/trusts.html>
Page 82 Ourselves
Page 189 Our Children

Lycos
<http://www.lycos.com>
Page 165 Our Children

Lycos Zone
<http://www.lycoszone.lycos.com>
Page 166 Our Children

Mayo Clinic
4500 San Pablo Road
Jacksonville, FL 32224
(904) 953-2000
<http://www.mayohealth.org/mayo/9709
   /htm/hyperten.htm>
Page 115 Ourselves

Medicare Rights Center
1460 Broadway
New York, NY 10036
(212) 869-3850
<http://www.medicarerights.org>
Page 346 Our Parents

Medicinenet.com
19651 Alter
Foothill Ranch, CA 92610
(949) 380-9800
<http://www.medicinenet.com>
Page 96 Ourselves

Menopause
Women's Health Center
(203) 735-1806
<http://www.menopause-online.com>
Page 123 Ourselves

Menopause: A Women's Rite of Passage
<http://www.yoni.com/cronef/menopause1
  .shtml>
Page 124 Ourselves

Mental Health Net
570 Metro Place North
Dublin, OH 43017
(614) 764-0143
(614) 764-0362 (Fax)
<http://www.mentalhelp.net>
Page 96 Ourselves

Money Central Investor
Microsoft
One Microsoft Way
Redmond, WA 98052-6399
(425) 882-8080
<http://www.moneycentral.com>
Page 31 Ourselves

Monster.com
(800) MONSTER
<http://www.monster.com>
Page 14 Ourselves

MSN MoneyCentral
<http://www.moneycentral.com>
Page 330 Our Parents

Multex Investor
<http://www.multexinvestor.com>
Page 55 Ourselves

Mutual Fund Education Alliance
<http://www.mfea.com>
Page 331 Our Parents

MyEvents.com
San Francisco, CA
(415) 362-8700
<http://www.myevents.com>
Page 6 Ourselves

**National Adoption Information
  Clearinghouse (NAIC)**
330 C Street SW
Washington, DC 20447
(888) 251-0075
<http://www.calib.com/naic>
Page 132 Our Children

**National Association
  for Continence (NAFC)**
PO Box 8310
Spartanburg, SC 29305
(800) 252-3337
<http://www.nafc.org>
Page 369 Our Parents

**National Association for Education
  of Young Children**
(800) 424-2460
<http://www.naeyc.org>
Page 141 Our Children

National Association of Life Underwriters (NALU)
1922 F Street NW
Washington, DC 20006
(202) 331-6000
<http://www.nalu.org>
Page 27 Ourselves

National Association of Personal Financial Advisors (NAPFA)
355 West Dundee Road, Suite 200
Buffalo Grove, IL 60089
(888) FEE-ONLY
<http://www.napfa.org>
Page 25 Ourselves

National Association of Professional Geriatric Care Managers
North Country Club Road
Tucson, AZ 85716
(520) 881-8008
<http://www.caremanager.org>
Page 282 Our Parents

National Association of Securities Dealers
1390 Piccard Drive
Rockville, MD 20850-3389
<http://www.nasd.com>
Page 26 Ourselves

National Cancer Institute (NCI)
National Institutes of Health
Bethesda, MD 20892
<http://www.nci.nih.gov>
Page 117 Ourselves

National Center for Assisted Living (ACAL)
1201 L Street NW
Washington, DC 20005
(202) 842-4444
<http://www.ncal.org>
Page 287 Our Parents

National Center for Complementary and Alternative Medicine (NCCAM)
National Institutes of Health
<http://nccam.nih.gov>
Page 120 Ourselves

National Center for Injury Prevention and Control (NCIPC)
Mailstop K65
4770 Buford Highway NE
Atlanta, GA 30341-3724
(770) 488-1506
(770) 488-1667 (Fax)
<http://www.cdc.gov/ncipc/ncipchm.htm>
Page 224 Our Children

National Center on Elder Abuse
<http://www.gwjapan.com/NCEA/index.html>
Page 294 Our Parents

National Child Care Information Center
<http://www.nccic.org>
Page 141 Our Children

National Cholesterol Education Program
NHLBI Information Center
PO Box 30105
Bethesda, MD 20824-0105
<http://www.nhlbi.nih.gov>
Page 115 Ourselves

National Citizens Coalition for Nursing Home Reformation (NCCNHR)
1424 16th Street NW, Suite 202
Washington, DC 20036-2211
(202) 332-2275
<http://www.nccnhr.org/>
Page 293 Our Parents

National Council for Adoption (NCFA)
1930 17th Street NW
Washington, DC 20009-6207
(202) 328-8072
<http://www.ncfa-usa.org>
Page 132 Our Children

National Depressive and Manic-Depressive Association
730 N. Franklin Street, Suite 501
Chicago, IL 60610-3526
(800) 826-3632
(312) 642-0049
(312) 642-7243 (Fax)
<http://www.ndmda.org>
Page 376 Our Parents

National Diabetes Information Clearinghouse (NDIC)
1 Information Way
Bethesda, MD 20892-3560
(301) 654-3327
<http://www.niddk.nih.gov/health/diabetes/ndic.htm>
Page 352 Our Parents

National Foundation for Consumer Credit
8611 Second Avenue, Suite 100
Silver Spring, MD 20910
(800) 388-2227
<http://www.nfcc.org>
Page 36 Ourselves

National Funeral Directors Association
13625 Bishop's Drive
Brookfield, WI 53005
(800) 228-6332
<http://www.nfda.org/about/#info>
Page 297 Our Parents

National Guardianship Association
1604 North Country Club Rd.
Tucson, AZ 85716
<http://www.guardianship.org>
Page 271 Our Parents

National Heart, Lung and Blood Institute Information Center
PO Box 30105
Bethesda, MD 30105
(301) 251-1222
<http://www.nhlbi.nih.gov/htm>
Page 233 Our Children
Page 362 Our Parents
Page 364 Our Parents

**National Information Center for Children
and Youth with Disabilities (NICHCY)**
PO Box 1492
Washington, DC 20013-1492
(800) 695-0285
<http://www.nichcy.org>
Page 151 Our Children
Page 152 Our Children
Page 218 Our Children

**National Institute of Allergies
and Infectious Diseases (NIAID)**
National Institutes of Health
NIAID Office of Communication
and Public Liaison
Building 31, Room 7A-50
31 Center Drive MSC 2520
Bethesda, MD 20892-2520
<http://www.NIAID.gov>
Page 231 Our Children

**National Institute of Neurological
Disorders and Stroke (NINDS)**
National Institutes of Health
PO Box 5801
Bethesda, MD 20842
(301) 496-5751
<http://www.ninds.nih.gov/patients
/disorder/dyslexia/dyslexia.htm>
Page 152 Our Children

**National Institute on Aging
Information Center**
National Institute on Aging (NIA)
PO Box 8057
Gathersburg, MD 20898-8057
(301) 446-1752
<http://www.nih.gov/nia>
Page 7 Ourselves

National Institutes of Health (NIH)
Bethesda, MD 20892
<http://www.nih.gov/>
Page 99 Ourselves

**National Institutes of Health:
Sleep and the Elderly**
National Institutes of Health (NIH)
Bethesda, MD 20892
<http://text.nlm.nih.gov/nih/cdc/www
/78txt.html>
Page 121 Ourselves

**National Kidney and Urologic Diseases
Information Clearinghouse (NKUDIC)**
3 Information Way
Bethesda, MD 20892-3580
<http://www.niddk.nih.gov/health/kidney
/nkudic.htm>
Page 357 Our Parents
Page 369 Our Parents

National Organization of Social Security Claimants' Representatives (NOSSCR)

6 Prospect Street

Midland Park, NJ 07432-1634

(800) 431-2804

<http://www.nosscr.org>

Page 317 Our Parents

National Osteoporosis Foundation (NOF)

1232 22nd Street NW

Washington, DC 20037-1292

(202) 223-2226

<http://www.nof.org>

Page 354 Our Parents

National Parent Information Network (NPIN)

ERIC Clearinghouse on Disabilities and Gifted Children

<http://www.npin.org>

Page 147 Our Children

The National Parkinson's Foundation, Inc.

1501 NW 9th Avenue

Miami, FL 33136-1494

(800) 327-4545

<http://www.parkinson.org>

Page 366 Our Parents

National Pediatric and Family HIV Resource Center

University of Medicine and Dentistry of New Jersey

30 Bergen Street—ADMC #4

Newark, NJ 07103

(973) 972-0410

(800) 362-0071

(973) 0399 (Fax)

<http://www.Pedhivaids.org>

Page 228 Our Children

National Philanthropic Trust

165 Township Line Rd., Suite 3000

Jenkintown, PA 19046-3593

(888) 878-7900

<http://www.nptrust.org>

Page 80 Ourselves

The National SAFE Kids Campaign

1301 Pennsylvania Ave. NW, Suite 1000

Washington, DC 20004-1707

(202) 662-0600

(202) 393-2072 (Fax)

<http://www.safekids.org>

Page 223 Our Children

National School-to-Work Learning and Information Center

(800) 251-7236

<http://www.stw.ed.gov>

Page 160 Our Children

National Strength and Conditioning Association
1955 N. Union Blvd.
Colorado Springs, CA 80909
(719) 632-6722
<http://www.nsca-lift.org>
Page 11 Ourselves

National Stroke Association (NSA)
(800) STROKES
<http://www.stroke.org>
Page 364 Our Parents

Nellimae
(800) 367-8848
<http://www.nelliemae.org>
Page 208 Our Children

Netguide
<http://www.netguide.com/Family
/spirituality>
Page 22 Ourselves

North American Menopause Society
PO Box 94527
Cleveland, OH 44101
(216) 844-8748
<http://www.menopause.org/about/faq
.htm>
Page 123 Ourselves

North American Securities Administration Association (NASAA)
10 G Street NE, Suite 710
Washington, DC 20002
(202) 783-3571
<http://www.nasaa.org>
Page 26 Ourselves

Northern Trust Financial Services
Tax-Wise Ways to Make Financial Gifts
to Minors
<http://www.ntrs.com>
Page 212 Our Children

Not Just Bibles: A Guide to Christian Resources on the Internet
9700 SW Capitol Hwy., Suite 120
Portland, OR 97219
<http://www.iclnet.org/pub/resources
/christian-resources.html>
Page 21 Ourselves

Office of Consumer Affairs (OCA), U.S. Food and Drug Administration, U.S. Department of Health and Human Services
5600 Fishers Lane (HFE-88)
Rockville, MD 20857
(888) 463-6332
<http://www.fda.gov>
Page 377 Our Parents

OmniList of Christian Links Gold
Private site maintained by Keith Arthurs
<http://members.aol.com/clinksgold/index
.html>
Page 21 Ourselves

OnHealth
808 Howell St., Suite 400
Seattle, WA 98101
(206) 583-8665
<http://www.onhealth.com>
Page 96 Ourselves

Parentsoup.com
<http://www.parentsoup.com>
Page 176 Our Children

ParentsPlace.com
<http://www.parentsplace.com>
Page 167 Our Children

PEDINFO
<http://www.pedinfo.org>
Page 219 Our Children

Peterson's College Quest
<http://www.collegequest.com>
Page 159 Our Children

Pharmaceutical Information Network
<http://www.pharminfo.com>
Page 380 Our Parents

PlanetRX
349 Oyster Point Boulevard, Suite 201
South San Francisco, CA 94080
<http://www.planetrx.com>
Page 97 Ourselves

Planned Parenthood
<http://www.plannedparenthood.org
    /BIRTH-CONTROL/Index.htm>
Page 240 Our Children

The Princeton Review
(800) 2REVIEW
<http://www.review.com>
Page 157 Our Children

Profiles of World Religions
University of Virginia
<http://cti.itc.virginia.edu/~jkh8x/soc257
    /profiles/profiles.html>
Page 22 Ourselves

Quicken.com
<http://www.quicken.com>
Page 31 Ourselves
Page 45 Ourselves
Page 321 Our Parents
Page 330 Our Parents

RealAge Inc.
11468 Sorrento Valley Rd.
San Diego, CA 92121
(615) 812-3800
<http://www.realage.com>
Page 7 Ourselves

**RESOLVE, The National Infertility
    Association**
1310 Broadway
Somerville, MA 02144-1779
(617) 623-0744
<http://www.resolve.org>
Page 131 Our Children

Restless Legs Syndrome
4410 19th Street NW, Suite 201
Rochester, MN 55901-6624
<http://www.rls.org>
Page 121 Ourselves

Roth IRA Website Homepage
<http://www.rothira.com>
Page 43 Ourselves
Page 320 Our Parents

Salliemae
(800) 239-4269
<http://www.salliemae.com>
Page 208 Our Children

Self Help for Hard of Hearing People, Inc.
7910 Woodmont Avenue, Suite 1200
Bethesda, MD 20814
(301) 657-2248
<http://www.shhh.org>
Page 360 Our Parents

Senior Alternatives for Living
An On-Line Service
(800) 350-0770
<http://www.senioralternatives.com>
Page 286 Our Parents

Seniors-Site.com
c/o Walter J. Cheney
5443 Stag Mt. Road
Weed, CA 96094
(916) 938-3163
<http://seniors-site.com/sex/index.html>
Page 255 Our Parents

**Sexuality Information and Education
   Council of the United States (SIECUS)**
130 West 42nd St., Suite 350
New York, NY 10036
<http://www.siecus.org>
Page 241 Our Children

Sexuality Later in Life
National Institute on Aging
NIA Information Center
PO Box 8057
Gaithersburg, MD 20898-8057
(800) 222-2225
<http://www.aoa.dhhs.gov/aoa/pages
   /agepages/sexualty.html>
Page 255 Our Parents

Sleep Net
<http://www.sleepnet.com>
Page 120 Ourselves

Sleep Well
<http://www.stanford.edu/~dement/>
Page 120 Ourselves

Small Business Advisor
Information International
Great Falls, VA 22066
(703) 450-7049
<http://isquare.com/retire.htm>
Page 44 Ourselves
Page 321 Our Parents

**Smartmoney.com—The Wall Street
   Journal Magazine**
<http://www.smartmoney.com>
Page 327 Our Parents

Smith Barney Investment Update
<http://www.salomonsmithbarney.com
   /inv_up/arts/two.html>
Page 43 Ourselves
Page 320 Our Parents

Social Security Administration (SSA)
6401 Security Boulevard
Baltimore, MD 21235
1(800) 772-1213
<http://www.ssa.gov>
Page 316 Our Parents

Social Security Advisory Service (SSAS)
271 Miller Avenue
Mill Valley, CA 94941-2862
<http://www.ssas.com>
Page 316 Our Parents

Social Security Benefits
SSA Office of Public Inquiries
6401 Security Boulevard
Room 4-5 Annex
Baltimore, MD 21235-6401
<http://www.ssa.gov>
Page 39 Ourselves

Social Security Disability Insurance
<http://www.kidsource.com/nfpa/social
.html>
Page 193 Our Children

Special Needs Advocate for Parents (SNAP)
1801 Avenue of the Stars, #401
Century City, CA 90067
(888) 310-9889
<http://www.snapinfo.org>
Page 195 Our Children

Split-up.com
Family Law Software, Inc.
831 Beacon St., Suite 2900
Newton Center, MA 02459
(877) 477-5488
<http://www.split-up.com>
Page 181 Our Children

Strong On-Line
<http://www.strong-
funds.com/strong/retirement98/ind/calc
/rothcalc.html>
Page 43 Ourselves
Page 320 Our Parents

Supplemental Needs Trusts
<http://www.seniorlaw.com/snt.htm>
Page 194 Our Children

T. Rowe Price
Shareholder Correspondence
PO Box 89000
Baltimore, MD 21289-0250
(800) 225-5132
<http://www.troweprice.com>
Page 32 Ourselves

Tad Publishing Co.
PO Box 224
Park Ridge, IL 60068
(847) 823-0639
<http://www.caregiving.com>
Page 284 Our Parents

**Technical Assistance Alliance
  for Parents Centers**
Alliance Coordinating Office
4826 Chicago Avenue South
Minneapolis, MN 55417-1098
(888) 248-0822
<http://www.taalliance.org/>
Page 148 Our Children

10 Legal Myths about Advance Directives
<http://www.abanet.org/elderly/myths
  .html
Page 266 Our Parents

Third Age Work
Third Age Media
585 Howard Street, 1st Floor
San Francisco, CA 94105-3001
<http://www.thirdage.com/work>
Page 257 Our Parents

Thriveonline.com
Thrive Partners
221 Main St., Suite 480
San Francisco, CA 94105
<http://thriveonline.com>
Page 97 Ourselves

Tips on Purchasing Life Insurance
<http://www.newyorklife.com/viewer
  /wsh-nyl/.hts/nyl/pfstch.html>
Page 82 Ourselves
Page 188 Our Children

Torah.org
Project Genesis, Inc.
17 Warren Rd., #2B
Baltimore, MD 21208
(410) 602-1350
<http://www.torah.org>
Page 21 Ourselves

Trans Union
PO Box 403
Springfield, PA 19064
(800) 888-4213
<http://www.transunion.com>
Page 35 Ourselves

Transweb
All About Transplantation and Donation
<http://www.transweb.org>
Page 381 Our Parents

**U.S. Consumer Product Safety
  Commission (CPSC)**
Washington, DC 20207
(800) 638-2772
<http://www.cpsc.gov>
Page 223 Our Children

U.S. Department of Education
<http://www.ed.gov/pubs/parents/index
  .html>
Page 158 Our Children

U.S. Department of Education

400 Maryland Avenue SW
Washington, DC 20202
(800) USA-LEARN
<http://www.ed.gov>
Page 37 Our Children
Page 58 Our Children
Page 146 Our Children
Page 204 Our Children
Page 208 Our Children

U.S. Department of Education

Office of Special Education and
   Rehabilitation Services
400 Maryland Avenue SW
Washington, DC 20202
(202) 205-4873
<http://www.ed.gov> (Site for U.S.
   Department of Education)
<http://www.ed.gov/offices/OSERS/>
   (Office of Special Education and
   Rehabilitation Services)
<http://www.ed.gov/offices/OSERS
   /IDEA> (IDEA '97)
Page 149 Our Children

U.S. Department of Labor

Fair Labor Standards Act (FLSA) Advisor
Wage and Hour Division
<http://www.dol.gov/dol/esa/public/youth
   /mwtour4.htm>
Page 195 Our Children

U.S. Department of Labor

Pension and Welfare Benefits (PWBA)
200 Constitution Avenue NW, Room N-5656
Washington, DC 20210
<http://www.dol.gov>
Page 40 Ourselves

U.S. Department of the Treasury

Office of Public Correspondence
1500 Pennsylvania Avenue, NW
Washington, D.C. 20220
(202) 622-2000
<http://www.publicdebt.treas.gov/bpd
   /bpdmap.htm>
Page 52 Ourselves

U.S. News Online

U.S. News and World Report
<http://www.usnews.com/usnews/edu>
Page 159 Our Children
Page 200 Our Children

Uniform Gifts to Minors Act

<http://www.invest-faq.com/articles
   /tax-ugma.html>
Page 214 Our Children

University of Pennsylvania OncoLink

OncoLink Editorial Office
University of Pennsylvania Medical Center
3400 Spruce Street—2 Donner
Philadelphia, PA 19104-4283
<http://cancer.med.upenn.edu>
Page 117 Ourselves

The Vanguard Group
PO Box 2600
Valley Forge, PA 19482-2600
(800) 871-3879
<http://www.vanguard.com>
Page 42 Ourselves
Page 320 Our Parents

WebMD
(888) 728-3702
<http://www.webmd.com>
Page 97 Ourselves

When.com
501 E. Middlefield Road, MV-041
Mountain View, CA 94043-4042
(650) 937-4145
<http://www.when.com>
Page 6 Ourselves

Widownet
<http://www.fortnet.org/WidowNet/>
Page 296 Our Parents

Women's Health Interactive (WHI)
PO Box 271276
Ft. Collins, CO 80527-1276
<http://www.Womens-health.com>
Page 98 Ourselves

Yahoo!
<http://dir.yahoo.com/society_and_culture
  /religion>
Page 22 Ourselves

Yahooligans: The Web Site for Kids
Yahoo!
<http://www.yahooligans.com>
Page 166 Our Children

**Zero to Three: National Center for Infants,
  Toddlers and Families**
734 15th Street, Suite 1000
Washington, DC 20005-1013
(202) 638-1144
<http://www.zerotothree.org>
Page 137 Our Children

CRISIS INFORMATION CHECKLIST

In the event of a crisis, you should have the following information available to assist those you care about:

Documents				
	Copy	Original	N/A	Location
1. Health care proxy/living will				
2. Power of attorney				
3. Will				
4. Organ donation card/instructions				
5. Cemetery deed/funeral instructions				
6. Insurance policies				
a. Health				
b. Life				
c. Disability				
d. Long-term care				
e. Car				
f. Home				
7. Trust documents				
8. Business (partnership/shareholder) agreements				
9. Deeds to real estate				
10. Recent tax bill associated with deeds				
11. Real estate appraisals				
12. Prior gift tax returns				
13. Last federal income tax return				

	Copy	Original	N/A	Location
14. Prenuptial agreements				
15. Waiver of right of election				
16. Other (guardianship papers, citizenship papers, military service records, visa/passport, birth certificate, divorce/separation agreement, adoption papers)				

Assets

	Copy	Original	N/A	Location
17. List of bank accounts				
18. List of brokerage accounts/mutual funds				
19. Retirement plan benefits				
20. IRAs/Keoghs				
21. 401(k)s				
22. Safe deposit box number and location				
23. Current beneficiary elections				

Professional Advisors

You should also have the names, addresses, and phone numbers of the following:

	Name	Address	Phone Number
Doctor			
Attorney			
Accountant			
Insurance Agent			
Financial Planner			

Note: *Check that you have current personal information on your loved ones, including address, phone and fax numbers, and e-mail addresses.*

ABOUT THE AUTHORS

Robert Abrams is the managing partner of the Law Offices of Robert Abrams, P.C., a mid-size firm located in Lake Success, New York. The firm provides legal services in several areas, including health law, elder law, guardianship law, estate planning and administration, and related litigation and business matters.

Bob is an active member of several professional organizations, including the National Academy of Elder Law Attorneys (NAELA), the American Health Lawyers Association (AHLA), and the New York State Bar Association (NYSBA). He is the former chair of the NYSBA's Elder Law Section and is a member of the Executive Committee of the Health Law Section. He is the current editor of the NYSBA Elder Law Section's *Elder Law Attorney* newsletter. In furtherance of Bob's understanding and sensitivity to the needs of the elderly and disabled persons, he founded Decision-Making Day, an annual volunteer program sponsored by the NYSBA and recognized by New York State Governor George Pataki. This program was specifically designed to advise New Yorkers of the importance of advance directives such as health care proxies and powers of attorney. Over the past few years, thousands of attorneys and tens of thousands of New Yorkers have participated in this program.

An informative and entertaining speaker, Bob has presented programs to a variety of consumer, health care, legal, and professional organizations on both the state and national levels. He has served as a legal expert for Fox Cable Television in connection with the U.S. Supreme Court's ruling on assisted suicide and has appeared on *Miller's Law,* a national show that is featured on Court TV.

Bob was selected by former New York Governor Mario Cuomo to serve as a New York state delegate to the White House Conference on Aging (WHCOA) in 1995. As a participant of the WHCOA, Bob was able to recommend national policy initiatives to his fellow attendees. The conference report was subsequently presented to President Bill Clinton and the U.S. Congress.

Bob continues to serve several community, advocacy, and public interest organizations in a variety of capacities. Along with the other attorneys in his firm, he has provided legal assistance to indigent individuals and non-profit organizations. He received national and international attention for his involvement in helping to secure appropriate care and treatment for the "Forgotten Man," an indigent individual who was improperly restrained to his bed by a public hospital for a six-year period.

Bob created and served as editor-in-chief of *Guardianship Practice in New York State* (New York State Bar Association, 1997), a 1,712-page book consisting of twenty-seven chapters, over one hundred forms and sample pleadings, a comprehensive list of guardianship cases, and helpful practice tips. The book has been praised by many professionals, including a law school dean who remarked that this book is "the most thoughtful and complete treatment of the subject to date."

In addition to his law degree, which he received as an evening division student at New York Law School, Bob earned a master's degree in Public Administration from New York University. He is also a New York state–licensed nursing home administrator.

Bob resides in Long Island, New York, with his wife, Linda, and their two daughters, Dana and Tracey.

Walter T. Burke was born and raised in the New York City metropolitan area. He earned his Juris Doctorate from Fordham University School of Law. Prior to his doctorate, Walter received his master's degree in English Education from Iona College in New Rochelle, New York. He also attended Manhattan College, where he received his bachelor of arts degree in English.

In 1988, Walter and his partner, Timothy E. Casserly, founded Burke & Casserly, P.C., a two-lawyer, two-staff firm, specializing in planning for all phases of life. Based in Albany, New York, their firm has grown to a mid-size regional firm, now known as Burke, Casserly & Gable, P.C.

One of Walter's primary areas of expertise is the burgeoning area of elder law. He is very active with the NYSBA and is a former chair of the Elder Law Section, which has over two thousand five hundred attorneys in

New York State. He also serves on the Elder Law Executive Committee. Walter had the honor of participating as coordinator of the White House Mini-Conference on Aging and served as an official observer at the White House Conference on Aging in Washington, D.C., in 1995. Additionally, he served as a delegate at the New York State Conference on Aging.

Walter is actively involved with the American Bar Association and serves as an assistant secretary to the Senior Lawyers Division Council. Within this division he is chair of the Elder and Long Term Care Issues Committee, a member of State and Local Bars Committee, and liaison to the Business Law Committee.

In addition to the many ABA affiliations, Walter has also been involved in many other organizations such as the National Academy of Elder Law Attorneys, the International Trademark Association, and the American Society for Industrial Security.

Walter also utilizes his financial and investment planning skills as a principal in Arista Investment Advisors, a registered investment advisor (RIA). Currently, the firm manages assets in excess of $40 million for various individuals, trustees, and retirement plans.

Walter has appeared on various public television and news programs dealing with his area of expertise and has lectured both locally and nationally on various retirement, elder law, estate, and financial planning topics.

Walter resides in Niskayuna, New York, with his wife, Mary, and their children, Daniel and Laura. Daniel attends New York University Law School, and Laura attends Boston College.

Timothy E. Casserly was raised on Long Island, New York. He attended Boston College in Chestnut Hill, Massachusetts, and graduated with honors in 1981 with a Bachelor of Arts Degree in Economics and Communications. In 1984, Tim received his Juris Doctorate from Albany Law School of Union University in Albany, New York.

Tim, along with his partner, Walter T. Burke, founded the law firm of Burke & Casserly, P.C., in 1988 (which has since become Burke, Casserly & Gable, P.C.); the firm focuses on estate planning, elder law, taxation, and estate administration. Tim also concentrates on financial planning, having received his Certified Financial Planner designation from the College for Financial Planning in Denver, Colorado.

Tim is also a founding member and president of Arista Investment Advisors, Ltd., a registered investment advisor with the Securities and Exchange Commission that currently manages investments in excess of $40 million for various individuals, corporations, pension plans, and not-for-profit organizations.

Tim has written, lectured, and appeared on television broadcasts on the topics of elder law, estate and financial planning, insurance, and investments. Many organizations and businesses across the country, including General Electric, the New York State Bar Association, the State University of New York, the International Association of Financial Planners, and the Institute of Certified Financial Planner Societies, have enjoyed Tim's informative and entertaining presentations. His lectures on planning for the elderly have been made available on tape through the College for Financial Planning in Denver, Colorado.

Tim's combined practice of law and financial planning, along with his presentation skills, has earned him the honor two years' running of being selected as one of eight mentors for the Institute of Certified Financial Planning's National Residency Program—an intensive one-week training program for newly credentialed CFPs.

Tim is very actively involved with both professional and community organizations, including the Institute for Certified Financial Planners on both a national and local (past president) level, the New York State Bar Association (chairing the Elder Law Practice Committee), the American Bar Association, the National Academy of Elder Law Attorneys, Volunteer Lawyers for the Arts, and his sons' sports teams.

Tim currently resides in Latham, New York, with his wife, Michelle (also an attorney), and their three young sons, Christopher, Daniel, and Ryan.

Barbara S. Nodiff is president of Associated Geriatric Information Network (AGIN), Inc., a health care consulting firm providing services to nursing facilities, adult homes, physician group practices, and managed care organizations in New York, Massachusetts, Connecticut, New Jersey, Ohio, and Florida. AGIN's services focus on regulatory compliance, development of new services and programs, and cost-effective operational management.

Ms. Nodiff is co-author of *Quality Assessment and Assurance Manual for Long-Term Facilities* (National Health Publishing, 1991) and a contributing author to *Guardianship Practice in New York State* (New York State Bar Association, 1997). She is well known to audiences of health care professionals, health care associations, and other interested parties as a speaker on issues pertinent to long-term care.

Barbara volunteers in the community, providing assistance with special projects to those in need. She was recently married to her husband, Ed, and they reside in New Rochelle, New York.

ABOUT THE ADVISORY BOARD

Ann Margaret Carrozza is a member of the New York Legislature, where she serves on the Aging, Insurance, Governmental Employees, Veteran's Affairs, and Election Law committees.

Ms. Carrozza has been the prime sponsor of numerous pieces of legislation focusing on child support collections, domestic violence, and senior citizens' rights. She is the host of a weekly cable television program on which she discusses budget and policy initiatives with guests. Ms. Carrozza is also a frequent guest on other television programs involving policy and political issues.

Ms. Carrozza has developed model programs dealing with social problems—most notably a day care–training program to provide women with much-needed job skills while simultaneously offering free and low-cost child care to needy families.

Ann Margaret Carrozza is also a practicing attorney. She received her J.D. from Hofstra University, where she served on *Law Review*.

Donna Glassman-Sommer is currently the director of alternative and Special Education for public schools in Exeter, California. She is also the principal of Kaweah High School, where she develops and implements alternative education models.

Mrs. Glassman-Sommer holds a master's degree in school administration with credentials in elementary and special education. In addition, she has had extensive training in behavioral and emotional disorders as well as organizational development.

Mrs. Glassman-Sommer is currently a national trainer for Character Counts!, a not-for-profit organization providing training to schools across the United States.

Donna Glassman-Sommer and her husband, Barry, currently live in California. They have two teenage daughters.

Philip C. Johnson is a certified financial planner and past president of the Capital District Society of the Institute of Certified Financial Planners (ICFP), the national professional organization in the financial planning field. He is also a registered investment advisor (RIA) with the Securities and Exchange Commission.

A frequent seminar and lecture speaker, he specializes in working with individuals and families, especially on education and retirement planning issues. He has been a regular contributor to *CNBC* and to *Kiplinger's Personal Finance Magazine*. In addition, he has been featured in *Money Magazine*'s "Guide to Colleges," in the *New York Times* and *Washington Post*, in *Investment Advisor Magazine*, and on *NBC Nightly News*. He is listed in *Who's Who in Finance and Industry* and is a member of the editorial board of the ICFP's *Journal of Financial Planning*. He also serves as a trustee of the Alzheimer's Association of Northeastern New York.

Raised in East Providence, Rhode Island, he graduated from Lake Forest College and earned a master's degree from the University of Rhode Island. Before becoming a financial planner, he worked in higher education administration for fifteen years beginning at Rhode Island College, then Union College, and then, from 1977 through 1984, as assistant to the president for university relations at the State University of New York at Albany.

Kyra Hollowell Morris began working in the financial planning field as an apprentice in 1983. She obtained the certified financial planner (CFP) designation in 1986 and began her own business in 1987. The analytical skills gained from her prior six years of experience as an electrical engineer and chemist have proven invaluable when solving complex client cases.

Mrs. Morris was one of the founders of the South Carolina Society for the Institute of Certified Financial Planners in 1985 and has continuously served in all positions on the local board. Since 1993, she has been serving in a national position on the board of the Institute of Certified Financial Planners. She was the focus of the cover story in the October 1995 *Dow Jones Investment Advisor Magazine* for her attention to detail when providing tax planning for her clients. Since 1994, Kyra has been named as one of the top financial planners in the country four times by *Worth Magazine*.

David G. Wolinsky is a cardiologist in private practice in upstate New York. Additionally, Dr. Wolinsky is a director of the practice's nuclear cardiology unit and the director of cardiac rehabilitation and women's heart disease prevention program at a local hospital.

Dr. Wolinsky was raised in Rochester, New York, and received his bachelor's degree in biochemistry from Columbia College in New York City. Thereafter, he received his medical degree from Columbia University and did his postgraduate training at St. Luke's Hospital in New York City. From 1983 to 1989, Dr. Wolinsky was in private practice in New York City. In 1989, he moved to Albany, New York, to join Albany Associates in Cardiology, P.C.

Dr. Wolinsky has written articles for many national publications and has participated in studies both nationally and internationally. In addition to being board certified by the American Board of Internal Medicine, he is certified by the National Board of Medical Examiners and the Certification Board of Nuclear Cardiology. Also, Dr. Wolinsky is a Fellow of the American College of Cardiology and a member of the Council on Clinical Cardiology of the American Heart Association; he is a founding member of the American Society of Nuclear Cardiology and member of several national committees in the society.

INDEX